WAMBA, COMEDY OF SOLDIERS FOOLS AND RATIONS

Keith Hulse

ISBN 9798356680663
Cover design by: Art Painter
Library of Congress Control Number: 2018675309
Printed in the United States of America

Dedicated to soldiers and lovers of comedy

CONTENTS

WAMBA, COMEDY OF SOLDIER FOOLS, AND RATIONS.

BY
Keith Hulse
123015 words 477 pages

Keith Hulse
Aberdeen
lugbooks@gmail.com
lugbooks.co.uk

CHAPTER 1 — WAMBA

Wamba
A story begins.

FUTURE

"We slander IT,
 Rowing galleys,
 Whipped by IT
 And marching in fog lost in wellies.
 Some idiot beautified IT.
 IT intercedes with our gads.
To scare away Harry Bros. PLC centre of all IT.
Pigeon droppings on statues of our gads.
While malicious drunks burned statues of IT.
We are blessed.
For Wamba Ordinary was IT.
A fairy with attitude and completely messed.
He had true IT.
A Garrison legend.
 IT," Satirextex the poet as the Brotherhood hung anyone in hoods from trees by the toes, for hoodies hide spots and knobbly knees, and when hung upside down, passing folk shouted, "Look his unmentionables have holes in them, buy new ones FINK." For Harry PLC disliked the Brotherhood as they wanted Wamba back to save them from Harry PLC, shops that charged inflated prices and blamed the weather.

Fairy citizens needed to believe Wamba still rode his piebald Old Nag in the clouds, waiting to be summoned by their nervous laughter to save them.

And why the Brotherhood disliked hoods as the hood salesmen wore them from top of head to cover unwashed feet, as soap costs cash.

And the citizens forgot they threw Wamba out of their city, Haliput, with flaming pitchforks as he was their King for a day, an ugly Burke if ever there was one, warts everywhere he had.

So here an Aslop fable, "Time is like a monkey with so many nuts to eat it forgets what the bright gold walnut tastes like, so gets colic again, serves it right, greedy thing."

For this was Futurism with a difference?

And who was Aslop?

A citizen hermit living on locusts palm fruit, honeycombs, ants and drank from pools full of liver fluke: spoke to imaginary thingamajigs and went advertising 'Doomsday,' so was an ignored nutter.

"Crank," good citizens called him and crossed the road and then threw bricks with deadly accuracy to chase the almond away.

Yes, the Bros. Plc. was the enemy of those in dark moth-eaten smocks, the Brotherhood who tip toe through streets full of broken bottles, exotic takeaways, snoring drunks, and canine unmentionables for this place found it could save money sacking road sweepers. A bad mistake but a wise move for it gave councillors cash to go on holidays with secretaries and not the wives. A holiday was not a holiday if the wife and sixteen kids tagged along; that was hell. A wife with curlers, an apron and fluffy slippers seen better days; a wife who had been a pretty secretary once and needed replaced.

DO YOU HAVE A SECRETARY?

And kids blamed their behaviour on dad with these words, "You are not a model parent so we model ourselves on Harry Bros." So, kids saved hard to take their floozy dates on holiday and not the girlfriend who was destined to have curlers and sixteen kids.

"I love children as they buy from me," Harry Blackhood, the

founder of Harry Bros Plc.

And Wamba in heaven hearing the nervous laughter of citizens would waken and fall off his cloud seeking justice for Ball, Mowpell, Fairyland, for these citizens were fairies, living ones that you could pinch to see if you were dreaming and they did scream.

Fairies walking about in multicoloured pantaloons and some pantaloons were tight and showed too much and belonged to the greasy hair fairies that loitered chippers at night. Them that threw chips at you then beat you black and blue with these words, "We wanted to protect ourselves."

And all had fluttering wings.

"Flutter," the wings and some had 'Hells Angel' tattoos so was best to let them throw all the chips they wanted and make them laugh as you caught them somersaulting passed the lit cigarettes they flicked at you, and as the bully tattooed fairies noticed you ate their chips, vanish quick.

So how did Wamba become IT?

PAST.

Once it rained a million toads, several thousand frogs, two newts, four dogs, an orange cat and green salamander while Wamba rested Old Nag on The Rift Plains watching the pink sky becoming a doorway to the Fiend Flat World beyond, a portal in other words.

"I am about to earn my pay," Wamba salivated while his dog Cur dreamed of rabbits, cuddly white rabbits that do not bite back, of shredding them to pieces in fields, and of Womba's leggings that reminded him he needed to sniff places then lick Wamba's face; yes, of eating unmentionables then being ill on Wamba spreading worms for he was a nasty DOG but still a loveable fun dog that boys need to play with for boys are made of pepper, sour cream, and worms of course they caught from the cat.

"I have seen little RIPS allowing one Fiend into our fairy world," Wamba mused for fools can muse. "Then we picnic eating sweetmeats, boiled tripe, red cabbage, gherkins, potted meat and all washed down with lovely warm mint beer and before we leave, hunt the Fiend down and throw him in a cauldron.

"Hurrah for Womba's Garrison border patrol, hurrah and three cheers," the frontier folk and slept well knowing Fiends would get a boiling as Wamba was on guard.

But this RIP was different because those salamanders and toads sort of thingies
raining down hitting you left red welts the size of melons, and the mess of an amphibian fallen from Heaven and them under your feet "squelched," and "popped."

The word was, "yucky."

It was stuff witches threw in cauldrons, while Fiends sat shivering behind outhouses for Fiends were excluded from what goes on in outhouses waiting to come through the RIP, afraid of the future. So out of sight out of mind and the cauldron lid was good and heavy and kept the Fiendish screams quiet.

They said Fiends peed from their fingers so never shake a Fiend hand. But we want to know where they got rid of the other stuff.

In a Fiend outhouse in Fiend Land and as no one had ever been there and back alive, some said, "Out their ears," "No from the mouth as they spit on fairies," "they keep it as a secret weapon against fairies," "no you are all nuts, Fiends are just like us and do it in an outhouse," and this sensible fairy was beat black and blue as no one wanted to hear such gibberish.

"Hurrah and three cheers for Wamba," the fairy frontiers folk and went back to bed with their milk maids and not the wife who got up at 4am to milk cows then churn the milk into buttermilk. Then make breakfast for sixteen kids and fall asleep feeding the cows so never saw the milk maid sneak away with a new PVC white imitation polar bear coat as is cold sneaking away at 4 am.

And Wamba was Ballenese and ordinary because he called Harry, "Brother," "Friend," and as said earlier watching the RIP widening, "I am about to earn my pay," and he was right but being Wamba did not know how right he was.

And the RIP was near the spot of the last big RIP druids said happened four thousand years earlier. A spot marked by a Give a Copper Harry stall selling plastic dinosaurs to unwary tourists like you. Unwary as the stall sold tea from an urn and uncovered fancy cakes where flies buzzed related to those that know how to get in a bakers shop and litter a butcher's window.

"Croutons are extra?" The greedy meat man and guess what the croutons where? "Blame mother nature she provides," the butcher again who is the meat man if you do not have a thesaurus, well he is the butcher.

"An extra blob of whipped cream and the citizens will think the crunchy bits nuts," the grasping baker.

"Plastic green dinosaurs are vogue at the moment," Harry's reasoning he who the Brethren hate, **he who made Harry Bros. PLC.**

And near the spot a bridge guarded by brave Garrison border patrol fairies.

"Flutter," went their wings and "flutter," too emphasise "flutter."

"Here is not that King Isisnaphut in that pink carriage coming this way as is not that his rhino crest?" One of the guardsmen and spat his tobacco so long strands of brown runny stuff splattered on one of them two newts that had rained down.

"Splat," it splatted.

But in the carriage a woman and seeing Wamba screamed for she had never seen
such an ugly fairy. So, King Isisnaphut next to her looked to see what was the irritation?

It was Wamba who seeing her mumbled, "I am in love, a love to let my friends guarding the bridge be heroes," and did not ask his friends for they knew what
happened to heroes. They ended up as forgotten volunteers in unmarked graves.

But he was Wamba and excited.

"Was she a princess?

A lord's foot warmer?
His mistress?
The chamber pot heater?
A cook?
Some fruit?
The floozy of Captain Hook?
A floozy with lots of suit?
Red haired and freckled?
Blond and curvaceous?
Big chested and bespeckled?
A thingamajig from the Cretaceous?
No just a pretty ankle.
Handed down from Uncle Frank?" And yes, this was another Satirextex ditty slipped in by accident of course.

"Come on Cur," and Wamba rode to her rescue for he was in love.

"Woof," Cur and knew Wamba was something?

DO YOU KNOW?

And behind the coach an army of Fiends loitering poking their noses, and worse eating what they found for they were hungry.

So belched and made much wind noises for they had no manners as not brought up by nannies.

"Flutter."

Then Wamba was amongst them for they were Fiends so deserved to be tramped
under Old Nag.

"Hey, watch my corns," and "You fat slob get off me," was heard often from them and, "Cur, you breath stinks of stale beer," "take you fleas back."

And at the carriage Wamba with massive hairy dirty hands that had even dirtier fingernails reached out for the polished door handle.

And the woman's eyes froze watching in slow motion the dirty massive hairy hand,
so saw her life pass before her eyes with these words, "What is IT?"

And Wamba grabbed her out of the carriage and threw her across his saddle and here saw moving creepy crawlies amongst his chain mail and faded plaid pantaloons so was mortified.

WHAT WOULD YOU DO?

She had met Wamba close like when you are ill with XXX and forgot to pull the loo chain. A common complaint amongst the alcoholic Garrison guardsmen the friends of Wamba.

And yes, if you are interested, she began to scratch for the creepy crawlies.

And Wamba rode into the pink sunset before King Isisnaphut could eat a snail which incidentally was his favourite snack.

"I have Gaullist ancestors," Isisnaphut hiding his nose.

And "My hero," Wamba waited from her red lips.

"Do you mind not staring?" She instead as she was aware he could not take his eyes off her bottom most parts that stuck up in the air; and worse the horse was looking too; and the ugly thing and horse, well their tongues were out.

And drooling.

So, spittle hit her in the face.

And Wamba's mental confusion was great for Harry told him girls want to be rescued by a handsome tall dark stranger, preferably a prince.

But locals whispered behind Wamba's back,

"Warty face.

And worse he needed hosed.

And shaved for perhaps he was not of the fairy race?

And the stubble on his chin washed.

"The girls love it Wamba," Harry told him lying.

"His chain mail squeaked for to clean it was a sin.

And made sounds like an animal baying.

Or perhaps that was Wamba rummaging in a bin?

And Wamba's teeth bright yellow.

And his hands big and hairy.

And his boots were chain mail and Stilton cheese.

So, his toes showed and were curly.

Big hairy like unwashed vegetables.

And he had a hole where he sat.

So showed his unmentionables that had a hole too.

"Pink daffodil print fit for a prat," Satirextex that poet again; when will his tortuous verse follow Pompei?

"The girls love you Wamba," Harry for he is a salesman so explains that.

And Wamba did not regard cauldroning Fiends cruel for he knew Fiends had no nervous system so felt no pain. A Fiend was something smelly a child could not hug like Roger Teddy. No, a Fiend would shred the child and eat her all up just like that. Yes, in that rancid butter sauce they smeared their snails in and garlic too for they believed garlic freshens the breath; but never bothered to smell it, that was left to you!

"We all have Gaullist ancestors," Isisnaphut who spread garlic on his toast.

A lot of miserable things can be said about Fiends like they are lovers of XXX, poke their noses publicly and wind too to clear queues at the discount store so they can be first in line.

Yes, Wamba knew what to do with Fiends caught on his side of the RIP, throw them in a cauldron preferably a druid's for Fiends had interesting thingamabobs more prized than dried newts to cure nasties caught at Common as Muck Filthy Big Bertha's Guest

House such as a bad cold.

And Wamba's King Charles Army Regulation BOOK told him just how many Fiends per cauldron too; and at the back a conversion page from Imperial measure to Metric. Even a of packet of stamps and strange seaside postcards to write home to mum on.

A BOOK Wamba consulted and told him everything is true and BOOK had interesting pictures, like pictures of the waitresses at Common as Muck Filthy Big Bertha's Guest House; oh, what an illumination! So, everything in Wamba's life was done by numbers for BOOK was army and volunteers needed reminding how to count. My when he visited the outhouse you could hear him shred the Ajax paper by numbers for, he was a volunteer.

So Old Nag thundered to the bridge where a Fiend desperately tried to remember why had he volunteered? A nervous Fiend for beside him Wamba's highly polished cauldron and under it fresh tinder and matches.

"Mummy," the Fiend moaned as volunteers do when they remember why they volunteered; and volunteered because they were soldiers needing medals to impress the waitresses at Common as Muck Filthy Big Bertha's Guest House for, 'WELCOME' was on the front door mat, so Fiends sneak in there to.

And when Wamba breathed as he must vile stale beer wafted over the beautiful girl who whispered, "An industrial plant has me?" For the girl was into cleaning up toxic waste and had a prize rose garden where aphids were protected.

And it was Old Nag the horse that knew the way blind folded back to the bridge for Wamba was gawking, ogling, and salivating all over the beautiful girl who grew
to hate him each second.

"Flutter."

And up ahead Cur imagining rabbits dangling from a stick in front of him, for encouragement to run for Wamba had told him Fiends ate feral dogs.

So, "Old King Isisnaphut the snail eater is here," Wamba shouted as he passed tourists.

"Nutter, they laughed," as they did not take him seriously so gave him strange finger signs and were never seen again as the Fiends caught them up and owned polished cauldrons too, for they knew fairies peed from their fingers and felt no pain.

Now Isisnaphut wanted the woman back and since the Fiend volunteer at the bridge was hiding shaking like a leaf under the bridge so ruined the heroic atmosphere of the story; so Isisnaphut sent a dark rider on a winged dragon that landed on the Fiend side of the bridge. This was to liven things up for now was the time for gallons of red squirting stuff and shrieks and yells to get the story going.

And he who rode the winged beast was a **Fiend** Flat Worlders and uglier than Wamba.

And he was nervous for he could hear singing at the other end of the bridge as the Garrison border guard sang,

"Mr Wamba Ordinary stands ten feet tall.

Ordinary is a lie.

Giant ape and built like a wall.

And loves to eat Fiend pie.," a Satirextex ditty so the Flat Worlders Fiend was worried as he was only a metre tall, so shook violently with these words, "I was full of XXX when I signed up."

"They all say it, for they signed up to see the world and floozy Pixy girls then come back and marry your daughters, plural of course," Aslop.

And Wamba was riding towards the Fiend so mud splattered from Old Nag's hooves and Wamba had let go of the reins for, "She might fall off," which explains where his hands where and were not holding the reins? Perhaps holding a cream bun?

Yes, Old Nag was old so tottered and did not gallop and ate fresh yellow daffodils and mushrooms and one purple toadstool with green spots. Now eating this had an effect upon the creature as it would upon you for suddenly flames shot from some place so it really did thunder towards the bridge.

Flames that reminded Wamba a place down below existed, a hot place for the **Fiend** at the bridge was waving a big two-handed axe in the air. And worse he had a green Mohican haircut and tattoos on his arms so at once we know what sort of **Fiend** he is?

I HAVE NO IDEA, DO YOU?

So, Wamba saw life flash by like how mummy sent him up cliff faces to steal sea gull eggs then sell to Harry, that *middle aged salesman* who owned a stall selling plastic dinosaurs at the bridge.

And with the cash earned mummy deposited them in a Harry Bank Account. And then mummy went back to working at Common as Muck Filthy Big Bertha's Guest House as cook.

And because Wamba was unusual never told him her surname or his daddy's name. So, all his lonely life asked, "Am I Wamba Son of Cedric the Dragon Slayer?" or "Son of Aelfric Champion of Jousting?" or "Carlsberg the Brewers Son?"

"Fat chance honey, just Wamba Urchin so get too like it," his busy mother cooking all those meat pies in Common as Muck Filthy Big Bertha's Guest House or by its respectable name, 'The Bridge Inn.'

"I am Wamba Urchin and with a name like that my daddy must have been a hero of quests in dark witch infested forests," Wamba and beamed, shame; and asked mummy, "Do I have a middle name?"

"Listen Burke mummy's busy, cannot you see the rich gentleman wants to try my sea gull eggs in mayonnaise, so go catch a fin so I can make fin soup." So, Wamba not only beamed but glowed, his middle name was Burke.

"Whatever honey, now I have clients waiting for some pie since you have not caught a fin," his busy mummy. And the four-year-old grew into a ten-year-old and Harry the salesman got a bit older for he was seen plucking grey hairs from his head with these words, "Ouch."

And Wamba was a hideous ten-year-old but do not worry he was so big was never bullied. "Why are you bullying freckled faced Brogan with the head full of red hair and buck teeth?" He did ask the bullies and because they were bullies and numbered ten were brave and silly. Silly because Wamba was not ordinary but huge and strong and did horrid things to bullies. He breathed on them for starters so they fainted so he easily got the better of them stomping here and standing there.

And was freckled faced Brogan pleased he had saved her?

"Mummy a Fiend wants to hug and squeeze me," the little girl ran home.

And Wamba knew girls hugged and cuddled those who saved them so ran after her.

But this is a happy story so freckled face Brogan got home. "Damn," Wamba and sulked away into the shadowy undergrowth.

And here a pool so Wamba decided to look at his reflection and a passing woodcutter all tanned with blond hair trailing behind, carrying his axe with bulging muscles passed the pool just as Wamba looked in.

"How handsome I am with my blond hair, never mind, it must have been a Fiend lurking in the shadows that scared freckled Brogan away for I bought this potion of beauty from Harry for he sells other things at his stall apart from plastic dinosaurs," Wamba and skipped away with these words, "Tar la boggy ," and picked flowers to sniff for he was happy and bees there stung him.

So, as he passed the bullies used them as footballs till, he bored for he was no longer happy with these words, "See how you like being stung by a bee?"

See we told you this was a happy story fairy tale for that made Wamba happy again.

And: "Drink this whole bottle when the moon is full and you hear wolves howling," Harry had instructed Wamba, "then go and kiss frogs at the pond for one is a princess waiting to marry you." And were lies but a middle-aged salesman never turns away a sucker's penny.

But a cloud covered the moon so Wamba kissed toads. And we are all told by our mummy's, except Womba's for she was busy cooking at the Common as Muck Filthy Big Bertha's Guest House, "Never kiss a toad."

"Here where have all these warts growing on my face and hands come from?" The poor boy asked so was more hideous looking than ever before.

"I feel somewhat responsible for this so have allowed him to use my mirror, soap and hairbrush for a small fee of course, and see Wamba looks handsome and sold him new clothes from cash taken from his bank account with me," and "there is no more money," and another lie, and "if you work for me for six years, I will buy you a horse to go with your new smart appearance," and was a cheap trick to get free labour so sent Wamba chimney sweeping so Wamba was dirtier and more fearsome looking than ever before.

And his other duties included picking up the litter left at the dinosaur stall. It was dangerous work; some fairies left their broken XXX bottles to cut poor Womba's shoeless feet to slithers.

"He has no cash in his bank account to buy shoes," the wicked salesman Harry.

Do you believe him? Yes? No?

So, six years passed and Wamba grew bigger but his clothes did not. And he got some education for Harry apart from sending him out in all weathers to takeaways for exotic foods let Wamba learn the menus by heart.

"I can speak Hindi, Chinese and French and other languages," and Wamba beamed.

And after six years Harry grudgingly gave him a horse, Old Nag.

"I have shares in the glue factory and a promise is a promise, so a horse I have given Wamba," Harry the evil middle-aged salesman for every story needs a wicked witch.

And Wamba left to find fame and fortune and at twenty joined the guards at the bridge here and because he did everything by numbers according to King Charles's Army regulation Book rose through the ranks to sergeant.

And now his men waited for him at the other end of the bridge and the **Fiend** waving the big axe waited for him at his own end.

And his men were fairies, real ones not the other type.

"Flutter."

Harold Gormless, private fourth class, all wrinkled and a real blond. A Viking he was and not happy for all Vikings know a man needs to row a long boat twenty hours a day to be blessed.

And because he was a Viking walked with huge knuckles in puddles for the roads of Ball are muddy, water soaked and full of leeches "Yes, Womba's our sergeant and there is none like him," Harold rolling his dice.

"And I am Corporal Conan, retired barbarian adventurer

and ravisher of women.

My hair patchy black.

My face a scar.

My knuckles walnuts.

My nose broken twenty times.

But I have teeth for I had the sense to shut my mouth while I got done.

And own the sword, Blade Runner.

You can see my blood red shot eyes,

Are full of XXX from that respectable eating house The Bridge Inn.

And see Wamba approaching so ignore him and roll dice."

"Sixes," Harold taking the opportunity to turn the dice by hand so not only did this fairy know how to lie, but too cheat so can straight away deduct he is a thief, murderer, blasphemer, womaniser, drunk and thick as toast.

"Yes, the fool Wamba is riding hard," Conan and wheezes, "for my chest aches for a sword nailed it so I retired to this easy job at the bridge, look Harold a Fiend with an axe waits for Wamba, what should you do?"

And Harold had to look so did not see Conan change the sixes to ones for Conan was a cheat too so straight away we deduct he sells exotic dangerous pets to unsuspecting kids.

And threw his own dice and they had lead in them so came up sixes and Harold knew he had been done for it takes a cheat to know a cheat.

"The pig is mine," Conan for they had gambled for it.

"Oink," a pig nearby waiting for a cauldron without a Fiend in it so would wait long and have many grand pig children and retire to a nearby pigsty at a ripe old age.

"Here what is that scream?" Harold for sure the **Fiend** had screamed for his waving antics had made him loose his balance and fall off the bridge into the moat under the bridge.

Moat water, very unhealthy so explains why the **Fiend** was screaming.

"Clatter," the noise of Old Nag crossing the wooden planked bridge.

"War, war with the Fiends," Wamba having taken his eyes of a bottom now knew what to shout.

"Flutter," went Womba's wings for do not forget these men are fairies.

And Mage Pee Wee Bat Wing attracted by the noise looked out his tower nearby.

"I am The Mage here and control Housing Building Applications and explains why everything is built near the bridge and more correctly Common as Muck Big Bertha's Guest House.

And here an Aslop fable: *"Beware the true intentions of zoo planners and where to place the monkey house?"*

And I wear white for I am a good druid and respectable and rid Wamba of some of his warts for I have many potions.

Potions a salesman would like to own but will not sell him just to be annoying.

And do not like our capital Haliput but do hear a blow dart blown. A blow dart aimed at Wamba by the **Fiend** in the moat water and will be the last thing he blows as anacondas live in that water; as well a hundred alligators, six hundred crocodiles, who knows how many fins and three hag fish and the water flows under Filthy Big Bertha's modern indoor plumbing works.

"Judas what is eating my feet?" The **Fiend** and splashed some water into what was eating him up eye's; and then added, "mummy," as the eyes of a hundred alligators, six hundred crocodiles, who knows how many fins and three hag fish glared back at him.

And the woman across Womba's saddle has petticoats billowing in Womba's face.

"Wamba, have you stolen a cook from Common as Muck Big Bertha's Guest House? Who is this pretty thing across Old Nag?" The Mage shouted taking an interest in frillies so straight away we take down the washing, well certain things in the washing when HE is about.

But the hiss of vaporising chilly air on a dart travelling at 1000m.p.h pulled his attention away from things an old man is past looking at; sunsets and passing butterflies so: "Warthogs abracadabra," The Mage shouted from his tower trying to be different.

And did the billowing skirts save Wamba from the dart? No, the hundred alligators,
six hundred crocodiles, who knows how many fins and three hag fish did for they ate the nasty **Fiend** all up except his sandals made of cheap plastic that cause constipation.

[CHAPTER 2] — — WASP

"In Ball a bush,
No flowers for a perfumed potion.
But lots of purple creeping mush.
Caterpillars doing the motion.
Caterpillars that are nasty and mean.
No leaves on the 'Yum Yum' shrub.
Just salty beans.
All Blackbird grub.
And why the caterpillars are abominable.
Its boiled roots taste tarry.
And why 'Yum Yum' is so hateable.
So only Cows like it for their tongues are big and furry.
But this 'Yum Yum' tree is famous.
It's in the tourist guide to the bridge," Satirextex that green Flat Worlders suffering boils who wrote cheap poetry about the 'Stupid fairies on the other side of the rip, vegetables with no nervous system that cheated evolution because the gads had been drunk at the Big Bang." So, this is Satirextex's ancestry? A Fiend in disguise and here an Aslop fable, *"Beware the hooded salesman?"* Is that slithery middle-aged salesman Harry meant? He who leaves a trail of London fog behind him and dreams of Ferrari chariots.

And malcontent Tom fishing in the bridge's moat, a place where sinks and latrines float.

And woolly things Wamba's feet had worn.

Said, "I caught a fish," to give an idyllic fishing atmosphere and at his feet a basket full of fins and hag fish, not salmon or trout, leeches also.

And wasps are silent so deadly because they quietly fly up and sting good heaps to be mean: whereas the bumble bee is a honey maker so is sweet and yellow and a friend to the gardener and only stings once. And silently a wasp found the

Fiend minding his own business in the moat fighting off a million leeches, the Fiend with the big heavy axe that had sunk his feet into the sludge, the rusty chamberlain pots, the bones of critters that fell in before the Fiend, and sneaking up on him, a fairy Godmother and not a Fiend Godmother so was pointing her magic wand at his back, covering it in carbuncles, leeches, spiders, and all things not nice that boys are made of.

The question was, where was the Fiend's Godmother to wiggle her magic wand and make all better and **is a secret** as no one knows.

Anyway: "I am stung," the Fiend assassin in the moat just before he vanished under
anacondas, a hundred alligators, six hundred crocodiles, who knows how many fins and three hag fish. "I am stung," the Fiend again as wanted some attention before he was erased. And the wasp stung him again for good measure.

"Titter, what have I done, giggle," the fairy Godmother who flew away to find Prince charming as she knew that poor girl Wamba carried needed one, at discount.

Now The Mage had wanted to interrogate The Fiend, you know hang him from the ceiling over hot coals, let hungry rats loose in his unmentionables, poke him in the eyes with V shaped fingers and what else, stuff a hot poker somewhere, oh yes amongst a spittoon of chestnuts as 'DELICIOUS WITH A HINT OF GARLIC BUTTER.'

"*And cruel reader, you thought it was going somewhere else, bad reader, naughty person,*" Satirextrex knowing the readers mind.

And this supposed to be a happy fairy story? Just remember it is called a **'Comedy of Soldier Fools, and rations.'**

And almost forgot Wamba's polished cauldron was ready for army food the dry biscuit mixed with corned beef, onion, salt and pepper and dried peas as the vegetable ration, and full of weevils for *weevils get about.*

And all agreed Fiends did not feel pain for they listened to Wamba who mouths,

"They scream they are fairy cousins so I will not simmer them with onions. And got
wings to buzz with like ours, wings they glued on with super glue," for Wamba knows all, everything in the world so why is called, 'IGNORANT BURKE,' behind his back.

And the assassin as said got all eaten up by anacondas, a hundred alligators, six hundred crocodiles, who knows how many fins and three hag fish, except his nose that the wasp clung to stinging the blazes out of; for wasps are psychopathic unstable disturbed insects that sting the blazes out of you for fun, and this stupid one was going down with the ship.

"And do not fret, The Fiend went back to The Source where fairies and all come from, and even at this moment is licking raspberry ice cream with chocolate fingers stuck in the ice, 'brr,' most enjoyable," Satirextrex unable to give up his Fiendish ancestry so describes a heavenly landscape where Fiend souls go, where Wamba does not exist,   paradise, *"and the wasp is dry relaxing on a cloud so be happy, this is a fairy story were extras all go to heaven."*

"It is war," Wamba posing on Old Nag for tourists with his tangled locks splayed out behind him as the girl on his saddle plans bad things for his future, like "Off with his head, broil it and stick it above this bridge as a warning to fairies, and his body quartered and a part sent to each shire of Ball, a further warning," and the poor girl did not realise there was not enough Wamba to go about and been watching 'Brave Heart,' *"and I watched it ten times, all them grisly parts and chop here and stab there,"* Satirextex a fan of FREEDOM.

"War, with whom?" The Mage putting down his garden plastic dinosaur for it doubled as a garden gnome, it had teeth.

"Them," Wamba fluttering his wings in triumph.

Was his surname not Ordinary and his middle name Burke?

"Wow," Tom watching *the dust of a mighty army with banners jostling the sky* and can be forgiven for he is the Garrison sweet innocent young recruit who has butterflies above his head, not a halo as has naughty thoughts about girl fairies as at that age, 'pukes,' bum fluff, acne, rabbit teeth, boy smell and farts too much thinking that is what BALD HEAD HARD MEN DO, fart and be darned.

Anyway, this is a Garrison sweet innocent boy? A boy with a Brill cream jar and comb in one back pocket and a packet of empty protectives in the other? *Is there a sweet innocent boy taking your daughters to a movie this week?*

Anyway: "Plastic dinosaurs going cheap," a middle-aged salesman at his stall. Yes, it was him, The Blackhood of Harry Bros Plc. That the Brotherhood wanted dead.

"Kill," the Fiend army chanted which was worrying.

"Do not worry me, a crowd is an excited crowd, thirsty, hungry, tired and easy prey to buy my plastic dinosaurs that double as garden gnomes, as have scary teeth, and if you want a gnome, got them too, see, ones with red hats and these others in bikinis for summer days," Harry.

Now Tom: "The Apprentice guard and fourteen. I joined to see the world, to get good pay, cuisine, and soft bed and Wamba lied so hate him and listen to Conan now."

"One brass Halfling for his X on the recruitment paper," Wamba and the Halfling was attached to string for Wamba had many commitments to pay Harry.

"Wamba what have you learned,
  To be a guardsman,
  A liar and thief when needed,
  And recruiting volunteers is needed," Wamba.

And Tom joined Garrison that never left here, shared a wooden hut, rotten mattresses, ate army biscuits full of weevils, and spent evenings at Big Bertha's.

Perhaps catching ideas about settling down with a nice frontiers girl, perhaps one of your daughters you wanted married off? Someone to give you sixteen grandchildren with expensive birthdays and a broke Christmas.

And dog Cur is listed private sixth class whose pay goes to Wamba, told you a thief.

"I just get ideas how to be a millionaire," Wamba and is

a common idea amongst the Ordinary and Burke's and, "I do not know what that word thief means so am guiltless, besides waitress service does not come cheap."

"*And a fairy poor lair,*" Aslop.

Anyway: "And who is this?" The Mage watching the slim girl stuff herself back into petticoats now Wamba had stopped on the fairy side of the bridge.

Had filthy Big Bertha remembered The Mage's birthday which tells us something about the goings on hereabouts?

"*And The Mage is a dirty old man,*" Satirextrex.

"What a pretty little nose?" The Mage also, "What pointed ears?" "What soft cheeks?" "What healthy teeth."

"I am Christina daughter of King Charles The Incarnation of god Ball, Defender of all fairies, Slayer of Flat Worlders, Invoker of Magic Realms."

"What idiot brought my king's daughter here?"

And the idiot remained silent.

And The Mage, "Why did I stay at Filthy Big Bertha's, why am a drunk?"

"Off with his head," Conan to be annoying.

"A real princess?" Wamba

"Wow," Tom and put on his innocent boyish look so disarmed the girl.

"Grr," a nasty dog and tore her petticoats to shreds and not a fairy stopped the dog.

"*Not only The Mage was a dirty minded fink, they all where finks,*" Satirextrex having a good look too.

"Kissing frogs is out, now I want a dragon to rescue her from and my future
secured," Wamba for see he was a Burke, an idiot.

Did not Harry who is called Give a Copper Harry tell him this to get rid of him from his dinosaur stall for Wamba was so hideous customers looked the other way and went to that other stall, an Offaltrex stall selling strange pies and drinks to the tired tourists.

"Recipes handed down from Granny Offaltrex," Offaltrex so knew his pies were made of everything that a possum was made up off and the thingamabobs that came out of sewers nightly with ringed tails.

And Harry the fairy with black wings fluttered for worrying about the opposition causes much wind and bowel complaints. "That is me and everyone but Wamba knows dragons do not exist," Harry, note BLACK WINGS that some salesmen have, a warning not to eat his curry pies as is scooping's from the moat drained and flavoured hot so ingredients is not noticed.

"But I saw one coming out of the rip.

 A big yellow one spitting fire.

With flat feet," Wamba insisted to be annoying for dragons eat fairies.

 "So, the Fiends have broken in," The Mage looking at the dust cloud with contorted face and everyone looked at him with respect and did not know his mind was empty.

"And I demand to be taken home," but a magic finger click silenced her, no royal sounds such as, "I am annoyed, off with a head."

"Wow."

And Harold salivated as his intestinal worms demanded notice. This was no lie as Garrison Men are prone to them. For those who make possum pie get licked by Cur the dog and use the outhouse and Filthy Big Bertha's and *never wash their hands.*

"My cooks wash and the gravy is hot and a little soap goes a long way," Offaltrex defending his hygiene record.

And Cur the dog admitted the girl was pretty by licking her good, then humping her right leg.

"Go away," the princess pleaded but the dog did not as jumped on her left leg.

And The Mage looked at his Garrison friends then at the stable, saw Bat Wing who had not flown in years his flying bat.

Either had he, "I am afraid of heights and fairies are supposed to fly. And doubt if the bat can carry me and the princess to Haliput.

"*Oh yeh, him and the princess, oh yeh?*" Satirextrex full of envy.

What Friends? Conan the cheat, Harold who rummages for grubs under my tulips. Tom who worships Wamba and needs putting down;" but The Mage was wrong, Tom kept a Wamba dolly in his secret place, full of pins for, *"He lied to me when I enlisted."*

Wamba whose name is Ordinary Burke Urchin?

"Oh yes, the dog? A dog that lurks behind bushes while I stagger past coming home late from Filthy Big Bertha's, then lurches at my feet and before I can remember how to click has gnawed me here and there.

Goodbye," and The Mage walked away and Harold thought he heard him say he was off to supper vented bad wind out of jealousy as Garrison Men eat boring food, corn beef three times a day with dried peas and weevils, and weevils are like you and me so poop and pee for flavour as is the vinegar effect added to the salt and pepper, is scrumptious. **For these fairies are army men and proud volunteers,** not conscripts like the Fiendish army coming.

Now where had The Mage gone?

To Bat Wing amid the sound of ZAP and ZOOM and VROOM and penguins complaining.

"And the bat would not wake up, even when I stamped here and kicked especially there, "Wake up," I screamed and pulled up an eyelid and saw XXX, "Blo****g Filthy Big Bertha again."

So was doomed to stay and be a volunteer and defend the bridge," The Mage.

"Looks like them thirty thousand Fiends are closer," Conan just to be annoying.

"Who needs bats when broomsticks can do, where is that salesman Harry?" The Mage knowing a true salesman has many deep compartments selling thingamabobs fallen off wagons.

But the salesman was nowhere near just an empty stall and not a plastic dinosaur souvenir to be bought for all was packed away.

"Never fear brave Guardsmen, my father King Charles will

hear of my plight and come save me," Christina the girl whom Wamba had rescued from Isisnaphut the Fiend King just in case you forgot; and did not include her father saving Garrison.

But they understood for they was army volunteers, expendables.

"My kingdom for a broom," The Mage fuming turning mushrooms into ugly toadstools out of meanness for he was desperate to flee.

"He was a dirty minded fink," Satirextex and better hope the mage never hears him.

"When you get a broom can, I come with you?" Harold showing big sad knowledgeable eyes of an orang-outang understanding its forest home is about to be destroyed by Fiends.

Now The Mage might like pretty ankles and have a collection of 'Mountain Treks with Ted,' magazines under his bed but he was really a decent old fink. "How can one turn Harold into a toadstool?" So calmed down and looked at Garrison as fond memories flooded him of singing acholic songs in front of a fire in Big Bertha's surrounded by apprentice Big Berthas with exposed melons, vegan drumsticks a plenty, alcohol spillage on the floor so the whole place and you stunk of XXX.

And that nasty dog Cur peed on The Mage's left foot and then was gone.

Just what had The Mage done to that poor defenceless animal to make it so horrid to him? It just hated all, was fed up eating corn beef and weevils, wanted new horizons, of green fields full of white bunnies to chew and passing milk maid legs to hit, hump and run.

"Wow," Tom in anticipation of the dog becoming a rabbit so it could chase itself.

The wand rose, Wamba held up pleading hands knocking the magic wand and a ball of sulphuric green smelly yucky landed on The Mage's tower which had rose vines growing, and tulips along the pathway to the front door **which had**

once stood where a tower had once been. Well, it was sort of still standing, bits; my you could see the loo and the tin copper bath.

Cur sniggered and 'hit, humped, and ran,' a princess.

And all The Mage's printed shorts were fluttering about on the breeze; and them magazines he kept under his bed; magazines, 'Origami with Ted, Father Ted and Ted that bear,' would you believe, I do not, remember what Ted represents in the movies, sex.

And all the fairy wings went "Flutter" and Garrison said, "It was not us but them Fiends," that came from years of passing the bucket; for they knew a wand would turn many Fiends into cross eyed newts so Garrison was on best behaviour.

"They have a powerful wizard in their ranks and he has my number, now that makes me annoyed and see the Fiend has done me a favour for see vermin leave my tower?" For The Mage had it in for cuddly vermin and he was right, mice and rats carrying luggage where filing down the garden path, he was also mistaken, no Fiend had sent magic to his tower, it was not Cur that jumped his leg, it was Wamba knocking him, just as well for Wamba The mage was confused, or be turned into Pinocchio with a long nose to dry his washing on.

"Wow," Tom and pointed at a valuable portrait of a woman with a funny smile carried on the back of a rat. And all had heard about The Mage's collection of art by masters and suspected he obtained them by the wave of a wand, where others had to pay to see them in a museum.

It was the perks of the magic trade see, a thief like Wamba.

Now The Mage softened for this was his home, why he saw a picture of mummy now upside down where a crack ran down a wall. Yes, this was his home and the
sad eyes of whatever Harold was bored into him. Who would feed Harold his nuts and bananas?

"Ouk," Harold appreciatively.

And a dog with a bad streak silently went behind The Mage and silently left an overpowering smell.

Will The Mage ever tell us what he did to that dog to make it so mean, **no, it is a secret?**

"Click," and "howl," for an invisible boot from nowhere booted the poor dog.

"Grr," the nasty dog hating The Mage just waiting to chew the wand too bits. A wand Cur hated but why, **it is a secret?**

"Well, " The Mage looking at the Guardsmen who seemed to look like discarded toys fit for the rubbish bin, "I am staying, and you Wamba will defend the bridge."

"Yes Wamba, you stay and defend the bridge," Conan making sure '**you**' was emphasised.

"What brave heroes," Christina and was a foolish thing to say for Wamba now knew he was a hero and that she did love him and her papa King Charles would promote him to general and give him his own yacht for his honeymoon with her.

It also awoke a devil on The Mage's right shoulder.

"Listen chum, look at them, you owe them nothing, go give the bat a taste of the whip and get out of here, just think of Haliput and the many 'Common as Muck Big Bertha's Guest Houses' under other names there! Remember 'Common as Trash Julia's Tea Rooms' for weary travellers and 'Rosemary's Infirmary' for cold seamen and," but an angel with a whip on the other shoulder appeared and *"Crack,"* and *"yikes."*

"He is in the gutter for he is gutter snipe. Do what he tells you and The Mage upstairs will send you to The Mage downstairs where it is hot, understand?" The angel that looked like a Cindy Doll in white frills so The Mage really wanted to go up.

"He was a dirty minded fink," Satirextrex whose envy was to want him to kill his brother fairy, The Mage.

"We will fight their Fiend king and be sang about," Wamba screeching.

And The Mage remembered their king was covered in pimples and suffered bad breath so had no friends apart from Teddy who never called him anything for Teddy could not speak for Teddy was stuffed and had buttons as eyes for Teddy was a Teddy Bear.

And Cur never told anyone about the Fiend he had seen

in the carriage Wamba had snatched Christina from. Was it because of the nasty streak, no because he could only say, "Woof, grr, bark, howl," sort of thing so only other dogs understood, and The Mage who if was not ogling could have used a spell so Cur could speak Balinese, then Cur could tell what he saw.

So, Cur went and humped a floozy leg in Filthy Big Berthas, and "Get out you filthy dog," and Cur was seen thrown out the front door followed by army boots, spittoons, corned beef dumplings, uncooked green neaps, and Ted.

[CHAPTER 3] — BARRICADE

"I was happy the mantle of leadership had landed on me," Wamba a delirious guardsman at the bridge.

"**Wow**," and in case you forgot it was Tom showing his innocence that was becoming annoying and to be annoying back did you know he slept with a plastic dinosaur under his pillow and sucked his thumb.

"He was just a baby," Satirextex, cooing the twerp.

And Cur dragged twigs to the barricade Guardsmen were building and Guardsmen were not happy for thirty thousand fuzzy jazzy Fiends was heading to eat them with garlic dip because 'do what your neighbour does to you.'

"Fetch," Garrison Men and threw sticks in the moat for they trusted the nasty dog not for it was not house trained and it remembered all the boots from them. So brought the sticks back for it was a dog, so the barricade builders were forced to keep one eye on the beast; and it was those eyes that saw thirty thousand fuzzy jazzy Fiends heading to eat them, with ketchup.

"Put your backs into it lads," Wamba giving orders from Old Nag for he knew generals never lifted a thing and, on a horse, could flee faster than them on foot who would naturally slow the Fiends down.

"But Wamba was not a general just a smart volunteer," Satirextex.

"That idiot thinks my papa will reward him with my hand in marriage," Christina whispering to the dog; for dogs are the friend of man so say "Woof" all the time.

"Woof," the dog with a nasty streak and sniggered to prove the point and "does not say the friends of women," so jumped a leg.

"I will throw my silk handkerchief in front of the barricade just as the Fiends reach it and knowing Wamba will pick it up and have no marriage worries," Christina confiding in Cur for she knew dogs never spoke so her secret was safe, "What are you doing you dirty dog?"

And the dog giggled this time and Christina must have it in her rose garden as an added attraction in her frog pond sitting on a lily.

But did not tell the nasty dog this who thought it was going to live a life of royalty in the kitchens. And here an Aslop fable: *"Dogs that have learnt to giggle should go a step further and learn to read."*

Anyway, "Come on Conan show us how many logs a barbarian adventurer can carry," and Wamba did not add at the same time so Conan had three on each shoulder for he was Conan, slayer of dragons and one of those types who had to prove it.

"Now where did that dog go?" Christina.

"Woof," Cur speaking to The Mage who had a jolly good laugh about Wamba.

And here the bit that fell off the last fable, *"Trust not stray dogs that giggle."*

"Puff poof wheeze," Conan taking a breather filling his body full of fresh tobacco smoke as he, "puff poof gasp" on his clay pipe. "Here Harold," and let the Viking
see a tasty peanut," for you when you carry them logs here, understand?"

"Ouk," Harold the retired Viking and had a jolly good laugh at the suggestion and tapped his head.

But they did manage to build up the barricade for The Mage knew without magic it would not be built before the ospreys returned to nest at the moat.

And a wine barrel rolled out of the ruined tower of The Mage, his best wine and the tap was correctly pointed in the direction of the defenders for their work was thirsty. And the tap flew off when a stone was met and the wine poured into the moat.

"Burp," was heard often from fish and Garrison Men who knew the XXX would kill off 99.9 % anything nasty the moat had, so filled their water bottles.

"The miscreants why I will turn them into missionaries," The Mage to be cruel to alcoholics.

And Wamba grinned at the princess and showed yellow teeth for the word dentist he knew not. Fangs flipped over his lips that advertised everything granny said about were-wolves lurking in neighbourhood trash cans true; they had High School thoughts towards pretty ankles.

And the lass knew he was in love with her, and the question that raced through her mind, **"Why me?"**

She also realised from that smile Wamba was a Burke. Mind you his men knew that for years but no one ever asked their opinion. Why they did tell you Wamba was fearless, brave, and drunk most nights at The Bridge Inn and popular for he bought rounds of XXX and then it did not matter if he was a Burke.

"And lucky for me The Mage never saw me roll that barrel out of his tower, why the last time I got on the wrong side of that fool he gave me rabbit ears for a week," Conan and "puffed sweated puffed" on his clay pipe and "click," as he became a were-rabbit with an insatiable craving for carrots in mayo.

"Click," and Conan never heard that and never noticed a floozy bunny in a field giving him a wink for he was refilling his water bottle with moat water full of someone's wine.

And The Mage clicked his fingers again.

"Poof," the magic variety and a trench filled with moat water in front of the barricade and there were crocodiles in it wanting to get out, but The Mage always thought ahead so made the sides steep so they were stuck in the moat.

"What happened to the wine?" Satirextrex not noticing the thousands of filled water bottles.

Do not worry, no cruelty was shown the crocodiles for the water was mixed with The Mage's best wine so soon many crocodiles saw pink Fiends approaching spinning for they were drunk reptiles.

"I must bottle that water and sell it at my stalls as 'Harry's Colic Cure," an oily salesman whispers hiding behind a big plastic

dinosaur otherwise would not be hidden.

And Harry did not cast a shadow.

Was he a vampire then?

No, just well hidden.

And Garrison was not happy for them types of crocodiles swallowed fairies whole so could not refill their water bottles again for they had the alcoholic shakes that only more XXX can cure. So hated The Mage something out of this world.

"Poof," again as The Mage turned himself into a fly and went scouting.

"Wow," Tom showing his innocence for he wanted to be a magician too and take bunnies out of hats and have a floozy girl take it away for the pot and share the supper with as the sun rose over a flamingo filled lake. To be a magician to turn Freddy Rex his plastic dinosaur into a soft cuddly dinosaur with a slit for a hot water bottle so Tom could love it more, hug and warm his pyjamas in. And magic to give it a voice so when hugged it would responded with, "Goodnight handsome boy, now say goodnight to Ted," for the dinosaur had a name, and when Tom fell asleep, Ted sneaked out the dog flap and:

"Oh, Ted you are so adorable.

Oh, Ted, you are soft and cuddly.

Oh, Ted you are funny.

Oh, Ted you are a drunk Ted.

Oh, Ted Cur taught you to?

Oh, Ted OUT, go home time," the floozy waitresses at Filthy Big Bertha's who thought it funny Ted was humping their legs. Then his humour ran dry as he was drunk and his speech slurred, so **'OUT.'**

Besides what dinosaur carries cash.

"Out."

It also did not help like all drunks, Ted vomited on them.

"Ugly sounds, bone crushing sounds, but Ted had stuffing so, the sound of stuffing been ripped his places and then a mop stuck in there and then used to mop his mess up.

THEN,

OUT,

As he was thrown out.

Anyway: "Buzz," a fly passing.

"Woof," which means snigger.

"Nice ears corporal," the princess passing him and Cur giggled.

"Buzz," went the fly with a nasty streak.

And Conan winked at the princess and she read that wink as meaning he was a dirty old bugger that meant to marry her. Was he not Conan of the Legends, was he not the same man as a freckled teenager she had allowed to sneak into her rose garden and pick green fly with her.

"Yes, there is a monster in Loch Ness?" Aslop.

But he was no longer handsome and fit to climb the steep wall of the garden; he was just a rabbit now that floozy rabbits in a field hopped over to wink closer at him.

And he spat tobacco at her red shoes. "Sorry princess," and he bent down and wiped it using a sleeve.

And he had a mirror on a ring so deserved the foot placed where one makes sounds.

And horrified she was for she realised the black sleeve was not cloth or leather but unwashed skin and the rabbits seeing that too hopped away to find boyfriends who washed, for rabbits are clean animals.

And something pinged onto her, a hungry ping thing. Perhaps it was a beautiful butterfly but more likely a nasty blood sucking flea.

"Kill," the thirty thousand Flat-Worlders Fiends chanted heading their way and should have been at the barricades ages ago, but they was Fiends and needed encouragement to "kill," so had stopped for tea and muffin in a nearby establishment: and because there were thirty thousand of them Filthy Big Bertha managed to pay of her mortgage with Harry Bros. PLC. In an afternoon.

"Life will be short here, let's boggy girl while we can?" Conan remembering picking green fly long ago.

"Daddy," Christina squeaked but daddy was the type that preferred a cheap bottle of meths to a daughter with pretty ankles. .

"Is not here, only Garrison," he replied.

"And rabbit."

"What do you mean?"

And now is the time to give a secret away? Yes, Cur the dog had a bad streak, encouraged to be mean and revengeful for when The Mage returned late from

Common as Muck Big Bertha's Guest House full of XXX he sent giant rabbits after innocent Cur. Hilarious so The Mage went to bed without nightmares but the dog whimpered in the common bed in the Garrison hut so woke all up.

So, Cur was thrown out the shut door but do not worry the moat ensured a soft landing and Cur knew how to swim so the alligators and leeches never had him for supper.

And being wet shivered and sneezed as flu bugs were about and crawled back into the hut to sleep warm and cosy amongst Garrison clothes for these fairies never hung or folded their clothes to go to bed. So, see a happy ending for Cur who laughed in his sleep dreaming of the day when The Mage would get his innings, from a dog.

A dog who had devil and an angel on his shoulders. A devil that should be called Gnasher for it had many teeth and with these words, "Woof," encouraged Cur to be mean, vicious and bite The Mage whenever he could after Cur licked his thingamabobs, for he was more than vicious, he was educated which meant he was dangerous.

Been brought up with loose magic which meant he had read The Mage's collection of 'Home Beautiful.'

No wonder it had 'hump' on the brain.

Thank you, Mage.

To jump on your girlfriend's leg and ladder her silks of course. And worse the devil had a tail and looked like a wolf under a heroes red cape.

And on the other shoulder an angel that looked like a pink dyed poodle under a Barbie white plastic cape and with these words, "Woof," encouraged Cur to be good and angelic and fetch

34

sticks, roll on the back and wag the tail hoping for a tummy rub,
to sleep and dream of you running with it across meadows

CHAPTER 4
COUNTERATTACK

Now remember The Mage went away as a fly scouting Flat Worlders, so was swallowed by flamingos, stung by bees, trodden by cows, soaked in a rainstorm, hit by lighting over a golf course, then reached enemy lines in a state of shock.

"Buzz," the dishevelled fly.

Now somewhere a brave fairy led Garrison against the Fiends in a counterattack for Book had given Wamba the wrong advice.

There were about thirty thousand Fiends.

"Here nice barbecue stick," and shows a mean streak in Wamba as he made sure Cur kept ahead.

"Woof," so cursed the night he was born a dog and added, "howl," for effect.

Now a certain barbarian knew of Wamba's cruelty and was distanced from fairy and beast for he was a volunteer.

"That is why I have a rope about that barbarian Conan's neck and he cannot protest as I am 7' tall and he is shrivelled up with arthritis," Wamba giving a new name to bullying.

And Wamba smiled and Christina was ill. "I will cover my face with false moles and put him off," Christina but was ill so did not follow her plan up.

"I feel responsible for that smile for I sold Wamba whitener. Do not ask me the ingredients apart form there is no chalk hereabouts." Harry's voice carried from his stall on a mystery

whisper.

"Listen Tom, we got to steal that Regulation Book of Wamba's and throw it in the moat and any second this rope will be off me and that fool will be one volunteer less," Conan and proves the point that when you think of someone, they turn up **just like that**; so "Shriek," as Wamba pulled the rope tighter for psychiatrists knew it was his resentment at being an Ordinary wanting to come out, that was OK and to be encouraged.

"Ouk," one of the roped.

"Here I will tie the rope to a stick and the fool will never now it is not us for see, the stick sticks in that hole and Wamba tugs as he thinks it is us resisting, ha he," Conan laughing the way a retired barbarian can then held his tummy for years of XXX made it loud, stinky, and agonising.

"What did the rabbit say, turn right," Tom and did and pulled the volunteers into the River Eiderdown.

"Fetch," Wamba throwing a stick over Fiends and Cur chased it.

"Woof," a dog with a nasty streak cursing this day.

"Kill," the Fiends objecting to Cur's presence.

"Woof," the cunning dog disappearing with a Fiendish lunch of roast goose, roast potatoes, and greens to keep Fiends healthy and shiny and shows no one likes Garrison rations are weevil infested biscuits.

Weevils instead of greens to keep the ills of Common as Muck Big Bertha's Guest House away, not antibiotics either.

"Here that dog is getting away from us lads, here nice doggy come to me," Conan wanting goose for Garrison are a greedy bunch.

"Woof," also greedy, eating all the goose, roast potatoes, and healthy greens just like that.

"I will do something nasty to that heinous dog," Conan.

"Buzz," and was The Mage and flew about Wamba who reading his Book had flattened himself so all the hungry peeved Flat Worlders would not see him; for he was reading, 'Field craft' from his Book,

"Here where is the rest of Book, it cannot end just like that? And what is this an order slip, 'From Harry's Bookshop volume 2,' here I need to know what to do next?" Wamba for he was thick as steak chips and needed to think for himself and remembered Conan's words of advice, "Never volunteer Tom, a general sends an officer who sends a sergeant who sends a corporal who sends Tom but since I like you lad tell Harold I need him."

"Oh, Harold where art thou?" Wamba sweetly.

And was a mistake for lying flat had been hidden from the Fiends who now were attracted to his sweet melodious voice.

And he pulled the stick to bring Harold up who he would volunteer but because he did not have volume 2 did not know what to volunteer him for?

For Wamba was a thick potato needing made into thick steak chips.

"Here I am all alone apart from this stick with no volunteers on the end of it?"

Wamba and stood up frothing and mumbling disbelief in these words, "You blooming selfish miscreants."

"Woof," and a dog with vermin blood in him ran between Wamba's legs with a rope that wound about Wamba for the nasty dog knew what it was doing. A dog bred with cunning but not looks for it had a face like a rat.

"Buzz," and flew away not wanting to see a grown man get nasties done him by thirty thousand hungry peeved Flat Worlders Fiends who wanted to eat Wamba as thick steak chips with salt.

"Hello," a Fiend thinking Wamba an offering of peace from the defenders of the bridge, for Wamba was tied up with rope.

"Hey, it is the Burke they call 'Warty,' behind his back another Fiend bravely.

"Aye, the one who smells of unmentionables who stole the princess from us, so let us show him our appreciation as we can go home," and put the boot in as King Isisnaphut was watching.

"I am Wamba strong and eat my breakfast so can with a

huff and puff break the ropes binding me," Wamba and the Fiends had a jolly laugh when he failed.

"He was a P.O.W. and perhaps was not the breakfast eating that did not save him, but his dislike of bitter Brussel Sprouts and metallic Spinach, so was not strong like |Pope Eye the Sailor Man, but weak like Ted the teddy bear with his stuffing yanked out being used as a mop in Filthy Big Bertha's.

CHAPTER

5   AMBITIONS

"Hello, remember me I am that beautiful princess Christina with a rose garden where I played Ambition with Lord Tootanfoot and then snigger behind his back, "There goes that ugly idiot Tootanfoot," and give him strange finger signs and pull faces so stretch my mouth and wiggle my tongue and look like Tootanfoot, an idiot, but I am a princess so silence.

I want to be queen for selfish reasons, the servants, a royal galley rowed by those I dislike, my own handy man the Chief Executioner for odd jobs, the dishes of Wild Condor Eggs sprinkled in deep sea star fish dust decorated with Great White Shark poached eyeballs.

Of course, I feel for those collecting my food, but look at the exciting career opportunities have created for those who make strange finger signs behind my back.

And have some strange friends like Tootanfoot and Isisnaphut and am afraid of Wamba for he is not my type. I fear he never washes just switches his unmentionables with revelers from Filthy Big Bertha's."

"I am Wamba and know Christina is my type. I love her

because she is a princess and can give me a palace and hundreds of servants to change unmentionables with."

"I am Corporal Conan and want rid of these rabbit ears then visit Common as Muck Big Bertha's Guest House and get waitress service with my curry fish head soup. Get full of XXX so I can eat those fisheyes, and never change my clothes for the exertion might give me the shakes and always undermine Wamba to save Tom."

And want to save Tom because of a dream that Tom is the product of a temple deep in a jungle that had a thousand priestesses to the swamp goddess that needed ravaged?

"I am Tom and want to be a sergeant like Wamba who is my role model in life."

"Ouk, I am Harold and fit for nothing and love peanuts covered in rancid butter sauce." And fit for nothing except to be a creepy crawly extra for the story.

"Woof," which means "I am Cur and want bones and more bones preferably the bones of The Mage."

"Buzz," "I am The Mage and want rid of them all."

"I am Lord Tootanfoot who people give strange finger signs too and want to be king and own a deep coal mine and send them who laugh to mine, "Here comes that idiot Tootanfoot," there without a union card so must work twenty hours a day.

"Isisnaphut and want to conquer the world, a common disease amongst leaders."

"And we the voices of thirty thousand Flat Worlders Fiends chant, "Kill anyone who is not a Fiend."

"I am the travelling merchant Give a Copper Harry who owns that depilated dinosaur stall and cannot please all my customers who scream, "Here these dinosaurs are just bits of plastic bottles stuck together," but by such devious means shall become the richest and greatest salesman ever," and perhaps sell you a water bottle for winter?

And we the Brotherhood are those types that failed society so set up our own, have dyed hair, have thousands of body piercings so make it difficult if not outright agony to walk, wear dark hoods as are ashamed of our tattooed pinned cosmetic altered faces, altered by Harry Plc. Cosmetic Surgeons whose other duties was to make plastic dinosaurs to sell.

Yes, we haunt the streets seeking Harry's aspiring cousins and stick them in sacks to trade with Fiends for rancid butter sauce that is good for the skin. And we give the aspirers to the Fiends as just do not have it in our souls to kill them.

And we Fiends sell the aspirers back to Harry at discount as cheaper by the dozen, so cheer, a happy fairy ending.

So, ambition temporally ends.

CHAPTER 7   THE FLY

An update: Roped Garrison Men had fallen into the moat and Wamba had been caught by Fiends. And a fly was buzzing about needing put down. And everything the princess did was OK as she had pretty ankles.

"Oh, beasties in the sky,
 Wish I were you.
 A disease spreading fly.
From flower to kitchen loo.
Buzz.
Big and black.
Buzz.
Blue or green I land on your sweaty back.
Spreading disease with dirty bristles.
With big black eyes.
I can answer to whistles.
Six creeping legs make crispy battered fry's.
And regurgitated food.
Buzzing.
From sugar lump to teacup when I take the mood.
Buzzing.
Spreading disease.
From latrine to me," Satirextex scribbled on a latrine wall waiting for paper but there was no attendant as Harry owned the outhouse and attendants cost money.

FUTURE
   And this inscription is on the plastic base of a plastic fly

at the modern-day bridge. A plastic fly 10 feet tall and is surrounded by vendor stalls run by priests to the fly god and they give 20% of profits to Harry Bros. PLC the future owners of the bridge for the privilege of working the tourists dry. *Selling plastic flies for "Dinosaurs cannot be fab for ever sniff sob,"* Harry very fond of T Rex that made him millions.

And after reading Satirextex you can see why he remains a forgotten poet. *"Never mind I come cheap and that is all Harry worries about, the cheaper the better."*

"I want to stay rich," the greedy salesman Harry whispers wondering when Satirextex will come out of the outhouse and get back to work.

And tourists come to the future bridge for they read the tour guide of Harry World Tours promising a wonder of the world and a plastic statue of a fly is a wonder is it not? A fly with monstrous bulbous black eyes and hair like life bristles so kids run screaming and work up a thirsty sweat, and Lo, Behold an ice cream vendor and with twenty ice creams bought, a free plastic fly.

"Blooming ugly," the art critics meaning Satirextex and not the fly that is borrowed from where Satirextex is, the outhouse.

But FLY does the trick as the tourists are too ill to eat so the eats is scraped back into the pot with these words, "Waste not as a hundred tourists to feed tomorrow."

And the fly is happy, well fed and a wooden outhouse to shelter in.

"It answers to Sheila, " Harry proudly.

And Harry dancing girls loitering the pavement about Common as Muck Big Bertha's Guest House with red lights above them advertising BINGO.

"Want young fairy girl sailor?" The gorgeous floozy fairy girl's mummy warned you about for every tourist is a sailor, soldier, tinker, undertaker, debt collector.

PRESENT

Anyway: "Grunt," Wamba making rude noises as he swung upside down on a pole after being captured by Fiends, beaten black and blue, poked places, and almost made totally useless to start a dynasty with his princess for Fiends know how to be Fiendish.

Now Wamba was a prisoner of Isisnaphut the Fiend king who was about to torture him for information.

"Give the prisoner a snail," and Isisnaphut indicated Wamba who accepted for Fiends knew how to disguise their food so we cannot blame Wamba for choking on the sinewy bits.

"This is what I joined for? Exotic food, too see China Town," for he was a Burke.

"How many men are defending the bridge?" Isisnaphut asked and a cook gave Wamba another chewy bit that might have been an ear once.

"The bravest," and shows Wamba can lie for his men were volunteers.

"You mean King Charles has his champions there?" Isisnaphut.

"How could he?" Tootanfoot disgusted Wamba was having a good chew on the other ear and forced himself to watch Wamba chew away for the ear was a Fiend who had accidentally fallen in the cauldron; for to say otherwise is too imply something nasty.

And Tootanfoot afraid of King Isisnaphut unpredictability was ill under his hood for he could never chew on a Fiend.

"Do not you fairies ever bathe?" Isisnaphut for he was upwind of Tootanfoot.

"Wonderful," Wamba finding things tasted better with chopped parsley and so never told anyone the champions was Garrison Men.

"And you have Christina with the pretty little nose?" Isisnaphut offering Wamba lots of wine for he knew XXX made people talk. But this was not ordinary people but seasoned drunks who visited Common as Muck Big Bertha's Guest House.

Garrison Men who cuddled up to pink elephants and not teddy except for Tom who had Freddy Rex for he was innocent.

And Tootanfoot was amazed Wamba drank a flagon of Fiendish wine that was peppery and sour for it was off so said in amazement, "What sort of men has my great, great, great, great, uncle reinforced the bridge with for the usual Garrison Men are those rejected from sitting positions in galleys. This tall ugly fairy with warts who has eaten the ambassador from Haliput; *(see Fiends are not cannibals)* and drank a flagon of disgusting wine cannot be one of the diseases that are Garrison Men?" Tootanfoot and saw the big hands of Wamba and, "This is he who rode single handily to my carriage and ripped the door handle off and stole Christina," and Tootanfoot began to salivate as he got dejected for, he could see Wamba's hands holding him down on the executioner's wooden block as the crowd shouted, "Encore."

"And I will not disappoint them as I am Lord Tootanfoot."

And a fly landed on him.

"Swat," as a fly swatter did its messy work.

Then an evil wizard joined the party.

Why bats flew about him for he was lofty.

And eyes red slits.

And little black lizards ran up his wizard's robes.

Green robes in a skull print design from Marks and Spencer's.

Grinning skulls.

And a dried scorpion hung from his belt.

And he wore a pointed black wizard's hat.

And a spider continually ran up and down it so must have been insane.

"Buzz," a fly, "my suspicions about a wizard are correct," and the fly crawled dizzily away to hide and cast spells to cure ache and pains caused by a fly swatter and to cause something bulbous and smelly to grow at the point of Tootanfoot's nose for the fly knew revenge was sweet.

Now every night Tootanfoot did have nightmares and see a giant fly swatter swatting him certain places. Nasty cruel fly that loved latrines without paper go away.

"Buzz."

And because the fly had aches and pains the bulbous smelly thing grew at the end of Tootanfoot's left foot so he had to hobble.

Nasty cruel fly that loved latrines without paper go away.

And because the fly was nasty put a carbuncle where Tootanfoot sat.

Nasty cruel fly that loved latrines without paper go away.

"I will turn the grovelling lord into a pin cushion not a smelly bulbous thingy," the wizard for he disliked Tootanfoot who everyone gave strange finger signs to behind his back.

Oh, poor Tootanfoot no one loves you for you are a creep that is why.

"And as soon as Isisnaphut makes Tootanfoot King of Ball for a day he will hear the patter of the executioner's small feet and I will be king and marry Christina for I have been picking green fly in her rose garden and see, in this locket a piece of her blond hair so I can swoon over her memory." For the wizard could look in a mirror and with a click of finger make himself Prince Charming until the spell worked off, and then he became an ugly lofty skinny freckled nerd of a wicked evil wizard again.

"And I will send Isisnaphut back through the rip covered in rancid butter sauce, and perhaps Tootanfoot as croutons to keep the water crest company and I laugh evilly.

And only one fairy can stop me, The Mage."

"Buzz," a fly on a spying mission.

Oh, yes?

Oh, no?

"Frizzle as Alicadabara the wizard thought flies were dirty insects for they could be found on the walls of public smelly places where there was no paper.

"Then I will trample The Mage," and Alicadabara trampled the fly good.

"Do not like flies do we Ali?" Tootanfoot and was a mistake to sneer for a wand waved and, "fetch," as the wizard threw a peanut and a monkey out off a green smudge appeared, "and since the monkey is a lord needs a donkey to ride," and Ali turned Wamba into a donkey *and this is a comedy distraction as Harry is approaching with dinosaurs.*

So was obvious to a fly, a lord and an Ordinary they were all in bad company.

And a Fiend tied a carrot to the end of a stick for a donkey to chase.

Anyway: "Buzz," a fly returning to a tower or more precisely the remains of a fine tower with windowsill flower boxes. "Buzz, this sun makes me lazy and there are no Garrison Men about so can land on that tasty biscuit crawling with weevils, no better from a fly's view of the world I see cooking remains behind my stove, lovely smelly dinner remains," and a fly had to buzz down and do what a fly must do.

Regurgitate.

"My from down here I can see the repairs to my winding stairwell are rubbish and that is what I get for hiring Harry. Wants to sell plastic dinosaurs well I will pool him into a disappointed tourist who just bought one; but was my own fault for I never looked at the building contractor's documents as I was at Common as Muck Big Bertha's Guest House playing a card game and could not concentrate for breasts the size of melons were pressed close to my eyes. It was a completely innocent accident as a serving girl tripped and landed on my lap," the fly.

"And it was a sting of an accident for 20% went to Big Bertha," a whisper and it sounds like Harry who adds, "I have pockets full of rabbit feet and garlic necklaces so am protected against The Mage's spells and I kept 80%."

"Woof," as a dog appeared and ate what the fly was eating for dogs that have kind streaks can smell something smelly and tasty lying on the floor for months, then come and lick your face good.

"Buzz, " a fly struggling to escape a dog's mouth full of sticky saliva and foul breath for dogs lick unmentionable places and sniff each other at the end places then lick you.

"Will I get a medal?" Tom to be irritating.

"Yes, but next time stay close like I told you," Conan and the fly wondered what the Garrison Men had been up to?

"I really showed that Fiend at the bridge who was boss did I not? " Tom persisted.

"Yeh why I can see him prostrating on the bridge from here looking for his head you chopped off," for a retired barbarian adventurer knew sarcasm. And the barbarian thought of Harry's stall and more tobacco.

"Water," and Conan knew things must be bad if Harold was not thinking nuts and had spoken a human word. And did not help put out the flames engulfing Harold as he had tripped into a carelessly left building contractor's charcoal heater. Just at the bottom of The Mage's tower, Harry Bros. was stamped on the heater.

"He has damaged the heater so will sue him," that greedy whisper.

"I have more important things to occupy my mind like to dry my tobacco and is all that Viking's fault drying himself out. Did he not amble into the Fiendish commando assault platoon crossing the moat because we had fallen into the moat?

So was in the wrong place at the right time because volunteers always are.

And one Fiend complained about the brackish moat water splashed onto his rations of grilled pike in rancid butter sauce. And then all the other Fiends complained and that ape who pretends to be a retired Viking replied, 'Ouk,' and went berserk for Garrison Men's rations are weevil infested biscuits; now if they did only provide ketchup?"

"Yes, and you fought with your bare hands when a Fiend shouted, 'Hey boys a rabbit, can make a change from all this grilled pike and duck and geese in rancid butter sauce that is Fiendish army rations," Tom to be innocently annoying of course.

"Yeh, the way Harold stuffed that pike tail down his throat is amazing," Conan jealous.

"And you was lucky you snatched the head away as you fell overboard from the assault craft," Tom being maddening.

"A head, with big eyes so am really jealous that Viking got all the juicy thingamabobs," Conan thinking of juicy thingamabobs?

"Help I am drowning you shouted too," Tom now exasperating.

"OK kid now let us not mention anything else," for Conan was afraid his image might be tarnished for Christina was about; her with the pretty ankles.

"And I wished I had Wamba's Book to tell me what to do as you drowned. I never knew barbarian adventurers were afraid of water?" Tom filling Conan's head with murderous ideas and could not escape as the kid held him.

"Let go kid here comes the princess," Conan.

"I want my medal for saving you, you said I could get one," Tom illustrating he was innocent of life and innocent of important things between his ears and **perhaps** between someplace else?

"Here is the princess," Conan with "pretty ears able to hear everything the infuriating kid had shouted. Wants a medal now does he?' Now Conan's private thoughts and they were ugly thoughts so are censored.

"And I used your famous sword 'Arnie' and slew the Fiendish commandos so am a hero am I not? " Tom to be sickening. "Wamba will be proud of me?" Even more sickening.

And Conan was ill and the princess shouted, "Hey look a rabbit that cannot hold its XXX," for she was more vicious and bothersome than Tom.

"Woof," a dog with a nasty streak and licked what Conan left and salivated all over the princess for dogs go with boys who together are made of defective stuff like pepper.

"Buzz," a fly escaping to the rafters with a lot more knowledge than it had before and because it was a fly went to where Cur went; then landed on a pretty ankle as desert for flies are made of worse things than pepper, like plague and cholera and food poisoning and a loo with no loo paper.

CHAPTER 8
ISISNAPHUT

Born Hal 895 and christened Ahmenton, "and loathed my name for it meant fairy king and wanted daddy and mummy done good for that. Did they not make me attend parties dressed as a pixie? And took my loathing out on the servants with daddy's bull whip for that is what servants are paid for?"

"Eek," the sound of servants running under a bull whip.

"And mummy put me in pink pantaloons and a sailor's hat.

"Fairy," my noble pals called me so ran out of chums for even a princely brat has his own executioner to run pitter patter to the block.

And grew into a monster who bought an even bigger bull whip from a plastic dinosaur stall.

Was I not beastly?

And tortured Ballenese tourists by making them watch plays Satirextex had written about Fiends being heinous.

Then sent them to our Circus Humours to entertain Fiendish crowds fighting lions and real dinosaurs.

He ha and see by my laugh I am an ogre with bad breath. "Save us kind sir," the fairy woman would shout and wink and show ankles but I cared not for I am Ahmenton in

pink tights. The Fiendish fairy that built greenhouses to have parties where all my friends came in pink pantaloons so we were all the same.

And our world on this side of the rip is green for the ultraviolet is green and makes our creamy parsley sauce yucky green so prefer rancid butter sauce.

Yes, the green has strange effects on us on this side of the rip, why just look at me and our giant snails that are feared because they are BIG.

And got numerous teeth and found out we taste nicer than cabbage.

No wonder why our god is Gastropodicus who commanded us, "Eat my kind in remembrance of me."

And we do in rancid butter sauce."

And the day came when a monotonous boy gave his parents poisoned apples to speed them off to happy hunting grounds.

"So, with gripe put them into Circus Humours and bribed the High Priest to denounce them as worshippers of King Charles of Ball. Any excuse will do, we like to watch rich folk get their Karma running from giant slimy snails. Much cheaper than lions as the snails get fattened for us to eat them at Xmas.

Oh, what a rotter I am?

And since I do not encourage corruption had an assassin mummify the High Priest while he slept and sent an assassin to lock the first assassin in a kitchen full of starving roaches to encourage employment for assassins.

And an assassin to push that assassin off a cliff while that assassin was walking his dog there."

"Woof," the dog jumping this way and now free to sneak into pedigree dog shows and cause an explosion in unwanted cross breeds.

And here an Aslop fable, *"Why calling a man a dog is a vile thing to do."*

"Yes, and the assassins assassinated till none could remember who was paying them; just what I wanted clean fingers and lots of cash in the bank.

Then changed my name to Isisnaphut after the goddess of love and in a name the character of a Fiend. And my nickname became 'Is he not lovely in pink?'

Then met this wizard called Alicadabara who told me about Ball that is flat and full of fairies, "Real ones sire," so burned with ambition to meet all these other 'fairies in pink pantaloons." And those I have met defending the bridge do not wear pink and are unwashed and smell of manure and have things moving about their heads; surely these are mercenaries from the human world? So still burn with desire to meet a fairy and by the way, the Fiendish world is so large it is hexagonal and uncharted; and somewhere there a sacred mangrove with trees with shrunken skulls, howling and heaps of bats flying about, the home of Alicadabara where a magic mirror hangs."

"Mirror find me the most degenerate powerful fairy lord," **Alicadabara** and the mirror showed Tootanfoot lost in a maze in a rose garden and pitiful thing, he was covered in green fly seeking revenge for plucking them off succulent roses. "So educated him showing him his new toady looks if he did not help me," Alicadabara.

"Never fear wicked wizard the Princess Christina is my betrothed. See I enter her rose garden and whisper, 'My darling' then ravage her ten times so now that we are friends, please get me out of this maze?" Then people whisper behind his back, 'Here comes that idiot Tootanfoot who lives in a fantasy world.' "And when I am made king by Fiendish troops, I will invite Isisnaphut to visit his younger brother in Haliput and boil him in rancid butter sauce and eat the ugly gastropod. For I am told all Fiends are snails and dream of going to heaven as snails but must be eaten by a fairy to achieve this," Tootanfoot a skinny aspirer who lives in a fantasy world like many do.

"And I Alicadabara am told fairies must be eaten by a Fiend to go to fairy heaven so have a cauldron full of carrots and onions waiting for Tootanfoot. Yes, here comes that idiot Tootanfoot."

"And I Isisnaphut know these stories are rubbish and if you want rid of someone just hire an assassin and many assassins till, they cannot remember who is paying them so get them free."

"And I Alicadabara know there is only one ruler of lands on

either side of the rip, me but it is not official yet."

"And before I hire a hundred assassins for, they come cheap in Fiend Land I will make Tootanfoot tell me his secret of virility by showing him a fire full of hot coals and a knife and fork," Isisnaphut not believing that idiot Tootanfoot lived in a fantasy world.

"And that is what Tootanfoot gets for telling lies so all beware out there," an Aslop fable.

"And that is what Ali' gets for finding the most degenerate lord ever and never heard nobles titter behind that lord's back, *'Here cometh that idiot Tootanfoot, titter ha he,'* Aslop again and laughs like a rat getting tickled.

"My virility is in this pouch full of dried healthy stuff a witch sold me. Purple mushrooms mixed with the front teeth of a crocodile, the wings of six barn owls, elephant tusks and the droppings of a rabid female fox on heat," to discourage any from seeking the witch and Tootanfoot did not tell them he bought the lucky bag from Harry at a plastic dinosaur stall for Harry got around.

"And I The Mage am fed up being a fly go 'POOF' and am myself again and shout 'Help,' for the rafter I pooled on cannot take my weight so I crash onto the stairwell Harry was supposed to mend.

And do not roll and somersault down the stairs there but go through them for twenty levels so shriek all the way down and moan when I hit the hallway floor with a loud thud."

"Here was that The Mage just crashed through twenty levels of stairs?" Conan being the most intelligent of the Garrison Men asked.

"Ouk." an intelligent reply.

"**Wow.**"

"Woof."

So, Garrison ventured forth to see what they could steal from the silent body of The Mage.

"He might have an expensive time piece that I cannot afford," Conan.

"A potion to make me a sergeant like Wamba," Tom.

"Ouk," someone hoping for nuts.

"Woof," someone hoping to see what eatables a mage had for mages did not eat ration biscuits with crunchy weevils, but fine French cuisine, chocolate eclairs, Belgian Chocolates and Gingerbread Men laced with certain mushrooms to help them communicate with the gods.

"Here that is my Swiss time piece," The Mage and made some rabbit ears longer so they flapped in the summer breeze.

"Blast," the rabbit, hopped about, left droppings, and came back and ate them as pet rabbits do that saving you a litter tray.

"Here that potion is to give one X ray eyes," The Mage warned Tom and did not say only when the moon was full every twenty years and for twenty years did have a boil some place too.

"Here give me some of that," Conan thinking of a princess and drank the lot.

"And has side effects for on full moons you grow fur and howl and rip and shred sheep good," The Mage looking for a silver necklace to ward off were-garrison men.

"Wow," an irresponsible innocent boy wanting a potion to heal the boil some place.

"Ouk," a retired Viking from the top of the tower but was ignored for it was breezy there and all had seen a mage shriek his way down recently so did not like watching repeats, perhaps in slow motion though?

"Here what is that dog eating?" The Mage seeing a string of his pheasant sausages disappearing down an ugly looking dog's mouth.

"Woof," a satisfied reply from an animal wanting more.

"Poof," as The Mage turned the dog with a nasty streak into a steak pie.

"Ouk," as Harold desperately tried to get their attention above.

"Here is that Viking throwing bricks on my head?" Conan who being thick headed did not feel a thing as was thinking of eating a steak pie.

"Maybe he found a bag of nuts?" A boy showing, he was not

innocent but an imbecile.

"Woof," a steak pie and bit The Mage some place important then fled up the rickety stairwell to hide above in rafters and beams.

"Here who threw this brick on my head," The Mage distracted from turning a fleeing steak pie into a large turkey for the pot, enough for everyone to silence complaints about eating something with vermin blood as they were hungry Garrison Men.

"Ouk," a reply as another brick bounced off The Mage who being a sensitive person felt it for sure he did, well lumps were appearing from his skull, and was bleeding, might have concussion, and looked like he needed a brain surgeon thanks to that imbecile above throwing bricks.

"He wants us to come up and look at something?" Conan not volunteering to climb those stairs he knew Harry never mended but took the money for the job. Yes, that was the type of swindler Harry was, a smart one.

"Poof," and just like that Conan found himself twenty levels up looking across a pretty landscape and did not appreciate the artistic beauty of the scene for there were no walls left to stop him falling over for the breeze up here was gusty; and Garrison Men were clinging to him for they did not want gusted away either.

"Woof," and a steak pie clung to him as well.

"Shriek," Conan as the steak pie clung to some place needed to sit in an outhouse.

"Poof," and Christina stood beside them for The Mage was one of these types who liked to share what went round with them that caused it.

"*A revealing side to his character that shows he was not a forgiving fairy but a person more likely to turn you into a pumpkin for he liked his puddings,*" Aslop.

"This is more like it," Conan feeling the princess cling to him places.

"Ouk," an excited whatever it was?

"Ah it is a donkey coming this way with an army of Fiends

behind it," The Mage for he was always kind to the retired Viking but why? Was he an animal lover, well we can answer that by looking at a steak pie who did not know it was a dog.

"It looks like Wamba in the lead," the Princess Christina never forgetting a wart.

"Chasing a carrot at the end of a stick," Conan.

"Is that Lord Tootanfoot riding him?" Christina afraid something of her ambition to be queen had gone amiss.

"My tea leaves revealed your entire plan to me," The Mage and grinned so all his gold and diamond fillings glittered in the summer sun hoping to impress her; for royalty are always broke.

And because the princess was distracted Conan got away with wrapping oily hands about her; or perhaps she had remembered a barbarian who years earlier had sneaked into a rose garden?

"Boohoo," a girl knowing a pretty girl only needs to sob and all the pretty girls' wrongs are swept under the carpet.

"I have reduced a fairy to a donkey even if he was a donkey," Christina and gave a big sigh and squirted some tears so there was a rush of sleeves and even a paw from a steak pie for her to wipe them away and give her nose a good blow.

And she knew she was forgiven for Garrison Men where offering her chewed gum, an unshelled peanut, a gnawed bone, and mirror that floated by itself for her to pretty herself up fresh.

Except while she looked in the mirror them lot crowded behind ogling and the mirror cracked.

It was revolting the grovelling coming out of these tough seasoned drunks who would now face the whole Fiendish army for her as volunteers and get killed. But they were men and were not thinking so deserved what they were getting.

"Who can blame her of wanting rid of King Charles who it is said bathes nightly in a bath full of XXX as floozy pixies sponge him down and feed him olives to the music of his enemies nailed to castle walls by hunchbacks in tight leather outfits; and other hunchbacks in fireproof outfits with hot tongs for putting places to get that music.

"And what about me? I am bored of being chucked aside for a bottle of XXX," his royal teddy complains, a cousin of the other famous Ted.

Anyway: "It was Lord Tootanfoot's idea as he wants to marry me and be an evil king who plucks the wings from fairies just before they are thrown from castle walls into fetid moats below," Christina knowing as a forgiven girl anything she said was believed.

And none saw anything treacherous in wanting to marry the pretty princess.

"As king he wants to be mega rich by taxing XXX," Christina and was lucky her nose did not grow like Pinocchio's so Garrison hated Tootanfoot for XXX was sacred.

"He intends what? He is a Fiend needing to visit a chopping board," Conan feeling withdrawal pains of no more XXX.

"A Fiend for me to chop off his head and get a medal," a boy showing boys were idiots and made of everything nasty.

"Ouk," a retired Viking jumping up and down and wringing his hands about an imaginary Lord Tootanfoot.

"Woof," a steak pie showing how nasty he could be to Tootanfoot and ripped apart a plastic dinosaur left behind.

"Poof," The Mage and sent a constipation spell to annoy Tootanfoot with his Fiend friends and had a side effect, the steak pie was Cur again.

"I will make a fortune selling prunes," a whisper on the wind and the voice was Harry's.

"We need the donkey," The Mage seeking volunteers for he had a plan and Christina was alarmed for it meant Wamba back.

And there was a scream as The Mage heard a volunteer with the only brains slip on untended stairs twenty levels up; a long way for any volunteer to fall.

So, Conan slipped into the world of nothingness and saw a white light at the end of a tunnel and people with wings waving to him there; so was happy knowing Heaven was full of fairies.

"Pigs can fly," The Mage and stopped Conan thudding into the cold unwelcoming floor twenty levels below and for atmosphere The Mage did not cast his spell till Conan was a foot above the cold unwelcoming stone floor. In truth, The Mage being a fink was waiting for Conan to wet himself. Twenty floor drop, any person would.

So, Conan appeared beside him.

"Is that it, pigs can fly?" The retired adventurer mightily peeved The Mage had waited so long to save him. And The Mage again revealed a bit of character, that there is a sadistic streak in mages, especially him.

"Well, this rabbit is not going alone," and Conan knew his volunteers were at hand to rescue a donkey.

"What a hero?" And a pretty princess kissed his cheek.

"Wow," was all a boy could say after he was kissed.

"Ouk," and was kissed by a princess with eyes shut.

"Woof," and was blown a kiss.

"Woof," and was picked up in gloves and kissed.

 "Woof," and thrown violently off a leg.

"Poof," and Tom appeared again so the princess kissed him again and behind a bush "poof," as this Tom became The Mage.

So, all were happy except Christina who gargled with fox glove to kill off infections.

And when the volunteers went down the slippery rickety stairs Christina the pretty princess threw away her expensive silken gloves and retched here and there and never noticed volunteers had fleeced the jewelled rings on her fingers, the gold earrings, and her diamond encrusted garter.

"We are Garrison Men and proud of it,
  Off to rescue a warty it.
  We are full of nasty its.
  If there was ever a wicked it, we, are it.
  And warty it is a gormless it.
  But mates look after their it.
  But he isn't a mate so is the other it.
  The BOSS bossy its.

So can stew as a cooked it.
So, Fiends can eat it.
  And we will be rid of it.
Free to be our own it.

Yes, it is, Satirextex.

We are what makes an army move.
We eat army food so got colic.
  And under the bridge frolic.
And got nothing to prove.

Wamba? Really?"

CHAPTER 9   A NASTY DOG

And Wamba was happy for in the reflection of a roadside puddle discovered 'pigs can fly' had removed his rabbit ears also.

"And missiles pricked volunteers.
  Who became mighty sore?
   Give us pay for beers?
   So, do we see four?
  And their liege Christina
  Led them to battle.
  Where is Aunt Wilhelmina?
  In her pram full of baby rattles?
  Who is this aunt?
   Supposed in a chariot pulled by wolves
   Supposed for she is a runt?
   Who needs figs to make her things move,
  And smote Isisnaphut good.
  So, he was rancid butter food ."

From a granite plaque at the modern-day bridge read by tourists and because it was the worst poetry ever tourists skipped the rest and had to see who wrote it, yes 'Satirextex' was at the bottom and it was his cousin Quick Draw Sampenciltrex made the cast for the plaque, he who worked for Harry and these two were responsible for culture in the Land of Ball. What Harry wanted you to think was art was rubbish for Harry not only knew how to sell plastic dinosaurs whose limbs fell off when rub a tub in the bath, but to run his own PR, and run fast from dissatisfied customers.

And Satirextex wrote this in Common as Muck Big Bertha's Guest House full of something, ale smells, the grunts of cutthroats and squeals of waitresses and priests begging successfully for charity, and Satirextrex was a Fiend himself hiding under a green hood on the enormous size to fool people into thinking he was big. But they knew otherwise because when he walked the extra high heels stuck onto his sandals gave the show away.

"Click," they clicked, "snap," they went.

Now here is the truth and was not written at Common as Muck Big Bertha's Guest House.

PRESENT

The Mage seeing Cur sniggering over Conan's reluctance to volunteer because of some 'poofing' found itself chained to a wooden cart used to pull manure to the fields.

"Woof," which means "what a stink woof."

"It was available," The Mage defending his choice of 1912 cart models.

"Ouk," a retired Viking thinking that funny.

"Wow," an innocent boy without wicked thoughts so is innocent as he has no thoughts; not even bum fluff to be daring or just stares when sees a bathing woman as is innocent.

"At least I am not volunteering alone," Conan and his prophesy came true for they all found themselves in the smelly 1912 cart now full of carrots.

"For the bunny," The Mage.

"What's Up Doc?" Conan replied and bounced.

And the cart pulled by Cur went to save Wamba.

"They fight for a copper piece a day.

A copper piece that buys them their bowl of runny gruel,
many pints of watered-down warm mint beer,
some strange tobacco and if they save hard
a guided tour of Common as Muck Big Bertha's Guest House
every weekend.

For they are Garrison Men and must stop them thirty thousand fiends and Tootanfoot marrying you," The Mage deliberately making **the pretty princess feel bad.**

"Sob," so she cried and of course on his shoulder.

And proves Aslop, *"Never trust a mage,' right especially a dirty old man under a long white beard walking about all day in a long white smock with a razor-sharp sickle tucked in his belt."*

"I know his kind, they sneak into the milking shed at 4a.m. and hide under straw to watch the milk maids work, never fear," the pretty ankle speaking unkind words and knew a tears on his shoulder would, "give me his bank account."

"Is lies, at 4a.m. I am crawling home from Filthy Big Bertha at that time," The Mage feeling nothing as he is, *"a man who can do no wrong."* Aslop.

So, both being preoccupied never saw the cart hit a mole hill and spill volunteers who did the sensible thing, come, and stand beside him and ruin the dirty old man's fun.

"Ouk," Harold the retired Viking offering Christina his long arms to cry in.

"Here baby," Conan offering an unwashed arm to cry in.

"Wow," a boy who just stared at bathing women, now with a man's intentions offering his arms to cry in.

"Woof," a dog wanting her legs for dogs know what to do with them?

"Hey, the dog is pulling a cart, cannot be two places at once?" A puzzled Satirextrex.

"Called magic friend," Aslop.

"Where did you lot come from?" The Mage about too 'poof' them to faraway places like a closed Theme Park; but the Fiends had other ideas. You can always count on a Fiend to save volunteers as they sent a cloud of arrows at the tower.

"Poof," as The Mage changed his spell and sent the

thousands of arrows back to their senders so "Yikes," "I am dead," and "groan," was heard.

"We are saved," Garrison Men not grateful to them Fiends full of arrows.

And a dog with a cart load of carrots reached a donkey, of course after running down a few Friends who took offence so the nasty heroic dog fled home with a donkey after the carrots and Fiends after them both.

"Kill," the nasty Fiends.

"Woof," the nasty dog enjoying the run.

So, Cur jumped the barricade with the cart without volunteers as they fell off earlier.

The donkey slipped in an unspeakable a naughty dog left behind.

Lord Tootanfoot fell off.

All those angry Fiends ran over Tootanfoot who moaned.

"Poof," The Mage making good usage of poofs so fire fell from heaven and roasted a few more thousand Fiends good so they stopped chasing.

"By the gods I am covered in unmentionables," Lord Tootanfoot cried eventually standing up covered in black and blue bruises, of course, you thought the other stuff, hey this is a fairy tale.

A needed Interruption

Just what Harry does to confuse tourist customers who have spent all their mule fares home on his plastic dinosaurs?

"Shows how real the dinosaurs look?" A Harry whisper to encourage spending and growth.

Yes, Satirextex and Sampenciltrex sold their souls to that salesman for greed is their bible.

"And I use them as stress dummies when angry mobs feel cheated when my potions I label 'made by a mage' cause noses to drop off and refunds wanted," The Great Salesman.

"So, our statues and poems are shredded and we along with them," Satirextex and Sampenciltrex knowing their well-paid jobs depended upon a little moans and groans.

End of Interruption.

And bandages of course.

And donkey Wamba 'brayed' all the way home as a pretty princess had nudged The Mage so his aim was off so fire falling from heaven fell on the donkey.

"*What a little b***h,*" Aslop.

"It was such an ugly warty donkey anyway," the princess.

"Abracadabra," Alicadabara stopping the fireballs from heaven so the Fiends feeling brave and threatened by him charged again.

"I draw upon the strength of my sword 'Arnie,'" Conan and swelled his chest and flexed his mighty biceps so Christina remembered swooning in them and forgave him for having unwashed filthy fingernails, and never saw the Austin Powers fake biceps wrapped about his biceps to enlarge them.

"*He has a cute bottom also,*" she whispered but Conan's rabbit ears had left him with super hearing so smiled and she read his smile and blushed. So, a jealous mage sent a horde of wasps amongst the charging Fiends and sneaky unnoticeable red ants to sneak their way up Conan's legs.

"Judas priest I am eaten alive," Conan as he scratched away, "scratch."

And a donkey clattered over the bridge just as the Fiends got to it and suddenly stopped.

They had run out of juicy carrots.

"I am worth more than a dirty old man lusting over a pretty princess old enough to be working at Common as Muck Big Bertha's Guest House. So have 'poofed' an image of the Fiend god Gastropodicus on the bridge," Alicadabara and now those Fiends who had stopped were pushed from behind into the moat were fins swam so never played a part in this story again. Pushed by their friends from behind chanting 'Kill fairies.'

A moat where dying lily pads floated with frogs with three heads sat croaking, and old shoes and Andrex toilet rolls floated and unused spells of The Mage lurked for volunteers.

So Alicadabara threw his wand down and stamped on it for he was having a tantrum for he was immature.

"Boohoo," he cried as he stamped and added, "ouch."

And since his wand was carved in sharp skulls and cobras with long fangs really did jump this way and that and scream 'V's' loudly too.

"Get down lad," Conan warning as V's screamed from a demented wizard foaming at the mouth are not to be taken lightly; so, V's fell upon the bridge pushing more Fiends into the moat where old mattresses thrown out of Common as Muck Big Bertha's Guest House floated to prove the moat was not a place to bathe in.

Why Conan threw himself on the pretty princess to protect her so gave her the biting ants.

"OoVoo," she squeaked then kneed the retired adventurer for even princesses must have dignity in public and added, "Judas I am eaten alive," as the ants got to work.

"Cur that hurt," a retired barbarian just before a jealous mage beat him good with his magic broomstick.

"By boiled newts I am eaten alive," The Mage as ants crawled up his broomstick.

"Retreat," Isisnaphut for his carriage had been coming leisurely up behind his army expecting victory and the slaughter of the brave defenders of the bridge that leads to the Land of Ball; where red tulips are big and butterflies flutter about dwarves singing happily going to work in gold mines for Sleeping Beauty only buys the best cosmetic expensive brands and that costs gold nuggets.

And behind Isisnaphut a salesman who seeing a rip had entered it to sell genuine plastic dinosaurs and sold everyone to Fiend kids so was returning home.

"Jingle to you jingle to you," the happy oily salesman we know and, "Listen mules," yes Harry spoke to his mules pulling his cart as princes with large ears
speak to their tomatoes, "you put the speed on or you will be glue."

"Bray," the mules sweating it up not wanting to be super glue.

And a lost Ballenese army patrol and wagon load of

tourists followed his tracks as his mules not wanting to be paste trampled a few more Fiends down as they raced for the bridge.

"Clatter," the mule hooves and was answered, "Ouch moan."

"Harry here?" Conan remembering dice bought that should have showed 6's but showed 1's so wanted a refund and violence like the violence done him.

"Harry here?" Tom remembering a potion bought to give him muscles like Mr Universe then be a Film Star but instead gave him Guinea worm so wanted a refund and rampageous behaviour.

"Bray," a donkey remembering a Book bought from Harry would teach him how to marry a princess and was just stuff about what fork to use at a king's dinner party so wanted a refund and bloodshed.

"Ouk," Harold the Viking remembering a monkey bought trained to hold a hearing trumpet and the first tree it ran off and threw the trumpet with excellent aim; and stuck some place for a whole embarrassing week: so, wanted a refund and brutality.

"Woof," a nasty dog with vermin ancestry remembering Harry had promised him a juicy steak if he had acted like a killer dog too protect Harry from dissatisfied customers at Common as Muck Big Bertha's Guest House; but the customers took offence that such a nasty dog was allowed in so beat the living daylights out of Cur while Harry sleeked away with the steak too.

So wanted sadism and a good free gnaw of Harry too.

"Harry here?" The pretty princess who had bought expensive imported toilet water and found it was real life-threatening toilet water full of cholera so wanted cruelty and the salesman to drink the perfume too.

"Harry here," a certain mage remembering cascading all the way down twenty levels of untended stairs so wanted a salesman to work for free to mend them so had the meanest intentions towards Harry The Greatest Salesman ever.

"Yes, Harry's here," Harry and smiled showing teeth just like Burt Lancaster had for Harry had sold the actor them made at a famous dinosaur stall by aspiring cousins who worked for free for their pay was cold runny gruel.

And the mean biting ants where happy Harry was here for, they ran up his legs biting places.

"Judas priest I am bit and will sue who ever let them loose," Harry and because he did not know who let them loose added, "Mother Nature and I am sending Cannymindtrex my lawyer to you."

But was a mistake as Mother Nature who is goddess Nerthus was her that was an abandoned single mum with heaps of orphaned lions, tigers, orangutangs and chimps to change nappies on so was not in a smiley mood, "Take this Harry," and sent him loads of diapers so Harry shouted, "Bananas what the blazes is this," but he knew as he was in a smelly mood and "no laughs please."

"Buzz," flies flying away for one diaper was Heaven but a thousand was Hell.

So, Harry stank.

"Here you forgot the biting ants," Harry trying a cheap salesman trick, "Nerthus you won online at Casino Crazy Addict."

"Bite ants," Nerthus replied and the ants bit for Nerthus knew her oily sales folk and Harry was the worst and here, so being a girl goddess and polite, covered her mouth as she tittered and giggled.

"Bite," the army ants.

"Did we forget to mention imported from Brazil, the worst ants ever," Aslop.

CHAPTER 10

Free Gifts

And Harry knew he had dissatisfied customers
because he was the Great Salesman.

"See my testimonials from King Charles complaining about clothes bought that were invisible because they were. Can I help it if the man is incontinent, sits in a large nappy, has a zoo of pink animals about his head, drools as is full of XXX so believes the dressed up pumpkin heads on the end of poles those he ordered Pitter Patter to, "Cut off their heads," and Pitter patter grew and the farmer who sold him the pumpkins grew rich and the condemned moved to Filthy Big Bertha's and became frontier folk.

For King Charles wore invisible clothes and often asked, "What is that wiggly thing?"

"Majesty, we see only your fine gold silks you wear," and trouble was some said, "It is your willy," and Pitter Patter was called and LIFE WENT ON.

And Harry's chain of barrow stalls made a killing selling toys of Charles, Pitter patter and the condemned and rubber axes, so, my employment agency made much profit hiring salespeople and had dissatisfied courtiers for the invisible clothes did not keep the rain off them, so said "Offaltrex, his idea, so Offaltrex the opposition got chased till puffing and exhausted, said, "It was Harry sold you them," but the puffers and panters chasing replied, "Puff pant," and collapsed, so Offaltrex athletically fit from being chased often, made one last puff and escaped.

Harry continues.

And here I am again with a wagon full of red frilly knickers, garters, stockings, a pair of woolly socks, three spiked maces and four whips studded with nails for the adventurous and a BOOK explaining what to do with the rubbish, for I have many strange customers and they are defending the bridge now. The sons of fairies and the son of a thing and a dog with vermin blood.

Why where there is exotic taste there is cash and am full of cash and can lie myself out of hell and will when I get there.

Always blame the manufacturer which is me and never tell the angry customers that and resell them the boil caused by candy ingredients under a different name such as, 'A cure for boils.'

And they buy for they cannot resist reduced prices for the bottles were dented so sell hundreds and cause a plague of boils needing my medicines. Medicines made from ingredients freely given from nature if I have mules and nearby graveyards.

And run a canvas sack business to support my Funeral Director and operate a pay up scheme for canvas sacks cost money.

And a popular DIY stitch your own canvas sack scheme for I am greedy.

A salesman must watch the interest rates," and did not add his rates and knew he was safe with these dissatisfied customers ahead for he had a secret weapon in the wagon. Why the secret is the **suspense** waiting to see what was under the blankets in the wagon.

"And have a case of imported garlic snails for Isisnaphut in case I have to change sides in a hurry for Harry gets around."

And his wagon came to a stop with an "Ouk."

"Here watch it, Jimmy?" Conan pulling Harold free and caressing wheel ruts out of him.

"Ouk," which means thanks.

And the salesman smiled for he knew success lay in making your customers happy.

And a nasty dog gnawed his legs and gnawed extra deep.

"Nice dog," and Harry knew to give customer's dogs a biscuit and kiss their babies. "Hello everyone, I am back," and threw back blankets to reveal more blankets and threw a dog biscuit amongst a thorn bush for extra good measure.

The suspense was horrific apart from the squeals.

Squeals? Yes, for Harold had been wheel rutted and Garrison Men now knew the ancestry of him and looked closely at Harold's bottom for the wiggly thingy; for they were fairies. Of course, only when Harold was looking the other way for it is rude to look at bottoms, unless that is your thing, IS IT?

"Howl," the nasty dog amongst the thorn bush where a biscuit had been thrown for good measure. And the dog would remember who threw the biscuit. For dogs have memories like elephants **so Harry beware.**

Conan fed up with the squeals and howls, "I feel like a bacon sandwich," so the squeals ended not to draw attention to the squealer.

Then Harry pulled the blankets back to reveal his secret weapons he knew the boys *needed to keep him alive*, AND ALL AT SALE PRICES.

And Conan saw the largest sword ever and heard a sing song voice in his head, **"BUY ME PLEASE MAN OF LEGENDS BUY ME,"** and he would.

And Tom saw a tin of 'Non-Smelling Best Armour Polish Ever' at discount price. And the strong Mr. 'Brassy' essence found his nose and he would buy.

And Wamba a book, 'The True stories of Prince Charming, Dragon Slayer,' and as much as he liked his name Ordinary, was not in the index under Princes? So, would he buy?

And The Mage a jar of the dried nose bristles of the 'Red Crested Yellow Spotted Rain Forest Newt, male,' needed for pile potions before winter set in, and if any drops left made stew gravy. So, was The mage constipated enough to buy?

And Harold a tin of juicy steak with red onions, mushrooms, and fabled yellow toadstools. 'Add water and tuck in,' the label read so added water and the foam went everywhere not to mention the hot gravy that splashed the eyes so he bought.

And everyone could guess the effects of eating yellow toadstools for Harold moved into the outhouse with an afternoons supply of The Mage's 'Home Beautiful' magazines and a bag of nuts.

And Christina smelt the purple decanter deliberately left open by Harry. 'Rose salts,' "I must have them for Garrison Men have strong stinky essences," so was a sale.

"Woof," and a dog saw a dinosaur bone so big and only Harry knew it was from a plastic model at the stall so, Cur did spend hours bunged needing a build-up of wind to act as a laxative.

And all the goods had bright fluorescent tags, **'1/2 price, Xmas sale, buy quick while stocks last.'**

The tags were big too.

And no one was interested in the secret weapon but these were the secret weapons.

Harry was honour bound to sell them here first before he sold them elsewhere.

"BUY ME PLEASE HANDSSOME MAN BUY ME," the sing song voice inside Conan.

And Conan did to the jealousy of his Sword 'Arnie' that decided to go on strike.

And his new sword was tin and the jewels glass beads so was cheated ha he Ha he.

And Conan liked the smell of manure wafting from Christina as it reminded him of home sweet home where barbarians rode horses all day, slept with their woman on them and brought up their kids on them and set many horses alight as they cooked on them.

Yes, the horse was important to a barbarian adventurer, a source of mince in times of famine when Conan would FIRST apologise to his faithful equine friend, then eat.

And Tom found the polish scorer bleach essence so ruined his armour so was wrath.

And The Mage discovered his newt was a female so would still suffer the piles in winter so was wrath.

And a dog full of blocked wind allowed Tom to boot it away, therefore releasing the pressure blockage and "Gods I am covered in stink," Garrison men for the humours of the air was bad. Not to worry, the sun did dry them off and LIFE DID BE NORMAL.

And when all Harry's customers were seeking him, he emptied their cash into a chest that smelt of money because it was full of money.

Then slammed the lid and locked it, "I trust no one not even the mules pulling the wagon. The world is full of thieves and not honest traders like me. Just annoying customers wanting refunds. But their money is mine and concluded all customers are liars. Yes, if only the world had more of my kind it would be a safer place."

And Conan's new sword went PING and became dust.

"I will kill Harry," Conan and a reply was on the breeze, *"Lovely compliments."*

"I will make Harry drink this rose water," and a reply on the breeze, *"I do not drink before sunset."*

"I will scour his bottom pink," Tom and a reply on the breeze, *"You can scour the dirty dishes."*

"I will curse him with piles," The Mage and a reply on the breeze, *"I have lucky rabbit feet and a chain of garlic so do your worst ha Ho he Ha."*

"Woof," and a reply on the breeze, *"I know where to boot a dog."*

"Ouk," and a reply on the breeze, *"I will sell whatever it is to a local zoo and own more cash."*

"Yes, I am The Great Salesman and beam pride as I see delighted customers and jingle their cash in my deep pockets."

"Jingle."

CHAPTER 11 SECRET WEAPON

And The Great Salesman knew he did have to disappear before complaints started and this was his secret too long life.

"But I must show them my 'Ultimate Sale,' the ultimate weapon against Fiends in numbered bitties.
In easy-to-follow instructions.

So do not be frightened by the thousand bits needing gluing.
It can carry volunteers into the midst of Fiends who did never know they were there and volunteers did never know they were in perilous conditions.
Enough room for an innocent boy, a barbarian, some sort of ape with a wiggly bottom thingy, Wamba, a driver experienced in magic as the thing do not run-on air and a foul-mouthed princess as navigator to turn mean when trying out a new scent just bought.
And plenty room in the bottom for a nasty dog.
Yes, a salesman's life is full of risks and I have been more successful than my rivals because:
They do not care about customer's needs.
They do not beat a quick retreat like me.
I give my rivals a fun time in Common as Muck Filthy Big Bertha's Guest House and as they sleep it off sell them to Fiend slavers.
Why I passed Virginotrex up in a balloon asking me to get

him down as had gone insane speaking to gulls, crows, blue tits, and silver fish in his clothes; because he had sold them pies and some mean oily salesman had told customers the pies were full of mole meat and a year old.

"So what?" The rural customer's.

"My mistake, it was rat," so stuck Virginotrex in a warm air balloon bought from me, and in the trade, one never informs on a brother salesman so one rival less Ho he ha.

And pretended not to see him up there with his bird friends.

And they pooped on me, even then I did not look up.

Even when he aimed a silver fish down the front of my hood.

Even when he threw a coin at me and bounced off my hood.

Even after a hundred coins bounced off my hood and he had no coins left to throw.

"Oh look, someone has dropped coins," I shouted gleefully and picked them up and scampered away.

"F' you," I heard, then, "I am sorry, please with strawberries and cream come back and save me."

"I knew he had no strawberries and cream up there so did not bother and spent his coin in an Italian restaurant and had leftovers to throw at my aspiring cousins as treats."

"*What an evil villain?*" Aslop stunned.

Anyway: These Garrison Men have no idea what to do with the Ultimate Sale apart from erecting it as a piece of modern art with a Viking begging in front.

"Sticking Harold out there with a tin cup beats robbing temples guarded by hundreds of Amazon soldiers armed with razor sharp swords.

"But will the thing work," Christina showing there is always one.

"Why you just throw Harold in it with a nut and roll it into the midst of Isisnaphut and he jumps out and beats Fiends up good," Harry and did not explain they were in it too.

And thirty thousand Fiends would do them good.

"Then what?" Wamba proving life could be dangerous.

"Your nights will not be boring as you can pull it to pieces and rebuilt it, even throw away the instructions and build form memory," Harry lying.

"I could drive it," Tom beaming pride so Conan nudged the volunteer into the moat and quick as a flash Harry takes from a pocket a ladder and saves him.

"Let the driver try the motor," Harry pushing Tom in and, "Conan you could hide in it as it is drives into temples for you to rob and Wamba fight dragons and rescue princess from it," **Harry with utter gibberish.**

"Only idiots would believe such tripe," a princess asking for a short life so a salesman threw a scent bottle in the moat hoping she did jump after it.

Woof," and threw a doggy chew as well.

And without doubters Harry sold Garrison his secret weapon, a DIY build it Wooden Gastropod.

"Here just to show my customers no hard feeling here is some free candy," and gave them rock covered in goose lard and sugar and The Mage looked at the Fiendish campfires and knew they did be famous like those in the Wooden Snail of Troy.

"Wamba, consult Book about volunteers," The Mage ever so quietly as to not frighten off volunteers.

But they heard.

"What about my donkey voice," and The Mage cured Wamba for glory.

"Now where are the others?" For volunteers had heard.

And saw rabbit ears sticking up from under the bridge where a dog that had slipped in the moat was drying itself, beautiful butterflies flew about.

"Gad leeches," a rabbit and was poofed just like that into the wooden snail,

And the dog into the exit.

And a peanut was thrown into the snail and "Ouk" was heard as something ugly went after the nut.

"I want to impress and win medals so walk into the snail proudly," Tom because he was innocent of life and a moron.

"I feel there are a hundred eyes leering at me from that wooden snail so want to burn it to a crisp," a princess fed up being leered at.

"Poof," so she joined the snail where she could be leered from inside and keep volunteers happy.

"Who needs woman?
  Volunteers do.
   Macho humans?
  And dogs too.
  And women.
  Women?
   To practice the art of woman.
   When they stick fingernails in man.
    And claw women.
  So, brother kills sister.
  Son his mother.
   The babysitter.
   The volunteer's father.
    All for a leer."

Satirextex and he and his third-rate poetry should be thrown in the moat.

CHAPTER 12 VERMIN

A plastic statue exists in the garden of a fairy lord in Haliput City of a warrior in a Field **Marshall Uniform riding a horse, and under the horse Fiends.**

"Oh, noble lord,
Saviour of our race.
Which we could not afford.
On your teeth that big diamond brace.
For you eat our carrots.
For you have a long face.
You the King of Faggots.
You the Lord of donkeys.
And donkey rides too.
And you lost the keys.
To a royal rose garden loo.
Much maligned and misunderstood,
For you must now cross your legs so,
And watch other donkeys eat your carrot food, " Satirextex and is one reason why the forgotten Brotherhood run about in hoods putting hooded fairies in stifling air balloons for they might be lucky and send away SATIREXTREX.

"Listen up fairy folk, why use a balloon?" Aslop asking already knowing.

"To send him back to Mighty Daghdha the Sky Father who has a vacancy for a jester," the fairy folk reply for your knowledge. Mean nasty fairy folk knowing Satirextrex did drive the god bananas, you know, round the bend. Then maybe

78

get a new goddess in a one suit leopard piece and," Aslop cuts these fairies off.

Another plastic statue exists in Grandholm Prison of a skinny fairy chained to a rock. My he looks ratty with a long skinny nose and beady eyes and apart from fairy wings has a stump of a ringed tail, and a ring with his prison number stamped on it.

"Oh, great and noble vermin,
   Destroyer of our race,
   the originator of sin.
   You lost all your face
   For a princess sent you to a donkey farm.
   For bent sinewy donkeys.
   Away from Harry and harm.
    For he wants to boil you to glue for monkeys.
   For monkeys to make scrap books.
   A complete whitewash.
   For Harry is King of crooks.
   And eats donkeys and mash.
   Of course, with tomato ketchup.
   Of course, with knife and fork.
   Of course, with Auntie's China cups.
    Of course, broiled donkey tastes like pork.
Of course, donkey is maligned and understood," Satirextex, where is the stifling air balloon.

And in the bushes an immortal, a god seen, with huge translucent wings, a huge cod piece and is grinning, and brandishing a sword, and is sweating and panting from what?

"The b*****d has pricked every hot air balloon in Haliput," Aslop needing his mouth washed.

A statue criminals cover in rotten vegetables and pigeons poop it and rats nibble the statue base and because it is plastic get constipated.

Both are of Lord Tootanfoot and one tells the truth.

And one day he bribed the Chief Executioner pitter patter to do a job? To meet a princess in a rose garden, Tootanfoot you traitorous melon headed FINK.

"I want to be the ruler of the world," a common disease amongst aristocratic vermin and his reason for the job.

"Already plebian vermin rule the sewers?
And air force trained vermin
To fly up and eat cupboards bare.
And love brewers.
For vermin like the XXX.
So, sleep cosy under beds
Full of XXX.
And in our beds.
At Filthy Big Bertha's.
For drunk vermin get the urge to breed.
And have strange names like Micky,
Or Mouse.
And some are blind and go in threes,
And to this day wonder castles lost.
And other vermin, big nasty types,
Live in the hut Garrison Men call home.

So, call it Home Sweet Home," Satirextex who gets around for he is cheap.

So Tootanfoot prospered in the palace of his great ancestor who did not know of his existence.

So, in the rose garden Tootanfoot possessed Christina's mind with ideas of ridding Ball of Uncle Charles and becoming a noble queen, his queen but this part he did not squeak to her. Nor did he tell her he was the biggest queen running about in vermin outfits.

So, visited her rose garden with cheese and crackers the staple diet of vermin for she was young, rich, pretty, and bored and lacking love so nibbled away.

"Nibble," she went.

And he managed to count twenty petticoats before she stood up and said, "Sir is that a ringed tail?"

"Squeak," Lord Tootanfoot.

So, the pretty princess who could do no wrong rolled down her twenty petticoats and said, "Sire, meet me at the fountain in the centre of the rose garden and I will yield to your demands."

"Squeak," the vermin thinking he did get all the cheese.

But the fountain was in a maze so the pretty princess ran home twittering and giggling like freckled teenagers do.

And the rat promised to count to ten before pursuing.

So counted to three but greed overcame him so he ate the last cheddar square before following so got lost in the maze and a month later crawled out muttering and foaming, "My gold ring for a bit of Danish Blue."

A skinny thing now to he was now.

And a passing salesman with a suitcase full of plastic dinosaurs took it and ran off without trading.

More Tootanfoot

"I will get her to meet Alicadabara who will cast a spell on Isisnaphut and the spell is the pretty princess who can do no wrong will lead the Ballenese Liberation Army to free Ball of her drunken daddy's rule," was Tootanfoot not a swine as well as vermin, and "make me king, no, queen, oh dear I am all confused."

"For Tootanfoot was a dandy who dressed in tights and gigantic extra-large codpieces, bright purple coats and gothic cosmetics, yes, he was a dandy with a ringed tail who bent forward because of the weight of the fish," Satirextrex.

"I am no relation to him, I only stole his gold ring," Harry whispers on the summer breeze, "fish, I can sell fish?"

CHAPTER 13
ORPHAN BOYS

Malice has it Tom and Harold are orphan boys who wondered into the Garrison Hut at the bridge. No longer hungry, as struggled through strawberry fields and the owners of them strawberries who chased them good waving pitch forks intent on grievous bodily harm.

Tour lads took the clothes off Scare Crows so were no longer naked, *"Oh Bloomers, what a thought,"* Satirextrex fainting as was of a delicate nature and explains why the strawberry farmers always never caught them, until they were clothed.

"Eat our fruits without paying? We will see about that," and set upon the poor unloved orphans with flaming sticks, the farmers sticking to a Hollywood horror script as always must be a flaming something.

"EEK," and "yikes," the unwanted orphans as flaming something is not wanted.

And when they ate what was called ration packs left about leading them to Conan and Wamba who threw a net over them, "Enlisted have we?" Conan and Wamba and a cruel dog that should have welcomed licking them cocked a leg and sniggered.

Yes, a dog that sniggered so explains a lot.

The new recruits had not slept in a bed for months and when shown their wooden planks knew they never would again.

They would get their own ration packs so would not be beaten and bitten good again except by fleas and bugs and them vermin living in their hut, those giant rats the size of cats so explains why the wise cats left them alone.

Harold was a Viking. Did he not steer the Viking ship left instead of right for he did not know what leeward and starboard meant and was deaf anyway. With barrels of XXX, sheep that could swim, waitresses that were rescued by other Viking ships, cows that jumped over the moon to dry land, and the Viking crew swam for it, ten miles back to land fighting off Orcas, giant squids, fins, and plastic dinosaurs cast into the sea by children when the legs fell off.

Now Harold needing a safe place for Vikings never forget and he was safe here for no respectable Viking did hole up as Garrison, so Vikings thought. And now he did not have to eat sea sprayed weevil infested biscuits for the weevil infested biscuits at Garrison were dry.

The bed plank dry from sea spray and did not roll left or right with the ship, and when cold that nasty dog cuddled into him. Allowed as one look into those bared fangs you just rolled over hoping the beast did sleep, and it did for it was smart see.

"Ouk, is that you teddy," Harold and "Slurp," Cur licking his face of course after licking its unmentionables for it was a nasty dog.

 Yes, now Harold was supposed to guard the bridge and collect toll fees from smugglers, tourists, and Harry but all crossed the bridge and did so by slipping past Harold lying on the grass sleeping. So, no toll charges were collected and no pay rise given.

So, the rest of Garrison hated him and if could write did send postcards to the Vikings telling them Harold was here.

But they did not know where the Vikings lived, and hating was easier.

And Tom was supposed to take a turn guarding but was sleeping on his plank in the Garrison Hut so no toll fees collected and no pay rise given and was hated also and planned to sell him to the Vikings when they came for Harold, when a post card was written.

"I just love these guardsmen," Harry whipping mules to slip past the sleepers.

And Conan sleeping in the water trough so no toll fees collected so no pay rise given, he was drunk and peed himself so Old Nag the horse hated him and with the others planned to sell Conan off to the Vikings when they came.

And a dog sleeping on his plank so did not wake any of the guards so was hated as there was no guardsmen on duty, but all were terrified of the nasty dog so did not plan but hoped the Vikings did take it as a mascot, when they came for Harold.

And where was Sergeant Wamba to muster his men and collect toll fees, asleep of course.

For they were Guards Men who were mates that sang nightly and drank swill in Common as Muck Filthy Big Bertha's.

And just left The Mage to hate them and spend a lot of cash on Harry buying bear traps, trap doors, and poisoned weevil infested biscuits for them, but Garrison always missed them for they were too busy sleeping.

*

And as an epitaph, "I wish papa were like Wamba then I would have grown up like Wamba," Tom and Conan replied, "A boy should be ravishing princesses not listening to turnips so is my duty to save Tom."

And because the turnip never mustered the men never got a raise in pay for their names were not on the pay slips, just Womba's for he was onto a good thing.

CHAPTER 14 OTHERS

And Offaltrex Purchtrix merchant was on a family holiday beyond the bridge, except it was not the wife seeing the wondrous sights of the 'Fantasy World of the Flat Worlders.'

Package holidays from Harry World Tours and a smudge the owners name prescribed by the civil laws of Ball, and the owner was oily Give a Copper Harry.

And Offaltrex decided if Harry could save his neck crossing the bridge, he would follow and break Harry's neck for, "I have read the smudge and although it promises an exciting tour of Fiend Lands it says nothing about feeding them, with ourselves.

If they get close, they can have the girl friend to save the wife ever knowing and me a costly divorce,

I will sue Harry to his last deep pocket."

And Offlatrex's heart was full of evil mischief and could not give a brass monkey's for the laws prohibiting grievous bodily harm on a greedy plastic dinosaur salesman.

And beside Offaltrex a girlfriend pixie floozy woman, Beautricianix who was, "That other woman, the scarlet woman of ill repute, the vamp." Who expected nightly dancing after seeing the brochure but got rain in a leaky tent in the middle of a field.

She had not read the smudge and should have asked The Mage about a certain building contractor, Harry.

And in her bag, pay packet from a vet, and knew what she was going to do to Offaltrex and Harry who were feral salespeople needing controlled.

And a lost army patrol under the command of Captain Moronicus Wondrous watched events and his men knew he would not go far in the military with a name like that. But he aspired to be a general and aspirers needed battles and his men preferred aspiring in Common as Muck Filthy Big Bertha's playing dominoes and Tidily Winks with the waitresses, honest, they even went to Church Parade and could be seen kneeling praying for they were conscripts, not volunteers.

"Officers that fight battles do not live long and we have families in many towns to support for there are many waitresses wanting to play dominoes," his men.

"We are lost but it is not my fault, it is Apes," Moronicus jerking a finger back at their mascot, a pet Tandoori Household Forest Gorilla who had a perverted liking to ink whether black, blue, or red if it was ink. So, the army map was now bare of little hills and rivers but covered in **lick** smudges.

Licked by a stupid primate that should be sent to Beautricianix so there be no little chimps running about.

And Moronicus filled with rage took the flat of his sword to his mascot called Apes who took the flat of that sword and beat Moronicus good and would have stopped at twenty beatings but was a mean big chimp, so lashed out sixty times; besides Apes never went to school so could not count.

"I make that thirty beatings," a Lost patrol member who never went to school either.

"Do not listen to him Apes, I counted ten," another.

"Judas Priest save me," Moronicus screamed but no one about had that name so was ignored. And explains Moronicus's glowing red ears and in case he had any ideas, Apes kept the sword.

Mean threatening primate that should be sent to Beautricianix quick.

And Apes now rode the captain's horse while the captain walked in torn sandals for Apes had lashed him two hundred times with that sword, so the captain looked shredded and torn and 'X' where his eyeballs should be.

So "moan" and "mummy" was heard often.

And no one wanted to object to Apes for that monkey was the worst bad-tempered banana eater any lost patrol wanted.

And Captain Moronicus was full of blameworthy evil thoughts towards King Charles who had given the patrol the ape for the king knew it was a psychopathic ape. A monster that molested his serving girls and drank all his sherry so had to go and needed an aspirer and as Tootanfoot was away Moronicus would do.

"Why that household Mountain Gorilla I was told can dance in a bikini, sweep floors and sing," Harry the salesman who had sold the ape to King Charles who full of sherry at the time was seeing double so thought two gorillas that could sing and dance a bargain for the price of one.

The alcoholic twerp so should have stuck to pink elephants.

And yes, the nasty ape swept the floors clean of anyone he disliked and there were many for the ape wanted ink to lick and better drink for there was something dark and nasty about this psychopathic primate.

It was evolving into a human at an alarming rate.

So King Charles was happy to get rid of Apes with these words, "Moronicus here is a mascot, see it is harmless and only wants a cuddle," and the king was a lair for from personal experience knew Ape's self-esteem was suffering a complex personality disorder; *simply stated the beast knew it was unloved so behaved like a delinquent child swinging from chandeliers and letting off bad winds that turned you green,* Aslop.

And Charles knew he could drink and hang his fairy citizens by their thumbs and fill their trousers with hot coals and they did put up with him; but to have Apes about would encourage revolution **and Moronicus had said**, "A cunning aspirer will put up with Apes and I will beat it black and blue and use it for my evil ends to become ROYAL he ha, he, ha," and he never laughed like a hyena again.

And Apes was at last happy for the men of the Lost Patrol

bought him juicy apples, big EEC shaped straight bananas so were bananas and bags of peanuts **and all laced with shredded glass for the men were not aspirers but murderers.**

But the digestive system of a Tandoori Forest Gorillas is strong so Apes after burping said, "Ouk," which meant more for he was a greedy unsustainable unstable nasty psychopathic primate.

So, the men bought yams laced with expensive arsenic and still Apes said, "Ouk," and the men said, "Here at this rate we will have no cash to spend in Common as Muck Filthy Big Bertha's and is that twerp's Moronicus's entire fault so shook their captain upside down till he had no money left then threw him into a thorn bush carelessly growing nearby.

"I am your captain and will hang the lot of you," Moronicus foolishly objecting.

"Oh yeh," his men who outnumbered him thirty to one so we see why it was a foolish reply so gave him the lead to Apes as punishment.

And now Apes led the Lost Patrol home to Common as Muck Filthy Big Bertha's for Apes liked to eat the termites there. And Filthy Big Bertha always welcomed Apes because of this and besides Apes always brought the Lost Patrol to take part in expensive art classes using her waitresses as models so got more termites to eat.

For they were the conscript sons of fairies and some the daughters and one an ape but were Ballenese and proud of it.

And have pity for the Fiends Apes bumped into on the way home for they shouted, "Hey a mangy monkey escaped from a zoo, anyone fancy monkey and mushroom stew," and learnt the hard way like Moronicus, Apes had sensitive feelings and exercised with weights daily and was an 'APE' not a 'MONKEY.'

"What bald hardman pushed your head down to where you sit?" Passing curious Fiends asked the funny looking bashed up Fiends with banana skins about them.

"Shish, it was called Apes," and tip toe away and did not chant, "Kill."

And nearby the merchant Offaltrex in his coach dreamed

of using a whip on Harry for the World Tours scam unawares Beautricianix was dreaming of a vets.

And the coachman above turned his crossed eyed beaked nosed face down to Offaltrex and smiled reassuringly and opened his toothless mouth, then his tongue fell out as he drooled and ogled Beautricianix.

"Gee up," and whipped the mules for speed for he had always been an extra in his famous film star friends movie and now had his big break for stardom.

"Whip," went the whip.

"Bray," the poor mules.

"Rattle splash zip," the stones flying under the carriage wheels.

"Judas Priest stop it," passing Fiends complained as the **coachman being crossed eyed** mistook them for mules so whipped them good and plenty.

"And because my name is not Judas Priestly, but Monty's cousin thirty times removed is driving and hate Fiends am putting on the speed," so the driver whipped Fiend and mule alike as his long tongue flipped and somersaulted.

"Bray" shrieked the mules.

"Judas Priestly," complained the Fiends.

CHAPTER 15 THE GREAT SNAIL ROLLS FORTH

'And the Great Snail rolled,
 Nostrils steaming,
And inside fairies all boiled.
So, fairies were minking.
Outside crisping hapless Fiends.
And the snails wooden udders needed milking.
So squirted Greek fire on any who was not a friend.
For god Gastropodicus was hungry.
Isisnaphut their king as well.
For Gastropodicus ate his subjects when angry.
Who called upon him to save their shell.
And punish the fairies,
But Gastropodicus ate them just the same,
And choked on the bits that were hairy,
So, Lord Tootanfoot was to blame,
For the donkey was doing the cooking.
So Gastropodicus put a carrot somewhere, " Satirextex who should perhaps change his profession to a lavatory attendant? Then be flushed away forever ha he HO he; a laugh borrowed from a Bolly Wood horror movie.

And Offaltrex Purchtrix should not have whipped coachman Monty's cousin thirty times removed who is driving who then would not have whipped the mules to run recklessly and so missed the Great Wooden Snail creaking and sweating profusely across the bridge as the timing was out.

They also might not have being going so fast.

'5 mph' the road sign in faded red lettering, faded is it was written in ink and a primate with a perverted liking to ink had been seen in the neighbourhood.

"Ouk," from a nearby out house.

But Offaltrex never read signs or obeyed them.

And Monty's cousin thirty times removed is driving swore the words, "Your blind," also, "You deaf bugger Harold," or, "I said steer right," come out the snail's mouth.

So, Harold steered the snail into the mules, and the terrified animals went further right and trod air for the bridge was not there.

"I am done," Monty's cousin thirty times removed who is driving watching the fetid moat water rise to meet him where hag fish waited for him and flushed toilet paper.

But was a true coachman to the end for he kept whipping his mules to the finish.

And inside Offaltrex cringed for Beautricianix gave him a look.

And a whispering chill blew across the bubbling moat that popped forth bloated frogs.

"Croak," the bloated frogs.

"Hold on, I am here," the voice of King Arawan, Ruler of the Underworld coughed as the moat's suction tried sucking his rising body back down.

And an orange peel hung from his mouth.

And an amused rat sat on his wet hair using perfumed hair gel.

And only the greedy merchant Offaltrex saw hell for that is Arawan, for it was his appointed hour to roast in a slow cook oven with trimmings to add flavour.

And so, a pale hand reached for Offaltrex who investigated death's grey face who feeds well on sins giving him free labour to cook his hot meals; and fling coals into boilers so always a constant supply of hot water as he walks about moaning, "It is hot down here."

And Death's hands are pale for the movies always have it so, for atmosphere of course and an organ hit the high keys.

And Offaltrex saw himself powdering sulphuric salt with a huge mortar, and then filling bags labelled, 'Harry's Sea Salt.'

For a certain greedy salesman got about.

But Arawan who was Death and Hell liked the meths and saw triple so took Monty's cousin thirty times removed who is driving. A man innocent of greed but Arawan did not care; a soul was a soul and was sure a man who had been an extra in an 007 film must have done something considered on the wrong side of the tracks?

So horrid popping sounds as Arawan vanished and Offaltrex rubbed his eyes disbelieving and a bubble rose and burst with these words, "Next time sunny boy," and Offaltrex was amazed a king could live in a moat that never emptied *so stank.*

A whole passing circus had gone down it as a certain brother to Monty's cousin thirty times removed who is driving who had a beaked nose and cross eyes too led his elephants along the short cut to Common as Muck's Filthy Big Bertha's famous pottery classes, into the moat and all the other crossed eyed circus coachmen followed and were never seen again, and lucky for the wobbling Garrison Men and dog they did as they were on the bridge waiting to be run down; so were saved for the story needs them but not cross-eyed Monty's cousin thirty times removed is driving or his elephant cross eyed driver brothers. They are extras so can be trod on, jumped there, and kicked here and elsewhere and not complain, for they are aspirers to be stunt folks who are set on fire, must swim fin infested lakes, eat mouldy food, and trod on, jumped there, and kicked here and elsewhere and not complain, for they aspire to be film stars.

And the moat is alive and is The Mage's fault for he dumped his unwanted potions **there** and did his laundry **there**, brushed his teeth and cleaned his plates **there**; *but a whisper* it was his slave white bunnies he conjured up out of hats that did all that **there** as The Mage knew how to abuse his magic power, and cute white bunnies.

Now you can "Boo Mages, karma to Mages, Boo," and throw empty sauce bottle at him.

The bunnies also emptied his chamber pot **there**, his spittoon full of tobacco juice, and fished for unwanted magazines thrown **there** by-passing fairy truant school kids, dried ironed them out, gave some to Harry to sell for a commission and some to the Mage in the hope of fresh juicy turnips to chew.

Anyway: Offaltrex, "That is what I have hirelings for; goodbye Monty's cousin thirty times removed who is driving. But the merchant's smile faded as the coach was sinking so he scrambled up it like the vermin he was and met death here, Arawan? No, Beautricianix was here.

 "Woman first chum," she said tossing him away.

"What goes up must come down," the wise merchant's words.

And the Fiendish commandos feared him as he headed towards them on their wooden planks as they sneaked silently across the moat.

"Row, your planks," their rowing song with, "splash grunt splash grunt, "for effect.

Yes, feared for the planks had a name upon them, 'Harry Timber Yards.' And the wood was snapping as for it was full of termites, wood taken from the rubbish heap behind Big Bertha's thrown there to keep Apes happy; for apart from ink the nasty rotten primate had a fondness for termites and might explain why it was in a vicious mood; all of them soldier termites inside his bowels nipping.

Yes, Harry had taken away the wooden planks and sold them to a Fiendish commando squad to cross the fetid moat with these words, **"You have my personal guarantee."**

"Bubble," the fetid moat as King Arawan waited for Fiendish souls.

"Yes, blame me," Harry and added, "I left some termites in Big Bertha's to spawn termites so I will be asked back to get rid of them. Oh, how lovely a circle is that never ends, termites at one end and deep pocket the other end," and gave an evil laugh, "He ha, he HO, grunt," sort of laugh for atmosphere and an organ hit the high notes.

Yes, the rotten wooden planks snapped just before Offaltrex landed on the Fiends and used them as steppingstones to reach the safety of the bank.

"Phew lucky for me I landed on them Fiends," Offaltrex and never thanked his Maker who would not forget.

Why he landed on the wrong bank full of Fiends with sharp spears chanting, "Kill," and *"whose cousins forty times removed you used as steppingstones"* Aslop.

"Oh, my Gawd," Offaltrex and Gawd would not listen for Gad never forgot; like Filthy Big Bertha's customers who did not tip the waitresses and were seen running across the deliberately planted nettle fields, *"shrieking as they went for a waitress not tipped is a dangerous woman,"* Aslop.

And a bubble appeared and had Offlatrex's name in red; "You cannot cheat Arawan," and popped.

And Offaltrex was ill as Fiends tossed him up and down like tossed salad for, he was salad too them so they took him to Isisnaphut who said, "An escaped Area 51 alien, throw him in the pot with carrots, Macedon vegetables and curry leaves, twenty Auntie Bessy Dumplings, and laxative to smooth the gravy." for the Fiends liked spicy food and Isisnaphut licked his lips, "an apple was needed to stick in the fairy mouth, celery sticking out the ears, a spiced parsnip stuck somewhere."

CHAPTER 16
JEALOUSY

"And Fiends worshipped gad Gastropodicus,
And Isisnaphut hid his rancid butter sauce,
For Gastropodicus wanted the circus,
A circus a bubble on the moat in the shape of a face.
Monty's cousin thirty times removed is driving
So sent Garrison.
Amongst his Friends who were hip hopping.
For Garrison used a whip belonging to Harrison.
So, Fiends were seen flopping and popping.
Someone give the Gastropodicus a clown,
Whip Fiends pleaded.
Coming a salesman knowing the clown had flown.
So, a lion he would give for Fiends needed bled.
Dragging that lion has made me blown," Satirextex again; is there no way to silence this poet?

And the great wooden snail stopped amongst Fiends and was silent.

Inside fairies sweated in fear Harold's worms did complain and expose them; why Conan had a hand over the mouth of whatever Harold was.

And that stupid primate Apes saw the great wooden snail and wanted to hug and cuddle it and led the Lost Patrol straight too it.

And Conan whispered, "Why are Fiends that carelessly

throw sharps spears about and who are as thick as sausages not fleeing?"

"Overdone sausages perhaps but thick never for they saw the humour in sending them a wooden sail," The Mage writing out a will.

For the Fiends unlike the brave Garrison Men sweating inside had read books a merchant that got about sold them, 'The Wooden Pig of Troy,' so knew what to expect and were building a fire underneath the wooden snail.

"They are putting out cutlery Mage?" Conan worried.

"How have I allowed Harry to send me to the pot in a wooden snail? I am a brainless sheep, bay, ma," The Mage banging his head on the inside of the snail, "Deluded by glory," he added and foamed at the mouth too and sought bandages in his deep pockets.

And Cur peed from that part of the wooden snail's anatomy to be nasty on the Fiends below.

"We eat that bit too," the Fiends shouted up so Cur whimpered, shame.

And Isisnaphut arrived with a cauldron of bubbling rancid butter sauce to smear on the wooden snail to help digestion.

And inside the snail Conan wished Harold were left behind for the smell of that rancid sauce was making whatever Harold was move; so was heading for that part of the anatomy where thingies exited for the salesman Harry had put in a door there.

"Let us worship Gastropodicus and thank him for this snail," Isisnaphut kissing his god's imaginary boots for Gastropodicus was a giant snail remember who might take offence snails were on the menu.

And none really knew what Gastropodicus looked like for visitors never returned to say what he looked like; perhaps he was King Arawan in drag?

And then Wamba saw Lord Tootanfoot and something dark twigged in his mind as he remembered this was, he who had sat next to his fiancée in the carriage.

Fiancée?

So, Wamba drew Conan's sword Arnie and fell out the place Harold was being held back by Conan from jumping down into that cauldron of rancid butter sauce.

Lucky for Wamba he went out sword first and pierced ninety-nine Fiends before he landed on a red ant hill.

"Wait for me," Tom who idolised Wamba for he was innocent.

And Conan did the sensible thing, he pushed Harold into the bit were Garrison Men had left blocking it.

"Why are you looking at me?" Conan asking The Mage who saw reflected there his own guilt.

"Better off without them?" The Mage.

"Sure," Conan wiping a tear away.

Then the smells of snails in rancid butter sauce wafted through the wooden snail for Fiends outside were basting it so Harold went nuts and burst from that place Garrison Men had exited as heroes and fell amongst the Fiends with this sound, "Slurp."

So, the awful sound of barbarian teeth grinding together as Conan realised, he would have to follow the idiots to hell and glory. "Mates who needs them," he complained as Fiends were coming in through that place to escape his mates below.

"Where is Arnie?" Conan fumbling for his sword.

"Take this," The Mage handing Conan something just before he slipped on rancid butter sauce and fell out.

Leaving Conan to beat Fiends with a flower for The Mage had a sense of humour.

"Bye handsome," Christina not wanting to stay at the deserted spooky moat nor inside the overcrowded wooden snail filling with Fiends for she had a sense of survival and knew a flower would wilt when Fiends were using axes and daggers.

So departed from that place to see Captain Moronicus and said, "What a handsome fairy," and got butterflies and forgot all about IT stuck in a red ant hill.

"I am in love," Moronicus proving fairies were all the same and he was another Wamba; perhaps a distant cousin for cooks did waitress jobs at Filthy Big Bertha's on Halloween when it was extremely busy, full of were-wolves, ghouls and Garrison Men so cooks where seen as sexy witches for the rooms were smoky and jammed full of drunks.

And Apes saw Christina and being short sighted swore she was a chimp escaped from a zoo and fell in love. It was the fault of her petticoats billowing as Christina departed for Apes had seen a girl floozy chimp ride a bike in a circus so she was a chimp and that was that. And if he had glasses would see the chimp on the bike was Monty's cousin thirty times removed who is driving doubling for the real chimp was ill; eaten bananas bought from a certain scourge of a salesman.

"Ouk," Apes in love.

"I always get the blame." that certain salesman ordering minor relations to throw blankets over crates on a wagon pulled by mules. And in the crates bananas, black skinned and mouldy, *"They fell off the back of a wagon,"* that salesman and the question was when?

CHAPTER 17 GREED

And Give a Copper Harry who is Harry was about to know fear for he had met Mistress Beautricianix and she smelled of the moat, had a baby octopus down her cleavage that Harry being a man did not fail to notice and her wet billowing skirts showed off her curves which was another thing Harry noticed with a grin.

"Slap," the sound of a female surrogate's hand, and in the clenched fist a rock.
"Yikes," the sound of a male chauvinist and teeth flew about.

And even as one hand slapped the salesman the other put an 'X' on a Harry sebaceous oily paper. An oleaginous oily business document that had cost Offaltrex four hundred thousand gold marks for the other women always has a spare set of keys to the family home, a set for the town house and for the house bought for her, keys for the newest carriages with flower boxes and more importantly keys to the secret safety box the wife does not know about.

So Offaltrex when doing his Month End balance sheet seeing spider webs only in his secret safety box would scream, "My heart gasp," and do it silently just in case his scream attracted the wife.

And Beautricianix had bought from Harry a 'Document of Immunity For Crimes of Passion' issued by Judge ImasleepasIambored of the High Court of Session Haliput the fairy capital.

And the mistress remembered the squid down her cleavage because of a Harry World Tour and did not blame the poor coachman Monty's cousin thirty times removed who is driving who did not know his left from right and was driving over the speed limit, and unless you forget, was a cross eyed driver, and in his back pocket a silver Celtic flask, for what, for keeping XXX but this one was empty, oh yeah!

She blamed Harry and stuffed in her red garter the baby squid.

And Harry could not keep his eyes of the red garter and breathed heavily and drooled; then saw the octopus crawling his way and still sold her the legal document for if there was brass to made from muck he was there' for he was The Greatest Salesman ever and a man who like other men did not think with their brains but other anatomical interesting thingamajigs, the bottom.

So, deserved what was coming for he was the muck.

Besides, he trusted the smudge all documents have; a smudge that said:

- Immunity was conditional as it must be a crime of passion.
- Committed under the 7th full moon when raining newts and frogs.
- There must be an eclipse.
- A were-wolf seen.
- An army of Fiends coming through a rip.
- A duck sitting by the moat on an egg.
- Something alive rise from the moat.

And ImasleepasIambored wrote the document before anything had happened at the sleepy bridge where Garrison Men stayed every night they could at Common as Muck Filthy Big Bertha's for that nasty dog was flea infested so infested the Garrison hut where they slept, so needed to sleep elsewhere. And they infested Common as Muck Filthy Big Bertha's where for a penny extra a waitress would scratch your but places.

Poor waitresses, wait a moment, these were tough girls and outnumbered Garrison men a hundred to one.

Now Harry saw Apes carrying Christina and The Mage riding the Great Wooden Snail and Wamba, Tom, Conan, and whatever Harold was and Cur running fast as Fiends was behind them so fulfilled 5.

And Harry saw the Lost Patrol carrying Offaltrex Purchtrix and with these words, "Lazy bugger," threw him into the fetid moat as they was in front of the other Fiends so wanted out of the way quick, besides the Offaltrex was overweight and slowing them down: so partial fulfilled 7.

And saw a singed Alicadabara throwing fire bolts, wolverines, and all things nasty at The Mage riding the wooden snail.

So saw The Mage reply with his own magic puffs of flowers and squirrels and all things summer so the two magic's magic combined made a were-wolf.

"Howl," the were-wolf seeking cuddly Garrison Men to shred as that is what they do so fulfilled 4.

And in the blinding puff of magic's saw Christina running lifting up her skirts so saw her pretty ankles and was happy, as it took a fairy's mind off dying.

"And Offaltrex rose from the moat," Beautricianix reading 7.

"Quack," and some duck was in the right place at the right time.

Then remembered there had been an eclipse today so fulfilled 3.

"I am safe for it has not rained newts and frogs," Harry wiping nervous sweat from his forehead using Beautricianix billowing skirts for a salesman always keeps his handkerchief in his breast pocket for show and blew his nose hard.

And a mage and an evil wizard dancing about were doing a rain dance so somewhat fulfilled 2.

And Harry saw the clouds part and behold the brightest full moon ever that a were-wolf was howling at so 2 was completely fulfilled.

And then felt the suction of a dainty ladies octopus kept in a red garter for emergencies and found himself looking into

Beautricianix beautiful eyes ImasleepasIambored did forgive; but now were full of blameworthy intent and he knew he was going to the great salesman in the sky so peed and giggled, waved his hands foolishly and said, "Breakfast coffee stains."

ANYWAY

"I am too smart for my boxer shorts," Harry still ogling the red garter thus proving he was a fairy to the end.

"Woof," and knew fulfilments had thundered into him.

"Ouk," Apes carrying Harry away for Tandoori Household Forest Gorillas have memories like elephants and remembered Harry was the bum that sold him a sacksful of bananas and was just smelly rotten banana skins.

"It was dark when I was filling the bag," Harry on Apes shoulder.

And Beautricianix was knocked into the moat.

"To the barricade," The Mage and did not need to shout as all were going there.

"What barricade?" Conan putting a damper on things for a certain salesman that got around had sold the barricade off as planks to certain Fiendish commando teams.

So, Fiends got on the bridge, "Kill."

And it was Harold that saved Offaltrex floating in a cauldron in the moat for the smell was tantalising.

"Ouk," whatever as Harold pulled the cauldron ashore licking his lips.

"Ouk," a disappointed "Ouk," as Offaltrex was in the cauldron.

"Ouk," an angry "Ouk," as Offaltrex was thrown away.

Poor Offaltrex that no one wanted unlike Harry who was loved as the creator of those plastic dinosaurs that *'Was the in FAB thing to have.'*

Because they were bright green and had a mouth full of teeth so you could shout, "Grr I am a dinosaur," for fairies had strange urges,

Anyway: "Click," as The Mage put the Great Wooden Snail

on its side as a new barricade.

"It is full of holes? Where is that ape?" Conan seeing termites in the snail for a merchant made sure his planks got around.

"My card," and Harry's card was a list of prices at inflated prices for he knew the termites would not go away without him.

And Wamba did something without Book; "Line up for volley fire."

And Conan spat tobacco juice at Harry who ducked this first shot but not Fiends charging ranting on the bridge so slipped on tobacco yucky, fell into the moat, and became bubbles on the fermenting surface, thus a GREAT VICTORY.

"And Tom threw his tin of Brasso at the Fiends and the stink of the stuff made Fiends fall off the bridge and gurgled away on the surface, ANOTHER GREAT VICTORY.

"Ouk," a whatever it was throwing nuts so Fiends clutched their eyes and fell into the moat and become whirlpools then vanished, ANOTHER FAIRY VICTORY.

"Grr," and the nasty dog lifting leg so Fiends complained before falling obligingly into the moat for they were extras and paid to disappear, OF COURSE A VICTORY.

And Christina rolled up her skirts so Fiends no longer shouted "Kill," on the bridge for they were all male so dribbled at the mouth and instead of hacking the snail into firewood stood still so more Fiends crowed into them, salivating, drooling, and ogling of course into the moat. You did think they never seen an ankle before, they had at Filthy Big Bertha's but this one belonged to a princess. YEAH, VICTORY.

Then she took off her red garter and pinged it at the Fiends who hacked themselves over ownership of the red garter for they were behaving like normally.

"Here that is not fair," a retired barbarian and charged the Fiends doing nasty's to themselves for Conan wanted the red garter about his neck as a scarf, no silly, to stop his tobacco drool going further.

"Here he is not stealing my red garter," an innocent Tom

who knew what garters were for the waitresses at Filthy Big Bertha's wore them to make you buy more carrot cake, so kicked Fiends out of the way.

"Ouk," the retired oarsman and swung off the snail to swing about Fiends for he wanted to show any Vikings the red garter was proof he pillaged and looted.

"Woof," a jealous dog and ran amongst the Fiends biting them in places needed for WIND where it could have bitten them on the leg, arm, or fingers, but we are dealing with a Garrison Dog, a psychopathic thing if ever with a vicious streak so bit them where they WIND.

And a were-wolf fed up howling at the moon jumped the Fiends with these words, "Yummy howl pass the ketchup."

"Ouk," that ferocious beast Apes as it throttled many Fiends looking for the red garter to wear for Apes was not the everyday Household Tandoori Forest Gorilla you know but something that knew what red garters were for! How sexy he did look in one.

"At them men," Moronicus leading his men onto the bridge to rescue the red garter and give it back to the princess for he was a grovelling aspirer.

And his men waited till the bridge was depleted of Fiends now floating bubbling gurgling dissolving in the moat before they stepped foot on the bridge for, they had many wives in every army town needing a red garter for soldiers get about.

"I do not believe this?" King Isisnaphut seeing thousands of Fiends in the toad, catfish, mosquito, dragon fly swimming in the crowded moat.

"I do not believe this," Alicadabara watching rabbit ears grow on his head as magic gets about.

"I do not believe this," Wamba watching a red garter float past his eyes as he filled a cauldron with Fiends.

"Mine at last," The Mage using magic to steal the red garter and smoked a pipe full of 'Condor' so said, "Satisfying," and added, "Wheeze choke gasp," for he was a none smoker but a stupid old man for he knew the image counts, "Cough gasp."

"Madam, look at this?" And Harry from a deep pocket

opened a pink brief case and Christina had to buy all the garters there, all the lacy stuff as well so, with a "Click," of her fingers directed at The Mage waited for his credit cards and knew she would get them; because he was of the same race as everyone else here, for males live in a world full bottoms for they are made of everything nasty, chilli, curry leaves, wet dog fur and what mice droppings and a pinch of sock.

Whereas girls are made of toffees, candy floss, cream and princesses royal double cream, butter toffees and giant whipped cream doughnuts.

"What the blazes," Harry feeling not wanting the dainty octopus making its way up his left leg. "My giant cod piece will stop it so am not worried," and flicked the animal away, but it had eight legs that wrapped about Harry's right hand and bit him, then let go and slithered into the moat.

"I need leeches, ah, always carry an emergency pack," and Harry covered his swollen fingers in leeches.

CHAPTER 18
WHISPERS

And these whispers were on the wind, amongst white clouds, behind trees and brick walls spread by fishmonger wives selling fish caught from the sea a hundred miles distant, beggar woman who were bored housewives, short sighted cooks boiling toy rabbits and bored females in general.

And by male chefs chopping mint, the watch before its afternoon nap, whipped rowers on royal galleys, real beggars fed up with the fake beggars.

"The Mage is a thousand years old? He bought a time share in his tower and drove neighbours out by littering the place up with old sinks, bathtubs, rubbish bags, loud music and his bat, Bat Wing's untrained habits on the grass.
"It was a huge bat," Satirextex watching Harry aspiring cousins with wheelbarrows and shovels filling 'HARRY BROS ROYAL ROSE GROWTH.'
"What a pong," his neighbours.
And the driven-out neighbours could do nothing for they did not want turned into fleas by him.
So, he got their properties cheap and seen given Bat Wing her share in tender moths, white chocolate mice, big T bone steaks and fried onions and fresh hay every night.
"He was a cheap gangster," Satirextrex.
And cleaned up by tossing everything into the fetid moat.

Why Cur hates him for the Mage gave him mange that spread all over the nasty dog that was ugly and now uglier for warts grew places, and because there was no fur, a flea circus seen, with trapeze artists, lion tamers, clowns and candy floss, all fleas, utterly amazing.

And he spent gold marks on gold wallpaper and a feather goose pillow for Bat Wing as encouragement to fly in all weather and under his bed a whip the bat had not met.

A Roman Bath in the basement for both and allowed Garrison Men and that dog to lick clean the empty lobster shells from his table as encouragement to guard the bridge in all weather.

And under his bed their pay packets just in case they refused.

And he brewed foul potions for all knew the meanest tasting medicines did you the best of good, and a salesman who got about sold them in Haliput, at inflated prices of course.

Harry medicines full of bat thingamabobs, snake venom, dust mites swept up, spiders from never swept rafters and the sweat of Garrison Men collected from their bandanas that magic gingerbread men wrung out into glass vials, then the gingerbread men were devoured by The Mage and Bat Wing covered in cinnamon butter and the spare sold to Harry.

"I am a respected medicine salesman," Harry whispers and lets loose a plague of infested rats with these words, "To encourage business for I own an undertakers."

Yes, The Mage was the son of a three-thousand-year-old mage who had partied weekends at Filthy Big Bertha's and this mage did not see why he could not live longer.

"Give me the secret of long life too," Conan had begged.

"We cannot all live forever son, some must die and some who know the secret of the Fountain of Youth potion will not," the selfish mage and added, "Look we cannot have thousands of your types living to three hundred years for imagine all the babies and the nappies needing changed, **the abandoned women wanting maintenance.**

Think of Wamba living that long and all the babies looking like him?"

And Conan knew The Mage was right.

But The Mage had a rival, The Leopard in Black Spots as Alicadabara was known in wizard circles.

The wizard who replaced his mirror with a cauldron that filled with socks and worms to ask if he was the best wizard ever, a true Halloween fan.

"No, The Mage is," the cauldron and in a temper, he emptied it out and filled it with iced water.

And the cauldron knew this was to be expected from the son of a fish monger who had joined the College of Black Arts and after turning all the teachers there into plastic dinosaurs for a salesman to dispose of the evidence fled through a rip; for things were greener on the other side with mean, smelly things that boys are made of, FIENDS.

And every full moon did sneak across disguised as a were-wolf and throw magic at The Mage who threw magic back so became a constipated were-wolf every full moon.

And Cur the dog hated them both for he grew a poodle's tail.

And Alicadabara found the other side had Prince Ahmenton in pink pantaloons so festered the youth's mind with ambition and we know the rest.

A prince who changed his name to Isisnaphut and was thinking of ways to change Alicadabara into an albatross so the nasty wizard could glide away and never come back. What do you expect of a fairy Fiend that wears pink pantaloons? For Isisnaphut had bought a book, "How to get rid of evil wizards," from a salesman who gets about.

"I sell that book under another name, 'Aunty Fairy's Guide to Healthy Eating.'"

"I am content and drink warm mint beer from my tower," The Mage before the tower was reduced to rubble remember.

"I am mean and unhappy for I want to rule the world and own Christina," Alicadabara.

"I already rule this part of the world so am content," The

Mage coming out of Common as Muck Filthy Big Bertha's.

"I drink potions to make me strong and handsome but give me warts instead," Alicadabara not understanding boys are already full of warts and everything nasty so was only encouraging them to appear and why he would never be like The Mage, clean cut and handsome and the spitting image of Clerk Gable in a long white beard.

"For I click my fingers and Garrison Men sweep my floors, wash my clothes, and pore my baths but do not cut my hair or shave me with sharp thingies for they are vengeful mean and dark; so, employ a gingerbread girl to do that.

"I have no friends for I eventually see they are happy so turn them into fruit flies for a laugh," Alicadabara.

"Ha, he has he," The Mage having a good laugh over the other's misfortune.

And there was a hidden factor that would decide the fate of both wizards; something
born years earlier, **Wamba Ordinary.**

CHAPTER 19
REINFORCEMENTS

And Conan said, "I am badly outnumbered six thousand to one and there's a slim possibility I can be killed," and thought of army rations which made him fight harder to escape across the bridge. But "There are six thousand Fiends wanting to slither me good over there so eating army rations cannot be that bad," so fought his way back across the bridge to Garrison Land.

And because he was near to death had a Near Death Experience and saw the temples he ravaged, the priestesses he did unmentionables to, the temple treasures he looted and sold to Harry who gets around, the cities he burned too ash and populations he sold to Harry for Harry knew many galley owners; and Conan should be a rich man, "But I am a barbarian and drank and womanised it all away boohoo sob."

And thought of his horse 'Whitey' for it was white and how it ran up scaffolds, kicked the hangmen places, and carried Conan into the sunset.

"Whatever happened to that horse?" He pondered blocking a Fiendish axe, "Oh yeh it was a bad winter and them horse steaks in onions certainly got me through to spring, and a salesman got the scraps for glue."

And wished he had a son as a Fiendish sword slid between his legs and knew one of them twenty thousand women, he had ravaged must have had a baby Conan?

"Did they call their daughters Conan after me? And cannot visit as all those babies need maintenance. Is not life hard on me?"

And smiled wickedly when he remembered the Princess who when patting Cur had asked, "What is that breeze?" And straightened her masses of petticoats for a barbarian must be quick to remain undiscovered.

"Maybe there is a little Conan about to grow up a prince?" Was he not Conan the son of Conan the son of Conan if there had been a Conan riding the Wilderness Trail causing havoc?

So realised little Conan needed some reinforcements if he were to grow up a prince and keep him in a life of luxury.

"Where is the regular army, never about when needed?" He shouted.

"You call me corporal?" Whatever was Harold asked holding two Viking axes dripping slippery red ketchup, "*for effect for this is a family story as the extras dressed as Fiends drank coffee in a mobile EATS and DRINKS,*" Satirextrex who drinks thirty coffee cups a day so cannot sleep.

"You call me corporal?" Tom dropping a Fiend at Conan's feet all covered in mashed red cherry stuff as this is a *family story.*

"Woof," a nasty dog cocking its leg on the Fiend and dropped a Fiendish hand at Conan's feet and the hand was covered in red dye as this is a family story. And the hand was made of paper mashie of course as this is a *family story*.

And he could not help himself for Conan plucked the diamond ring off it before the nasty dog could see for a barbarian must be quick.

And above a sky darkened as Fiendish arrows blocked out the sun and thudded into a shield Wamba hid behind.

"Mummy," he mumbled.

And Conan thought of the plundering amongst the dead and the dead owned you as hacking was heavy work. Yes, there were many diamond rings out there.

"Who needs the regular army then?" He asked the dog and fairies for Conan was a retired barbarian adventure riddled with arthritis and wrinkles, warts and bad wind attacks so was not as quick as he thought for, "Woof," from the nasty dog expecting a share of a diamond ring.

"Hello Conan," and was Tom wanting a share of the ring.

"Ouk," and was Harold wanting some cash.

So, forgot all about his little prince needing kittens, puppies, ponies, and pet dragons bought, and all the birthday parties were hundreds of celebrities needed fed, and the schools for rich kids needing paid, yes, he forgot all about them twenty thousand ravaged woman and Christina patting Cur.

"I am sure that blur was Conan?" Christina wanting a share proving Conan THE Conan of legends was just BAD WIND.

CHAPTER 20   DUKE

"The Grand old Duke of Haliput.
Had ten thousand men.
And were called the Duke's Halibut.
And had names like Ben.
Marching to the drum.
This way and that.
Uphill and downhill full of army rum.
All XXX prats.
So needed The Fairy AA anonymous.
But preferred Big Bertha's.
For the waitress service was fabulous.
Especially from Martha.
So, the Grand old Duke of Halibut and chips,
Never had ten thousand men," no not Satirextex again?

An inscription from a stone edifice at the bridge read by tourists two hundred years later.

And a messenger headed for Garrison in bright clothes and, "I am not a parrot," so ripped the clothes off and that is why a salesman had wagons behind the Duke's men for he was in the Rag Trade and the Duke's men were not parrots either.

So, there was a naked messenger running about the countryside giving country folk a bad name.

"I love the Duke for he is senile and sell him what his men throw away. Why look at these million red trainers needing feet, and those purple felt hats with yellow feathers in them, and these pink pantaloons needing fairy legs to prop them up, and all these flower printed boxer shorts, yes, my mule wagons are full and is a never-ending cycle and need not own a single Mill or pay a thousand Mill workers, spinners, and weavers," and Harry dribbled as he jingled the cash made from the Duke and his naked men and choked as the dribble went down the wrong way.

Naked men he sold chain mail taken from all these bashed up Fiends lying about and sold the Duke all the swords needed to fight Fiends with too.

Swords he sold to children at his dinosaur stall for they were rubber.

"How are we supposed to kill Fiends with these?" The Duke's men asked.

"You beat them with them," Harry's voice drifted to them from a safe distance.

And the weapons did the Fiends no good either for they bought them from a certain salesman who got about, no wonder The Fiends had not broken through Garrison?

And Lionel Mathews the naked messenger saw the bridge and heard the screams, "I am not going down there to give a message to something Ordinary and I need cuddled and wrapped up in warm blankets and given hot chocolate to drink to calm my nerves," so headed for Common as Muck Filthy Big Bertha's for he had not thrown away his sporran where he kept his pennies for the sporran covers important places as this is a family story.

"Deliver your message son," King Arawan hoping he did fall in the fetid moat; but he was drunk so Lionel ignored him as that is what you do to annoying drunks, especially one's that smell of meths and relieve themselves in public.

"Only the dead can hear my message and they are dead and so cannot hear anything so my message is delivered," Lionel Mathews the bad naked fairy messenger and entered Bertha's where giggles and raucous laughter drifted out the windows and doors.

And King Arawan sitting on the driver's seat of his own

wagon full of collected souls, in this case all Fiendish cursed his luck, "Meths is cheap burp," and his white, red eared hound bayed and all heard and knew Arawan had escaped the moat so trembled.

And he wanted a certain salesman to sell Arawan something for that dog's constipation so it would stop baying.

"Howl," the bunged-up hound bayed.

"I will not go near the vicious brute but have a wagon full of cotton balls to stick in ears," a Harry whisper and as the breeze carried the whisper was free advertisement.

And any dog baying like that needed a nasty name.

But priests said Arawan's mind was dim with meths so had forgotten the dog's name. Others said they heard him call, "Red Ears come here," just before they died and Arawan threw their souls in the back of his wagon singing, "Hi Ho hi Ho collecting trash hi Ho hi Ho another soul for hell's fires," while others heard "Flea bag," "Filth come here," and "Mange," or "Dribbler," "Gnasher," all heard on their death beds, some at the end of a poppy addicts mugger's dagger, some under the wheels of a drunken mule wagon driver, perhaps Monty's cousin thirty times removed is driving before he went in the moat? Others frozen to death in a bad winter for they had been evicted by a certain salesman for rent arrears in the slum apartments he owned. You see to hear Arawan you must have a Near Death Experience.

And you never forgot it, the sound of that nasty bunged up dog baying, the creaking of a wagon needing goose lard and the smell of meths was overpowering.

And "Everyone is dead," Lionel Mathews sent a message to the Duke from Big Bertha's while drinking chocolate for, he knew they could all go home then. "Here wait a minute, what do I want to go home for? I have a wife who after giving me sixteen kids has lost her figure and these waitresses prefer me not to wear clothes drinking my hot chocolate."

Yes, whether fairy Fiends or dogs the male race had a one-track mind; how to win the lotto.

"Men, now is the time for glory, go sell your lives dearly,"

The Duke upon hearing Lionel's message for dead Fiends could not fight back.

"Here wait a minute; someone said there are thirty thousand Fiends down at the bridge chanting, "Kill," so am staying right here, where is the trade union?" A soldier just bought scratchy furry trousers from a merchant who knew how to turn scratchy furry door mats into trousers to sell naked soldiers feeling the cold.

"Put my tent up here," The Duke ordered and the strikers obliged for they were civilised strikers and busied themselves digging latrines nor did man the pickets for the smell of hot chocolate had drifted to them.

And a sweet little rose scented waitress was seeing delivering hot chocolate to The Duke in his tent. "Pizza delivery," she replied.

And Filthy Big Bertha made all the fairies and Fiends in her house swear not to slither each other for cash was cash whether from a fairy or Fiend, it paid the heating bills for the place had many naked guests for some reason; and waitresses needed lots of expensive rose water and pizza.

"I am rich," Harry filling glass bottles from the latrines and sprinkling some rose petals in them.

And neither Isisnaphut nor Alicadabara knew about the hot chocolate for such an establishment was below them.

And Lionel Mathews wrote in his diary:
"I scouted seeing Fiends,
 Charging stout defenders.
 I reported to Duke.
 That swarthy warrior.
Who immediately ordered trenches dug?
And stakes sharpened to stick Fiends' places."

And his battle of the account of the Battle at the Bridge was stolen and given to Satirextex to inspire national pride amongst fairies: so, they did buy Harry's plastic gnomes that looked like Wamba.

To buy Harry's cauldrons whose handles looked like

Harold's mouth and the brim his teeth?

Or medals with pictures of Tom on them.

And cute pink poodles that named Cur.

And mantel piece stallions called Old nag.

Made by Sampenciltrex that artist responsible for culture in Ball. And clay swords you wind up to hear 'Arnie' sing but turned to rubble instead.

And jars of 'Eat a bit of Isisnaphut' for they were pickled snails and ingredients were too small to read but Harry had nets outside the latrines to catch flies.

And models of all the characters of the battle whose limbs fell off and eyeballs pinged out so the kids would scream in terror.

And the Christina look a likes disappearing into Harry's Cactus Jack's Casino nearby with tourists.

Yes, dart boards with Tootanfoot's grinning face as the Bull's Eye. Mugs with Lionel Mathews face on them drinking Harry's bedtime chocolate.

'Harold's Bags' of peanuts with something apish on it and cuddly Ape soft toys for kids to rip the arms off for all knew Apes deserved what was coming.

And square toilet squares with Alicadabara's face on them.

And a 'Harry Carpentry recommended by The Mage,' so folks bought chest of tools, saws, hammers, nails, and stuff, nope, was sponges to clean the toilet, cotton balls to remove ear wax and stuff, but was TOOLS.

And The Mage was so respected and ALIVE he sold vials to Harry Medicines and they were vials of vile.

Yes, it all could be bought at the dinosaur stall.

"Gee up," King Arawan heading for the bridge as Red Ears bayed and in his hand the message someone never delivered.

"Help is coming."

CHAPTER 21
HOLD ON

And the Fiends attacked the defenders until some Fiendish hero slipped on tobacco and crashed into the bridge railings, went through them, hit the timber supports below, supports riddled by termites, so all fell and landed on Mistress Beautricianix floating on a plank below, a plank riddled by termites also.

"Them insects is my gold mine," a whisper belonging to Harry.

And from underneath flew the long-eared bats that lived there doing what they do best, getting in the hair of Fiends so they screamed, "A rabid untrained bat is in my hair," and fell off into the moat because they were extras.

And not a single bat got into the hair of the defenders for they were the good guys.

And all the centipedes, earwigs and silver fish left the planks and crawled up the legs of the Fiends about places they should not be so more Fiends fell into the moat.

And magic from The Mage and evil Alicadabara fell amongst the Fiends only because Alicadabara needed glasses and refused to admit it so more Fiends fell into the moat.

"Volley fire lads," Wamba encouraged his men as the words had got stuck in his mind.

"Splat," as more slippery tobacco fell amongst the Fiendish feet so more Fiends slipped into the fetid moat and there was lots of tobacco to chew for tins of it lay about a dinosaur stall at last year's Xmas price.

"Still making a profit even if it is mixed with tea dust," an oily whisper, *"hey wait a moment, Conan is not paying argh my chest."*

"Splat," as Tom threw Ladies Foundation found at a dinosaur stall so it got into Fiendish eyes so they could not see and fell into the nasty moat.

"You thieving boy Tom," Harry on oxygen.

"Splat," as Harold threw empty cauldrons lying next to a dinosaur stall and they had price tags on them, but Harold did not notice that. So, Fiends' splatted as the cauldrons was made of cast iron and fell into the microbe infected moat.

"Viking monster," Harry having run out of harsh words.

"Splat," as that horrid dog lifted its leg after drinking many bottles of fizz found lying next to a dinosaur stall and they had sale prices on them.

"MY fizzy drink made from fizzy unsold vile vials cough the dog is not related," Harry his mind flipping.

"Splat," as Wamba in a panic threw Book at the Fiends and threw it so hard, he knocked them down like skittles into the frothing moat. Never mind Harry had many copies of Book for him to throw at inflated prices.

"Ah, I can rely on Wamba to give me resuscitation and am so happy again," Harry.

"Somebody save me," Christina screamed as that is what a terrified princess is supposed to do and emptied bottles of perfumed rose water into the moat so the fumes did drive the Fiends away.

"I am going to afford that white galley with a swimming pool when I bill her," a certain salesman so full of excitement he became temporarily incontinent and asked, *"Here this is not supposed to happen to a smart salesmen?"*

And whoever was authoring the story had Apes catch Harry and drags him to the top of The Mage's tower and tied him to the flagpole there for Apes was a revengeful primate that remembered a sack of banana skins.

And magic was about so Harry grew elephant ears.

And mooed at the end of his words.

And his trouser bottom split as a monkey tail grew there.

And heard an ape snigger.

"I will sue the story writer," Harry promised so the author made his nose red and enlarged.

And below: "Reinforce men," Captain Moronicus wanting to impress the princess and when all the Fiends were dead rescue her and become a handsome prince so added "please."

But his men looked the other way pretending not to hear him and saw Apes coming down the tower towards them so fought the Fiends to try to get away from Apes so Moronicus did not have to add, "with strawberries," and humiliate himself further.

And all that weight on top of wood infested with termites was too much so with a mighty roar the bridge collapsed sending Fiends into the treacherous moat but not a single Garrison Man for they were the good guys.

For Fiends are made of worse things than boys so got what they deserved.

(Do not worry, Fiends are extras and even now drying themselves and drinking hot chocolate at Big Bertha's, naked of course as their clothes are drying.)

But not the fairies made of less harmful ingredients for they are fairy boys.

So, Wamba hung onto the last plank with groaning fingers that groaned because Conan hung to him by his belt and Tom hung to him but not from his belt.

"Shriek," was heard often and, "let go you fool Tom."

And Harold hung onto Tom's medals so they pinged off into the moat.

"For my collection? How kind," King Arawan incredibly happy for business was brisk.

And Cur did not have fingers to grasp thingies so used his teeth on Harold so "Ouk," was heard much and, "Let go idiot I needed seven hundred corn flakes tops for that medal," and then swore a lot but that is censored for Tom is portrayed as a sweet innocent lad who sells toffee on street corners to support 'Homeless Girls of Filthy Big Bertha's.'

"Hey, this fairy is wearing Superman printed

unmentionables?" Captain Moronicus admiring what Harold wore as he clung to whatever Harold was.

Then added, "Shriek let go off those," as his Lost Patrol clung to every part of his anatomy for the moat was below.

"O," was not the call of a female Tandoori Forest Household Gorilla and was Mistress Beautricianix wobbling on her plank as she stamped on Fiendish fingers trying to get the plank from her to save themselves. Selfish Fiends for not trying to save a delicate painted woman first.

"Ouk," Apes replied and swung down Wamba and stuck his massive toes places so Wamba screamed, "Yikes that is not a banana," for he was afraid for he knew primates ate bananas.

So, Apes ignored Christina with the pretty ankles for she was bland compared to the new love in his life so rescued Mistress Beautricianix.

"When I am queen that ape will visit a taxidermist," Christina peeved.

"This ape has fleas," a member of the Lost Patrol and just like that the fleas were biting and everyone needed a good scratch and lots of flea powder.

"I am finished," Wamba managed to gasp, "Gasp," as his fingers stretched so those at the bottom dipped into the swirling moat waters.

So, all scrambled to the top over him.

Poor Wamba Ordinary was just a ladder to everyone and not a fairy with ambitions, feelings, needs and nightmares, yes just a ladder as uncut fingernails clawed places; and many boots dug places so, "Gawd almighty," was heard often and, "Have pity on me so let go," but the clawers were not fooled for the dark deep moat was below.

"Gurgle," from the deep moat water.

But not too worry Alicadabara just for spite threw one last magic spell at Wamba and missed for a breeze was on the air and hit Harry.

So, he turned into a Dwarf Tandoori Forest Household Mountain Gorilla with a monkey tail, in a light blue ballerina dress.

"Ouk," Apes holding Mistress Beautricianix up for closer inspection and was horrified to see the mascara had smudged, the red lipstick smeared, the dye run from her hair, the foundation had fingerprints in it, her hair needed a shampoo to untangle the million knots and clumps, her clothes were ripped and covered in nasty looking stains and the rose water smelt of something bad, and paper mashie was stuffed in her bra so the melons looked BIG, so Apes said, "Ouk," which meant "Harry again."

And unable to look upon the haggard woman tossed her to the elements, but not to worry just before she hit the moat snatched hold of something.

"Oh, sweet mummy not again," Wamba shrieked.

And Wamba was not the only one shrieking for Mistress Beautricianix had put on weight eating all those strawberries and oysters on holiday; and with a "Splash," all hit the moat water.

Perhaps it was the rose water but the moat spat them out, except for the Fiends for they are the bad guys.

"Saved," Wamba groaning lying flat on the embankment and should not have lain still **but sought cover for what is spat out must come down.**

"Marvellous, who are the actors?" A member of the regular army drinking warm beer at Common as Muck Filthy Big Bertha's in a deck chair.

"Retreat," Isisnaphut with his accountant beside him who had told him, "All those war pensions needing paid so no more midnight swims in swimming pools full of Champagne and floozy Fiend girls, fairies, pixies and brownies and scrub-a-dubs Highness."

And Lord Tootanfoot coming up the rear of the Fiendish army was muttering, "Why does no one love me?" "Is it my big ears?" "All I want is to rule the worlds seen and unseen, is that asking too much Gawd?" So never heard the Fiend army screaming coming his way, "No more hacking today boys," "Line up the XXX at Common as Muck Filthy Big Bertha's," **so trampled all over he who was muttering, "What the blazes?"**

"Hi Ho, hi Ho, off we go making souls out of muck," King Arawan sang happily nearby tossing Fiendish souls into the back of his wagon, you see, all alive again, just in HELL.

"Bray," his mules nibbling carrots bought from a salesman so after a few nibbles spat them out for they were nasty tasting Brussel Sprouts dipped in orange paint.

"Is not the season for carrots," a lame reply from someone on the wind and jingled his sporran protectively.

"Ouk," a furious primate who hearing the jingle thought of Xmas and presents bought from a travelling salesman and the boxes where empty.

"What does an ape know about presents, the time needed to remove what was in the boxes, the hours spent wrapping the boxes in Xmas paper? It is after all only an illiterate thingy?" Harry who did not whisper and since he was in the arms of Apes was heard so got battered good and Apes ripped a sporran off.

"Shriek," as the sporran almost took away something else for sporran's hang in dangerous places.

And not only did the greedy salesman get battered he got his chips too for the magic wore off so Apes saw it was Harry.

"Blooming heck wish Apes did hurry up rob that salesman," a soldier buying a Fiend an XXX at Common as Muck Filthy Big Bertha's for he knew Apes did stop by and trade, a peanut for table of XXX.

"Maybe I can go home now," the Fiend seeing there was no bridge left to fight over and showed the army man his photos of his green wife with 49DD breasts, the seven kids with fangs and the pet crocodile wanting to eat you.

"These are my lot," the army man showing the Fiend a picture of a dancing girl then six more of the same but they were not the wife.

And Alicadabara bit his nails to the core in nervous frustration so screamed when he bit into bone and added, "They did not teach me this at The Black School of Arts? They told me evil always wins so I want refunded."

And Isisnaphut in a royal rage stamped on all his snails so

would not get his supper that night. "Never mind there is a table reserved for me at Common as Muck Filthy Big Bertha's where Fiends are not judged by the colour of their horns but by the jingle in a sporran."

And it was all because of termites and a greedy salesman that won the battle at the bridge.

"How can I get Satirextex and Sampenciltrex to turn ugly bulbous termite white insects into heroes kids need reared on?" Harry and in his pocket a Chartered Surveyors report to the last nail how much King Charles did have to pay to rebuild the bridge.

"And at no extra cost can rebuild it in a night," and added, "that ape is on a one-way ticket to a zoo, all I need is volunteers to get it there?" And a brainwave, "I will add termites as the crunchy bits to my famous white chocolate and white because of milk and TERMITES," and Harry laughed so much his tummy wobbled and his shoulders justled so his hood fell off his body and watching floozy waitresses nearby at Big Bertha's thought he was a peeking Tom and did him black and blue.

"Gasp, I need an ambulance, hey wait a minute, they cost cash, ah found it, my emergency jar of leeches."

CHAPTER 22
COUNCILS OF WAR

And after dinner where King Isisnaphut ate Cottage Pie made from vegan haggis, with a salad dish of fresh cut grass and washed it all down with iced lemon tea, as that grass was fresh and so was Cur a bit on the leaky side, he went and sulked on his golden throne, a giant snail crafted by craftsmen but Fiends was supposed to live in grass huts so they must have stolen it from fairies who knew how to make such things.

"All I know he is welcome here any time," Common as Muck Filthy Big Bertha jingling for, he pays in gold not I.O.U.'s like some broke faggot Garrison Men.

"And he tips well," the waitresses adjusting their strap thingamabobs as they jingled the gold nuggets he gave out as tips and juggled other thingamabobs that did not need paper mashie nor juggling but was doing it as show-offs.

And the heavy golden throne was carried on poles by sweaty pole bearers the criminals of the Fiend world so do not feel sorry for them.

"What a weight?" A children's bank rubber moaned.

"Cannot he fall off and have an accident?" A white-collar swindler of granny bank accounts hoped.

"Yes, the smell down here is overpowering?" A mugger of those in wheelchairs overcome by unhealthy essences drifting down from a royal above.

"Rprt," from the royal as eating snails, rancid butter,

vegan haggis, fresh grass with Cur's fingerprints on them, well, it was obvious there did be a royal essence.

"We get gruel to eat while he gets waitress service," a Fiend dwarf miner who ran off with the mine now scraping gold flakes off the gold poles.

"Gee up," the task masker and sent the whip in; a thirty foot long one to reach hidden places.

"Yikes," the Fiendish criminals and jumped to it.

"Blast I dropped the gold flake," the Fiend dwarf miner and bent done to pick it up and was never seen again as the other pole bearers stomped forward.

"But be happy, a squeak was heard from the road," Aslop, "Fantastic I got trampled down to Australia and OPALS, opals, drool, Australian opals," the happy dwarf.

And Isisnaphut was going to meet Alicadabara and tell him what he thought of his magic that did not work, **perhaps not a wise move?**

And Alicadabara was fuming in bandaged feet holding his glued stomped wand carved in cobra mouths, with sharp fangs. And because it was a magic wand the fangs had been full of nasty venom so explains why Alicadabara was covered in boils and red spots and seeing triple for that tantrum where he stomped his wand.

And beside him Lord Tootanfoot sitting on a red spotted toadstool and we know what is said about them, *'Do not eat toadstools, especially that variety.'*

"I am in a thousand bits and my plans of toppling Drunken Noddy and becoming King of Ball in tatters because his magic does not work," **a foolish unloved Tootanfoot.**

"He needs a diet," the toadstool once a Fiend but there had been so much magic lately? And that should have been a cue for an unloved mangled broken up lord needing the emergency ward quick; but do not worry even if the whole Fiendish army had retreated over him as **this is a grown-up fairy story where no one really dies**, so all that magic healed all Tootanfoot's million broken bones and squashed thingies inside him.

"Zap," Alicadabara fed up with the complaining unloved lord and sniggered. **What spell had been used?** *"Find out in a later instalment when buying chapter 36 at no extra cost of course,"* that salesman hoping for a sale.

Anyway: "Who is Wamba, is he General Wamba, where did he come from?" Lord Tootanfoot carelessly promoting Wamba.

"Half my army in the moat, calls himself a wizard, why if I was green apple pie covered in green slimy custard, I could work better magic than Alicadabara," Isisnaphut from his gold throne.

"We will see about that," and was a deliberate mutter so heard and a broken wand moved and all the labourers carrying the throne became green slimy custard.

"Needs cream," a certain Lord who was one of those types that loved his puddings.

"We have no bridge; we need a merchant to sell us a D.I.Y. easy assembly bridge?" Isisnaphut not noticing the colour of his pole bearers.

"Delicious," a certain lord that loved auntie's apple pies.

"Hello," and Harry tied up his mules for a successful merchant must have good hearing, be fearless when dealing with disillusioned customers and carry a Fiendish dictionary in his pocket.

And in a flash Harry had shown them in the back of his wagon the best packaged D.I.Y. Bridge with a garage on the upper level for mules.

"I cannot afford that?" Isisnaphut being a difficult customer.

"Yes, it should be free for all those rotten planks you sold us?" Tootanfoot on his last slimy custard pole bearer.

"For you," Harry giving the dangerous customer cream on the house, cream that was the white froth lathered on his mules' coats for Harry knew speedy mules got him places first, and first meant no competition for the competition groomed their donkeys and horses and fed them oats, and when cold put electric blankets on their beasts of burden and gave them names, "Goldie Locks," "Banana Rama," "Sir Oliver," and such tripe, *whereas Harry used the whip and named them all "Glue bags,"* the horrid man and in cold nights sold their blankets to cold frontiers people living near the bridge.

"I can click a bridge out of the clouds," Alicadabara in the huffs still so "Gee up," was Harry's reply as he left the wizard to it.

"Wait, bring it back, **I will give you anything for it,**" Isisnaphut using the wrong words to a salesman, so was Alicadabara's fault Isisnaphut bought without bargaining for:

"Sign here," Harry and the king signed 'X'.

"Gee up," was heard in the distance as Harry crossed the moat in a hurry with these words, **"No mouldy hay tonight for you Glue Bags if you do not hurry."**

"How did he do that?" Alicadabara amazed but was a salesman secret for those that owed him had prostrated themselves across the fetid moat so his mules and wagon could cross, **in a hurry of course**; for they hoped he would let them off a month's H.P.

But it was Harry the greatest salesman ever they were dealing with and just as well he sold splints and bandages as his wheels rutted here and broke and squashed places.

"Oh ah," was a moan from Conan needing a splint in a prominent place.

"EEK," Wamba shrieked and might shriek for ever.

"Crock," Harold as a wheel rutted his mouth so did not "Ouk."

"Woof," and was the last woof for many an hour.

"I will be innocent for ever and never know adulthood," **Tom and was a lie.**

"Should know greedy salesmen are greedy salesmen," an Aslop fable drifting by.

So, them who needed bandages hated Aslop as well as the salesman for his smart words.

And the Fiends began to assemble their shiny new bridge. And the instructions where in Chinese and Harry had not sold them a Chinese dictionary for, they had no money left.

And across the fetid moat another Council of War as The Mage and the regrouped defenders figured out what to do. And they held their talk in Common as Muck Filthy Big Bertha's so were distracted often by FLOOZY waitresses so never saw Harry jingle his cash.

"We won, we actually won, here baby come sit on my knee," Conan knowing war and shared difficulties dissolved social barriers so pulled the princess to him. But he was wrong for they were at peace again, the war was past so she slapped his face so hard his lips hit the opposite wall with this sound, "PING."

"Just what I like, a woman with spirit," and Conan's lips puckered for a kiss but Wamba full of rage beat him good with these words, "Ugly pensioner, touch her again and I will beat you, understand," **and beat Conan good to make him understand** but he was Conan of the Legends so did not lie down so stood up as fairy men do so got beaten up good again so was beaten up good three times, the idiot for Wamba was jealous and no fairy Guards Man friend kisses his wife.

"WIFE?" Aslop and Satirextrex and his friends, staff, and customers at Filthy Big Bertha's?

"WIFE?" A princess.

"Click," and The Mage turned them into butterflies so he could have peace to read The Times.

"What children," Captain Moronicus pulling Christina towards him now the Ordinary was a butterfly so was kneed good then in went the right uppercut.

So, his lips hit a distant wall too and the customer there was offended, so beat Moronicus black and blue and stuffed blue cheese places for he had been eating cheese and crackers. So, the two of them would be ignored by the waitresses for that cheese stinks.

"Ouk," Harold swinging from the rafters as Apes was curious to see what made such attractive noises and Harold swung fast for Apes was swinging behind him.

So, banana skins fell upon the Lost Patrol playing a certain card game with the waitresses so were happy the skins covered places now bare.

Yes, it was a Council of War for Tom was nowhere to be found but giggles and titters came from behind the wooden curtains. **Being innocent he must have been swapping marbles or trading Marvel comic picture cards?**

And Common as Mucks Filthy Big Bertha's pedigree poodle was nowhere to be seen either and nor was that nasty dog Cur.

"Hello all," Harry entering and from a bag gave all trinkets, *free of course*, for he was rich from the bridge sale so knew it was Fiendish money that bought these gifts he needed to pacify these good fairies with or nasty things did happen to him, for he could remember Apes.

And the trinkets were that, collected from the bottom of Corn Flake boxes but the fairies were happy for fairies liked free thingies.

"What peace?" Harry but his customers did not hear him as they laughed playing with their toys. "Who sold them toys?" Harry.

CHAPTER 23 HELL

And Arawan is the element hell and doors lead to him from poor cold street urchins huddled under hot bakery windows at night for bakers work funny hours; perhaps they are funny people for they make funny face cakes and angel cakes and gingerbread men and toffee whirls so like to whirl it up.

"Recruit them young, I make no excuses," Arawan looking for a new meth bottle for he has recruitment signs over the bakery window; 'Fresh bread,' and is a lie and is just a lure to get the poor cold orphans huddled under the window for a trap door exists right there.

And guess who pulls the string to open the trap door, which is when he can get a swig of meths to steady his hands, a red eared hound that it took thirty hours to teach and knew what to do in an hour.

Shame and bad wicked Arawan and hope you catch something bad some place.

"And is not a cruel master as allows them to lick the steam off the hot water pipes when they get thirsty and there are geysers here that shoot up steamed fish but they must catch their own. I do not employ domestic staff for can you imagine how many cooks did need paid to feed the zillions in hell. Let them live off the larva that is what I say.

And since business is so good at the bridge have allowed everybody a cup of meths to liven things up. A moment for them to forget where they are and better not breath out as meth fumes is highly inflammable.

And here is Red Ears gnawing a leg belonging to a fairy murderer Mr. Tinker Horn. Gnawed till the end of time for Blameworthiness dictates the sentence.

In this case he had none; he strangled his poor defenceless mother-in-law. Did her when she slept. No provocation, his murderous action was full of reckless wicked intent, yes, a class one murder and he goes straight to level 9 Hell to shovel sulphur into Harry bags for Harry has contacts in the chemical industry you know.

But I need meths for my goddess mother-in-law is mitigating circumstances too......so felt sorry for him and let him work his way up to level 1 then send him back to 9. **A change of atmosphere does staff wonders.**

And need not worry about his leg, it will grow back, all bits do beyond the veil.

And needs his legs to wash my soul collecting wagon as is gory work.

And see here the Most Wanted Posters and all are at the bridge.

And use these moles as darts," and he flung one at a poster but because he was drunk hit a newspaper and somewhere someone felt a cold breeze run up his spine; death was coming to collect, all busy no time for holidays Arawan as he drove the wagon DRUNK.

"I am innocent honest, wake the drunken Burke Arawan up quick," but a royal snore, windy and belch greeted the protester as ghouls in black hoods in a wagon driven by Monty's cross-eyed cousin thirty times removed is driving approached, and a red eared hound jumped off the wagon and humped his legs.

And the innocent was not dead yet and kicked 'GNASHER' back to Arawan who rolled off his seat and fell on red ears who offended went to find a leg to gnaw elsewhere.

"Ha, he has he, not again, I cannot stand this," Mr. Tinker Horn somewhere in hell as a leg is gnawed, a fake plastic leg for Harry has a contract to supply them to Hell.

CHAPTER 24 A PUSHING WE GO

"Oh, wondrous metal beastie,
Shining black,
No termite finds you tasty.
Pure Ballenese railway track,
Erected by fairy sweat.
In freezing snow.
So, with much fret,
As fairies froze you know.
As they made a beastie upside down.
For Fiends don't read Chinese.
So Isisnaphut wore a frown.
"Why wasn't it written in Ballenese?"
So cleared off to Common as Muck,
To have his hot chocolate of course," Satirextex who has escaped assassins and giant rat traps to write again.

And all lies for a salesman knows the public loves to believe lies.

"Heave Ho a pushing we go," Fiends shoving the DIY Bridge towards the bridge and Garrison Men lost in thought as those about to die do.

"I am Conan and feel the wind of the steppes in my blood and want to run and tame wild horses there but the stripes on my arm make me responsible for Tom that innocent boy and

Book needs burning and Wamba gagged?"

And Wamba had a copy of Book in his back pocket and had no idea what to do for the writer of Book had authored Book drinking hot chocolate and eating dried toast. So, all Wamba could do was parade his men when seeing fifteen thousand fiends pushing a steel bridge towards him; should run and plant mushrooms somewhere, marry a freckled farmer's daughter and have twenty kids to do farm chores as you take it easy.

And Cur was gnawing at the string Wamba had tied him to a peg in front of them all, for he knew the dog was selfish and would not lay down its life for friends, so would bite any Fiend foolishly enough to get near and for effect, lathered the mouth with whipped cream so looked rabid.

And Harold was happy for he was half blind for a certain merchant had sold him glasses that where designer sunglasses so could not see any Fiends coming so was happy eating famous Harry pork pies. Strange pies with ringed tails hanging from them.

"The spaghetti bits," a lying salesman throwing a blanket over traps in his wagon. Pork pies thrown in free if glasses bought. Pies fit for the bin for they was green and the salesman knew if he ever met Harold again, he did need to sell Harold proper glasses to see Fiends with as they were getting close.

False teeth as Harold did not have any but a salesman knew the crusty puff pastry did wonders for gummy gums hard as steel, shredded them.

A hearing aid to hear the better the wondrous items for sale on a mule drawn wagon.
Mules of course as kids love to give them sugar cubes and say, "Nice horsy." Sugar cubes bought from a salesman.

And a bottle of purgatives to get rid of any pie left and no guarantees it would work as only Harry and the mules knew the ingredients.

"Bray," but sugar had been added for taste and a sprinkle of cinnamon for aroma so it was an expensive bottle of purgative.

"Come and get your just deserts Alicadabara," The Mage at the top of his tower. And Alicadabara would like many deserts for he was fond of lemon pie, apple pie and chocolate sponge pudding and lots of ice cream and custard.

And behind the Garrison Men the Lost Patrol behind their oval shields with spears bristling for Moronicus had read their minds so told them poisonous worms lived here and attacked anyone walking; so, they stood still listening for the grass to rustle for it does when a worm appears so they could stamp on the poisonous worm and send it to Arawan below.

Poor cuddly worms and maybe goodbye Arawan.

"These fairies are too used to riding horses on goose feathered saddles, of eating fine food at Common as Muck Filthy Big Bertha's, of having waitress service and this time will fight and I will be noticed by King Charles who will give me Christina in marriage," Moronicus illustrating why he was called Moronicus.

And was all lies apart from the good waitress service.

And the oval wooden shields and spears had been bought from Harry made from planks infested with termites, oh fear.

"We do not want shields and spears to last a lifetime but replaced at a decent price," and was a whisper from you know who?

"Is the princess worth my horse to flee to safety?" Moronicus who wanted to flee for he was a selfish self-preservationist. Beside Apes had got fond of that horse as riding beat walking.

"Listen kid go get me some chewy tobacco," Conan and Apes knew when a stripe sent the kid to the rear things must be bad.

"Ouk," Apes swinging off to find a wet warm Tandoori Rain forest and floozy girl ape to make heaps of nasty gorilla babies with tremendous strength. But saw Mistress Beautricianix and Offaltrex Purchtrix arguing with Harry and Apes remembered banana skins so screamed: "Eek Ouk," and the Fiends heard that savage shriek and stopped but the

Fiends behind kept pushing forward shoving them in front into the boiling moat.

Kept pushing for Alicadabara was behind them turning them into butterflies and worse, was riding a giant black bat cracking a bull whip to make Fiends shout louder, "Kill," when all the Fiends wanted was to go home to the wives and sixteen kids and read the Sunday newspapers and eat cereal biscuits for energy to cut the grass.

And up front The Mage was turning those Fiends there into runny treacle as Arawan had sent a message to him: 'Need molasses for my jam sandwiches.'

Then Wamba thinking hard knew what to say as the fiends was piling up the moat allowing Fiends behind to cross and hundreds of butterflies too.

"Retreat," he shouted.

"About blooming well time?" Conan and spat chewy tobacco at Wamba to show his appreciation.

And Tom was not there to salute Wamba for he was long gone from listening to Conan.

But Cur was for he had gnawed his way to freedom so bit Wamba somewhere so there was a loud "Shriek;" to show his admiration for his sergeant.

"Ouk," and something big in dark glasses and fury swung over Wamba and unable to see did Wamba good in case Wamba was a Fiend and being deaf did not know what Wamba had shouted so was empty of appreciative thoughts apart from where to find peanuts and a Viking ship to row away to Greenland and retirement for there was none here?

And Wamba lay where he was floored admiring all the butterflies above him just as the Lost Patrol took a chance and ran across the grass and across Wamba for everyone was heading to The Mage's ruined tower for it had many levels to hide in; so perhaps the Fiends would not see them and "Kill," them.

"Gee up," Christina on Apes' horse and galloped over Wamba and one Fiend said, "It is the famous Bengal Lancers," and it only takes one and the Fiends were in full retreat and were so numerous Alicadabara could not turn them all into butterfly's quick enough so made some flies before he was deservedly trampled.

"Buzz," they went away home to be swatted by the wife.

"The Fiends became afraid.

For they thought which was dangerous,
For they were soldiers and worse fiends,

So fled," Satirextex words inscribed on the spot Fiends became winged insects. And near this plaque a hot pie vendor for Harry knew tourists liked Scots Hot Pies and was also into vermin control. *"A lovely hot pie full of minced pepper meat and runny gravy and only me, the hunter and them vermin and the butcher knows what ingredients are, and almost forgot the mules but a glue factory is nearby,"* a Harry whisper but sales in purgatives are good.

Is this the future we glimpse where the world is controlled by Harry Bros. PLC that sees the world as a sale? No wonder the Brotherhood exist, people all ,bunged up unable to work with gripes, cholera, dysentery, parasites inside and HIS FAULT.

And across the bridge a Toll House and a Harry cousin selling tickets to 'Garrison Men Theme Park.'

"Mine all mine," Harry when selling Harold, a plastic dinosaur covered in gravy so became his motto. Yes, all the pennies were his and there was a hundred pennies to a gold mark and all his. "For a salesman needs to think ahead," and with his disgruntled customers he needed too. "I accept I.O.U.'s for they are valued behind the veil and will pay for my green pixies dancing about in tights for they are floozy pixies that never made it to that other nicer boring place where you must listen to loud organ recitals.

I will run hell and feed Arawan meths so he sees pink elephants always and not me taking bribes to open the gates to leave with my maps. Maps showing the road to the other place but is the rear exit to hell. They do not know that but I do.

So, send Arawan angel cakes stuffed full of floozy devils but He sends them back. What is wrong with Him? Money makes the world round and have already bribed the fates so all fate lines come to my stalls.

Yes, I know how to make money and these Garrison Men do not know how lucky they are to have me as a friend.

Now what do I see? Wamba has got to his knees and a thousand Fiends are in front of him. I cannot look but will; perhaps I can sell the Fiends an axe sharpener?"

And all the Fiends thought Wamba crazy not to flee with the rest to The Mage's tower and wondered why he was not afraid.

"Ga," escaped Wamba for he was not with this world for he ached something after being trampled all over and sucked cream he had given Cur, as a treat for his million bruises.

"He is not afraid because that is a rabid General Wamba," a Fiend and only takes one so the Fiends tip toed past Wamba afraid that if they slithered him his ghost did come back and haunt them, besides, he had rabies, just look at his foaming mouth.

So, Fiends counted how many Fiends bobbed up and down in the moat as they went by. And just then Christina appeared on Apes' horse and threw Wamba across her saddle.

"I do not believe this, that puny little delicate girl lifted that Ordinary onto her horse?" Alicadabara and pulled hair from his head so was bald, "Ah that is so painful."

"Hi ya baby," was all Wamba was allowed to say before he was dumped at The Mage's tower door just next to where a spoilt dog did its unmentionables so he was not pleased. And he was not happy as Christina urged her horse to enter the tower over him. Then misery set upon him for Conan to save Tom from Womba's corrupt influences shut the tower door.

On the side where the Fiends had recovered their composure and where chanting "Kill."

"Here let me in," Wamba pleaded banging on the door.

"When do I get paid?" Tom replied pretending not to hear.

"That is the spirit," Conan.

"Kill."

And a spear parted Womba's legs so he trembled for the spear was high up near thingamabobs.

"This is more like it," Alicadabara getting happy.

"If you want in, push paybooks through the letter box," Conan and was immediately popular and a nasty dog waited under the letter box for dogs know what to do with the mail and newspapers.

And another spear thundered into the wood above the last spear so Wamba afraid pushed Book through the letter box.

"Stop that, that is army property," he heard Christina and hope rose in his heart. "I love you princess," and well she did not hear him! And she saved Book not for Wamba but because she was afraid there was no discipline amongst the Garrison Men apart from her riding crop that Garrison men always wanted to polish.

Yes, strange things occurred with waitress service at Filthy Big Bertha's it seems and perhaps were taking horse riding lessons and not how to improve your knitting.

And Book was pushed back to Wamba's tattered and bruised and then the door opened and Apes took hold of Wamba and swung away to the rafters, and here shook him upside down to see if any pennies fell out; but it was a Garrison Man he was mugging so dropped the penniless thing six floors up.

"Here why are you looking at me like that?" Conan asked Christina.

"And why is Harold picking mushrooms off my back?" Tom worried.

"Woof," and a dog scratched a potato off its head.

"Ga," Wamba managed trying to get up as that was some loud thud, he hit the floor with.

"Here I am not captain to vegetables?" Moronicus as the Lost Patrol sprouted them.

"Ouk," Apes panicking as onions grew on his bottom.

"What has that idiot done?" Conan forgetting whom he addressed going after The Mage.

"What a sweet old man, how I love white beards," Christina lying but knew how to grovel as she went after The Mage also and, "The nice old man has put a wall of magic about us and any Fiend that gets too close becomes market produce," and plucked Italian produce off Conan with these words, "Minestrone soup tonight boys."

"No one makes soup out of me," and was Conan's last words as he was on the steps a salesman never repaired so hit the wooden dining table below and bounced off a rubber chicken Harry had sold Harold so his fall was broken, **lucky fairy.**

So, helping hands pulled the chicken off his head as Fiends fell down the stairs for The Mage had opened the trap door to let dinner in. Tomatoes for everyone, to be added to omelettes or eaten raw.

"I have had enough," Conan sitting down to smoke his tobacco and Christina asked for some and surprised he gave her and together clouded the room up.

And his fury arm oiled its way about a princess *for any girl that could smoke his tobacco was meant for him.*

And he was wrong, for any girl that could lift Wamba onto a saddle knew how to deal with fury oily arms.

"Come on girl, untie me," Conan begged as Christina knew how to make knots out of burly fury oily arms as she was a sea cadet.

And Conan saddened for any girl that could make mince of him was his girl, a girl to ride next to him never washing so they did pong the wilderness trail together.

Yes, the Fiends could have the bridge and Common as Muck Filthy Big Bertha's as well and Wamba thrown in as extra; Conan was coming out of retirement and thinking of The Mage's bat, Bat Wing and escaping with his girl to litter the Steppes in litter.

A girl that could make mince of him, smoke his tobacco and was full of other tricks but not the type of Conan expected. Did he know she had black belts in all the martial arts and a cooking degree and a home economics diploma.

Yes, he should have asked her if she wanted to escape with him.

CHAPTER 25 BAT WING STRIKES AGAIN

And Harry has the sympathy of all salesmen, bank managers, social workers, elected bodies, fishmongers, and ticket collectors after receiving customer complaints head on and not via a secretary.

He had no idea what the shouting was above his head or where he was?

"Must be sea gulls squabbling over a rubber chicken," he *assured himself. "And were the first words that flowed into his temples, for he was a CHEATER,"* Aslop.

But he was wrong for they were nowhere near the breezy sea.

And Harry with wide eyes spied Bat Wing with many escaping passengers aboard and said, **"I am not one of them."** And he was right for he had been left behind as a brave rear guard without getting asked, perhaps a volunteer.

Then the horrid Fiends had him and were to chop him good but heard his magic words:

"Summer sale, credit cards accepted, everything must go," so the Fiends put down their choppers and put out the flaming torches about to set the Garrison Hut ablaze with all its bad pongs and rancid essences, bed bugs, spittoon air fresheners and fleas so Harry did not do his friends any favours: for they wanted new accommodation like the regular army boys of the Duke get. [*Oh yes and a half gnawed lonely rubber chicken lay on the hut's floor.]* Running baths for orphan boys run back and forth to the moat. Good army food of six and twenty black birds in a pie; and the fancy clothes the Duke's men wore. [Not to worry kind folks, the black birds had been bought from a butcher who supplied Harry, so were chewy and indigestible but filling, and laxative sales went up and behind the butchers big oil drums steaming away with melted rubber and plastic, yes Harry had pet chickens behind his stall, "Lucy have a chocolate bar," "April nice unwanted pies for you," "Fatima give me more eggs, listen up chickens, a hundred eggs per week or Harold will not be eating rubber chickens, ha Ho, He Ha Ho," the SCALLIWAG.

And Alicadabara and The Mage wanted Bat Wing brought down from where sea gulls glide for it like the magnificent birds of the air, was free with the waste bits.

He was mean and knew it was a long way down for escapees to fall into a field of nettles for Alicadabara had a dark streak on him, well the bat was above.

And The Mage because if anyone was escaping it was him so was mean too.

So Alicadabara waved his bandaged wand and pooled red pixies with little black aprons on in front of Bat Wing who was not afraid, and whereas Harry had chickens running amok in his temples, Alicadabara had pixies, the FINK. So, cursing for FINKS think it makes them BIG WIZARDS pooled a red dragon with black soot smudges. And Bat Wing knew she was not dreaming for her passengers screamed, "Let us get out of here," or "There is a fire breathing dragon up front," or "How do we get this stupid bat to turn about," and "We are dead" and "Banana roaster," which is gorilla for dragon.

And The Mage sent a strong homing instinct to his bat.

And left the tower to see what Wamba was doing for he was not on his bat and found him lying near in an untrained dog's unmentionables at the door, he was needing a wash with soap.

And is why Bat Wing suddenly dived at 800 mph for the tower and those aboard **were terrified.**

Why Apes fell off or *might have been pushed* and fell through the tower roof for it had holes you know. And hit a thick oak rafter below that stopped him crashing into the solid cold stone floor

"First one down," The Mage

But did not see Apes fall off the rafter and through a hole in the solid cold floor and land in an XXX barrel that The Mage was brewing for he sold it to Harry who sold it to Common as Muck Filthy Big Bertha. Now Apes was in it with bits of gorilla fur, drowned fleas, squashed papaya fruit and an XXX cork: adding JUNGLE FARM flavours.

"Ten green bottled rats floating in wine," a rat swam happily near Apes.

And Apes swam across the vast barrel and swallowed much XXX. And he knew when swimming to keep his mouth closed so had no excuse to stagger out of the barrel and fall face flat on the cellar floor with this sound, "Burp thud."

And inside he was angry for falling off a bat at 800 mph. hitting an oak rafter, an XXX barrel and almost drowning for not keeping his mouth closed while swimming; so, wanted to "Kill," **for temper and XXX do not mix.**

He was blind drunk like daddies on weekends.

So started the long trek upstairs for each step was a mountain to legs that tottered that belonged to an Ape seeing pink bananas.

And was lucky for everyone there were a thousand steps to climb so was exhausted when he got to the top; so now just wanted a quiet corner to lie and whimper and suck his thumb for his head ached something and his tummy wanted too empty.

He was hung-over and serves him right for swimming with a gaping mouth.

But before he collapsed allowed something in at the front door, something that had been lying in unmentionables.

Something Book belonged to so Apes was unpopular but because he was a drunk gorilla no one complained.

And Bat Wing zoomed by within reach of the Lost Patrol

who wanted on and did get on for they outnumbered Conan thirty to one and he was no longer Conan The Barbarian but Conan the Incontinent; he who should have asked Christina if she was his WIFE to escape on Bat Wing to populate The Wilderness Trail with little Conan's. But he had not, just thrown her over his shoulder and jumped on Bat Wing with blunt spurs, and any bat seeing spurs does not need being told twice to get going. Long sharp silver spurs for kicking were-wolfs met on the Wilderness Trail out of the way, but spurs thrown into the back of a locker and needed polished and sharpening, so do not fret, Bat Wing is oaky.

Except a primate fed up with shaking Wamba for pennies saw a better life elsewhere **for when a stripes sends the kid to the rear it must be bad,** 'We are all about to die and there did be no little gorillas swinging from banana trees.' So, Bat Wing seeing Apes coming did not need telling thrice to get flying and as he flew past a rafter Apes jumped aboard with these words, "Ouk."

"I am still not one of them passengers," Harry moaned selling plastic dinosaurs to Fiends who thought they needed them to gather dust mites on mantle pieces.

And the Lost Patrol hung onto anything so Conan screamed and shrieked these words, "Let go of me Yee Burkes."

While some hung onto each other's thingamajigs with these words, "Odoo," so were true fairies indeed and some to money belts that burst, showering Fiends below with manna from Heaven so Harry was happy too, for more floating plastic dinosaurs to put around the bath was bought and real soap he sold Wamba.

And soon the Lost Patrol realised they had not been saved for a red dragon with snoot smudges was up ahead breathing fire on them.

So many instantly became bald needing wigs.

"I can supply those," a salesman's whisper.

And since money belts had twanged away there was nothing left to hold up the pink pantaloons that dropped away to a salesman below who would sell them back as soiled goods.

And yes, the Lost Patrol it seems where responsible for many essences as they had not changed their unmentionables.

The foul regular army boys, conscripts, cadets, volunteers, the boots on the ground lads but not our boys, The HEROIC GUARDSMEN, the Border Patrol.

And The Mage who had used an electric whip on Bat Wing many times but also fed it oysters so was a paradox himself, so sent a rain cloud to cool the bat down and put out dragon breath.

And Bat Wing slowed down by the extra luggage found she could safely follow Apes through the hole in the roof, hit a rafter and splash below in an XXX barrel and get drunk.

"I will murder it," The Mage a paradox for on his chest a 'Be kind to dragons' button.

And The Mage was wrath for he could hear many regular army men in his barrel polluting it in their unwashed unmentionables.

"Never mind, I will buy it reduced as damaged goods and sell it to Bertha's clients as hundred-year-old XXX at a top price," that salesman whispers as he buried his cash taken from happy Fiends returning home with sacks of plastic dinosaurs, and real soap.

And a peeved red dragon with soot stains needing to vent its stress on a stress dummy saw Harry so singed him crisp.

"Why me, I never done the world a wrong turn, I make everyone happy with my plastic dinosaurs," Harry and was not whispering but shouting as he jumped about on fire for dragon's breath had covered him.

And all his disgruntled customers pretended they never noticed him; my they had shoes to polish and suppers to make and linen to change, dogs to take out for whoopsie, cat litter to change, a quick nip into the neighbours and *"yes, a neighbour, yes I understand,"* Satirextrex and wish he did tell us the secret.

"It is a secret as should not be in the neighbour," Aslop enlightens us.

And Harry luckily fell into the past its sell-by date moat and the fire was put out.

"Why if it is not Harry?" Arawan.

"Go away," Harry meekly.

CHAPTER 26   FOOL

"And from this spot an advantageous view,
Of the Ariel dogfight.
Commonly called aerial stew.
To see Conan's might.
And brave Christina
Of royal stock,
but with a laugh like a hyena.
And red dragon pure vintage hock.
Of Alicadabara lineage.
And on the spot
Eat pickled meats of great age.
Of course, hot.
And see the nasty red dragon slain,
And be turned into a plastic dinosaur," Satirextex and was all lies but a salesman knew lies sold.

Lies made fairies feel warm safe and cosy and buy plastic dinosaurs to litter the fireplace up with.

And the plaque was below a plastic statue of a handsome knight slaying an ugly dragon. And the face on the knight resembled Harry, and told Sampenciltrex this as Harry wanted fairies to ask, "Is that Harry, did he kill the bad dragon?" Sam' an artist who watered his oils because he was a seventh cousin removed of Harry that means Harry had Fiend blood in him and probably explains why he wanted to rule the world?

"Fiend ears," and "Fiend breath," Harry had been called at school and now the bullies worked deep down his plastic mines never seeing the light of day.

"Ouch," and "eek," drifted out of the mine mouths. "Crack," whipping sounds also.

Anyway: Conan ran up the rafters for Apes being a drunk needed a barbarian to make black and blue. And a girl seeing the look in the dirty old man's eyes had run up stairs needing repaired for mummy had warned her about dirty old men with white beards in white smocks, especially them that turned barbarians into rabbits.

"There is my honey," Conan and ran after her and threw her on his shoulder for she did what good girls do, fainted when she should have kicked him places and stuck her fingers in his eyes and pushed him off the rafter to fall in a dry XXX-barrel twenty floors below in a cellar because his friends had drunk it.

And Conan found it cold up here for a breeze howled through the holes in the tower so he ripped off Christina's petticoats and she awoke and sighed, "I am too be ravaged at last."

But the selfish barbarian wrapped her petticoats about himself for warmth.

So, Christina twittered, tittered, shivered, and ran here and there thinking she was being chased by a muscular tanned barbarian but she was not for he sat on his hunches with these words, "Chatter I am freezing."

And the smell of her rose water Harry had sold her awoke memories of mummy who sent Conan out to milk the goats at 4am and churn the milk into butter. "These are nightmares," so fled from his past.

"He chases me, I must pretend to be out of breath," the princess and panted so but he did not catch her but crashed into her running from nightmares, and together fell amongst the rafters and landed on a cuddly thingamabob.

"We have somehow landed on Bat Wing," Conan so used

these words, "Gee up," then noticed a rose tattoo on a royal thigh so was distracted so did not see it was not a **bat he was putting the spurs into but the dragon.**

And explains why he and Christina ended a thousand feet up above the tower and saw Harry escape the sour moat for a royal drunk Arawan was too drunk to stand on his feet and take him to a reserved seat in a galley that went up and down the River Styx in hell. No breaks or pension scheme just row all day and night for exercise is good.

So watched Harry bury his cash made from selling dinosaurs underneath a latrine with these words, "No one will look for treasure underneath a loo?"

And in years to come had Satirextex change Conan's words from, *"Unmentionables is this a fire breathing dragon?"* To, "Never fear I will slay this dragon," and *"I have wet myself,"* to "I am wet in dragon's blood," and *"Arnie my chicken sword will not come out,"* to "Arnie my sword will slay the beast," and *"Christina do something,"* to "I will save the princess," for Harry knew fairies wanted lies to make their lives tolerable for they spent all day working to pay of their debts to him, for dinosaurs in a mantel piece was a sign of wealth and the in scene.

And because Harry was wiping his hands on the grass for burying treasure under a latrine is not the best place in the world to dig, so never saw Christina fall off the bad dragon and drop a thousand feet through the hole in the roof Apes had gone through and land softly on Apes, luckily for her and lucky for Apes was out cold with XXX so never felt a thing or might have shredded Harry because no one shreds a princess with pretty ankles so Harry was a substitute.

Then Conan followed her and landed on Wamba who was knocked senseless so never remembered what happened to him.

"If you had bothered to ask?" The Mage pointing at Bat Wing eating oysters for The Mage supported animal rights and only used spurs and whip as had a mean dark streak and needed Filthy Big Bertha's Fish Head Curry Soup.

And soon The Mage returned rabbit ears with these words, "Did not mummy teach you to cover your mouth when coughing and spitting for it spreads germs?"

"No old man," Conan so The Mage gave him extra-large ears for cheeks.

And Christina spat on Conan for she had not been ravaged by a handsome tanned barbarian and wondered where that barbarian had gone. Then heard arthritic joints, a deep wet cough, a loud fart, and a disgusting smell come off a burp and knew.

CHAPTER 27 HALIPUT
5000 PLODS

And is easy to guess what plod means? And the above is taken from a signpost pointing the way home; perhaps Garrison Men might never go home? Who would have them? Smelly things that did eat the shirt on your back; so, **deserved no home.**

And Wamba watched a Fiend struggling to carry a mattress out of their hut door and scratch at the same time; so, Wamba showed he had a malicious side for he smirked for he knew what lived in the mattresses found in that hut.

Bugs got angry when sleeping off their meals so all those Fiends thinking they were smart looting and pillaging were taking thingies back to Fiend Land far away behind the rip in the sky.

"They are stealing my biscuit boxes," and Tom was wrath and wanted to "Kill," but let Conan hold him back for in those boxes his medals and coupons for more medals from Corn Flake makers.

And Christina felt pity for the innocent lad and hugged him and slapped Conan for she felt her bum pinched, so did not see the smirk on innocent Tom's face. He was Garrison and had a corrupt side to him for he drew waitresses for he was an artist so paid like Garrison at Common as Mucks Filthy Big Bertha's for what he paid for, models to draw, plastic dinosaur model kits, origami packs, instant noodles, and such. Did not his posters cover bedroom doors illustrating what was on the menu behind?

"I will sneak into Filthy Big Bertha's and rip them down and sell them in a gallery," an oily voice.

"There will be a loud shriek if I catch that miser in my establishment for, he sells us strange meat with ringed tails," Filthy Big Bertha.

"Ouk," and Harold was wrath and jumped up and down on nearby mushrooms as Fiends ate his walnuts and took back to their lands highly contagious germs; never mind they was just Fiends and the only good Fiend was a dead one.

"In those flames is my freedom away from this place," Conan and grabbed Christina to head for The Wilderness Trail but she was disappointed for she had not been ravaged; so, kicked him hard somewhere so he doubled up and did not see Cur cry as it watched its new toy rubber chicken get bitten and stretched between Fiendish teeth on the way back to their lands, a rubber chicken covered in doggy saliva and germs picked up where doggy mouths go, everywhere. Never mind soon be no living Fiends in Fiend Land?

And Cur cried too because he had nowhere to call home and needs you to adopt him, please?

He knew he was just VAGABOND now.

Like the Garrison Men already were!

And the Lost Patrol saw Fiends pushing Harry's army supply wagon back across the rip and were happy for the wagon was full of surprises, rubber swords, basketballs, basketball nets, basketball stadiums, robotic Japanese dogs, and blow-up celebrities.

"They sell like hot cakes at my dinosaur stall amongst the kids," a certain whisper needing gagged.

Then all moaned for they saw a long war ahead and lots of marching up and down hills in soggy rain when they wanted waitress to serve them 'Bosch soap,' margarita pizza, carrot, and potato mash and XXX.

And "Ouk," as Apes mashed a banana between bugling

knuckles wondering if he did ever see a floozy girl chimp again?

Never mind Monty's cousin thirty times removed is driving a circus wagon with a chimp dressed in a flower print bikini and goes round the spectators selling banana flavoured candy floss. If Apes could only get a ticket to the circus? But no one told him a circus was nearby so all missed the chance to get rid of this murderous beast.

"If I can bribe Harry to get Satirextex to write poems that the Fiends are retreating because Captain Moronicus defeated them, King Charles will by popular demand give me Christina," a Moronicus who did not have enough pay to bribe a salesman; perhaps even buy the last plastic dinosaur as a collector's item?

"I am certainly going to flay him alive," Mistress Beautricianix looking in a pocket mirror for every floozy girl worth her salt carries, and she meant Apes for he had given up undoing her corset and now it was just a knot and Beautricianix showed belly rolls, so added, "I will not him and throw him in the moat," she could dream, this was Apes she was on about.

And Bat Wing beat her chest which then hurt something for she missed a handsome red dragon with soot smudges.

"I just want rid of them all," The Mage and gritted his teeth.

"This is my entire fault," Christina who was a good girl at heart, really, she was and added, "I should be spanked," and Conan and The Mage being worldly came forward to offer their services.

"I wanted rid of Drunken Noddy my daddy and be queen and have my subjects adore me and return their love with good government," And Wamba was happy seeing his love returned and Conan spat tobacco at him and Cur lifted a leg on him.

"But things went wrong, for Alicadabara and Tootanfoot who wanted to marry me and bring in extra racks, electric chairs and gas chambers to tax my fairies," and Moronicus was gagged by his men.

"I am broken hearted for Book says I must be loyal to King Charles," Wamba but cheered for The Mage shut Book.

So ogled Christina who too be an annoying flirt lifted her petticoats so Wamba shook but these were not ordinary fairies apart from one, for Cur shook violently so fleas went onto others so they scratched. And Harold could not pronounce "Ouk" for the sight of pretty ankles had rejuvenated parts that XXX usually do not, his sense of smell.

And Conan recovered seeing slim ankles made to throw Christina on his shoulders and run to The Wilderness Trail but got kicked somewhere important so doubled up again. "That man just will not learn," Christina observing all men.

"Ouk," and the gorilla shook firsts from the sight of silken flesh then from seeing what happened to Conan so changed its mind about swinging off to the rafters with the princess.

"Wow," Tom showing he was innocent.

"I am off to pack and leave," The Mage.

"Leave when there are millions of fiends wanting to kill everyone one of us?" Conan asked.

"Why not?" The Mage and went to stuff teddy into his overnight case.

And Conan spat tobacco at his shadow but because of his weakened condition the breeze blew it upon Apes who with these precious words, "Ouk," went bananas on Conan.

"It is 5000 plods to Haliput and home," Christina seeing the sense in getting away from this place, a place with no scented baths, no hundred chefs to cook breakfast, no credit card facilities and no handsome millionaires looking for a sweet little freckled girl to shower with expensive presents.

Yes 5000 plods to Haliput and the patter of the Chief executioner to get rid of horrid Garrison.

CHAPTER 28
LONG HIKE

And The Mage stepped out of the tower's front door after clicking of course to change any lingering Fiends into lingering mushrooms. Behind him roaches carried his expensive canvas overnight bag; expensive because it was signed 'Johnny Walker, your friend.' So, we know what was in the bag.

And he began to plod along the way to Haliput with Bat Wing behind him with tears in her eyes. In her paws a red scale plucked off a red dragon with snoot smudges.

And no one else in the tower followed for they saw Fiends snoring on the lawn.

Licked cauldrons clean.

Seeking latrines for what they had eaten was Garrison food.

And others digging for grubs to dip in chocolate fondue cauldrons.

And many others staring aimlessly at their feet having counted their toes now waited for excitement and only takes one to find it.

"Here gobble wobble cluck," which is Fiendish, "for here look a stall selling plastic dinosaurs."

"I will put an end to this dinosaur looting," and was Harry enraged and so stuffed a $10 dollar gold mark bill in someone's back pocket. A pocket that had a rip in it; a $10 bill attached to a string.

And Wamba put Book away and Conan saw him and feared the Ordinary had read it.

"It says in Book we must protect businesses, so volunteers needed," and he got them for he was using a big baseball bat with knots in it.

And in his bag pocket a shiny $10 gold mark bill.

So, the volunteers did not line up outside amongst the visiting Fiends but ran after The Mage and the Fiends would know what to do with Mr Ordinary.

"I have paid you to protect my dinosaurs, protect or give me back what is mine?" Harry in the shadows. And Wamba found his bribe was gone, so was the string and, in the shadows, a $10 bill was being stuffed next to its cousins, $100 bills in a greedy salesman's wallet.

"It will take you ten years working in my hot plastic factory with the dwarfs doing sixteen hour shifts to pay me back my $10 dollar gold mark piece," Harry now under a table but still in the shadows.

"Ha Ho," I will not pay you and there is nothing in the world you can do to make me pay, so there, rasp," Mr Wamba Ordinary so sure of himself he made a rude sound.

"I will tell Garrison I bribed you to risk them protecting my plastic dinosaurs," Harry now under Wamba but in Wamba's shadow for he did not want exposed to the glorious sunlight; for perhaps Harry was a were-thingy, or vampire needing a coffin or just perhaps his head was so singed from magic so now needed one of his wigs. Also, he had cauliflower ears where Apes had pulled them and his clothes tatters, and he smelt of spilt rose water.

"Ha so the little smelly twerp thinks he can tell me what to do?" Wamba towering over the little salesman twerp who suddenly stood aside and behind him muscle men hired from a passing circus wagon driven by Monty's cousin thirty times removed is driving.

And while one kicked Wamba in his ordinary shins so he shrieked another kicked him that place elsewhere so he shrieked louder. And a louder shriek came when another boxed his ears and the loudest shriek was when one poked his eyes.

And because he had fingers in his eyes never saw Harry open the tower door so his hired help could push Wamba towards his plastic dinosaur stall and Fiends.

And Wamba went and used the knotted baseball bat on the Fiends at the stall except that was what the other Fiends where waiting for, some excitement as counting your toes gets boring after you done it a hundred times.

So, Wamba was done all over so he ran screaming after The Mage with these words, "Help."

"Him as well?" The Mage just coming to terms he was not travelling alone so clicked and a 10-foot brick wall grew in front of the Fiends so they ran into it. So did Wamba but fear had him for Fiends were piling up on him and they had not bathed; and why Wamba used them as a ladder to get over the wall

So, Wamba grovelled as he kissed The Mage's feet so did not see Harry gently stroke the stressed out $10 dollar gold mark bill; a bill attached to a string.

"He did only spend it in Common as Muck Filthy Big Bertha's but now I can spend it there," Harry leaving the tower and added, "Here what do you burly circus men want?" Hoping they had become confused and believed they had lost their wages to sort Wamba out.

"Polanski? " Which in Magyar where all good circus horsemen come from means "Wages mate or else?"

And The Mage did not help Harry when Harry shouted, "Help," for he remembered stairs never mended.

But sighed as an object thrown through the sky landed in front of him.

"Harry's here," The Mage and walked over Harry on the road to Haliput.

And so did Garrison walk over Harry and Apes left a banana skin for Harry to slip on for the Ape was mean.

And Harry with a yell slipped on it and Apes threw another

and after six slips Harry asked, "Here where is everyone?"

"Invisible Harry, I made them invisible," The Mage replied.

"What about me, them Fiends can see me and think I am crazy talking to myself," a disturbed Harry needing the funny farm.

And a banana skin wrapped about his face as an answer.

"To think I left the wife for you," Harry heard a voice from nowhere and was Offaltrex Purchtrix about to die.

"I turned down a waitresses job at Common as Muck Filthy Big Bertha's to holiday with you," Mistress Beautricianix just before she burst into tears so all the invisible Garrison men and The Lost Patrol comforted her.

"That woman would make me a good wife," Harry seeing she could fleece anything in trousers and as the husband he would be legally entitled to spend her riches.

But forgot she was legally entitled to spend his.

And Christina too show she was kind gave Beautricianix the rose water she got from Harry so soon Beautricianix was left alone with Offaltrex Purchtrix who began to "EEK," and "Yikes," quite a lot for she was bigger than him.

"At least I am not alone in my misery," Harry cheering and he was correct for behind him Fiends had followed the trail of banana skins to an invisible Ape just in front of Harry.

"At least I am not alone in my misery," Offaltrex Purchtrix cheering at the sound of many Fiends plucking some more hair from Harry so the singed bald patch got larger. His ears too as Fiends pulled them 6 metres out and then let go so, they twanged back. Oh, the nasty Fiends how could they do this to their friend Harry who sold them rubber swords?

"Go and help him, Wamba?" The Mage becoming tired of the sound of "Shrieks" and "yikes" from behind.

*

"The army is composed of
Generals to privates sixth class.
And a mascot called Apes who fell off,
A stool seeking a ballerina chimp lass .
And a nasty dog.

But no merchants.
For they hid in the fog.
"We are monks," they chant.
So cannot enlist.
Unless they sign the dotted line.
 By mistake in the mist.
Thinking it free shares in a gold mine.
 For Ordinary is a cunning recruitment serge.
" *So, enlist for thirty years with Ordinary,*" Satirextex who escaped the vets so still has a deep Fiendish voice.

And Wamba showed Harry the enlistment papers and a quill to sign them with; and when signed he could become invisible.

Now Harry might be singed and having Fiends examine where his tongue began but he was not enlisting.

"Stuff the quill up your hairy nostrils mate," the foolish merchant.

But would sign for night was coming and the Fiends had got bored kicking him to see how far he could jump and where bedding down and cooking mushrooms; and snails in rancid butter sauce and one was boiling a rubber chicken to see if that would tenderise it.

And the aroma's reached Harry whose stomach gurgled with juices wanting to digest food. Food that was invisible but smelt of roasted vegan pheasant, rosemary, acorns, peanuts, sage, onions but not any pheasant, for it was shooting season, and the aroma of Xmas pudding for many are always found at the back of cupboards, and the aroma of boiling tripe for Harry's gums were tender and the bad Fiends had taken all his teeth as were real ivory, so needed that and some watery gruel.

But out of deep pockets he produced a new set of teeth, gold crusted and a silver spoon and forks to eat with.

"Sign here," Wamba answering the digestive juices of the merchant who was showered in plastic dinosaurs from where no one knows?

"Never, do you know who I am?" Harry so was not made invisible so heard merry laughter from those feasting, pulling crackers and reading aloud Fortune Cookie Notes inside, cracking jokes at his expense and jollying it up. And it was at his expense for a certain supply wagon had arrived at the exact spot in time when The Mage had made them invisible; so, there was plenty of tobacco and rose water to go about.

As for the plastic dinosaurs, well no one wanted them which explains who threw them, FIENDS. And the supply wagon belonged to Harry but because it was invisible could not see it so he was spared a tantrum.

And Harry felt the night chill and shivered with these words, "I am a poor unloved merchant who just wants a cuddle and warm cup of milk, can you help me?" And help was at hand for he spied a public latrine on the road to Haliput so sheltered there.

"Food at last," Harry eating the flies he found.

"Warm at last," Harry wrapping layers of scratchy Ajax loo paper about him.

"Hello, my name is Harry," Harry speaking to paper fairies he made. "Stuff you then," Harry shredding the paper fairies he made when they did not reply.

"Boohoo sob now I am lonely," Harry putting it on so do not feel sorry for the miser.

See a giant Indonesian centipede crawling from the splintered wooden seat onto Harry so now Harry is not alone.

And when the sun came up, he was thrown out of the latrine by Fiends so got no breakfast inside his hiding place for the centipede ate all the flies.

"Let me in," he begged Wamba and The Mage replied, "You sold Isisnaphut the DIY plans for a bridge, go away Harry." And Harry smelt the kippers in hot butter and went bananas so the Fiends came over to see what was up and some slipped on banana skins and fell in the loo that was a thunder box so were a bit annoyed.

"Gobble wobble," the Fiends screamed in Fiendish which translated means, "Gawd what is this stuck to me, oh it is a yellow plastic duck, which is alright."

And Alicadabara came also for banana skins do not come

out of the clouds you know? Maybe the back of a wagon with an ape on it.

Anyway: "That foolish swindler will expose us all in our invisible world, it is about time to send him as a crispy offering to King Arawan and be done with his plastic dinosaurs," The Mage revealing his nasty side. You see all because he had a fluffy white beard and wore a white smock tied at the middle with a large leather belt and sandals with a sickle do not mean you are all white and made of sweets. And the truth is in the original Red Riding Hood there was no wolf but a Mage with a sickle.

A dirty old mage in a grubby white smock trying to get a sweet little girl to turn his kitchen into a fitted kitchen on the cheap.

"Spare him; enlist him as private eight class and this is how to do it?" Christina with butterflies coming out of her mouth with each word showing she was pretty inside too.

"Here Book says there is no private eight class in the army," Wamba showing he was a man of regulations.

"Silly Wamba did not anyone point out you have the old version of Book and when we get to Haliput you can buy one in gold print," The Mage and tweaked his cheek and spoke to him as if he were a Gaslamp which he was.

And so, Wamba offered the papers and quill for Harry to sign.

"Stuff it up somewhere," the nasty merchant's reply.

"Trust me he will sign," the beautiful princess who was all good inside apart from when lost that time in her rose garden with Tootanfoot and Conan and many thousand other times.

"Oh, dear perhaps I spoke in haste," Harry about to regret for:

1...."Suit yourself then," The Mage.

2...."Ah ha," and was Alicadabara puffing up recognising Harry as he who sold him the dud plans.

3....A red dragon with snoot smudges appeared also and Alicadabara ordered it to find out who Harry was speaking too.

4....And an army of Fiends was ready to give Harry cauliflower ears again and stretch his lips and steal his new set of teeth with the gold crusts.

"Eat him," Alicadabara just like that to the red hungry dragon that unlike Harry had not been eating flies.

And still Harry kept his mouth shut as he was taken to a lofty treetop to be eaten by a ravenous dragon who liked plump merchants.

But the Snake god of salesmen favoured the dinosaur seller for his unmentionables tagged a branch and stretched mighty far and wide and with a twang sent Harry at the Speed of Light through the sky.

"Where is my dinner," a ravenous disappointed red dragon with snoot smudges.

So, Harry landed miles away in a ditch beside a road and read a signpost.

"Haliput this way weary traveller."

"Kiss," Harry kissing muck as he kissed solid ground.

"Oh, snake god of salesmen I will sell more Harry's Prayer Books to the customers so they pray for discount but actually pray to be ripped off, for you grow fat on complaints up there in the clouds and give you my word as a vendor."

*

"Here he did not enlist?" Wamba vindicated over eight class private and there was booing.

"Who cares, he has gone?" The Mage and there was cheering.

"Wait and see Wamba," the beautiful princess who could do no wrong and there were sighs, sweet little birds chirping and real perfume smells.

"Sigh," and it was a long, lonely sigh and from Bat Wing for that red dragon with snoot stains and The Mage knew a vet was needed if that dragon was going to date his pet; especially one with unsure pedigree.

CHAPTER 29 X

" And rained toads
For magic was about.
So, fiends became wet sods.
And got batted out.
And amphibians did croak,
On the Garrison cricket field.
And a merchant slipped into a black frock.
For disguise and changed behind a shield.
But toads were there so a merchant did wart.
For toads were numerous.
For they multiplied so became the in art.
And the cricket field became toady poisonous.
So giant annelids came forth.
And slid up a black frock to escape toads.
Annelids full of annelid wrath.
And Harry was allergic to segmented thingamajigs.
So, he shouted, "Let me X," a Satirextex tapping the grass to
see if it that really brings out the worms.

And Wamba's burly arm appeared from thin air holding
the enlistment paper and quill.

"What is this smudge," from a master smudger so the arm
vanished so annelids fell upon he who hated them for they
wiggle and look like vermin tails.

"Is that rose water I sniff," Harry added not sure he wanted
to be invisible after all but then a fiend spear went between a
remaining head hair.

"Shriek," he screamed.

And from Invisible Land an empty peanut shell pinged off

his nose.

"Ouch," the salesman cursed.

Then a spear thudded in the ground between the parts needed to make a lineage of great salesmen so he shook all over.

"Kill," a fuzzy jazzy and sent another spear so it parted Harry's legs a little bit higher up.

"Enough of this I want like any salesman little salesmen in nappies for my aspiring cousins to change, so will sign my X."

But the greedy salesman had left it too late and so had the fuzzy jazzy because Apes appeared and shredded the spear and the fuzzy jazzy so Harry could not sign.

"Why did you shred the enlistment papers?" Harry asked.

"Ouk," as an ape never forgets.

"Oh Harry, a friend of yours has arrived," The Mage showing his dark side.

And Harry who had already been sooted was sooted again as that red dragon with soot smudges appeared and sooted him good.

"Soot," which means in dragon tongue "Where is my Bat Wing?"

"Let me in let me in," Harry the salesman as a dragon sooted him to crisp.

But the salesman found empty peanut shells instead and that dragon suffered from bad breath as did not gargle with mint mouth wash.

"Sign here," a burly arm and a salesmen's X was signed.

Eight class private and then big muscular fingers grabbed the salesman's neck and pulled him into Invisible Land.

And on the other side Harry found the world a purple haze and guitar music played, "Groovy," Harry and floated away till his sergeant kicked his parts and said, "You have enlisted son."

"I am not your son," Harry replied and added, "Wheeze gasp pant that was some kick?"

So, the sergeant kicked the son again somewhere so a loud shriek was heard and the son knew he had enlisted.

"I never employ such underhanded means to get my railway tracks laid?" The salesman and was a dirty lie. In his broom closet whips in varying lengths and many minor relations to use them, relations found collecting warty toads for a salesman had advertised, 'A cure for plies,' and illustrates a dirty lie for warts grew next to the piles so much moaning was added to the howling on full moon nights.

CHAPTER 30   DOUGH

"Ta governor," Wamba said to King Arawan.

"Stay with me and be cool," Conan advised innocent Tom.

"Look into my eyes for CBN news," Arawan replied to the lot of Garrison.

"I have one minute to gaze or will become baker's dough," The Mage seeing Arawan had cast a spell.

But "Tick tock," came from behind The Mage who said, "You blooming chimp you have eaten my watch?"

"Here a quick sale, an egg timer with one owner," and Harry flashed a red timer upfront with a horn to squeeze and make sounds.

"Give me," the silly Mage.

"A thousand gold marks and just X here and pay monthly and will be cheaper than your monthly phone bill," the salesman.

"X."

And Harry snatched the X away **for the egg timer had 4 owners and a hole** in the bottom cup.

So, The Mage trusted foolishly the grains of time or whatever?

"As every salesman knows gold marks buys one out of the army as I am not putting up with an Ordinary shouting at me," Harry but till he got his marks Wamba made him do a hundred press ups as Wamba stood on his salesman's head, to encourage closeness to 'Mother earth.'

And in Wamba's hand a potato peeler for the wagon full of potatoes needing peeled. *"A Wamba never forgets a book sold to an Ordinary,"* Aslop.

"Sweet blue bells," Harry swore for Wamba had tacks in his boot soles.

"And here are my customers to buy me out of the army," Harry seeing Garrison about him counting his press ups; "all I need is something to sell," and he had 1penny naughty postcards strapped to his back, and lots of change in his deep pockets and a wind me up viewing machine glued to the lining of his coat and it took 1shilling pieces.

But he could dream for customers queued so he dreamed of the thunder god Tanaros's chariot pulled by goats, goats that would eat his gold for cash to goats was tin sent from Heaven to fill their tummies.

And suddenly a ball of baker's dough for The Mage had trusted the grains of time in a holed 4 owner egg timer, for Arawan had given him ONE MINUTE to gaze into Arawan's eyes and watch CBN news.

And thanks to a salesman who sold him a faulty egg timers gazed longer.

"Show me a guaranteed replacement slip, why there is none, he paid cash," the salesman not taking any blame The Mage was dough.

"Slurp," Harold licking his lips as liked gooey dough sticking to his teeth.

"Fetch," Christina throwing a cinnamon coated stick towards the moat so Harold chased it for she knew The Mage was dough, so saved him; for his spells were needed: Thai mushroom noodle soap was on the menu tonight.

"Gobble wiggly," the fiends for they had heard The Duke's regular boys had come to an agreement overpay and now wanted a fight on over time rates.

"Never," The Duke believing over time was done out of loyalism.

So, the regular army left Common as Muck Filthy Big Bertha's and believed Lionel Mathews all were dead, the idiots for there were many Fiends out there chanting, "kill," for Lionel not wanting to be disturbed puffing a Havana cigar in the bath as a waitress served him Thai noodle mushroom soup had lied to be rid of the army boys.

"*The bigger the lie the bigger the tip as every waitress knew,*" Aslop.

And lies were the in scene as Isisnaphut had sent strike agents to prolong the strike but seeing all the lovely Thai noodle mushroom soup served by waitresses had gone on strike; and now lay across wooden tables singing, "Oh what a lovely war," as gastropods crawled over them in rancid butter sauce but they was too XXX to devour them.

So, the gastropods escaped and with slugs infested your gardens and this is the reason why.

And The Mage saw all but he was a piece of dough so was unable to help.

And that is what he gets for trusting an egg timer with more than one owner.

And a salesman who sells plastic dinosaurs.

CHAPTER 31
CHEAP LIES

Now Harry owned Dog Publishing House that churned out stories all about heroic fairies, godmothers, Tinker Bell healing dust, Tinker Bell Romance Tales, Tinker Bell Runs Off With A HUMAN, Tinker Bell Silhouette Drawings, and nasty human murder mystery novelettes; just the stuff readers liked to read so bought as all a penny.

"Jingle," your cash in Harry's pockets.

And Satirextex authored the stories on the back of loo paper squares and had none left for what he needed them for, he was La Imbecile. Stuck in the outhouse for he frequented hot pie stalls owned by HIM, Harry.

A vendor chain that sold meat pies. And at the back of the stall empty cages where vermin caught the night before had been eating socks stolen from laundry baskets by aspiring cousins of a certain salesman, for real cheese was expensive to catch rats.

"My meat is all fresh," Harry defending his health and safety record. Do not worry another aspirer cousin was a vegetarian so let the rats escape, especially the cute dormice and pet hamsters. What did she replace them with, unwashed socks mixed with chopped onions, garlic, and diced green neeps mashed into cubes.

"And the gods chose you Harry to spread their fame for could you imagine Wamba running your publishing business empire?" And was a whisper steeped in meth fumes.

"Choke," Harry reaching for a light to clear the air.

"BOOM," and Harry, singed and wiser stood there wide-eyed holding ash shaped as a matchstick.

And Harry was now afraid for he did have to give royalties to the gods which he had not been doing.

"Millions you owe us Harry, why where do you think Satirextex gets ideas about a purple other world and a doorway to it covered in purple branches from? Why the bum is unfit to call himself a poet and should be left in the outhouse," King Arawan knowing how to be nasty.

"There are more gods than Arawan over here?" And the voice was stern.

"Who are you?" Harry sniffing to see who he was speaking to but the air filled with butterflies and harp music so Harry trembled so his innards sounded like bagpipes.

"Daghdha the Boss so grovel Harry grovel," and Daghdha was surrounded by floozy goddesses feeding him grapes so Harry was illuminated about the other side. "Fairies have simple minds Harry so all Wamba Ordinary's believe what Satirextex writes. Just as well because you do not?" And was an accusation and the gawd added, "For when you shout, 'I do not believe in gods a gawd gets a chest pain,' and **'then drops dead.'**

So, Harry stopped trembling for he knew this god was an idiot to tell him that secret, and then saw all the floozy goddesses admiring silks in the back of his wagon pulled by mules.

So shouted: "All at sale prices," he just could not stop himself so the gods bought for they knew if their floozy Goddesses were not happy, they did be shredded by sharp tongues and nail files goddesses keep in handbags.

"Here Apes a banana in it if you carry the loot," and Apes carried a heavy sack with LOOT in red stitched on it.

Only a fool would rob Apes and the fool **was a secret.**

And the deities were so happy with their glass beads they lent everyone transport, chariots pulled by cats and goats that squabbled amongst themselves and scratched anyone foolish enough to try and say, "Gee up," **and the muck was something else.**

And a boar pulling Daghdha's chariot vanished as Harold belched so Garrison being quick thinking and afraid of Daghdha stuck Harold next to the other boars to pull the chariot for he was so ugly the god would never realise a boar was missing.

"Ouk," Harold so perhaps the gods might.

"What is this?" Christina asking Harry.

"I have enlightened the gods in commerce, which is your higher purchase agreement, 5 gold marks a day for the chariot," Harry's replied and did not tell her the gods had loaned the chariots to them for nothing; for a salesman is an oily greedy thing.

"And if you want a chariot, give me my enlistment papers to shred?" Harry holding out a salesman hand that remained empty for Wamba would not let him be discharged.

"For once I am proud of him," Conan remembering all the tobacco smoked and suspected ingredients that did horrid things to his insides.

"You should have this?" And Tom pinned one of his Corn Flake medals on Wamba for he remembered Harry ordering him about, "Go and clean the outhouse for Satirextex has been there all night without loo paper so hated Harry who was only an eight-class private.

"Woof," and the nasty dog lifted a leg on Harry for it remembered Harry booting it somewhere to take his stress out on a poor defenceless doggy just needing a cuddle.

So, Wamba gave Cur, Harold's rubber chicken for Harold would not need it with the boars being boring so Harold gave Wamba a filthy look for the boars where not house trained.

"Walk then," and Harry meant all of Garrison.

And the road to Haliput was not a road but a track through brambles and stone so the Garrison was heard to, "Gasp," and "pant" to keep up with the chariots.

"Rip up his enlistment papers," Conan wheezing.

"Shred them well," Tom finding his nights sleeping at Common as Mucks Filthy Big Bertha's had not prepared him for exercise of this type.

"Woof," and the nasty dog showed how nasty he was and bit Wamba good.

"Ouk," a boar fed up being a boar.

And Christina felt pity for them for she was a good pretty princess till she read a cleaning charge for any trash found on her chariot so trash walked.

And the chariots distanced themselves from the trash for out of mind out of pity.

And a pile of dough rode Christina's chariot by her ankle so was happy for the ankle was attached to a long leg.

And the dough was The Mage remember waiting to be turned back into himself.

"There is nothing I can do, Book says he is enlisted and that is that" Wamba obviously liked being bitten, have plods of earth thrown at him and ridiculed behind his back for there was a strange, perverted streak in him that needed a dentist to remove, without an anaesthetic of course.

And the soldier in question wanting discharged rode the chariot pulled by boars so used the whip a lot on one boar for he suspected it was one of them, Garrison.

"Ouk," the boar in question pleading for the enlistment papers to be shredded.

"Never," Wamba, "Whip away."

"Ouk," a terrified boar.

And Harry was happy; it was fast approaching the time when he would be awarded the 'Top Salesman of Ball' trophy that he won every year.

And he was not going in Garrison uniform that was just rags sold to them from a wagon pulled by mules that followed The Duke's men who threw away their green pantaloons and felt hats.

"There is none like him
Thank the good god Daghdha.
Who has the last laugh, he has he ha.

Harry made on a flimsy whim.
And Harry deserves this award.
A gold $vase with his name inscribed on it.
And sent Apes out in a drunken fit.
 So, all the competition is in hospital wards.
 For the price of a banana.
And he sold his parents.
Their swine he took as rent.
The swine troth he gave to the waitress Anna.
So kept the farmyard clean.
"Cash not a troth I want."
 The troth is for Garrison who cannot
  Pay so leave them lean.
 And HE hires urchins to push his barrows.
To catch fresh meat.
So keeps the plague down in the summer heat.
Yes, there is none like Harry,
Thank the good God Daghdha," and Satirextex wrote this one night he was in the outhouse longer than usual for he had eaten three pies.

And Harry knew he would be discharged soon for in his deep pocket he had a secret weapon; it was an eraser to rub away his X.

"Oh, my corns," he heard Conan.

"My blisters," he heard an innocent boy.

"Woof," and then "shriek" as Wamba got bit.

"Ouk," as Harry gave more whip and was happy for, he had just put the price of the secret weapon up.

"Oh, boys look what I have," and a cruel grin spread across a salesman.

"Give me give me," Conan but the eraser was just out of reach.

"Nothing is cheap in life, twenty gold marks," Harry so his gold fillings dazzled.

"Son of a circus flea," Conan replied but dust answered him as a boar being whipped put on speed.

"Shred it never, it is army property," Mr Ordinary so plods

were replaced by stones and one bite was replaced by a savaging.

"Ping," also as a portion of rubber chicken kept bouncing off the back of Wamba's head.

And Wamba saw the mouth of Cur was green and slimy and feared the hacksaw not leeches.

"I have to buy a vile potion of secret ingredients from the salesman to cure my bites," Wamba but the salesman shouted back, "Forty gold marks for the eraser and sixty for the potion," to be mean.

"Ping," as a ping vibrated through Womba's empty bit where sweetmeat should have been as he heard Tom snigger with the malcontents.

"Woof," one of the malcontents.

"I will never volunteer again," Wamba heard Tom so became depressive.

"Eraser?" And was Harry from the back of his chariot pulled by boars and Wamba erased.

And Wamba bought on I.O.U. and Harry was happy for Wamba did be wiping the soles of Harry's boots clean till the end of time.

And not a single Garrison sniggered for they were not totally heartless fairies.

But friends again for they clapped Wamba on the back with these words, "The rounds at Big Bertha are on you friend," Conan.

"Woof," and his bites were licked by a mouth never washed but Wamba was not afraid for he had drunk the potion of Harry's on I.O.U.

"Ouk," a boar wanting freed.

"I will polish Book," Tom being really sickening.

But they was Garrison again and sang,
"We are off to that wonderful city of Hal."
"We are off we agree," the chorus.
  "Off to Drunken Noddy.
  We are his loyal fairies see.

Hi Ho, hi Ho," they sang.
"We are indeed off," the chorus added.
"And none did disagree.
 Woof.
We are Moronicus's mules.
We beasts and boars of burden."
"Rubbish we are Ballenese," the chorus correcting.
"Woof.
 Loyal to the king.
Hi Ho, hi ho.
And to the gods.
Hi Ho, hi ho."
"Not ruddy likely only loyal to Bertha," the chorus.
" We got pox.
Ticks and fleas,
Love warm beer.
Gruel.
And weevilly biscuits."
And got lice too," the chorus.
"Woof.
We fight dragons.
 Ravage princesses.
We are Ballenese Garrison.
And proud of it."
"Fairies," the chorus.
"Woof.
 We eat anything moving.
 And not moving."
"For they are Ballenese," the chorus.
And just who was the chorus?

CHAPTER 32   THE WRATH OF THE GODS

"When I dream of you
  Daghdha.
Riding the sky in your tartan chariot.
Daghdha.
Eating your boars,
Daghdha.
And want some too.
Daghdha.
When I have nightmares,
Daghdha.
  I see Morrigan
Daghdha.
  Riding here chariot,
Daghdha.
  Pulled by cats.
  Daghdha.
Alley cats too," so, get shredded good," of course such awful poetry can only belong to Satirextex attempting modern verse; and is an inscription under a statue of Daghdha sculptured by Sampenciltrex, and is cast in brick made from stuff collected from the fields and dried, for a salesman was paying.

And Daghdha is holding a scroll of the law.
'Do not cheat on the wife.
Do not cheat on the mistress.

No murdering unless a merchant.
No stealing unless it is free.
No lying unless it is to lie.
No patronising orgies unless you get away with it.
Do not speak to travelling merchants unless to spread gossip.
Do not lick the bottom of cauldrons unless you are alone.
Leave sin to the gods,
And always read the smudge.' and Daghdha made Wamba to scourge fairy kind.

"For making him I will ignore your pleas till the end of time," Daghdha wife so the god hated Wamba.

So Daghdha sought solace with his mistress Morrigan and bought her beads from a merchant.

"You louse, I am good enough to dance with but cheap enough for plastic beads," and kneed Daghdha somewhere so, he groaned as floozy woman are used to diamonds.

And lighting hit the skies so fairies knew a woman was at work in the heavens, working on a poor defenceless god who spent his days off modelling human SIMS to sail his model boats.

"Fetch me the roach Harry," for Daghdha knew the merchant's lowly origins for he made his ancestors out of clay.

"I want him spitted till he is goose crackling," Morrigan swinging a laced up black boot with a foot in it so there was a shriek from Daghdha.

Also, the sound of many teeth falling to the floor but Daghdha did not mind for the leg attached to the boot was very pretty, now if it had belonged to the wife, that would be a different matter for they forget to shave legs for they have beads not diamonds.

"And I want his head so he can see himself cook," for Morrigan was a nasty bit of stuff for mistresses usually are for they are, "That other woman," "Scarlet woman," "That bitch," so are nasty as hell.

And since Daghdha was prostrate she trod all over his

fingers and he did not mind

for from down here he could see up her leg; the pervert god and she knew he could for she was a calculating other woman thinking of diamond tiaras he did buy for privilege.

"I want hell," she hissed and Daghdha who would not give the wife a new mop said, "Anything you want Babe," the cheating miscreant and, "I will give you Harry who sold you the cheap beads," and saw a way to get rid of a certain drunk who always had a bucket next to him, smelt of meths, loitered chip shop corners begging for pennies to buy more meths, mugging them who did not give pennies and staggering home to hell singing, "Ba, Ba Black Sheep." And in case you do not know who, Arawan that binging alcoholic, "and Gnasher will make a fine addition to pulling your chariot as lead puller."

So Daghdha crawled after his bit on the side with these words, "Hell is yours Babe, trust me for I love you more than I do the wife, I was only joking about Gnasher honey" for he knew the wife was busy elsewhere changing smelly diapers'

"No more fun if you do not," she replied twisting his ears till he was on his belly.

"Groan," and was not his cauliflower ears making him dribble but her belly button where he could see her diamond pin, he gave her. '**I can get it back any time,' the fool thought.**

And Morrigan reading his dribbles beat him up good with these words, "Lousy

Indian giver," and she got away with it for she was not the wife whose belly button was covered in stretch marks put there by the god's sixteen children.

So Daghdha hit a brass gong and assembled all his warriors and told them to mount their dead mounts and follow him but did not invite the wife who was delousing the sixteen kids for lice get about primary school children.

And Daghdha sent a bottle of meths with a note in it for Arawan inviting him, especially him to come along.

"Unless you are torturing souls."

But the meth was good vintage so Arawan came hoping for more.

And Daghdha got in his spare chariot pulled by a representative of every living thing except Harry for the salesman was unique.

So Daghdha blew his carnyx horn and went hunting and some dough on a chariot remembered magic so "Poofed" itself back into The Mage.

"Please remove your teeth," and Harold did for he found dough without sugar unappetising to eat and "Mage you have sprouted up my elastics," for the dough has been at her feet and before he could click, he screamed, "Argh," for our princess remember was a martial arts black belt and when she was finished with him, he stared at bent knotted fingers and swore he did never ogle a pretty ankle again. Thing was, there were two pretty ankles next to him?

CHAPTER 33   POKER

"Gee up lazy slug eaters, brothers of worms," for Daghdha knew how to encourage his chariot pullers with words and was lies, by his side the longest whip ever. So, his chariot crossed the purple sky of the other world for he sought he who sold glass beads, beads that fell off and splintered so glass went into the god's bare feet lacerating them something bad so he jumped high forgetting he was a god and with a click all was better, because he had HARRY on his mind.

"You have customers Harry," Conan combing Cur's matted fur.

"What can I sell you?" Harry bowing and smiling.
So Daghdha pored the beads down Harry's mouth for Daghdha kept it open and
the beads were dry, for there was no ring-tailed gravy to wash them down.
"Give me water," Harry pleaded as Conan drank from a leather pouch. And Conan belched and showed mercy, for there was one last drop of water left that went "Plunk" onto Cur for a comb should be wet when combing matted hair.
"Greedy swine," Harry with a dry throat.
"Burp," Conan for his feet had many blisters from running while others rode chariots.
And the goddess Morrigan threw one of her cats onto Harry's back who now knew what it felt like when a cat with long sharp claws shreds you, painful.
"Help me Cur," Harry begged but the dog cocked a leg instead.

"Mage help me with strawberries please," Harry being sickening.

"Cannot do, this is the business of the gods," The Mage remembering untended tower steps and no refund given.

"Wamba friend?" Harry.

And the Ordinary picked off the snarling ferocious cat and gave it back to Morrigan with these words of charm, "Yours?"

Of course, with a big smile that would disarm any woman but not goddesses and princesses, so Morrigan was livid and would turn Wamba into a mouse, a lethal occupation since a snarling ferocious pussy cat was on the loose.

"Forgive him Great Queen of the Heavens, he is a Gvssaimph," The Mage and Wamba beamed pride.

So Daghdha squirmed for he made Wamba.

"Drunk were we at the time?" Morrigan asked so Daghdha whistled, "Humpty Dumpy had a fall," as he stared at the sky counting passing crows so never saw the back of her hand but did disappear over the side of his chariot with a "Thud."

Then as he opened his black and blue eyes the crows let loose their unspeakables.

But it was OK it was the mistress not the wife who had back handed him.

"Get Harry," Morrigan shouted and Harry did not like these words but a true salesman to the end kept his smile as Morrigan removed his chest hairs handfuls at a time.

Not a squeak passed the professional salesman's lips.

And the gods shredded Harry's clothes so he was naked and kept his trained smile and the gods felt ill looking at him for he was lumpy and 'Moley' and his unmentionables were pass me downs from regular army men.

And still Harry kept his tutored smile for a sale might occur at any time and he knew **the customer is always right unless wanting a refund.**

And the gods ripped up the chariot hire agreements and stuffed those places so Harry cried for he loved the jingle of cash that would not jingle any more.

And no Garrison helped for this sensible reason, "We do

not want his fate."

"Give me water," Harry begged and the gods smelt meths so let Harry have a drink for the gods are not cruel.

And Daghdha ordered Arawan to take his drinking buddy to level 9 hell and roast him.

So, the deities left chuckling for they knew what happened when the swine was heated up in swill.

But Harry was a true salesman to the end even if drunk and knew how to turn the cards and get a sale.

"Poker," he cried out and opened a deck of cards and a crate of meths from the back of a wagon pulled by mules.

"Lovely," Arawan breathing in the fresh air and almost passed out for the meths

was cheap meths made at roadside pools as crows passed over.

And Arawan got so full of meths he was a danger to the others and Conan was banned from smoking.

"I do not like this game," Arawan complained as he lost his shirt that Harry put on as it was silk and "Very soft to skin mauled by a ferocious cat," Harry and gave the god a 4 Leafed Clover for luck.

"There are sixty leaves on this clover," Arawan his vision spinning for cheap meths has that effect when drunk by the bottle.

So Arawan passed out amongst the empty bottles that Harry was throwing onto the back of his wagon for he knew shops that gave 2 pennies an empty glass bottle and took Arawan's trousers and his unmentionables for the gods had shredded his hand me downs.

"Yucky, those unmentionables are stained?" Conan fearing his might be seen.

"Yes, Arawan has no washing machine," Tom being innocent and a salesman noted many aspiring Chinese cousin launderers here and promised them a laundrette if they washed Arawan's thingamajigs but where souls so Harry did never have to keep his promise.

Anyway: "Very nice, all velvet, even the boxers," Harry and stuck and lit Conan's pipe in Arawan to be nasty for a shredded clawed salesman never forgets so Arawan disappeared in a flaming "Bang."

And Garrison fled for they did not want to be near Harry when Arawan woke up.

And The Mage raked his brains for the spell to make them nonvisible and return them to the world of Alicadabara and sanity.

And away from nasty gods and vicious cats and stained unmentionables and haggling Chinese aspiring cousins of Harry's threatening with choppers to make Harry Chop Suey.

CHAPTER 34   UPDATE

"Haliput Zoo is the eighth wonder of the world,
For it is full of apes,
Put there by Him who cares?
Offaltrex Purchtrix."

Of course, Satirextex was scribbled at the bottom and was hailed greatest verse of the century because it was short.

And Apes would tell you about his parents and forest home with these simple words, "Ouk," for he was behind zoo bars.

And he was ashamed he did not know them, just a passing banana fling where his mother was concerned and as for daddy, another conquest between Banana Ice Cream Sundays.

"Ouk."

And Garrison would nod sympathetically and say, "Ten apes swung down from the vines and ravaged mum so which was mum?"

"Ouk," Apes refusing this version of birth.

"OK one was taken by skinners and now is stuffed in a bell boy suit at the Paris Hilton?" Garrison for they had been at someone's meths for they had spent all their wages already at Common as Mucks Filthy Big Bertha's.

And they cried for such crimes to be committed against one of their own.

"Only ten and orphaned," they muttered and gave Apes bananas, oranges, and unripe melons to cheer him.

And Conan moaned, "Was in the Tandoori Forests ten years ago with rum not this rubbish meths; a barbarian practising ravaging jungle temples and priestess."

That made Apes remember a book he had found on the jungle floor.

"Conan the Barbarian."

And Apes had caught a trapper and made him read the book, and the book was 48 volumes and the trapper was there many a year for he had to translate it from English into Ballenese then Apish.

So, Apes listened and developed ambition to be like Conan for he saw no difference between the species.

"Let me go and I will take you to Conan," the trapper fed up eating mushy bananas and having the runs from raw fruit and worse no Andrex loo paper for no nearby supermarkets.

And so, Apes was sold to Harry who sold him to King Charles who gave him away as a mascot and now Apes had Conan before him so no longer wanted the barbarian life. A life full of bowed legs from riding horses, and ills from ravaging temple priestess on horses while fleeing temple guards.

He just wanted to be Apes, "Ouk."

And how did a future Apes end up in a zoo?

See here Offaltrex Purchtrix had costly divorce settlements from more than one wife and at the same time so built a zoo and revolving restaurant at the top selling revolting food.

And because Offaltrex had been bruised by Apes so desperately wanted revenge on all monkeys so stuffed every cage found full of them.

"Lions," but was monkeys.

"Crocodiles," but was chimps for Offaltrex never went to school for he was a self-made millionaire selling tripe in caramel sauce from his stalls. And was popular for feeding the wife this tripe got you a divorce so could ogle the other woman in the park.

So, completely screwed up the education system of Ball for even a python was a cute spider monkey and explains why the pythons of Ball ended up fat and well fed.

And by the way the trapper giggled all the way to Common as Mucks Filthy Big Bertha's and spent his mark on wine woman and disease and, travelling home was ill on Garrison and a nasty dog **so Karma visited him**; for he was beaten black and blue.

And fell in the moat and landed on a jolly rowing boat that drifted away to Haliput where because of his ugly cauliflower ears could only get a job as a muck cleaner of zoo cages, and because he had nightmares about Apes would scream, "I am not an Ape, go away Apes," so, "he is a monkey in a human zip up suit," and just takes one idiot, so was thrown in a cage with monkeys where he was fed mushy bananas.

KARMA for what he done Apes.

KARMA for giving Apes to Garrison Men.

And there was one cage for a vicious primate, empty now for, "I must catch him first and throw him in and you will thank me and tell me to throw away the key," Offaltrex.

"He will never catch me," a whisper belonging to Harry.

And one cage had a Japanese battery Ape toy playing a trumpet, 'APES,' was at the bottom of the cage.

"A lot less dangerous than catching and stuffing the real APES in that cage," Offaltrex showing wisdom.

"I will show the world my decent side but at the click of a thumb will replace Madam Beautricianix with Madam Universal." Offaltrex.

"He can dream but strapped to my garter not a pistol but scissors so I can hear his heart tremble and know I will always be his Little Bunny," Madam Beautricianix the vamp.

CHAPTER
35   HALIPUT

And Garrison fled the gods on blistering feet for the chariots were gone and the road full of nettles and thistles waiting to rip you to shreds as is Hay Fever Time.

"Eureka," The Mage shouted and made the Hay Fever sufferers jump higher.

"I need the crest from a newt, rock bat droppings, horned toad extract, and jumping cobra fangs and then we shall be in Haliput just like that, **any volunteers to get the ingredients for the magic spell?**" The Mage and all looked at Harry and thought The Mage a ratter for not remembering sooner a spell to whisk them away on an 'Easy Magic Carpet Flight'.

"The newt crest causes green spots for a week," the princess knowing she could not be a volunteer for then she they would not have something pretty to ogle over and dribble saliva and bump into each other when they should have eyes to the front.

THEY WERE SOLDIERS.

"And bat droppings cause drooping mouth for a week," Conan fearing for his rabbit ears were a reminder of the venom of mages.

"No Conan, which is what Dracula spreads about to keep you away from him as is a bat you know?" The Mage knowing here was a volunteer.

"A bat," Conan holding his neck as if Dracula bit him and

The Mage threw him a garlic round, "keeps Dracula away, completely safe now."

"And them toads make your hair stand up for a week even if they are tasty to eat," Harold unintentionally offering his services as a volunteer.

"Just take these laxatives," The Mage finding another volunteer.

"And when that snake bites you die," Wamba trembling.

"No, Wamba just triple vision so you will see three princesses for a week to ogle," The Mage knowing he had a volunteer.

"Book," Wamba wanting to ogle over three princesses and Garrison looked in Book as well for there are always legal loopholes when a smart expensive lawyer is hired for lawyers make the law; but they cost money and we are dealing with Garrison I.O.U.'s.

"I think this is the page you want?" The Mage dryly.

"Splat," as Conan spat tobacco at the page to destroy it.

"Click," and "Splat," as magic sent the vile tobacco juice back to the chewer who gagged, foamed, and said, "That juice is like acid, why do I smoke? Quick Mage give me a cream to soothe my skin," Conan the fool.

"Sure VOLUNTEER," The mage replied to the fool.

"The page says you must help a mage when he needs help," The Mage and did not add, "Under a full moon and be rewarded," for The Mage was a cheap skin flint.

And The Mage did something unkind, he SMIRKED and The Lost Patrol smirked for they had Moronicus by the shirt with rubber swords pressed against him if he volunteered to aspire to be a prince.

And no one was sure if Apes smirked as he was eating bananas and making a real yellow mess.

"Do not fear I can sell you lucky charms like this eagle egg," Harry and from nowhere a wagon pulled by mules.

"Stinks like it died a thousand years ago," Conan.

"Yes, a thousand-year-old pickled eagle egg to ward of lice and when you are hungry you get to eat it," Harry polishing up the egg and added, "gem necklaces to dazzle the cobra so it bites the bugger next to you"" and there was silence as all the buggers next to Garrison where Garrison.

"Lucky chop sticks to pick up poisonous bat droppings?" Harry showing plastic ones made in Gung Zhou Province, "chop sticks you can use again at any Harry's Chinese Takeaway vendor," and to show how accurate they was at picking up small droppings, Harry from his wagon took a dish of special fried rice and ate single grains of rice.

"Wow," a stupid innocent boy and Harry knew he had them.

"Dried Siberian Yak bitties that newts love to chew and while they are chewing you catch them for the thingamajigs will make them bloat and harmless," a no-good salesman who was not a volunteer.

And sold to the Garrison Men all these wonderful lucky charms and threw in rabbit foots each that had not been lucky for the rabbits.

And Wamba lined up the volunteers who mumbled horrid unprintable words.

And cursed their enlistment day.

But they were volunteers.

"Jingle," the sound of cash in a salesman's deep pocket.

CHAPTER 36 WHAT LUCKY CHARMS?

And the Other world is a mirror of the real world and the gambleholic gods created fairies to bet on and all the ingredients in the real world are here but nastier than those in the mirror world of the other world, blah.

Just something The Mage neglected to mention to the volunteers.

"A pond," Tom innocently.

"And is that an amphibian basking on that rock?" Conan terrified.

So, the terrified drew straws and the shortest went.

"Bullocks," Wamba and Cur smirked as the buggers stood back to distance themselves from what he would catch.

"I will eat all the Siberian lucky charm bitties," and the crumbs he gave to Cur and just like that threw a stick at the newt and Cur chased the stick.

"Oh, jolly brilliant," the other Garrison spectators and clapped.

And the newt caught the stick and Cur caught it.

And Wamba expected his friends to return but they did not but pointed at his bare feet for his shoes had holes in them for he was a poorly paid Garrison Guard, which is lies, he just spent his wages in Filthy Big Bertha's who wore polished cowgirl riding boots, especially good for booting Garrison Men out screaming 'blue murder,' for her aim was deadly.

"Woof," a friendly dog wanted patted for returning the stick and horrid newt.

And Wamba saw great big green spots on the places mange had rotted away on Cur's fur and was afraid **for the lucky crumbs had not worked**, so ever so gently picked the newt up to drop in a canvas sack.

And Cur being playful chewed Womba's feet so he felt much pain but not as much pain as he squeezed the newt.

A newt with sharp spines on its crest so he screamed like a teething baby.

And knew he had green spots for he heard one burst and the smell was vile.

"Woof," a happy dog no longer alone as a leper in the cruel world of fairies.

"That is what I like about you Wamba, you share the hurts of your men," Conan lying for he thought Wamba a nerd and geek.

"Three straws left," Wamba showing an insane smile and kicked his dog now and again to show he was mean and the dog bit him back for no one kicked him.

And to be safe the men distanced themselves from these two, and then the blessed Siberian lucky thingies took effect and there were no latrines so distance was made further.

And later they came upon a cave and smelt bat droppings for the wind was from the cave so blew the essence of Wamba and Cur away.

So, curses and groans were heard in the valley downwind below.

"I can say something stronger than Bullocks," Conan with the short straw, "just nothing to it; I just scoop the bat droppings up with these lucky Chinese Chopsticks."

Except Harry had not sold him instructions how to use chop sticks.

"Whoops," Conan dropping droppings in his boots and just for good measure many bats flew out the cave and did things all over him.

"I am done," his stoic thinking.

So, Conan as hard as he tried could not spit tobacco juice so swallowed it and would cause colic and there was no latrines nearby.

And just across the way the cobra waiting to bite a volunteer.

"Hiss," the creepy crawly snake.

So, Tom clutched his lucky gem necklace that was beads made from melted down plastic dinosaurs.

And Harold ate the smelly eagle egg that tasted like the pickled eggs at Fifthly Big Bertha's because they was.

"Is that an elephant?" For The Mage had not told them these toads are huge.

"Here lad, let me do the snake and you get the toad and do an old Viking a favour?"

"Bugger off," from the innocent boy.

"Eeee's leaaaaaaaarning," [He is learning]Conan as his jaw swung dropping from the effects of bat dropping essences.

And Harold put on glasses bought from Harry and saw he could see nothing for there was no glass in them; so, with determination stumbled forward as his mates sat on a high rock eating weevil rations.

"Hurry up Harold we are bored," the mates.

"Woof." a dog laughing.

"That toad is the size of two elephants," the mates also to encourage Harold to be quick.

"Woof," a dog sniggering.

And being bored Tom threw a weevil infested biscuit and hit the toad some place.

"Snnnnnorthiss," the toad sort of snorted and jumped up and down on Harold.

"Ouch," Wamba said for Harold.

And Harold to get from under the lazy toad that was just sitting on him passing wind plucked a horn free and still his mates would not come and help him.

So, the buggers played poker while Cur dozed under a sun with a tongue reaching to the grass for it had been coiled inside in secret organs a nasty dog has.

And the limbs of Harold stopped twitching.

"Better help him then?" Wamba.

"Help whoooot?" [Help what?] Conan.

"Him under the toad," Wamba fearing he might have to get the horn.

"Whatsek toadeeee?" [What toad?] Conan knowing, he was to get the horn.

"Here is a volunteer?" Tom showing true intuitive as he held a sleeping dog's rat like tail.

"Swing him like this and then let go like this," Wamba swinging Cur this way and that and the dog hit the toad in the eye a biscuit had made sore.

"Looooook thereeeees Harooold," [Look there is Harold] Conan swinging his jaw and indeed all saw Harold for the toad was coming at them snorting and gnashing teeth.

"Blooming hell fire," Garrison running for it and added, "Bloody dog, always causing trouble."

And the toad landed upon Tom's spear and a horn pricked Conan.

"Oh, blooooody heck," [Oh, bloody heck] because Conan had a dropping jaw.

"A toady soul is a soul," and Arawan appeared and, "Help me Wamba," meaning too throw that toad in his wagon and Wamba got pricked for only an idiot would help. **"Oh, blooming hell and more Bullocks."**

So, the toad fell off and pricked Tom.

"I never hurt anyone so why me?" The innocent lad but was a lie for he had broken many hearts amongst the waitresses for he just wanted free mushroom soup.

"Woof," as a horn raked Cur and all thought it Harold's fault who just lay there allowing Arawan's wagon to rut him as it went home.

So, the mean Garrison Men used all the Lucky Charms and ingredients got and did Harold good.

"Hiss," the cobra that Daghdha the good god had made long and mean.

As it waited for a volunteer.

"Your turn lad," Garrison as they shoved Tom forward with swords and axes and "hiss," went the nasty snake waiting too bite Tom good.

And the bad snake leapt through the air and bit Tom and one of its fangs snapped off and pricked Harold.

So, all Garrison went rabid and stuck each other with fangs and horns and ate bat droppings and sang:

"We want home.
Back ta da bridge.
Wis cash buys respect some.
Where were-bugs live.
And Filthy Berta.
Girls who like green spots.
Drooping jaws.
And lots a cash.
With lice and nits for you.
But is home," and they was all Garrison afflicted with green spots, drooping jaws and hair that stood straight up and saw everything in triple vision.

And they sought The Mage who had remembered he had given them the wrong lucky charms and being volunteers would come back with ingredients.

Of yes, the effects lasted three weeks, never mind The Mage was sure for the sake of the Fairy Land they would be proud to wear their aliments.

But he was wrong?

*

"Here is the spot The Mage led Garrison out of the other world back to Ball," a futuristic tourist guide.

"Mama it's a swamp," a little boy not wanting to be guided through the mosquitoes.

"Look sunny, its costs money to drain the swamp, plant date trees, build swimming pools, not to mention the golf courses," the guide.

And there was no imagination required to imagine Garrison popping out here for nothing had changed:

"Get ost," [Get lost] for Conan could not pronounce the L for his jaw swung as he shouted at midges that lived in the swamp. All female mosquitoes needing his veins to satisfy their blood lust so they could lay baby midges.

Baby midges that did not wear nappies but knew how to bite.

"Dey bit," [They bite] Harold and being slow in shutting his swinging jaw a trillion midges flew in and all heard "Crunch slurp belch," and a satisfied smile spread across a Viking's face.

And the midges wizened up so ignored him and ate everyone else.

"Help dear God, I cannot stand it," Wamba and leaping here and there jumped into a bog, the quicksand variety. "Help I am sinking," he shouted so someone kicked Cur to him. What a shot, right on Wamba's head Cur pinged.

"Old the rat's ail," Hold rat's tail] Conan having difficulty with his words and that is when he pushed Tom forward to hold the part with the teeth and the idea was for Wamba to use Cur as a plank to crawl over to reach safety.

"'ere I am not olding this en?" [Here I am not holding this then?] Tom complained.

"I got stripes so yee is," [I got stripes so you is] Conan throwing rank.

And then Apes arrived, just what was needed, a strong friendly chap to pull them all to safety.

"One banana in it for you, OK?" Conan bribing the primate who took the fruit, ate it, and wrapped the skin about the stripe's face. Then being an unfriendly chap shook and vacuumed Conan upside down and seeing no more bananas tossed the barbarian to Wamba.

"Ouk," Apes disappearing **which meant bananas to you.**

"That was not nice?" The Mage missing the volunteers for he was sure many exciting adventures would require them.

"Snarl," the unfriendly ape about to shred the druid but seeing a wand begin to stir fell to the ground and kissed The Mage's sandalled feet.

Cleaning them so they sparkled.

And The Mage shook his distant ancestor off so Apes jumped onto Moronicus for Apes did not like the squelchy swamp mud running between his long toes. And leeches ran up his fury legs and attached themselves to a place no other would look at, a big gorilla bottom.

And Apes was so panic stricken he thumped Moronicus who slowly sank into the swamp ooze so a little cute green frog with yellow spots jumped into his mouth.

And the yellow spots spread from the cute green frog to him.

So, he looked horrid.

And since Offaltrex was stuck in mud Mistress Beautricianix came out of swamp mist and fleeced his pockets and to make sure he did not call for help, she used this signpost on him:

"No swimming SHARKS."

"Thump," the music behind a black fin in the sinking sand so those in the mud trembled and shrieked and The Mage knew he did better use some magic and cure them of drooping jaw sickness so they could speak correctly or they did drive him nuts, and you did not want to be a nut about when an ape was nearby!

And Christina shook many creepy crawlies out of her petticoats so Harry was peeved for they were the ingredients The Mage needed to summon Garrison out of the sinking sand; ingredients he hoped to sell The Mage.

But Apes made up for lost sales in bugs for Harry sold him a jar of miraculous ointment to scare away midges. And Apes bought many and signed his X to a labour contract to carry Harry across the swamp for he had no money as gorillas never do.

So "Ouk," and Apes bought sixteen jars and covered himself in swamp mud full of medicinal leeches so even Harry decided to walk in case they wanted him.

Never mind a sign in the swamp mist said and pointed, "Haliput oh weary travellers this way, good luck," and a grinning skull lay at the bottom of the sign whose luck had run out.

*

And Alicadabara knew Garrison was ahead for banana skins, girl magazines, hair curlers and The Times with a filled up cross word puzzle littered the road.

"Attack kill," Alicadabara shouted at the Fiends who did not.

"Sorry is muffin time," Isisnaphut and all Fiends know that they must stop what they are doing in the army mobile latrine and go eat snails, and while chewing the chewy bits meditate on the snail god Gastropodicus.

"Pass the cream old boy," Isisnaphut to Alicadabara who fumed and cast a spell for Fiends to kill fairies stuck in a bog and throw Isisnaphut there.

"Hiss," was all he heard as god Gastropodicus was annoyed for Fiends must meditate on him so the god threw Alicadabara and any near him into the bog.

Do not worry the fin needed company as The Mage had rescued Garrison and now Ali's magic wand lay next to Ali, slowly sinking in the quicksand, and behind it the black fin and a mouth full of teeth.

"Mummy," Alicadabara.

CHAPTER 37   LEVEL 9

The Future

"It is a stove mummy," a kid with chicken pox complained.

"But not any stove sunny?" The guide of Give a Copper Harry PLC as he pulled out a baking tray, "a nickel per baked cinnamon soul kid, ask mum while cheap?" And made sure the kid saw and the paints nearby to buy to paint the cinnamon gingerbread man, and war gamers rules and a catapult to use on the gingerbread men to smash them to crumbs, then you got to lick the crumbs up, cinnamon delicious .

And then buy tickets for holidays into Arawan's Burning Department, where girls wear naught for it is so hot and wicked, level nine hell and sweat so much for anti-deodorant is not available; so, the word is stink not sweat.

Holidays were singles are catered for, pensioners and family groups.

And the fairies booked for they could not resist such holidays of a lifetime and because fairies just cannot resist buying bargains like plastic dinosaurs.

"Ha, squark," King Arawan for there were no return tickets and laughed like a penguin.

Anyway: "That gingerbread man is not Wamba as the guide at the gates of the pearly other world sold me a gingerbread Wamba angel so Wamba cannot be down in level 9 hell," the smart chicken pox kid.

"Listen son, this guide have red hair and freckles?"

"Why?"

"That is my cousin Give a Copper Harry Liar thirty times removed and tightened his oily arm about the kid so the kid went purple.

"Mummy," the kid and "wheeze."

"Hiss," the guide, "and for a penny will tell you your future and the true story of Garrison in Level 9 Hell, hiss," the guide as his legs wrapped about the boy.

And mummy paid the price and used her handbag on the guide so the oily limbs fell away off her chicken pox son.

"Madam do you mind hiss," the guide at mummy's feet and mummy used her stiletto heels this time so there was no more "hiss."

*

Present

"This is not my doing even if I added an extra drop of Cobra venom," The Mage as he could admit his mistakes publicly as he had a magic wand to silence complaints.

And Conan carried Cur for the dog was cooking and hissing steam and the barbarian was not all cruel and did not like his dog overcooked for he was a man of The Wilderness Trail, even if he did eat his friend, his horse.

And Cur kept quiet as fur fell away and the tail exposed was truly a rat's.

"Yes, it is your fault, you clicked us here with a promise we did be in Haliput," Offaltrex Purchtrix the idiot not knowing when to keep silent.

"Sue the druid," Harry infected by greed and was mealy and dribbled at the mouth as his fingers worked his calculator.

And there were two poofs and rabbit ears appeared on fools

"The mage is correct," Arawan from nowhere, **"welcome home boys."**

"Who do we sue then?" Offaltrex needing a bunny tail to match his ears.

"Him," Arawan jerking a finger at Alicadabara swimming in hot vindaloo for they were in Level 9 Hell just like that, and all looked at The Mage, when it was Arawan who was Hell, who had materialised had materialised HELL just for them.

Complicated yes, no, meant to be so your mind enters Vincent Van Gogh's dream world.

And beside the wizard Lord Tootanfoot baying as a donkey kicking fiends into the pool.

And Arawan swigged from a bottle and breathed out and his breath ignited and singed Cur something bad so the air smelt horrid.

"Howl," the poor nasty dog.

"I fear you sweetheart," Offaltrex as Mistress Beautricianix neared.

"You have nothing to fear honey," she lied for a red imp behind her had given her garden scissors.

And a wagon stopped next to Offaltrex and a yellow imp drove it and the wagon was full of dead Fiends in curry sauce for hell is a hot place you know.

"My dearest what do you want?" The merchant Offaltrex.

"Everything and the garden sprinkler," Beautricianix and the imp added, "the gnomes too."

"Then I want the clothes you wear," Offaltrex for the yellow imp was advising him.

And Beautricianix being into voyeurism threw them at him.

"Woof," a dog too young to be out late.

"And I want the gold fillings in your teeth to buy new clothes from that vendor," Beautricianix and her imp yanked the merchant's teeth out so he yelled terribly.

"Help me," he begged Harry but Harry shock him off for Beautricianix held garden shears.

Exceedingly long ones that glinted in the heat.

And Offaltrex fell at Ape's feet begging help and offered him a banana.

"Ouk," Apes wondering where the juicy yellow fruit had

gone for, he had eaten it and was thick.

"What is this?" Offaltrex reading a note Apes had handed him, "a year's supply of bananas," and signed when garden thingies landed between his legs.

"So, shred her," Offaltrex to Apes but his happy mood changed to wrath as Apes swung over to Beautricianix and she signed him up to a two-year supply of bananas from the vendor Harry for she owned everything Offaltrex owned so could afford it.

So Apes the swindler landed on the shadow of Offaltrex who had fled into the sulphuric mist of level 9 hell screaming "EEK."

And behind him Conan spitting dry tobacco gagging, and behind him Wamba was eating Book page by page so Book screamed "Mummy," and behind him Cur was eating his tail to hide the evidence of his ancestry, and behind him Harold was drinking a whole pool of madras sauce and shouting "Help me I am hot Ouk."

And not a Garrison did help so The Mage poofed but his thumb caught fire instead of clicking and so did the nine others next to it.

"I will save you," a Burke and Wamba jumped in to pull Harold out but was in fact wanting to satisfy his greed so slurped happily away, for only the Waitresses at Bertha's knew he was a secret curry fan.

"The seven deadly sins have us by the brass monkeys," The Mage as Arawan bumped into him spilling half a bottle of meths on him so he went BANG loudly and was lucky it had not been a whole bottle of flammable meths, was not The Mage lucky?

"Dance dear," Arawan asking Christina who accepted for she was full of lust and BRAZINESS so flashed her ankles and worse undies. Clean undies for celebrities always keep a spare tucked in the red garter for emergencies.

And Harry was not infected by lust as he was full of greed anyway and either was the other cunning mind The Mage for cunning minds never are.

And a band appeared from a hot geyser and soon Christina was doing the Can Can and kicked the Lost Patrol everywhere.

And Apes drank many bottles of meths carelessly left by an adult drunk and ate the glass too and soon imagined Arawan as a female Tandoori Forest Gorilla and Arawan went along for the joke.

For this was hell level 9.

And the other cunning mind stopped the music for it saw a chance to make gold marks; even pennies would do if it jingled.

"Watch me," this other cunning mind full of arrogance and boast.

And The Mage sighed as his magic was useless against a god.

"Grr," Arawan's red eared hound.

"Chase," Harry and threw a rubber chicken portion into the madras and two hounds chased for Cur could not help it.

"Bbbbbbbuuuuuuurrrrrgggggggeeeeeerrrrroooooffffff," Apes warned Harry to stay away from his dancing partner and fiancée.

"Fruit fetch," Harry and threw a banana into the madras and Apes could not help it and dived in.

"Gasp," the big hairy ape wanting water and got none.

And Harry produced a pool table and leaded balls from a salesman's pocket and from the wagon more vintage meths.

"What stakes," the alcoholic gambler.

"Why all of us," Harry smiling and needed volunteers to get chairs, bags of crisps, green lamp shades and ash trays for the players.

"Where do I get that from?" Wamba in charge of the labour.

"Use your imagination," **The Mage but forgot Wamba had none so Harry sold them a map to guide them to a general store, 'Give a Copper Willy's General Store,' just a distant cousin who was waiting for them for he smelt them a mile off.**

*

"Do not worry lads, we will not freeze down here," Wamba as he carried bags of crisps on his back naked for Give a Copper Willy was a fleecer.

"Is not here I am worried about," Conan and spat tobacco on Womba's rump and stained it brown for soon Christina would be appalled at a grown man needing nappies.

And what had happened to their clothes?

"Such good customers get free invisible clothes and I get their rags to sell to Harry who will sell them back to Garrison at inflated prices as is supply and demand and demand will be big he ah he ah Ho," and was an insane salesman's laugh only a Give a Copper Willy could laugh.

And Wamba proved he had imagination and he could see the shiny boots on his feet and silk trousers fit for a prince, why Christina did be happy to have the Burke next to her when she met daddy.

"We are five idiots,
   We are Garrison,
    Brave and imaginative.
Naked as babes.
Someone gave us Wamba.
Our fairy serge.
Please do him good.
We are five idiots," and sang to the Disney *"Hi Ho hi Ho off to work we go."*

And Harry rushed to sell them fig leaves to show they had no imagination and clothes must be haggled for.

"We have no money?" Conan the heat fizzling the hair on his knees.

So, Harry pointed at the giggling women so accepted I.O.U.'s at 2 gold marks per fig leaf for front and bottom and some goose lard for the fizzled hairs.

"And I am not heartless and will let them work off a gold mark in usherette outfits selling crisps and kebabs," Harry jingling cash.

But Cur did not get any fig leaves but some

unmentionable long Johns to cover his purple skin and Harry got from Willy his cousin; rags that had been Womba's closest thingamajigs to him so Cur was ill.

"Let us play," Arawan winking at an usherette with knuckles dragging behind for Harold's looks had been improved.

CHAPTER 38   POOL JUST LIKE THAT?

"Pool," Arawan taking an extra swig of meths to steady his pool cube and the meths was not his usual rot gut but vintage rot gut so he imagined dwarf Harry's on the balls so missed his aim.

"!804," Harry opening a meth bottle of that year and Arawan drank the lot and threw the bottle that landed on Conan because Garrison always get the worst.

And Harold licked it clean inside with his long tongue and threw it away.

And Cur licked it spotless with an even longer tongue.

And Christina and Beautricianix lounged like floozy woman asking Arawan when he was buying the next round for the hostess wanted the host plenty drunk.

And Wamba, Conan and Moronicus Christina's suitors were not happy when Arawan invited her upstairs to see his stamp collection.

"Here Apes a banana in it if you put this blond wig on," and Apes did for Apes was jealous his floozy women were ignoring him and needed to know if it was his hairy arm pits that drove woman away or the smell of them? And none would tell him why for they did not want beating good and shredded too.

So Arawan could not concentrate and missed all the balls in front of his eyes seeing triple green floozy ankles but when the blonde appeared he foamed at the mouth and desired her to see the family photographs; since the ploy about stamps had not worked and all boys love a blond except Apes who is into chimps.

"Who is this gorgeous wench then?" For he was blind drunk and deserved what he got.

"*Twenty gold marks and she is yours,*" a whisper from nowhere and Harry got richer.

"Listen Apes play along and I will give you a free holiday in hell level 9 that exotic place for lovers," Harry and Apes played along for the primate was thick for this was level 9 hell.

And none heard The Mage ask, "Who has escaped on Bat Wing my bat?" For she was missing.

Now wanting to know he cast chicken bones on the grass and mumbled mumble jumbo and there was a red 'poof' and in the poof an image of Bat Wing in the arms of a red dragon with a sooty smudge.

And not grapes but bird seed the red dragon was feeding "that floozy bat," so The Mage cursed and threw purple powder amongst the chicken bones so of course a purple "poof" happened and he stuck his face in the purple "poof," and now Bat Wing saw his face, took fright, and cleared off fearing being locked up at nights; then she would not be seeing her handsome boyfriend the red dragon. A boyfriend who was peeved his girl was gone so breathed fire upon The Mage.

"By the gods I am burnt crisp," The Mage complained but not too worry he knew magic so with a click was himself again just like that. And The Mage was annoyed and having a dark side took his anger out on Garrison and crisped them too.

Shame.

"Why us," Garrison complained fed up being volunteers and that was the answer to their question.

And Harry's leaded balls sank into all pockets so won all the souls except Arawan's.

"Come on Garrison we are off to Haliput," The Mage happy again Garrison had shared his crisping; and did not include the Give a Copper.

"Here I have won everyone's soul except the drunks," Harry

and took the drunk by the throat with these words, "Give me give me your soul," and the drunk had a red eared hound whose job was to gnaw annoying pool players.

"Get off," Harry unable to shake the hound off his right leg, and it had long sharp teeth too.

"Ouch," Harry.

And got no help as his customers were heading for a sign "Exit this way," out of level 9 hell.

"Daddy," Harry as the red eared hound was about to swallow the last of him but Harry was made of what a salesman is, swindling thoughts and Hire Purchase agreements so the hound coughed Harry up in the fashion of dogs.

"I am off," Harry covered in slime so slipped his way out of EXIT and landed on his head.

"Ouk," Apes trying to get out of the clutches of a drunk addicted to meths.

"Here what is this?" Arawan having pulled off a blond wig and "Good grief you have a hairy face and a flat nose and your whole body needs shaving woman."

"Ouk," which means "Bye."

"Here I swear by the gods that woman is a chimp," for Arawan never went on Safari to deepest Afrika or used his imagination when playing with rubber zoo animals to fill up Noah's Ark so had no idea what a chimp looked like; except this one was really big.

Now the hound being mean was not content chewing Harry and covering him in slime and sank its long sharp teeth into Harry's butt as he slipped out of hell so printed flower boxer shorts could be seen by all.

"So that is what a salesman wears?" Mistress Beautricianix.

"Titter giggle," Christina in the fashion of freckled girls.

"Ouk gee up," Apes driving Arawan's wagon and beat the horses with bananas to make them gee up faster as a drunk waved his blond wig and threw banana skins at him.

"Come back monkey I will buy the peanuts and cinema tickets," for Arawan had gone through all the dating agencies and been thrown out of them so was one lonely desperate guy. Even seen talking to Tootanfoot at night and offering him a carrot to play in the park.

"I do not accept carrots from strangers," Tootanfoot, "especially from him."

And "Burp," and was him that drunk Arawan breathing meths that was in danger of igniting.

"Run," Wamba saying something sensible for once.

And Garrison ran and that red eared hound was just in front of them wanting to gnaw for gnawing is addictive so was trampled and kicked out of the way so landed

back in hell in a pool of hot Madras with no rice; never mind the Animal Welfare Officer was in Madam Filthy Big Bertha's but not here though.

And Gnasher saw spinning bones and rabbits not stars.

So, all escaped to Ball again into a rainstorm.

"I am fed up being wet," The Mage and clicked and sky was full of sparrows and

bright sunshine and no one agreed behind his back, "Yes The Mage is a wet," for they did not want rabbit ears.

CHAPTER 39 DREAMS

"Haliput this way," a dented sign being read by Garrison and under the sign a skeleton of a horse, not any old horse, but of those that pulled Arawan's soul wagon and died dancing for they had been drunk.

"Old Nag dear where are you, nice juicy carrot in it?" Wamba tired of walking but Old Nag saw the glint of spurs so was nowhere to be seen. "Here monkey a banana in it for you?" Wamba for his boots where not made for walking!

"Ouk," and the primate took the spurs and stuffed them some place.

"Cur blimey," Wamba shrieked.

"Walking, are we?" Conan to be sarcastic.

And Bat Wing landed on the sign and did what pigeons do for it was a bit confused.

"Cur throw a sack over it," Conan and added, gasp give me air," and bought a peg for his nose from a salesman.

"What a stink," Tom and bought two pegs from a salesman.

"Blooming unhygienic should be put down," Wamba and had no cash so bought no pegs so added, "please lend me a peg?"

"No," a cruel salesman.

"Ouk," and whatever Harold was got a peg.

"It might turn vicious if I refuse," that oily salesman.

"Woof," that nasty dog.

"Animals to the back of the queue," that salesman and the nasty dog turned viscous.

And The Mage jerked a thumb indicating he wanted a lift and the bat since the fling with a certain dragon knew about independent living; so, bit him on the nose.

"If you turn it into a taxidermist's animal, we will not trust you for you might turn us into plastic dinosaurs to be sold at a vendor's stall?" Conan and Garrison nodded agreement so The Mage did not click and spared the modern woman in Bat Wing.

"Walking, are we?" Conan to be sarcastic.

"Hi Ho, hi Ho," Garrison and the rest joined in except for The Mage who was in the sulks.

"Oh, to Haliput we go.

Where bargain sales exist.

Stir fry smells."

"Latrine essences," Conan to be sarcastic.

"Where rose gardens and princes exit," Christina throwing freezing water on Wamba.

"And expensive lawyers," Beautricianix and Offaltrex trembled.

"Hi Ho, hi Ho," Garrison chorused.

And The Mage knew when they entered the South Gate at Haliput he did sell Bat Wing where a local restaurant knew how to make Bat a la' king, and he did reserve a table for himself and then see who had the last laugh about one-night stands. Oh, what a mean druid he was, meaner than Alicadabara who wanted to turn everyone here into snails in rancid butter sauce; so there must be a moral here and it is, "Do not trust

wrinkled old men needing a haircut. I mean old men waving wands about muttering strange sounds; perhaps needing to be put away in a local asylum?

But The Mage could dream and Wamba dreamed of King Charles promoting him to a prince so he could marry Christina and live happily ever after on a pension from her daddy.

For Wamba had no trade, was unemployable and a Burke and worse; Garrison but he could dream and his king to make sure his type stayed away from Christina would send Wamba to a war galley.

And Tom the innocent boy dreamed of helping Conan stand at a bar getting full of XXX and then going upstairs with a waitress for a private meal of fish and chips.

And the bar would collapse as it was full of termites so Harry was in their dream as well selling the landlord termite infested wood to make a new bar.

And upstairs the waitress would pore XXX into poor innocent Tom who did stink of XXX. "Gorgeous," Tom would slur as he was a future alcoholic and gorgeous had curlers in her hair and a moth-eaten bodice and no longer slim but shall we say, nicely plump and as he admired her assets a shadow behind Tom got nearer and nearer and then STARS and Tom woke up hours later in the gutter, mugged.

That should teach him but he was a future fairy man so crawled back into the establishment that provided soups and waitress service so the Town Watch would be called to get rid of him and send him to a certain war galley.

And was a dream and Haliput had many such restaurants waiting for innocent Garrison boys.

And Harold dreamed of the other type of restaurant that served steaks and provided false teeth in jars to eat the steaks with.

Big juicy steaks stuffed with salmon slices stuffed with chicken cubes stuffed with ducks from the pond stuffed with rats plaguing the alley out back, for the bins were not emptied regularly.

And for desert mango laced with cream that should have been given to the rats; "is sour cream," the waiter wanting a tip.

And Harold did wash it all down with warm XXX and being on Garrison pay could not afford such stuffing's so the Town Watch was called and he was dragged off to a war galley at the docks.

But were dreams and the stuff of nightmares.

And Conan had nightmares for he knew he did be caught

horse stealing while stealing Christina to ride away into The Wilderness Trail and be sent to row a war galley slowly finding an engine.

And all war galleys need a mascot so Cur was thrown down where the bilge is to make sure there were no store a ways and rats.

"Woof," the dog woofing as it was a nightmare when he should be dreaming of chasing white rabbits and Red Riding Hood.

And Captain Moronicus and his patrol would be sent as marines as King Charles feared aspirers.

"Ouk," Apes dreaming of bananas and someone shouted, "That ship is full of mangoes," and Apes loved mangoes more than he loved bananas so found himself in the crow's nest. "Ouk," he did say to passing crows but it was just a dream, or was it?

"A passage to the Americas too escape daddy's spanking," Christina and fled aboard the war galley and took over the captain's cabin for she sprawled upon its double bed.

And The Mage was not popular for the Ballenese missed the rain that turned their roads to mud where newts and salamanders crawled up your leggings. "I must seek passage out of Haliput before assassins are sent from The Assassins College to do me permanently. At least a sea cruise and tanning in a deck chair will inspire me to remember the spell to make rain again," The Mage dreaming of future adventures that involved Garrison so was ill.

And Harry saw possibilities with the sunny climate, valleys full of grapes to provide rot gut XXX for innocent Toms to lose their innocence. And would Harry dream of joining a summer cruise on the high seas? No, he dreamed of Harry Bros. PLC that owned all sales in the land so he could live in a mansion with a heated swimming pool; while you lived in a tenement he owned. A tenement overrun with vermin and leaky lead water pipes and roaches in your food for after paying his rent the roaches were the dinner.

And Harry did charge tourists a gold mark for the privilege of to be guided around his palace. Surely this miserable Scrooge must be sent out of Ball on a war galley.

CHAPTER 40   BOOK 2

And is tempting to call Garrison horrid beasts but that is unfair to the crawlers living in your linen or coming up the bath plug.

The beasts that run riot in your shack when you are at the market buying noodles.

So, it was a Zoomorphosis met the travellers because it lived next to the Haliput Road in a stinking cave because of inswept remains of travellers that made up its menu. And a Zoomorphosis has bad breathe as it is not choosy between beggars with boils and merchants covered in Harry's rose water. Besides no one ever got close enough to whisper, "You have bad breath," and live.

"Sniff," this winged beast sniffed and, "I smell the blood of a fairy, several, Christmas is early," so swung its scaly legs over a stone bed, stretched talons, yawned, belched, and let off a stinker, "Oh pardon me," and giggled for these Zoomorphosis are sensitive; then tidied its chained pillow that squeaked as it was a bear. Which shows how big these Zoomorphosis are?

And expected Bear to air the blanket that was the fur of a mastodon that had been picking yellow daffodils as it walked innocently along the Haliput Road when Zoomorphosis had jumped it.

"Got you," were Zoo's precise words.

And skinned it and had many steaks for a long time so was happy, full, and content so ignored the travellers on the road who, "phewed," with relief.

"Here why has not that monster not eaten me?" A traveller

wondering if the pongs of travelling were too strong.

And the Zoomorphosis did not get dressed, it had never found a tailor on the road to make him clothes but that was a lie, he had, he was just greedy and ate first then questioned later.

"Grr snarl," Zoomorphosis in front of his mirror.

"Who is the handsome boy then?" He asked the mirror.

"Christina," the foolish mirror so was done well and illustrates how bad-tempered Zoomorphosis are.

"And where is this, Christina?" Zoo' kicking his pillow that shrieked.

"On the road outside," the mirror and did not tell Zoomorphosis that Garrison walked with her, no that did ruin the surprise!

"Oh, in that case I am sorry you fell out of my hands and broke into a hundred bitties," Zoo' lying to the mirror for he had thrown it down remember? "Dwarf will glue you together, here Dwarf where are you?"

So, Zoo' yanked on a chain that disappeared into the depths of his cave till he could yank no more and then resistance at the end.

"What is it now?" Dwarf shouting from the depths of the cave

"Fix mirror," the only reply and Dwarf had one look at mirror and knew he was for supper.

And while Dwarf hurried to find paste, Zoo sang melodies, picked daisies outside, blew kisses to blue tits, flicked some white cabbage butterflies off his herb garden, and then told Dwarf to lay out the best cutlery as guests were expected.

And Dwarf pasted up mirror, set the table and went back to filing down his chain:

Escape
Was on his mind.

And was more relaxed since guests were expected.

"I have been filing down this chain for twenty years, but tonight feel lucky."

"What about me?" The pillow hoping to be taken along.

"You will be promoted to my job," the selfish dwarf.

Now the pillow thought about this and after an hour replied, "Not if I tell Zoomorphosis that you plan to escape?"

And Dwarf beat the pillow with his file and quickly regretted it for pillow was a Grisly Bear.

A Grisly Bear that made Dwarf put twenty years of filing practice on **his** chain so Bear was freed. And shows why dwarfs are becoming extinct for they tend to go berserk against bears, Zoomorphosis, pink elephants, and themselves when they cannot make up their minds who to berserk on?

"Now you can have my vacancy," the bear walking away with the file.

So, Dwarf got mad and this is a suitable time to point out this one had a nasty temper and was on the road to self-annihilation.

"Give me it back," Dwarf and walked towards the bear foaming, his eyes black, his ears red, his ribs bruised and patches of hair gone from the last meeting with Bear.

And Grisly Bear tossed Dwarf out of the cave.

"And the chain snapped.

"I been filing twenty years and that stupid bear snaps it just like that?" Dwarf much peeved.

"Plunk," as Grisly Bear pulled Dwarf out of the mud.

"Should have asked twenty years ago," Grisly Bear so Dwarf got mad.

So got beat up good again the stupid Dwarf.

"We cannot keep meeting like this?" Dwarf aching all over.

"Why not?" Grizzly Bear not a scratch on him.

But then the bear ran away just like that.

"Ha, I won," Dwarf and then slowly his brain began to think as he realised, he never won against Grisly Bear. So, was it the bad breath coming up behind him that made him run after Grisly Bear?

And he jumped this way and that, landed on nettles, Venus fly traps and all made him jump longer so he landed on the back of Grisly Bear at last.

"Gee up," Dwarf and from deep pockets where he hid

things from nasty Zoomorphosis took out spurs.

And Grisly did not have an hour to think where those spurs where and the faster he ran away from them the faster Dwarf used them; **for bears are as thick as thick toast.**

And they were running straight to a Zoomorphosis menu straggling on the Haliput Road.

*

"By the gods, who is this handsome man?" Mistress Beautricianix putting her faith in a mole in her cheek and obviously was short sighted for Zoomorphosis was ugly as sin. "Wait a minute, it might be well endowed but is a huge beast with no manners, very rustic and maybe quick tempered," so she kicked Offaltrex to be in front.

"This is the thingy that eats little girls in red hoods going through forests with recipe books," Christina and someone threw a red hood stolen from a wagon pulled by mules over Harry.

"Who did that?" Harry wanting gold marks for the hood but silence greeted him as the fairies stood grooming each other and it was some job as Garrison never washed.

"Never fear sweet princess Captain Moronicus and his Lost Patrol will protect you?" **An aspirer.**

Why Christina asked the obvious, "What Lost Patrol?"

Why Moronicus played with his wobbly sword bought from you know who for his Lost Patrol had vanished.

"Where are you?" Moronicus looking in roadside bushes for his men so knew he was promoted to a war galley.

"That twerp is laying it on a bit thick lately, is he not?" Mistress Beautricianix to another woman.

"Ouk," the reply.

And Apes was wearing glasses hoping Beautricianix did buy them from him with Mangoes for Apes was a secret aspirer. Glasses he had picked pocketed from a certain oily salesman.

"Get lost 4 eyes," Beautricianix.

"Yes, fairies are all the same," Christina.

"And here are the fairies," Mistress Beautricianix as

Wamba made Garrison form a shield circle about the women.

But Apes threw bananas into Zoo and got him in both eyes so poor Zoo flew into the ground so only his scaly reptilian tail showed.

And Cur did what dogs do on trees.

"This is not supposed to happen," Zoo cursed to the worms.

"A Zoomorphosis just what ingredients need," The Mage with a dark side.

"Do not read Book, just chain the thingy," Conan whispered to Wamba so Wamba would not lose face.

And Zoo was not chained up; Garrison used string as chains bought from Harry were expensive.

And a foolish worm crawled through the beak holes of Zoomorphism and "SNAP," and "That was not very nice," Wamba who kicked the beak to teach Zoo what goes about comes back.

"Judas let us get out of here," Conan to Garrison **as he knew what goes about comes back to volunteers.**

CHAPTER 41 WHAT DO WE DO WITH IT?

And a genius need not ask but Wamba was not a genius.

"Do not know," Conan and dropped a stone on Zoo's head hoping to send him to Zoo Heaven.

"Very interesting," Conan as the stone shattered and was afraid so his intestines made noises.

And was obvious Zoomorphosis was eating the string so would be free so Garrison 'POOFED' away.

"Wamba come back and tie Zoo up again and please," The Mage and was popular amongst non-enlisted Garrison as only Burke had been asked for.

Those that support power and are called aspirers.

"Here where are you going?" Wamba asking Garrison sneaking behind a bush to hide.

And Zoo was free and towering above the Ordinary about to eat Wamba uncooked.

And Wamba failing his hands in the air over Garrison slapped a beak real hard.

And Cur winced as slapping a beak was like kicking a nasty dog places.

And Zoo fainted and fell across a bush.

And they did not have a chance.

And Zoo winded so gassed those underneath.

And here an Alsop fable, *"Never enlist."*

"Come on Lost Patrol, it is dead," Moronicus and appeared

alone with a wobbly sword.

And only Apes appeared proud to be considered a fairy at last.

"My hero," Christina and swooned.

But who did she swoon over?

"By the Snake god let there be a metal cage and hurry please," The Mage knowing always to say 'please' when speaking to gods and sometimes Wamba.

Then poured the contents of a black pouch about Zoo and the contents smelled badly so Zoo kept fainting like any normal person would.

But The Mage forgot to add newt livers so the cage landed on top of a wagon.

Volunteer fairies were needed to lift Zoo that weighed 2 tonnes into the cage.

"Here who will compensate me for my ruined shoddy goods?" Harry looking at his wagon.

"Garrison," The Mage knowing the government never would.

But Garrison were all squashed now.

"Volunteers," an aspirer Moronicus.

"Must mean us?" Garrison trained to answer with pride.

And appeared for Zoo was fainting continually for Garrison creaked under him.

And takes one to shut the cage door with all inside and some idiot threw the key away and he was Captain Moronicus.

"Here get this bum off me," Tom loudly for he was innocent for bums were everywhere in the small cage pressing against him.

"CSSs you will wake the monster up," Conan wisely.

But Zoo awoke and went nuts.

"By the gods it will with one bite be free of the string, help," and Conan was not ashamed to ask for help for once freed outside the cage would forget where he got the help from and be a barbarian again ogling the ample riches of a pretty ankle?

"Yes, it will be free soon," all the other non-Garrison enlisted people.

But Zoo went quite for a Dwarf riding a Grisly Bear appeared for Zoo was amazed.

"Dwarf's the name," and held out a septic hand that came from twenty years of filing.

"Grr," Grisly to be ferocious.

"Wonderful a circus bear," Christina and clapped her hands.

"Wonderful," Conan and spat hot tobacco juice on Zoo's bottom so it smouldered.

And a flying bat appeared and perched on the top of the cage and forgot about a handsome dragon with soot stains for Zoo was handsome indeed.

And Wamba bent down to examine why his men could not crawl out from Zoo's bottom, and the answer was they had more sense.

And Cur licked Wamba's chin and was ill for Wamba had not shaved for days so Witchery Grubs, butterfly cocoons, a birds nest were stuck to Cur now.

CHAPTER 42
PROFESSIONALS

They sang happily, *"We are Duke's ten thousand,*
Marching up and down hills.
For we lack imagination.
Sometimes run too.
Away from fiends
As that comes naturally.
So isn't imagination.
And count sheep to sleep,
For marching is knackering.
And eat sheep too.
And have a union.
So, strike when cities burn.
For we leave fighting to Garrison.
Yes, we are the Duke's ten thousand,"
and the regular army staggered down the Haliput Road to fight Fiends. *"They are making a remake of Indiana Jones so are looking for extras,"* and was a whisper and a lie spread by a certain you know who to make them buy mascara and laddered pantaloons for a merchant we know was wanting a new pink wagon with the latest mules; and that costs cash, preferably yours.

"Face them with a stiff upper lip," the Duke at the front of the ten thousand and hoped he would get the leading role as Mr Jones.
"Ha,"

"We will right the wrongs the Fiends done our wives," The Duke who could afford many wives.

And the ten thousand did not think of their wives who bore them litters of squealing children as were plump cigar smoking women wearing aprons as a baby sucked away; the Fiends could have them; it was their girlfriends they would fight for, girlfriends who took all their pay in silk stockings and Belgian chocolates.

"There is Isisnaphut," the Duke who could not tell Apes apart from Isisnaphut for Apes was driving Arawan's wagon.

And because there were ten thousand men, they charged the handful of Garrison coming towards them.

The silly fools so was a Bonsai charge.

"Wamba form a thin red line," The Mage who had seen too many movies.

"With what?" Wamba sarcastically.

"Here are spare keys to that cage where a zoo sits on your men," Harry and jingled them in front of Wamba who bought so put his X to parchment agreeing to sweep Harry's mule stables clean at 5a.m. daily for the next three years for keys do not come cheap. And Wamba knew he was lucky for at 5 am. the mules were fast asleep so no cleaning needed.

"Wait till he sees my new stables in Haliput home to a hundred mules," that horrid whisper again.

"Captain Moronicus get your men and join the thin red line," Christina showing she was good at her job of ordering those below her about.

But The Lost Patrol got lost in nearby bushes.

"You will need these not them," that whisper and Harry showed Wamba many padlocks and chains to chain Garrison together into a thin grubby line.

And Harry sold them to Wamba for 100 gold marks that Wamba did not possess.

"An emergency situation requires Garrison to defend rich salesmen like me, so make allowances and after they are all killed will come down and get the padlocks and chains back,"

Harry the miserable rotter.

And Book told Wamba to throw away the keys and then flew away into nearby bushes for Book was a girl and The Lost Patrol was men.

"I can see everything from up here," Harry on top of the cage and prodded down at Zoo with these words, "Look plenty of food for you," hoping the zoo did fight and get skinned for Harry wanted a trophy on his wall so could boast, "I shot it in East Afrika."

But Zoo was not daft and stayed in the cage and to show Harry it did not like being prodded with a stick ate the stick and spat the shavings at Harry.

"Ouch my Adams Apple," the oily merchant and said ouch a hundred times as he pulled a hundred slithers out.

"Count me in lads, no Dwarf ever missed such good odds," Dwarf joining Garrison.

"Thinks he can do everything without asking me, well I am joining too," the silly Grisly Bear.

"We are Ballenese
 And proud of it.
 Fools more likely.

Volunteers," Garrison sang and Christina on top of the cage shed tears for she was proud of them.

And beside her The Mage made himself invisible and was tempted to ask her to join him for remember he had a dark side to him and should be ashamed for he was old enough to be her great granddaddy.

And Bat Wing crawled under the wagon and found herself next to mules and Old Nag and was the only female so enjoyed all the presents and attention.

"Charge," the ten thousand as they got really close to the grubby thin red line that needed a wash and stopped; so only those not looking back ran up to Garrison and seeing they were alone apologised and went back to the ten thousand.

"We are on strike," the ten thousand seeing the thin red line was dangerous.

"Oh, its uncle Ducky," Christina and waved.

"Why it is Little Greenfly," the Duke waving back.

And The Lost Patrol appeared with Moronicus and waved a standard and snarled and spat like soldiers do.

And Harry sold Duke a long table and with a click produced waitress service and all were invited except for Garrison for they smelt of wet dog for Cur was with them, and since they smelt did not mind Dwarf with them for twenty years filing without bathing sure as hell leaves an essence. And Grisly Bear stank of Zoo for he had been a pillow for twenty years.

"Pass a biscuit," Conan and Tom that sweet innocent boy gave him a ration weevil.

"Pass a biscuit Little Greenfly," The Duke and she passed a chocolate Éclair.

"Some were born winners like me," Harry sipping tea from best China and scuffing chocolate cake and "some like them were born volunteers," as volunteers drank their tea from plastic mugs and crunched weevils in biscuits.

CHAPTER 43
HALIPUT CITY

Now once upon a time there was this road sign fill of arrows and a skull was at the bottom.

"Haliput
Thou stinks," and yes was Satirextex who needed to be taken to school and given basic lessons in literature. *"But is what the plebeians want, rubbish, jingles to jingle*
with my gold marks deep in my pockets," a greedy whisper.

And beggars line Haliput streets with tin cups and mangy dogs nastier than Cur
ready to bite those not giving; and monkeys in funny hats holding tin cups to jump on non-givers too and pull all your hair out by the roots. Monkeys who get a bag of peanuts and the beggar 5% of the Harry Bros. PLC wigs bought by new customers.

And behind the beggars limbs hastily hacked off to match the beggars signs, "Was a soldier in the Duke's," so pennies given; and more pennies if the limbs were hacked off in front of an adoring crowd plus the nasty dog nastier than Cur was dancing with the monkey with the tin cup.

"What about the thingy above the leg," some joker hoping.

"I do not replace those, how lowly you think of me so am deeply hurt and offended," an oily whisper and thought of XXX to paste over the boring paragraphs.

So, quirts of tomato sauce went everywhere and the crowd

got in the mood for fish and chips with vinegar too.

"Hack him good lads," a one-legged man with a parrot on a shoulder and the crowd did and the beggar what's his name was famous for his bits and thingamajigs were stuck on pikes in all the major city gates of Ball.

"Great show," the sailor with the parrot.

"What was his name?" A posh woman holding a scented hanky.

"Beggar Fred," another beggar claiming the now vacant spot and kicked the nasty dog away so got ripped down to interesting bits. Then the parrot flew down and pecked the nasty dog to crackers and my these is not pets you did like to introduce to the girl friend, **but yes, the mother-in-law**.

And King Noddy encouraged such hackings as it was a form of population control.

And those that did not hack themselves where thrown in the back of a wagon, "Army Recruitment, come and see the world," and found themselves amongst the ten thousand so fermented strikes and were not grateful they could afford waitress service at Common as Muck Filthy Big Bertha's and catch illnesses.

"And I hope a million Fiendish arrows find Duke for he is a relation with an army and might object along with the citizens to my sitting in a rose garden, spying on Lord Tootanfoot," Drunken Noddy, "and here pick my nose and eat what I find and order lobster in peanut sauce. They say I am mad as a March Hare but I am just lovingly different.

Ha he Ho he has Ho.

Did they call Cleopatra dim when she bathed in ass's milk? I want a hundred asses in my bath for continuous milk supply for I am a nut.

And asked a night watchman what was in his canvas bag?"

"An asp," as the idiot emptied the snake out and it crawled into my milky bath and the hundred asses got out.

"Fetch it or else," King Charles who is Drunken Noddy and pitter patter was heard as The Chief Executiuner ran along the corridor to the royal bathroom.

"I am bitten," an unhappy night watchman and hated his king.

"Majesty?" The Chief Executioner.

"Chop off his head," and the night watchman got to see bird's eye views and had long conversations with beggars spread about on pikes; but at least the snake did not get to bite him again.

And Haliput hated the royal drunk and royal fleas jumped on his sclerosis swollen liver and had a bite.

"Arg," and was a royal moan as the king scratched away and made his liver red and raw. Fried onions he laid atop his belly and not leeches for a cure.

"And have fitted trap doors in every royal room for assassins to fall in and get shredded by wild beasts below.

Ravenous wild beasts as there was so many trap doors the king forgot where they all were, so never fed them.

And only pitter patter the chopper loved his king for he took bribes not to chop thingamajigs and stick them on pikes at city gates to have a lengthy conversation with a night watchman.

Yes, he was a corrupt bum who had two axes, a sharp one for them that paid to get a clean job and a blunt one to draw the chopping out all afternoon for skin flints.

"I did not chop up the royal steward as I needed a serf on my olive orchard and olive and citrus fruits are rave since The Mage stopped the rains and Grand Marshall Wotanic still lives for, he bribed well; for now, I live in his town house of 60 rooms and 4 swimming pools and he still pays for the staff and many waitresses needed to serve the guests tomato soup," the Chief Executioner all smiles.

"I am going to complain to The Brotherhood," Wotanic about the Brotherhood not assassinating that royal drunk Noddy so Wotanic thought up some lies which comes easy to aspirers for they dream big.

"Noddy is coming to arrest you Big Ears," for one of the brothers had enormous
ears.

"He will stuff us all in lions," Big Ears snatching his socks back from a waitress.

"Yes, many lions need stuffing," some idiot swinging from the rafters while a waitress practised circus acts.

"We must get The Duke to join us or we are tinned cat food," Wotanic adding,

"I sent a carrier pigeon with a message saying Christina has joined us in The Brotherhood so bring the army quick," but did not mention he would marry the

princess and still feed lions with this lot for not only was he an aspirer but a bum.

"You must be our leader," Big Ears and Wotanic was happy, he did lead them all to pitter patter and win his town house back.

So led the Brotherhood along the Haliput road to meet The Duke.

And the other army come out of Haliput was under Barbarossa, the palace guard Noddy had foolishly entrusted with these words, "Save me and you can marry Christina with the pretty ankles."

And Barbarossa would marry her anyway, of course after hacking everyone else to shreds.

For that is how they got rid of the opposition back in them good old days.

And The Mage and Garrison were on that road too and Isisnaphut and what remained of the Fiendish host after falling off the bridge into the fetid moat.

And in the sky Mars a red planet was happy war was coming. It was smiling as it was the comic relief.

"Gee up, must not be late, souls to collect," a drunk swigging meths and fell back

into his wagon to sleep it off.

"Howl," a red eared hound stuck under him.

"Bray," his mules and had a carrot break.

"Crack," a carrot being broken in two and was covered in chocolate.

Yes, it was a something break.

CHAPTER
44   WAITER

"A pot of iced tea please," a tourist at a tea stall near the bridge under the hot Californian sun The Mage created when he banished rain and muddy roads from Ball.

And the tourist was with Harry World Tours PLC about to watch a re-enactment of The Battle of Haliput Road played out by the Haliput War Gamers Club.

Fairies in cardboard armour running about fluttering wings at each other.

Of course, a stretcher lay on the grass nearby for even Harry's bendy swords went places.

And the day was hot for Harry's relations organised the battles on the hottest days to make sure plenty of iced tea was bought.

"No cash no tea," and the sibling jingled the ice cubes that melted so He that great salesman did be furious for he liked his ice tea with a slice of ice.

And the battle was always late for those inside the cardboard armour were not daft and were waiting for the cool sunset. So starving tourists bought cucumber sandwiches.

"Here this sandwich is green?" A complaint.

"That is cucumber," the sibling in a waitress outfit and was a lie.

"This bread is green, and the Canadian steak slices are moose steaks and the moose tastes like the cat for we Ballenese know what to eat when a harvest fails, and the sour cream floating on the coffee is really sour and full of germs to give me the runs," the complaint and was all truthful statements.

"Look at the others tucking into their lunch and because they are eating get this free sachet of brown sauce so complaints wanted what was free so ate.

And he used the sachet of brown sauce and very soon had to run for the outhouse where other diners were queuing and passed a piggery and the swill was brown and nearby orphans filling sachets of brown sauce.

"I have many siblings and relations to feed," Harry explaining he must use what is available as there is a recession and shares have collapsed.

"Oh, my tummy," complaint lying on the stretcher but there were no stretcher bearers.

"That means extra wages," Harry sternly.

And much earlier in time Wamba put Book away for Book was refusing to open for Book did not want shredded with arrows.

And Conan spat tobacco at Womba's bottom and stained it brown.

Tom gave Wamba strange fingers as he counted butterflies.

Harold was eating grass for he had two stomachs.

Cur was gnawing a stick that had a name, "Wamba."

"Parade shun," for Wamba could think of nothing else and used a whip hidden in his back pocket to get Garrison too parade.

This is the first manoeuvre of the Battle of Haliput Road.

Then a messenger from General Barbarossa of the Palace Guard arrived demanding the arrest of Christina.

"Her with the pretty ankles, you must be almonds," The Mage answered as Christina flashed an ankle at him for pretty girls know how to get what they want.

"Barbarossa wants to ravage me in his tent and proclaim himself king," Christina and sobbed and threw herself on The

Mage's chest and he was a male fairy so was affected so clicked a finger and made a carnation grow on the messengers nose.

The first hostile action of the battle.

"Not to glittery I hope the tiara," Christina adjusting The Mage's tiara in a pocket mirror all girls keep to see who is ogling them from behind.

And Conan spat tobacco and hit the messenger in the left eye so it swelled and went green and black and was horrid.

And so, the enemy filled the air with arrows and a passing flock of geese and ducks saved Garrison but not themselves so Harold dreamed of many roasts.

"Thank you Snake god," Harry filling his wagon with duck and geese to sell to the hungry Garrison men. "Someone must pluck the feathers and clean the innards out and baste them with goose lard, and that costs times," Harry defending his stealing of the manna.

"Here Wamba I am not standing here because there is no more ducks and geese to stop them arrows," Tom and inched away and Conan was proud of him.

So, Wamba looked at Book and Book felt sorry for the Burke so opened its pages and was shredded with arrows; so, should have remained shut and uncaring.

So, Wamba was wrath and Garrison inched yards away for he was PREDICTABLE.

And had tied Old Nag nearby for that horse was PREDICTABLE also.

And Wamba mounted his unfaithful horse, drew his sword, and shouted,

"Gvssaimph."

And disturbed a flock of starlings that flew overhead just as enemy arrows came so more food fell at Garrison's feet.

"I must collect those as well for Garrison eats anything and can sell the rest as Dwarf Chicken to the ignorant of Haliput," that greedy salesman again for he knew fairies were not found of starling roosted or broiled.

"Who is that?" Isisnaphut.

"Wamba again," a reply for the Fiends knew Wamba well.

"Send in the champion," and a mighty warrior was given a donkey to ride and the donkey had fairy wings for none had turned Tootanfoot back to his original self.

"He was so annoying as a fairy, at least as a donkey he can do useful things like carry the kitchen and drums of cooking oil, the firewood needed to cook the cauldrons he carries as well, and not to mention all the food needed cooked and eaten by us," Isisnaphut wanting you to agree and not feel sorry for the donkey who "never gave a child a ride on any beech."

And to make sure Tootanfoot went the right way a honey basted parsnip was attached to a stick and waved under his nose.

"Bray," Tootanfoot trotting towards Wamba and "this parsnip is not washed," he complained.

"Ha he Ha," and was Wotanic watching and then a bee stung his mount and he was off to meet Wamba also with his armed Brotherhood waving assassin weapons, sling shots, darts, lassos, and guard dogs trained to bark loudly.

And the bee belonged to a swarm of bees that just flew amongst the archers so no more arrows fell upon Garrison except one fired last, and it landed on the bottom of a greedy salesman who shouted, "No discount for whoever did that, for ever."

"Cannot wait to stuff them in my lions," Barbarossa who kept hungry lions as pets and fed them anyone who annoyed him, so his lions were well fed, fat and lazy so Garrison could outrun them any time.

"My men will strike," The Duke so sat in his deck chair and sipped cool fizzy drink.

"And we are sitting on the grass drinking cool fizzy drink also," his ten thousand who knew what was good for The Duke was good for them.

"I am rich, ten thousand soft fizzy drinks and in this hot day they will want more, my there are many customers out there," Harry and organised his supply line of cool fizzy drink from a nearby pond.

"Here there is a tadpole in my drink?" One of the ten

thousand.

"A free toy," Harry and threw extra cinnamon into the pond and caramel for colour.

"He is heroic after all but so ugly," Christina warming to Wamba on Old Nag.

"Are you not you going to help him?" Dwarf watching the Brotherhood swarm about Wamba with pitchforks and machetes.

"Help who?" Conan and pretended to look for someone needing help.

"Him," Dwarf as Barbarossa led his men into the swarm of Brothers with spears and long Halberds.

"You mean Tom, why no he is big enough to choose his own waitresses," for waitresses had appeared to serve muffin cakes to those buying cool fizzy drinks with toys in them.

"Where is he?" Dwarf no longer able to see Wamba for Isisnaphut champion was jumping up and down on Wamba with these words, "Bray."

"All right I will help," Conan and was alone for Garrison had vanished.

But not to worry he bought a banana from a waitress and threw it amongst the bodies about Wamba.

"Ouk," and an ape swung down from vines and soon sorted the bullies on top of Wamba out for the banana was in amongst them somewhere.

"Bray," a donkey getting the bung by Apes.

"Here this is not fair?" Barbarossa finding Apes bigger than a lion so was stuffed by the primate needing that one banana to fill the hole in his tummy.

Now it was not all due to Apes Wamba was saved; it was due to Conan carelessly leaning on a latch that opened a cage where Zoo was. A Zoo who was hungrier than a primate for bananas never filled any tummy, why fairies covered in gravy was needed and there were many about.

Even Fiends in rancid butter sauce sounded tasty.

"Here is that Apes sailing through the air?" Offaltrex who being a merchant let others do the fighting.

"Is that King Isisnaphut Apes landed on?" Mistress Beautricianix seeing Apes in the corner of a mirror as she smeared on layers of Foundation for a floozy woman must have full red lips always.

"Here we are never invited for any fun, come on Grisly Bear," and Dwarf dug in his spurs to make sure Grisly Bear jumped in amongst the Brethren Brothers.

"No one asks me if I want to play?" Grisly knowing this was not fun; fun to a bear was being part of a circus act jumping through flaming hoops, diving off the tent pole a hundred feet up into a barrel of water, of being lashed to a spinning table so he could see the knife thrower throwing axes at him blinded folded. Yes, that was fun, not tearing limbs from limb Brothers with flaming pitch forks and machetes.

So Grisly Bear was not happy so took his anger out on anything within reach.

"Hallo lads," Wamba now clear of nasty people wanting to shred him.

"Have some tobacco?" Conan hoping, he would not as tobacco cost money and a merchant we know stood near rubbing his hands in anticipation of tobacco prices going up.

"My hero," Christina and shut her eyes to swoon in Womba's arms for she did not want to see what held her for Wamba had long hairy warts.

And because her eyes were shut did not see Zoo eat till he was bloated and could not move.

Lucky for Wamba because his men were walking off to South Gate Haliput where many inns waited for them that had cousins of Common as Muck Filthy Big Bertha living there and a girl on every corner with these lines, "Hi handsome, want to drink iced tea with me?"

"Where are you going without me?" Wamba wanting home to The Bridge and thingamabobs. "Cowardly Zoomorphosis's that is what you are, reptiles with scales, "the foolish sergeant who was too busy opening his mouth to see Zoomorphosis was offended at being likened to Garrison that was unwashed and unclean and ate anything.

So was annoyed and jumped out the cage and did another misdemeanour on Wamba.

So, even Fiends thought a rowing trip healthier and followed the sneaking tip toeing Palace Guard of Barbarossa to South Gate, "Siss, let that Burke deal with Zoomorphosis," they whispered.

And the sneaking became a rout and routed all over Wamba and Zoo, lucky for Wamba yes.

Why Zoo was flattened flat and could not eat Wamba for Zoo was seeing stars and spinning ketchup bottles.

"Gee up," a king on a wagon swigging meths.

And lucky for Wamba King Arawan threw him in the back of his wagon and headed for South Gate for he got a lift; because the king was blind drunk and did not know where his mules were going as they had been at his meths to, they were drunk mules.

"Here you are Garrison you are not welcome here," the City Watch at South Gate afraid of Garrison who it was said were troublemakers, stole your women from under you, ate your supper while you visited the outhouse, bought thingies from a certain merchant, and charged your account while you were at the movies so Garrison was unwelcome.

"Here lads, they are heroes, the crowd wants them," the merchant wanting thingies bought and charged to who was at the movies.

"Gee up," and all made way for Arawan.

"Hello," Wamba wakening up at the wrong moment and was recognised by the Haliputians as the worst troublemaker ever so set upon Garrison but not Barbarossa who was a hero for trying to stop Garrison entering Haliput.

Nor The Duke whose men because they had wages were welcome to ravage their daughters and drink too much XXX and be ill on the pavements where you did slip the next day and incur an expensive doctor's bill for the leeches used to cure your broken leg.

Even the Brother Hood were welcome in their hoodies so were not recognised as they loitered markets holding machetes and pitch forks looking for monsters.

"Fiends this way," an entrepreneur who knew Fiendish gold was as good as Ballenese gold and Harry showed them certain houses down at the docks to hide the Fiends away and fleece them at the same time.

"Matches anyone," King Arawan giving away free boxes to the crowd for Garrison was not welcome.

"He is indeed an ugly thing but so muscular and big," that daft princess who should be dyed brunette and stuck in a tower to grow her hair long! **Was it she who saved Garrison from a roasting?**

"Ouk," Apes swinging amongst the crowd so Zoomorphosis would not find him? So, **did Apes rescue Garrison?**

"Belch," Zoomorphosis arriving in the crowd looking for Apes but then saw Wamba who had likened him to Garrison and then saw Garrison sampling pies bought from a pie vendor so must have some pies too.

"Lovely, a soldier marches on his stomach," Conan licking the gravy off his fingers and then saw Harold eat his third meat pie and there was a ringed tail sticking out of the pie.

"Without my pies the streets of Haliput did be overrun with rats," that man again who jingles your cash.

So, who saved Garrison from a roasting?

Was it Zoo ill from eating a hundred pies with ringed tails sticking out of them?

Perhaps it was the hundred rats running loose without tails?

Who saved Garrison?

Was it you?

CHAPTER 45
PITTER PATTER

"What do you mean a Zoomorphosis is in my city?" Drunken Noddy.

"He has eaten many that live in South Gate," General Elfrid and hoped the creature did eat his king who kept sending him to Pitter Patter who now owned his wife, his twenty girlfriends, his sixty children and rowing boat so could not afford any more bribes to stay alive.

And was so unimaginative he could not see Pitter Patter had done him a favour, why had given him a second chance at life again so should be grateful to The Chief Executioner. He was free to visit Filthy Big Bertha's every night instead of weekends only. He could stop planning to leave a pile of his outdoor clothes on the beach and sneak away to start a new identity, he had FREEDOM without being drawn and quartered.

And did not tell his loathsome king whose breath curled your hair as it was 100% XXX, that Haliput had taken a shine to Christina with the pretty ankles.

He and the twenty million fairies that lived in the city would keep it their little secret. Twenty million plus those about to be born for fairies knew how to spend their time wisely.

"Here my King your breakfast," General Elfrid and gave Noddy cheap green stuff that had fallen off a wagon the night before.

"Gad I am dying," Noddy being used to Champaign for royal XXX's drink upper class XXX for breakfast.

"I will marry Christina and have palaces not a rundown town house and a galley and not a rowing boat," Elfrid and should have made sure the king was dead by poking his liver, but he was drooling over Christina's pretty ankles because he was a man and men think of nothing pure.

"Off with his head," Noddy recovering and lit a cigar so there was a loud explosion and still Noddy was standing and proved the saying correct, XXX makes drunks rubbery so when they fall off a skyscraper they bounce away and drink another day.

And a singed General Elfrid was led away to the chopping board muttering Christina my love where Art Thou? So, perhaps had played ambition in a rose garden with Tootanfoot?

And all about him the mob was rioting to make Christina queen and Harry was wrath for it was a jolly excuse to loot his shops.

Eat his pies, free the rat cages out back, steal Satirextex's writing tools by shaking bags of peanuts about and even by mistake of course, carried Harry to the docks and dumped him with these words, "Bye Drunken Noddy."

"I will recoup my loses as I own many Funeral Parlours," that man who sells you plastic thingies as everyone looted everyone to be in the scene and did not hear the city watch copying pitter patter as they "pitter patter" to arrest and end FREEDOM.

And a lit tobacco was dropped by someone fleeing for his life and was Conan. So never saw the dangerous thing roll away into a stable filled with straw.

"FIRE," the mob screamed.

And Wamba bending down to tie up his leggings was kicked into the stables and the doors kicked shut.

"Bray," the donkey responsible then eyed up a horse.

"Blink," the horse blinking an invitation and was Old Nag

who thought the donkey the sexiest thing ever seen.
"Bray," the donkey making a run for it.

Shame and double misery that poor horse only wanted some attention; cruel Tootanfoot in his donkey suit.

CHAPTER 46   HE
LET HIM IN

In South Gate Haliput a statue of a camel and not any camel, this one has vampire teeth, bat ears, a dragon's face and muscular body, a devil's tail protrudes from some place smelly and smoke drifts from the mouth; and of course, the feet are hooves.

"My finest work," Sampenciltrex and none did disagree for they knew that certain salesman paid his wages.

A plastic plaque made from melted down dinosaurs read,
"Zoomorphosis," and was the only lines
needed from Satirextex thankfully.
And the artist forgot the rat tail Zoo liked to hide for vermin are secretive beasts.
"Women faint over vermin tails," Sampenciltrex hoping to catch a few.
"And never was a vampire?"
"Women need their necks bitten by handsome vampires," Sampenciltrex hoping to be that handsome Dracula, *in his dreams maybe?*

And decades earlier Zoomorphosis had demolished most of South Gate for he was inside the city while he should have been locked out.
"It was Garrison's fault and explains why they are hated," Harry experimenting with a cigar, for the image of course.

"Cough wheeze gasp, why am I smoking this horrid thing, oh yes the image."

And the city council was paying ten thousand to fight Fiends and in negotiations over wages so was broke so borrowed from Harry Bros. PLC to rebuild burnt houses and Harry built slums with outhouses hanging over canals that emptied into the breezy sea.

"Fish for sale," a fishmonger.

"It smells," a slum tenant.

"Do you know what fresh fish smells like," the vendor.

"No."

"It smells like this fish," and obviously had to be a relation of you know who?

"We will charge a toll at the new gate to pay Harry off," a yuppie councillor hoping to impress Harry and get a job on the board of Harry Bros. PLC.

And Harry demoted the yuppie to the new job of toll collector as he was a noticed aspirer. "Bright minds are dangerous so must be swatted quickly," Harry explaining his ways.

And Harry was so rich he did not have to work but knew everything was his by divine right. Why the kids playing with the pigs in farmyards needed his management and cures for Swine Fever jars of his medicinal leeches.

"Slurp," Harry overcome with greed and embarrassed wipes drool of his mouth.

And Sampenciltrex would chisel gargoyles on every street corner so all fairies did know who was watching their every move, HARRY.

He who looked like the gargoyles, he who made slurping sounds over his cash.

And the slurpier gazed at the stars and saw the future, the new gate would collapse as it was made of paste and paper mashie and the new loan to the city would have strings attached.

Strings that made him mayor and a key to the city cash box,

"ha he HO," Harry.

*

And Apes was blamed for letting Zoomorphosis into the city and was a lie.

Once upon a time General Elfrid was for the chop and bribed pitter patter to let him have a leak with these words, "I need the other business as well," and was lies as we all know everyone for the chop goes to the outhouse first as not to disturb the proceedings of chopping.

And General Elfrid with maniacal giggles found Zoomorphosis outside South Gate and held up a sign in big red letters for Zoo to read.

"THIS WAY," the sign but Zoo could not read but came anyway wanting to tear Elfrid limb from limb and eat him all up.

So, Elfrid seeing the foam at Zoo's mouth cleared off quick and melted away in the crowd waiting to be torn limb from limb by Zoo entering the city.

"That demon from hell will eat Drunken Noddy and I will be king and marry Christina and if she has pretty ankles her knees must not be knobbly but pretty too," the pervert Elfrid.

"Where is he, it does not take anyone that long in the outhouse?" The Chief Executioner fed up waiting for Elfrid to return and get chopped.

"Honey, I will marry you and be king," Elfrid a mile away explaining things to Christina whose face slowly curled up so Elfrid began to wonder if her digestive juices were not working.

"Never fear sweetheart this book I bought from Harry the merchant says a Zoomorphosis favourite meal is a cauldron of sea anemone and the beast has reason and if promised regular meals of sea anemone will be obedient," but Christina was not listening for she had joined Garrison nearby.

"They can join the sea anemone for my princess is too high birth to walk with Garrison," Elfrid and found two slaves and a cauldron.

"They are star fish but he has never seen a star fish or anomie," a fishmonger who would give Harry the Boss a cut of cash later.

"Here nice beast, a cauldron of sea anemone your favourite dish," Elfrid.

"Snort," Zoo sort of went for he hated sea anemone but loved slaves so ate them before he ate Elfrid who believed everything he read.

But Harry's book was the only one on the subject so sold a million copies overnight and Satirextex was up all-night copying and went through a packet of crackers for the parrot.

"Here can I have a tea break?" The poet huddled under a candle and when that went out in moon light for candles cost pennies.

"Crack," the answer as Harry ate Coffin Pie from a table but knew how to use a whip as he ate a chicken's head; never mind the entrails were next and some thing's toes, a lost thingy for vitality and the pie was only fit for the strongest souls, those who could sell you a plastic dinosaur; but it was Coffin Pie and guaranteed to put you in one.

*

"You set fire to our city," a man selling garters shouted at Garrison.

"Does he work for me?" Harry attracted by the shouting.

"Caught it in the moat," a woman shouted who took a break from washing unmentionables.

"A Chinese laundry with her the washing machine," Harry dreaming.

"Now no one will buy my meat pies as sea anemone is the craze," a pie seller and Harry noted he must do something to increase the rat population to make his pies wanted again.

"And that pie seller is not one of mine, slurp," for cash was being mentioned.

And the pie seller threw one of his unwanted pies with a tail sticking out of it and a man caught and swallowed it tail as well and was Harold always willing to try a free supermarket sample.

"How much for your rats?" The pie maker asking a nearby hunter.

"A penny each as no one wants one," the hunter.

"Make it a penny for two," the pie maker and bought a sacksful.

"He does not work for me either," the slurpier visualizing one Guild for all workers and anyone working needing a licence and as mayor he would get his cut: and those that
did not join, there was zoomorphosis who did be on his payroll or else.

"And for just now must send in hired help to make those with loud voices join my new Guild."

And the hired help knew what to do with the hunter's legs for he needed them to run after rats, and they knew what to do with the pie maker's hands that he needed to make pies with. And the washer woman they did not know what to do with so just threw her in the moat with cement.

"Splash," and a big splash for washer women are always big with lots of wet petticoats.

And because Zoo found beggars with hacked off limbs nearby who could not run as fast as the other fairies, he ate them. And because the rats had nothing to eat now, they bred and crawled up your legs when you sat in the outhouse; and worse got in your bed when you thought your luck was in with the neighbour's wife.

So, the rats had to go and since sea anemone stank lying in the bottom of cauldrons fairies desired meat again, with ringed tails.

"Coffin Pie is selling well," that greedy merchant " as the tails are not noticed amongst all the gore," that miser Harry and "Coffin Pies sell well because fairies want a bit of everything so everything goes in except the best cuts of meat, and who is too notice with all of them tails swimming about under that pasty?"

"Buy Coffin Pie," soon became a popular jingle.

"And wiggle a tail," and yes was Satirextex earning his keep.

CHAPTER 47 A
MATCH WAS LIT

"And we got Harry Bros. PLC to thank for these fine tenements built after The Great Fire of Hal 945," a tourist guide in an open wagon while an usherette sold candy for tourist teeth shatter on; and the tourists were not impressed for the fine tenements looked like the slums they lived in, and a front with a Harry Dentist Plc with a welcoming door, but inside no more walls, just a mule whose tail was attached to string and stocks for the sufferer to sit in, and never mind.

And a chimney pot fell off and silenced the guide and the tourists were immediately happy.

"Let us party," one tourists and fizzy drink was opened and hip hop music was beat out of a plastic dinosaur.

"My dinosaurs have many uses and why are so popular," that $ whisper again.

And although the Harry's might control what you bought; they could not control Haliput's druids so did not control history.

And sometimes a white rabbit jumped out of Harry's pocket or he grew bat ears so showed he was trying and an H letter would illuminate the city at night as a search light roamed the sky; give the miser his due he was trying.

And the truth of history was that a watchman lit a match and handed it to the crowd who wanted to roast Garrison.

"It is out," was heard often as the match was passed

around.

"Fire," some fairy and "why are you breathing on it?" Another as Arawan breathed 100% meths so the fire spread quickly.

"I must organise a mincer to work a sausage machine, why all the rats are cooked and just need collecting in plastic buckets," and it was Harry from his black book seeking addresses of minor relations.

SO.

"Hot dogs one mark," a minor Harry vegetarian relation pushing a mobile steamer and swinging those buckets under the barrow vegetarian neep dash hounds and, on the barrow, an unused mincer.

"Everyone will thank me, why vegetarian sausage dogs are fit for nothing except being eating in hot chili sauce," Harry defending his plummeting hot dog sales.

"No, forgive me Boss," a vegetarian aspirer being hauled away to be replaced by a rat devouring aspirer for Haliput loved MEAT.

"Argh," the sound of a vegetarian aspirer thrown to her new job, to give Zoomorphosis his daily wash and dry followed by teeth flossing.

"Ha Ho ha that will teach my aspirers to think," Harry and the aspirer was so loved by Zoomorphosis the fink changed his eating habits to eventually become a vegetarian. **Now, the rat lovers happy and he vegetarian readers satisfied?**

Anyway: "Is not this cheating?" Conan as Garrison was left as all the citizens had run away with their beds and mistresses but left the wives as the fire spread. Never mind the wives ran away with the savings.

"Certainly not," and Arawan handed Conan a paper and Garrison pretended to read it before it was snatched away.

"A mandate from Daghdha the good god to clean up this city," Arawan.

"We can read," Tom.

"But not that for it was in pictures," Conan.

"The language of the gods," Arawan.

"It had pictures of us," Wamba.

"Oh, you noticed," Arawan and shuffled his feet guilty so Garrison was worried. Then all Garrison plus the eyes of that nasty dog glared at Arawan who became a shuffler. "Look but it is not important," and he lied for he knew Daghdha had grown fond of Garrison who were brave and never spoke with a forked tongue so had spared them the flames and was not cricket as Arawan had been after Garrison for years.

Harry as well for he wanted paid.

Yes, Arawan could scream his disappointment but the meths was sharp so could not, and his imps ran between his legs with flaming torches setting him on fire; by accident of course for he was the cruel Boss.

"Pardoned?" Tom wanting rid of his innocent boy next door look.

"Pardoned," Conan glad he was granted more time to ravage.

"Pardoned," Wamba and was not surprised as he never did anything wrong.

"Pardoned," and Harold roasted mushrooms off Arawan who was jumping about as he did not like what he dished out to others, it was Karma.

"Woof," and was doggy for "Pardoned," so Cur bit the roast mutton out of Arawan while he could.

"Ouk," and Apes stuck two bananas in Arawan's eyes for he was mean, nasty, and liked to act big and tough for the primate was.

"Gad my eyes," a natural response from Arawan.

"Here what is good for some flea-bitten chimp is good for a dwarf," and Dwarf got Grisly Bear to do 'The Mashed Potato' dance on Arawan.

"I am mashed," the only reply from Arawan and sought comfort in meths.

"Here wait for me," Moronicus running after his Lost Patrol who did not want to be drafted as fire men for that was heroic work and these marines were selfish, slobs, suffering colic for they ate with their fingers as never washed the fingers after a visit to the outhouse that belonged to Harry Plc that charged for loo paper, so was lots spare.

"I never forget the bottom of a boot," Arawan knowing they did meet again one day.

"Haliput is on fire, better put the fire out lads," and was a whisper fearing his warehouses full of plastic dinosaurs might catch fire.

And Wamba had no idea what to do until he saw Book on the back of Arawan's wagon lying next to dead Fiends and crisp fairies so stole it and stuck it down his trousers. And still had no idea what to do for he had not read a page.

"Use the cauldrons full of sea anemone to put the fires out," the whisper as a warehouse exploded and showered plastic dinosaurs down.

"Here those idiots are not supposed to do that?" Morrigan the Queen of Heaven as she drove by in a chariot pulled by cats.

And Daghdha was worried for it had been his idea to spare Garrison that was now putting out the fires with cauldrons of sea anemone.

There were many cauldrons with sea anemone put out for Zoomorphosis to eat, so there was no need to fill the cauldrons with moat or open sewer water that might have caused the fire to spread as Arawan used those places as little boy places and Arawan was pure meths.

Which explained why eels and carp floated on the surface quite dead from XXX poisoning?

"Here what have I done?" Harry realising, he should let Haliput burn to the ground so his builders could cram more slums into the cleared areas. Why the empty parks did be warehouses, the museums sweat shops behind a cultural façade, the schools places that taught children how to sew and become cleaners so Harry was not happy with himself.

CHAPTER 48
SHUFFLERS

FUTURE.

And tourists file through King Charles throne room admiring his wooden throne and have free menu pamphlets from Harry Bros. PLC the only thing free.

'Charles the XXX lover who taxed his citizen fairies gold marks to drink more XXX and ate from plastic plates for he drank your gold marks. Sat on a wooden throne for he fermented your gold marks. And because he gurgled your gold marks, he had stewed rabbit and vegetables between emptying barrels of XXX while you could only afford them pies with tails hanging out of them.

See the hammock King Charles swung in snoring with his twenty-six wives and they were your wives on a rota.

See his loo, wood and splintered and was a lie, he stripped it of its gold plate to buy imported African XXX made form bananas.

And you had to use an outhouse and deep hole that you often fell in.

For our houses do not have electric light switches.

See his loo paper, leaves so you can imagine what your ancestors used?

See his daughter's rose garden and the hundred skeletons of suitors who could not find their way out of the maze there, a maze she tempted gardeners in to play dominoes while your," but the guide became afraid for Christina was a popular memory for a hundred films has been made about her ankles; so, the guide whispered in true Harry fashion, *"while your ancestors read tax demands as they walked the open sewers that were the old streets of Haliput before Harry Bros. PLC laid down roads."*

A future where the roads where not laid down where weeds grew and monkeys threw fruit at you from window guttering. So, Harry had to make the past gruesome for the future was hell come to Haliput.

A future where a weak puppet king sat on a wooden throne while Harry's descendants played Cluedo till the night there would be no Muppet King?

*

And skipping back in time Christina skips into the throne room followed by Wotanic and others who had a vital interest in staying away from Pitter Patter.

A bottle of cheap meths rolled at the feet of Drunken Noddy.

"Snore," from the royal drunk; so, Christina because it was daddy pulled his feet so the snorer rolled down his steps that led up to the cheap wooden throne.

"Who did that?" The head when it stopped bouncing.

"She did," for the others in the room feared Pitter Patter.

And the drunk went nuts and spanked his daughter good so the others in the room fell to their faces and shuffled backwards covering their ears hopping not to be recognised.

Like Mr Salomatrix who sold fish in the slums so Noddy was not his customer ever.

Or Mr Plaguetrex whose bread never rose and was full of baked roaches and Noddy never bought from him.

Or Mr Veilo the butcher who bought ingredients from a hunter and since Noddy had no friends except a green bottle never ate his meats with tails.

But the others could not help themselves looking for Christina was being spanked and they were a bunch of dirty old men deserving Pitter Patter who could be heard in the corridor outside.

"Pitter Patter."

"You should not have down that daddy?"

"Why not?"

"I am a big girl now," and did not mention she had a black belt in Kung Fu so Noddy screamed some as Christina did a mental number on him.

"Ga," was the ending sound as she made him swallow the glass beads, he gave to her mummy but she stashed the diamond tiara he had bought for a waitress in her pocket.

"Business will be brisk," Pitter Patter outside looking at a catalogue of new yachts.

And the shufflers stopped amazed.

"When he wakes up, we are chopped," and it takes one shuffler so they all shuffled backwards at great speed right over Pitter Patter trying to decide what sailor hat to buy from his bribes to come.

"Here what happened?" Noddy coming too.

And the shufflers being curious stopped to listen better.

"This?" Christina and showed Noddy.

"What was the answer?" The shufflers shuffling foreword again over a prostrate Pitter Patter.

"Gee up," was heard in the corridor and a strong smell of meths as a certain king approached for a Pitter Patter lay peaceful with a dozen axes in his back, three dozen cheese wires about his neck, sixteen knives in his chest, yes there was a murderer amongst the shufflers who had it in for the Chief Executioner Pitter Patter.

"Long live Queen Christina," Wotanic suddenly behind the throne and showed the shufflers he was a cringing twerp of an aspirer.

"Sniff," Christina realising he had down much shuffling himself so smelt bad under the arms that were held high holding the crown.

And in hell Pitter Patter was plucking arrows and axes from his legs when he heard "Revenge baby," from many past clients he had used blunt axes on for they had not bribed him enough and many, "have we got a surprise for you sweetheart," from those who bribed and being a lazy Chief Executioner had not used an axe but just opened the lion cages so he could have a long lie in being a weekend execution.

Bad executioner whose clients expected the best from you, a sharp axe not sharp teeth gnawing the wrong places.

And Arawan was a king who listened to his subjects for he did not want a revolution so turned his back and did not hear the screams as he slurped and gurgled from a green bottle of meths.

See even amongst fairies there is Karma at all levels of society, what goes round comes round.

"Refreshing stuff this meths," Arawan and gurgled happily away sucking the vile stuff out of a baby bottle. "Suck," he sucked.

*

Now mention of a fairy must be made whose military upbringing made him fearless of shufflers.

An utterly selfish man and a survivor.

And worse, ambitious, Wotanic is his name a son of a general the son of a general, the son of a mule Skinner.

"My kingdom for a mule," Wotanic still believed was good advices for kingdoms come and go but a good mule is hard to replace.

And that ends that unwanted interruption about this unloved unwanted creep of a fairy man.

Now mention must be made of Dwarf who rides a Grisly Bear so that explains a lot for a start.

I mean would you or I ride a ferocious Grisly Bear?

And Dwarf sees bears as flea circuses and hates them especially this Grisly who wants in on all the fun Dwarf is having so Dwarf uses extra-long sharp spurs.

And Dwarf believes gold is under Haliput and needs him to dig it out. Why he is the son of a gold miner and inherited that cave and was seeing gold in the dim candlelight in the cave when Zoo arrived.

"I will chain him up without a fuss," Zoo and he was right

for Dwarf was sure he was digging for gold nuggets that only existed in his mind.

So traded his pickaxe for a mop and apron and became Zoo's Hygiene Personal Assistant.

"He is bigger than me so must do what I am told," Dwarf sensibly so washed up thirty years of dirty dishes and when he dusted the pillow well, it was Grisly and is to horrid to describe what happened next.

"I hate that bear," Dwarf's famous words.

CHAPTER 49   CORPSE

FUTURE

There is no X at the spot where the gods discussed business.

For in the future Give a Copper Harry wanted it secret, he who sits on a gold throne while relations huddle the long table slurping up tasty watery gruel.

For in the future Haliput is ruled by a dead thingy whose hands get hairy under a full moon and Harry's relations feed it vile potions, a most dangerous occupation so why Harry sits on a gold throne, for he is the one full of potion and the dead thingy to.

And a creature under the moon howled for viler potion and was Harry.

"Yes, we the relations tremble for look fangs have flipped out behind those rubbery gums."

And Harry in the future had a shaky voice for he was old so squeaked, "Never repeat what the gods said or it will undermine our rule over the puppet boy king. The gods that met in the Sparrow Inn because there was waitress service available while their wives were at Bingo , and they drank and ate Coffin Pie thinking Haliput was burning away but Wamba was out there with cauldrons, making me safe to breed and carry on the Harry lineage,"

*

PRESENT

"What is Wamba up to?" Morrigan next to Daghdha at the table and the good god patted and squeezed her knee under the table for Nerthus the wife was present, sucking the claws off a chicken foot for the wives had returned unexpected for Bingo was cancelled. Never mind the husbands were delighted to see them back early.

"Lovely," Nerthus as she sucked away, "Coffin Pie lovely," and next crunched away at a cow's foot.

"Judas," Daghdha going red as Morrigan not to be fobbed off had skewered a certain hand with a fork under the table.

And Morrigan's cats that pulled her chariot scratched the blazes out of Tanaros's goats that pulled his chariot, who went nuts and kicked the stuffing out of the boars that pulled Daghdha's chariot, who needed something to tusk so did the green stags that pulled Cernunous's chariot he being the Green Man here and in the melee demolished South Gate.

And there was no rain a pity as the fires might have been put out for some Mage had given Ball a Californian climate .

And saved all those tenements with nappies drying on strings from burning, saved wives cooking pasta on hot stoves who snatched kids playing football in the narrow streets and saved themselves, and gone playing in green fields once the fire burned the place down. Saved Harry the trouble of repairs but not the cost of building new slums.

Now Morrigan went for walkies as Daghdha tried to explain what a fork was doing in his hands to the wife.

And Morrigan was happy thinking of doing Wamba and then noticed the fires out and empty cauldrons about and the stench of sea anemone.

"The smell of a stagnant sea that leads one to the fishmonger," Aslop wisely.

"Hi honey," and Morrigan smelled meths as burly hands threw her into a wagon where a red eared hound waited to gnaw her.

"A soul is a soul," Arawan croaked and was the last croak he croaked in many a night as she beat the blazes out of him. "What have I thrown in my wagon," and shrieked as Morrigan pulled him places.

"Well boys we put the fire out," Wamba looking at a pile of exhausted Garrison that wanted him away from them.

And one of them threw a cauldron at him but missed and hit Morrigan, lucky for Wamba as it was made of brass and not cast iron.

"I smell Garrison and now a war galley is moored in Dockland," Morrigan rubbing her head.

And the creak of wheels made her look and see saw a coach pass by on its way to Dockland.

And Dockland was named that because docks and ships could be found, and jars of cockles and mussels and jellied eels and gutters full of snoring sailors full of XXX.

"Here," and Morrigan threw the cauldron back just as Wamba was bending to pick up a penny.

So hit Garrison who staggered away muttering things such as, "My legs are broke," "My arms are twisted," "my wooden leg has fallen off," but where all lies for, they had seen who threw the brass cauldron so were sneaking off playing possum, sneaking
towards a war galley that had no oarsmen now or sea dog to gnaw rowers to get the speed up.

"Here I do not believe you," Wamba knowing any fairy with a broken leg could not walk so stood laughing the Burke.

Then Morrigan about to beat the living daylights out of Wamba sniffed him for Wamba smelt of rotten sea anemone and socks and unmentionables for he did not know what the word 'bath' meant.

"Daghdha can sort you out, I am off," Morrigan and pooled away in a sulphur cloud for she was nasty not good, so no chirping sparrows or sunshine about her, just smells that wafted from Wamba.

"I am going to be sick," she was heard to complain in the green mist and "Does he never wash?"

"I am out of here," Wamba worried she might be ill over him and then the princess did think he never washed.

"Here wait for us," Conan grabbing Womba's belt so was dragged behind for he was feeling lazy.

"And me," Tom that sweet innocent kid grabbing Conan by his left foot for Garrison could not afford to buy new shoes often.

"Ouk," Harold and sat on Tom and urged him to shriek and moan as the excited retired Viking beat Tom's back with his massive fists.

"Ouk," the arthritic Viking being reminded of snowboarding in his homeland.

"Ouk," Apes swinging down on Harold attracted by the drum beat on Tom.

"Banana for you friend," Harold and was sickening as Apes replied, "Ouk" and Apes took the banana and started to beat Harold who replied, "OINK," and kicked Apes away for retired Vikings who say "oink" are a tough greedy bunch.

Then a nasty dog jumped on the top of Ape's head so Apes could see nothing and Cur ate the banana to see what banana tasted like.

"Woof," the hitching hiking dog which meant, "better in ice cream and chocolate sauce."

And Garrison never saw the coach stop at the docks and the soldiers on it held out hands for gold pennies that had Drunken Noddy's head stamped on them, pennies in the hands of the press gang paying the soldiers. For a certain war galley at harbour needed two hundred rowers and now had none.

So, the coach door opened and the smell of cheap XXX wafted then Noddy rolled out and kept rolling off the pier so he dropped into a jolly rowing boat below.

"Crunch," the sound of wood breaking so the little boat sank.

"The captain needs rowers and he is one and I am not," the press gang leader so kicked his men below so they screamed in the water where fins lived to save the drunk below and put him in another jolly rowing boat.

"Here where are the sailors to row this drunk out to the war galley?" The press gang leader and then suggested, "We better row or we will take his place," the foolish fool for a war galley needs two hundred rowers and with the drunk and them would then have ten.

FUTURE

"What I have told you never tell anyone," Harry in the future then howled for viler potion? Was he the one who let fangs flip out from rubbery gums? What was Harry in the future apart from the greatest salesman ever and just what was in those vile potions that let him be in the future when Garrison was just plastic statues with pigeons sitting on them doing pigeon things.

Vile potions made especially for nasty boys that grew into oily salesmen bought from Mages who lived three thousand years.

*

And in the future a poet sat in candlelight thinking of fine poetry that did not come for he was dim witted.

"Oh, Haliput under the rainbow.

A rainbow of vice," for Satirextex was at work.

"How do your citizens sleep?

For the streets are full of bugs,

Vermin,

Muggers and drunks.

And dinosaur vendors," and Satirextex threw a cream cracker at a parrot chained to a bird perch and the parrot put down a quill and ate the cracker and gasped for water.

"Another twenty lines for a glass of water?" Satirextex giving away the secret of his horrid poetry and when the lines where finished pulled a cord and an urchin appeared fresh from the street below.

"Deliver this to Dog Publishers," and gave the boy a slice of lard as payment.

"Yummy," the boy and ran as fast as he could for perhaps then Harry who owned Dog Publishers did be so impressed, he did spare some salt and pepper on the lard to make it tasty.

And nearby a spider monkey put down a chisel and stood back to admire its work, an armless woman called Armless Venus.

"Catch," Sampenciltrex throwing it payment, a nut that it missed and the nut rolled away into a dark corner, "never mind when you finish David over there, I will give you two nuts."

And the spider monkey being ravenous went to work on the statue of David and made David nude for the monkey was thinking nuts, walnuts, almonds and Brazil's, any nut if it was a nut.

And Satirextex and Sampenciltrex saw Harry as a philanthropist who built slums for the poor to breed in and demand slums for their children to live in. Yes, without Harry they did be two unknown relations begging, of course after using a hack saw on the legs to get the crowds sympathetic.

"Personally, I do not understand all the fuss about a picture with parrot droppings on it?" Harry soaking in a bath of gold marks. "Or why fairies want to buy statues of some sailor at the top of a column?" And Harry made sure all the gold marks in the bath with him got a good wash so he could see them sparkle.

CHAPTER 50 SOAP, TOWEL BATH PLEASE?

Now after the fire the remains of the classical public baths was a swinging door for fairies believed in unisex, why even the public outhouses was unisex, but fortunately an outhouse allowed one in at a time.

Why Conan treaded hot embers to find a clean bath for it was his yearly bath time.

And Harold said, "Ouk," and swung to the top of the swinging doors that Garrison left till he fell with a splash into a bath full of soap, water, and soot.

"If you clean up a bag of nuts in it?" Wamba lying.

And Conan found a bath full of sooty water and said, "Lovely, all I need is to dip my toes in it and the soot matches my clothes."

"Woof," a dirty dog needing bathed in flea shampoo and found none so jumped in with Wamba.

"Cur I am been beaten to death," Wamba as fleas sought refuge on him and they would have been safe till he thought of Christina smelling of roses and wonderful things girls are made off?

So sank in the soapy water and drowned the flea circus on him, no that was them pinging away though an open window to fresh air and FREEDOM and your pet.

"Hear princesses love smelly barbarians living on the back

of a horse to ravage them," Conan and was a misconception the idiot believed in because he was a barbarian idiot.

"Here you cannot come in here without paying," and was the bath attendant wearing a Job Worthy Cap form the days of Ester Ransom when those who obeyed the smudge on the bottom of the page wore a cap.

So, he was a mighty big fool for this was Garrison that paid for nothing except for waitress service for them girls knew these magic words, "No credit giving."

"Move buddy if you want to live," Tom and was this the sweet Tom we know?

And Wamba flipped a penny towards the attendant who knew he did get a farthing from it and Harry the rest for Harry Bros. PLC had many tentacles.

Slimy oily tentacles needing chopping off.

And as Garrison washed none of them noticed a hooded figure slip into the baths and rub a dub himself with soap.

"Here that smells of coin I recognise?" Conan being a ravaging temple looter knew what coin smelt like.

"Yes, like the coin the waitresses give me to come upstairs and play SNAP with them for I am so handsome and innocent," Tom and **was so sickening.**

"Yes, like the wages we never get?" Wamba giving his nasty dog a good soaping.

"Woof," the nasty dog biting Wamba and translated means, "That is Dirty Harry PLC?"

And it was him come to collect the penny given the attendant.

"These baths will be built to Olympic size so can harvest more pennies," that greedy whisper.

"Moan," from the attendant not wanting to hand over the penny he hid in the soap but the hooded one had sneaked up to the penny holder, grabbed his ears, and boxed them good till the penny came out the attendant's nose.

"A cheap magic trick," the hooded one we know as Harry.

And the penny being soapy slipped from his grasp and fell into soapy water.

"Ouk," from him who stood in the soapy water?

"What am I to do?" Harry fearing to be near the retired Viking oarsman.

"Ouk," an answer from the rafters as Apes sought bananas from, he who had a wagon pulled by mules.

"Here fetch," Harry throwing a banana amongst the soap.

"EEK," Apes as Harold thought a retired Viking woman had joined him for them that live in those cold freezing climates must be hairy and big too withstand the cold?

"EEK," Harold realising his mistake.

"I will always wear a black hood as I see the potential of disguise," Harry always after a free penny said. From now on no one was safe, for BLACKHOOD was about.

Beggars begging will be mugged for they are easy prey to BLACKHOOD.

Your washing stolen from washing lines as an easy prey to BLACKHOOD.

The washer women vanished as an easy prey to BLACKHOOD.

Chinese Laundry owned by BLACKHOOD.

Chinese rail workers siphoned off by BLACKHOOD.

"They make the best washer women," BLACKHOOD.

"Also rail workers," BLACKHOOD.

Yes, a howling would occur in the future as BLACKHOOD wanted to stay young and breed like vermin.

For he was a salesman so explains why there are many HP agreements waiting to entrap your descendants in the future for BLACKHOOD was not taken to the vet!

BLACKHOOD HP brown sauce a must to squirt on greasy sausages.

BLACKHOOD HP agreements to divert your wages.

BLACKHOOD political Party to make sure his puppet king remained a Muppet King.

BLACKHOOD tomato sauce to make sure Harry stayed rich and you, poor.

BLACKHOOD was fab.

And Blackhood was about to be screwed for a lot of pennies

for Daghdha awoke with a sore head that follows the XXX so screamed, "Aspirins quick," and Morrigan knowing he would never divorce the wife Nerthus pushed his head down so it bounced off the goblet he had drained of XXX the night before.

"Lovely," he moaned but if it had been the wife that had down such a thing?

"Here where am I and whose silkies are these?" Daghdha before he realised the wife was lying next to him holding garden shears.

And quick as a comet across the sky stuffed the silkies onto Tanaros whose girlfriend Aphrodite would find them, never mind as long as they were not found on the good god Daghdha, the fink?

"Garrison put out the fires," Morrigan and since the wife was still asleep adjusted her brassiere so Daghdha gaped drooled and salivated and was disgusting but it was OK he was macho divine.

And Morrigan let his nose get so close then let go the elastic so a nose was caught somewhere.

"She," meaning "wife," might wake up?" A terrified god for garden shears lay close by.

"I own 50% of Harry Bros. PLC and planned new temples and baths and lots of slums for rent," Morrigan letting more than cleavage slip, "now because of Wamba the fires are out and Harry has bought me out because he had lawyers who are afraid of him, and are you afraid of me, dearest?" Morrigan so squeezed Daghdha's nose and pulled his ears then stamped places and got away with everything because she was not the wife who had born Daghdha the good god twenty kids so showed it.

"Who will rid me of Garrison?" Daghdha the good god showing some gods are not good. For all Daghdha the good god could think of was the melons his face was pressed up against, the dirty old god.

"Who will rid me of Garrison, draw, hang and quarter them," the good god Daghdha asked again.

"A war galley needs volunteers and Wamba loves to

volunteer and I will rid you of Wamba but in return Haliput is mine for two hundred years," and was not the wife but Morrigan the stuff on the side wanting what she could out of the miserly ugly beast before she ran off with a Tom Boy god like the new winged Mercury wo wore flying sandals and shiny pants.

For some wrinkles had appeared on Morrigan and rolls of lard on Daghdha.

And Daghdha looked at her and compared her to the wife, the fertility goddess Nerthus, with bosom swollen with milk and ten babies wanting fed from them, and the stink of nappies was rotten, and her hips the size of a walrus for childbearing and her blond hair in pleats and, "agreed," the good god for he knew Morrigan would give him the last dance for he had made her happy.

And Morrigan had essences of expensive perfumes, the invitation of silkies and the allure of wink about her.

"Volunteer Wamba shall," Daghdha drooling at the mouth.

"Hear wipe it," the wife giving him a hanky and he did with these words, "Yucky," for Nerthus being so busy with ten kids hanging from her chest forgot which was nappy and which was hanky.

And Morrigan gave him a look, "Who wears the pants?"

"And tuck your woolly vest in, do not forget to use hair gel on the hair, blow your nose clean and take some salts to settle the wind and do not be late tonight," Nerthus suspicious another woman existed.

"Oh sorry," Nerthus tripping on Daghdha's feet so she dropped the hanky on someone who represented howling on full moons, lies, cheating and dungeon racks and no was not that salesman but Morrigan.

And Morrigan said nothing for gods were present and all regarded Nerthus as "mummy."

"Later I will stuff that nappy some place," Morrigan hissed doing snakes justice.

"And take those hands from underneath the table?" Nerthus fed up and disgusted Daghdha could just sit there ogling Morrigan.

"Here love of my hearts," and Daghdha pushed a diamond ring towards Nerthus and Morrigan fumed.

A diamond ring taken from one of her cats that wore diamond leather gear for the gods always gave Morrigan gifts; for she was that sort of girl and they those sort of gods.

"Cheap bum," Morrigan knowing Nerthus had won coup and coup she would on Daghdha when next she met him privately. Hot tongs and cement about the ankles for starters till she extracted many diamonds out of the good god.

"Meow," the nice pussy cats that pulled her chariot looking forward to ruby and emerald tiaras for cats must look their best all times; tabby mangy ally cats might be ogling them from behind garbage bins!

And as Nerthus showed off a diamond Daghdha tried to follow Morrigan out into the night.

"What is that sound?" He asked.

"Garrison," Morrigan threw back in the wind as she cleared off to find a kind Sugar Daddy without a wife.

"Rub a dub and keep still Harold," Wamba as Garrison fed up with the smell of unwashed Viking unmentionables held him in an open sewer with soap and towel, they had took from the Public Baths.

So being preoccupied did not hear the 'thump' music as a fin parted the sewer water.

"Hiccup gee up," a drunk splashing about the orange peels and Andrex Rolls floating in the water.

"I will beat them black and blue," Daghdha and fumed and strode down to where Garrison was and "Splash," for in dark nights the open sewer is not a place to go fuming.

And landed on the fin just as it was about to eat Harold all up.

"Let go of me Arawan," Daghdha warned as the drunk seeing double thought Apes had come back to him so planned a church wedding.

And in the distance a war galley creaked and at a single oar a drunk slept it off and dreamed of servants pouring a bath, of feeding him kippers while he was scrubbed by a waitress that was the servant, of a cord to pull at any time to summon Pitter Patter who he did not know had met a slimy end.

And when the drunk woke with a mighty headache and screamed, "Aspirins," silence did greet him for he was the only one aboard ship: a lonely engine cog.

"Squeak," and was a rat who being the only rat aboard and lonely did squeak away night and day till Noddy went insane.

"Squeak."

CHAPTER 51   SUMS

And because South Gate was ash and the watch messy thingamajigs on the road because Zoomorphosis had passed by, so Fiends said, "Hey boys there is no guard at the gate," which even for Fiends could make for one answer only, "Does that mean fish suppers tonight?" The Fiendish soldiers hungry and afraid they did meet Garrison again.

And Isisnaphut thinking this a jolly idea agreed so Fiends sneaked into Haliput in single file; and were an exceedingly protracted line for they still numbered hundreds.

"Why do I work for these snail eaters?" Alicadabara stamping his wand again, just never learns that lad so shrieked.

"I make that three hundred and thirty Fiends sneaking by," Conan bored of watching Harold fight the fin in the open sewer.

"Three hundred and sixty," Tom proudly showing his arithmetic workings to Conan who replied, "A barbarian does not need to know how to count just how to burn cities to ash."

"Ouk," Apes appearing handing Conan bananas to count with.

*

FUTURE

Now a plastic statue was built where Wamba lined his volunteers into a Saxon Shield Wall and was made by Sampenciltrex without Harry's permission.

"I was drunk so out of my mind with spinning waitresses so had no memory of making it," Sampenciltrex.

"An empire must have authority and discipline or supermarkets will open next and I will not own them," Harry so sent heavies onto Sampenciltrex.

"It was the monkey that chiselled the statue," Sampenciltrex so the sweet little cuddly monkey wished it were never born.

"Phew," Sam,' "that was quick thinking."

"Ouk," the monkey disagreeing.

So that explains the statue and it was based on true events: **PRESENT**

"Parade shun," Wamba looking at Book so Garrison knew they were volunteers.

"I do not care if you turn me into a snail we are going home and going through that open sewer to sneak back out of Haliput, a Zoomorphosis is about," Isisnaphut telling Alicadabara who was King and Boss.

"Ha he Ha he," Alicadabara having come this far to marry a princess and become a tyrant king was not having any of this squeaky stuff.

"Squeak," Isisnaphut adding effect.

"We are not carrying this throne in that muck?" A pole bearer and there was puff as Alicadabara turned him into something that could swim.

"Quack."

And he did it to be nasty and was warming up for the final.

"There is a fin in there?" Isisnaphut terrifying his army.

"And a royal snail on the throne," Alicadabara and did not lie for he had turned squeak into one.

"Plunk," Alicadabara dropping the snack into a canvas bagful of snails for Fiends knew what to eat on the move.

"Slurp," was heard as the royal snail sank through layers of rancid butter sauce.

"Bray here come Garrison," and it only takes one donkey that could speak.

And Alicadabara lifted his wand and saw a mangy dog.

"Ha he Ha he," he laughed thinking a dog could not do

nasties to him, the great wizard of Rip.

And Cur ripped him up good for he was a nasty animal having learnt to fight dirty in the alleys and in a hut full of Garrison.

"Oh, good the brute has stopped gnawing me," Alicadabara standing up looking for his wand to turn the nasty dog into a cat so it could be gnawed by a passing nasty dog.

"Meow," and was several feline sounds as a chariot passed and the cats pulling it could not resist sharpening their claws on Alicadabara.

"Judas," Alicadabara complained.

"Baaaaaa," the goats having a go at Alicadabara for these animals eat any rubbish.

"Help," Alicadabara getting butted here and there.

Then the boars wanted to be nasty for as all Safari Parks know boars should be behind fences.

"I am finished," Alicadabara lying as he was still breathing.

"Bray," a donkey putting the hoof in for revenge for being pooled into an ass.

Had the local zoo emptied, no they were the animals that pulled the chariots of the gods and liked to taste foreign food.

And in front of Alicadabara Garrison were coming behind a solid wall of shields; four to be exact.

There was Wamba, Conan, Tom, and Harold and behind them a huge ape throwing rotten fruit at Alicadabara.

"I am off," a donkey.

"For medals and beer," Wamba.

"We mash Fiends up," Garrison.

"We do not like that bit," Fiends.

"And I own 50% of Harry Bros. PLC," Morrigan pulling her cats off Alicadabara not wanting to be in the middle of this punch up, she had manicured fingernails to worry about so took her kittens to eat Burgers filled with sardines from a vendor nearby who must be a Tartan Army football supporter for he had a red wig of hair and a tartan cap, worse a red moustache and beard needing trimmed.

A vendor she did not recognise but one that had oily hands and smelt of cash? And was too small to be Harry but those ears, like mini cauliflowers, and that nose, long and narrow like a rat, and those hands, skinny like vermin, and those feet long and big like a pet vulture, and that ringed tail? So Morrigan rubbed her eyes, had she been eating too many strange pies with ringed tails perhaps?

Yes, the minions of Harry get about for the Boss sent his many floozy Give a floozy girls wanting silkies and chocolates from the Lowlands to the Highlands in exchange for plastic dinosaurs. "The silkies and chocolates I will take 90% and sell in Haliput, the girls can have the laddered silkies and melted chocolates for I am a caring Boss."

CHAPTER 52   A NOSE

"What is that racket?" A potbellied female victim of the fire stuffing cream buns into her mouth. And she had just been woken up after being asleep for ten minutes. And like many had crawled out of a cardboard box and was lucky The Mage had changed the climate to California where grapes and grapefruits labelled Arnie Schwarzenegger grow in sun drenched valleys stuffed full of Big Foot.

"I am the Terminator," could be heard up and down the Jolly Green Giant gardens.

"We will complain to the landlord," a skinny man who did not get any cream buns for that woman ate them all and the landlord was elsewhere but his heavies returning from a monkey where about to silence complaints.

"There is the racket," the potbellied woman and thought the gods upon them for musicians led a procession where task masters cracked whips on a hundred sweating convicts pulling a throne on twenty log wheels, while maidens sunbathed on platforms flicking grapes at red eyed potbellied victims just crawled out of cardboard slums.
So got red eyes as grapes got stuck in them.
And on the throne a stunning woman with lots of lipstick while two naked barbarians fanned her in invisible clothes for movies without skin do not sell.
At her feet courtesans blowing her kisses.
"Do not look dear," the potbellied woman covering a little man's eyes. And he peeped through the fingers so screamed as

the wife clubbed him with a plastic dinosaur saved from the fire.

So, he fell forward just as a hundred Brethren marched over him, then logs also so never saw the six panthers that sharpened their claws on him, one tiger that gnawed him and two lions that played jump on him, or the duck that laid an egg on him, or the two elephants that walked on him and did something strong on him.

Then behind the litter on logs a hundred horse men and the horses did what horses always do on parades, worse than the elephants as there were only two elephants.

"Hey, look it is The Mage," and was not surprised mushrooms grew from him.

Then a single black horse reared on him and heard, "Hey it is that fink Wotanic."

Then heard "It is the Duke," as a white horse cleaned its hooves on him and the ten thousand marched over him wearing brand new spiked shoes Harry had just sold them.

"I want a divorce," the poor man moaned.

"What was that, why you ungrateful swine after I gave you the best years of my life," that wife again and stomped what was left of him.

And the maidens sang,
"Christina the Great, make way for her,
 Fall on your face for her,
 Bend the knees for her,
 Adore her.
 Look not upon her.
 You are not worthy of her.
 Grovelling worms for her.
 Unclean fairies for her.
 Welcome your queen because she is her."
And then repeated if all for her for was on a loop.

And a new Pitter Patter could be heard coming up the rear of the parade.

'Chief Executioner was written in yellow on his T shirt and red paint had been splashed on the axe for effect; and the night before had been a beggar eating out in royal trash cans.

And in Christina's hand a note, an offer of shares from Harry to buy into Harry Bros. PLC and Christina was angry for if anyone was fleecing her city it was her.

And because she was fuming did not read the smudge that said the shares where Morrigan's for Harry hoped the two would do each other and he did be free of two domineering females, free to poke his nose in public, to wind and let the breeze spread it elsewhere; for he was a swindling oily fairy with a nose full of bogies.

And the procession turned a corner and halted for it had met Garrison fighting Fiends, a goddess in a chariot and her savage cats.

"Fall flat upon your faces," the maidens and trumpets blared.

"I love her," a Burke throwing Fiends back in the open sewer.

"She is my girl," Conan and spat tobacco and the wind carried it to a man flat on his face with divorce papers stuck some place, who was fed up moaning and groaning and accepted life's free latest blessing for he liked a good chew.

"What legs," Tom that sweet innocent boy ogling places for his mind was warped from being Garrison so perhaps was not sweet like we think but someone you would not want to escort your daughter home?

"Ouk," Harold opening his mouth as grapes where thrown in.

"Woof," a dog and shook the cats off its back.

"S**t," the naked fanners as the cats landed on them.

"Bray hello sweetie it is me Tootanfoot," a donkey and Alicadabara cursed the mule for drawing attention to him.

And he bowed low for he was an aspiring twinging wicked evil wizard.

"Lost Patrol salute," the other aspirer and his men gave him strange finger signs ruining his aspirations for Christina could never marry a man who could not rule a platoon?

And a big juicy ugly blue bottle flew off something floating in the open sewer and buzzed happily to a royal finger.

"Chop its head off," a courtesan and Pitter Patter had his first customer.

"Buzz," the flies last words.

And Christina had vision, she wanted suspension on the logs, hanging flowerpots on the throne and incense burners for the open sewer stank and cod pieces on the naked fanners as protection against cats.

And perfume sprayers for Garrison was about.

And as crowd control alligators on leads.

And a cockerel crossed the royal shadow to ogle and chat up a grape eating hen.

"Off with its head," a courtesan and Pitter Patter would be eating roast chicken tonight, the perks of the job.

CHAPTER 53   A STILL VOICE

"I warn you I am a cheap back street wizard," Alicadabara to Brethren wanting to shred him into shreds.

"Fizzle," is all that came out of Ali's stomped upon wand.

"I warn you I was top of the class for spell casting, go away or I will turn you into flies," and was the wrong thing to say as many Brethren wanted to be flies and land on royal knees and such for they were those types mummy warns you about, the fishmonger that offers you kippers for a smile, the baker who offers you a pasty for a wink, the ice cream Brethren who offers you a wafer and cream for a scratch.

"Buzz," and there was a plague of flies swarming about Christina.

"Fly swatters, I will be mega rich," an oily whisper amongst the buzzing.

Then the log pushers were afraid, Garrison was just ahead. Did not Dog Publishers say Garrison foamed at the mouth, slept in coffins, and did not think decent like ordinary fairies who wanted to be flies.

"Hallo Alicadabara and Wamba lifted Ali to his feet for there had been many Brethren wanting to be flies.

"Moan," came from Ali.

And a royal finger twitched and those naked barbarians ran out from Christina with chains and Wamba tossed them aside for ,"A galley needs him." And thought nothing about the shocking naked barbarians that shocked fairies so royal tax collectors fleeced the pockets and when the shock was gone and when you came out of the shock, "Hey I swear I had ten gold marks in this pocket with no hole in it?"

"That Burke has sent us somewhere nasty," Conan warning Tom as he sneaked away and Conan could not guess where?

"An example must be made of him," Wotanic meaning Wamba and Christina had memories of Wamba and Garrison.

"A war galley needs oarsmen," and she repeated the words for an oily whisper was in her ears and he who spoke would tear his last hair strands from his head when he realised Garrison were his best customers. Where not the pockets of his black hood full of I.O.U.'s? So did not jingle with cash but rustled with loo paper for Garrison used those squares for everything imaginable.

"Here Christina they might be Garrison and we do not want them as neighbours?" The Mage shouted up forgetting whose side he was on; but had he, was this not the dirty old man loitering mistletoe grooves with a sickle so should be locked away some place? Perhaps he was slightly schizophrenic and hated Garrison so much he wanted them on a war galley.

"The crowd will back him and pull you off your log throne, quick send him to the war galley," that whisper again forgetting where he got his vile potions to make him live forever from?

"Woof," and that nasty dog made a big mistake for it lifted its legs on the logs.

"Exterminate it, it has vermin ancestry," that oily whisper.

"Woof," Cur pleaded but saw stern royal authority that replied, "I am not amused," so Cur was muzzled and dragged off to a war galley.

"You do not need to worry about that arthritic barbarian and indecent boy Tom they have sneaked onto a war galley to hide from you," that whisper.

"Ouk," Harold crawling up her logs.

"It needs quarantined on a war galley," that hellish oily

whisper.

"Ouk," and Apes swung up the logs.

"Quick leave a trail of bananas to the war galley and keep it away from me," that whisper that had experience of Apes first hand.

But Christina was basically a good girl whose judgement had been clouded from getting rent from eight floored overcrowded slums to replace the four-story present slums and cardboard boxes.

"Remember the profits of one family per ten square feet," that whisper and she repeated it for the whisper wanted her unable to think just dream of cash and more cash and the means justified getting it.

"They are my friends," Christina and saw Conan ravaging a priestess of the sea god Mann so they could expect tidal waves sweeping dockland clear of ship rats and floozy girls that gave girls with pretty ankles a bad name.

There was Tom the innocent sweet boy sneaked off the ship and lifting an orange sellers skirt to see her ankles and knew he was Garrison.

And saw Cur shred a teddy bear belonging to a little cuddly girl with blonde hair and big blue eyes now filled with tears for teddy had a name, "Hen," for teddy wore skirts and bras.

"Without them you can build new schools and charge the poor kids entry, think of the new hospitals filled with patients wanting Harry Cures PLC that you have shares in, and shares in Diseases PLC that think if new germs to spread about," and the whisper was louder for it had gained confidence.

"That poor man," Christina watching Cur scrambles up Conan to stop sinking in the mud that was a road.

"Them types foul your pavements and need dog wardens paid to round them up, just throw it in a war galley and send them all away on a long cruise to foreign lands," the whisper worried Christina was not infected with greed enough.

"They were my friends," Christina remembering the past.

"A great queen has no mates, just a royal finger and Mr Pitter

Patter," the whisper pushing luck.

"Hey, wait a minute I am your friend," and was Wotanic and did the whisper a favour for Christina saw in Wotanic many aristocratic desires centred about her and was ill.

"Send him to the war galley," and her finger went crazy so naked barbarians dragged the aspirer away screaming, "Dearest does this mean our engagement is off?"

And Brethren noticed their new leader was now the queen so dropped and did a hundred press ups and was disgusting as was grovelling at the extreme, for a nasty dog

had passed, and three hundred mummy's changing nappies also, and since it was a parade all the school kids had been present waving flags and eating ice cream.

Yes, it was sickening and Christina felt good that others were squirming so an Aslop moral here, *"royalty never changes like a leopard changing spots."*

"Meow," and was the first warning Morrigan was here.

The second as cats used the Brethren as scratch poles.

"Lovely," the Brethren the best grovellers about.

"I want Garrison for ruining my plans, send them to Arawan now" Morrigan.

"No one tells me what to do apart from Harry who is now known as Blackhood," and the whisperer gloated with pride.

"Your roses will be covered in green fly," Morrigan.

"I have many soldiers."

"I will fill your bath not with milk but leeches."

"I have Brethren to take my place."

"Crocodiles will leave the sewers and eat your citizens, beggars first."

"No one tells me what to do."

"Carbuncles will visit Haliput."

"Guards arrest this goddess,"

And an empty crisp packet floated by.

"Give her Garrison," the whisper changing its tune.

"I want more shares too."

"Look at your citizens filled with the plague of FEAR Garrison gave them," that whisper up to something?

And citizens appeared from hiding places and nodded agreement.

"Do as Blackhood advises, give me Garrison."

And a nasty dog took hold of the black smock and there was a ripping sound so Blackhood was exposed, all pink and hairy for it was hot under that smock.

"Hello Harry," Wamba waved.

"When cash is at stake there are no mates, gone the days of selling plastic dinosaurs, now I own a queen," Blackhood hurrying away for a replacement hood.

"To the war galley with them," Morrigan commanded for that is all she wanted to do, show which woman was in charge.

"We were going there anyway; I do not understand Conan?" That sweet innocent boy so perhaps he was innocent for nothing existed between the ears.

"Pack your alligator bags," Morrigan to be bossy like any woman is.

"It means only one can have pretty ankles and get worshipped by men," The Mage using magic to get ants to carry his luggage to the war galley. He also tried a sneaky "poof" on the goddess but because she floated about clouds all day his magic just went "Poof."

"Send me a post card boy," the mean wicked bossy goddesses stroking her savage cats feeding them sardines.

Sardines she had helped herself from a Blackhood stall.

"A wise salesman knows when to give away a tin of sardines," Blackhood knowing Aslop fables.

"Glad we were not down there," Bat Wing to Old Nag on a nearby hillside.

And a bag of snails began to scream as Harold ate his way through them so long strands of rancid butter sauce splattered everywhere.

"Missed me," a royal snail in the bag.

"Manacle that one, it has long hairy arms so perhaps is some sort of monkey," Morrigan not recognising Harold.

"Here what have you done to my snail?" Harold annoyed as he had been pushed this way and that so the snails in his pockets were a mess and showed his annoyance when the tomato sauce sachet burst and he threw his captors into the open sewer so fins chased them.

"Meow," the sound of cats near Harold and Morrigan peered closely at him and used these words, "A Garrison."

And it is said Morrigan's hair became snakes and her eyes hot coals.

"I am off," Harold wisely and fled with these words, "Ouk."

"Eat bananas," Morrigan annoying Harold.

"Ouk," Apes jealous he was not invited so swung down from a log and threw Harold towards his mates going off to a war galley.

"Ouk yummy," Apes enjoying the free fruit and never noticed he had been chained and was being carried towards a war galley.

Now it takes an aspirer to survive so Wotanic hid behind one barrel of herring then another till he was at the bottom of the log throne.

"For you dearest," and waved flowers he had bought at Christina, and she ignored him, a bad sign.

"Take these, they are roses not weeds like his," Blackhood behind her throne and gave her roses, freshly cut by minor relations sent into a royal rose garden. And the relations had been given fresh clothes from beggars found with plague for Harry wanted them to go to the grave with their employer's name a secret.

"Handouts, the relations should be grateful I clothe them," Blackhood.

And Brethren had been stamped on their unmentionables so Harry would not be blamed.

"Here these are my flowers?" Christina knowing each flower by name.

"And some have Wotanic tagged on their stems, his guilt is there for all to see," Blackhood revealing his evil genius for he knew there must be one power in the land, him.

"Dearest please?" Wotanic grovelling licking the soles of royal shoes, sickening for what had Christina been standing in earlier?

*

FUTURE

And in the future: "And here the Knights Bridge Peoples Shop of Offaltrex Purchtrix, wonderful women's clothes at affordable prices," the tourist guide bribed by Offlatrex's descendants legitimate and illegitimate but all with his long nose.

And in the distance a dry-docked war galley, a museum piece run by Harry Bros. PLC, but in the harbour a brand-new galley with a seat reserved for the bribed guide who would not be welcome any more at the table where Harry did his howling.

 And Offaltrex had been in his city house hiding in a cupboard during the Great Fire for the wife was after him with a chopper.

"I told his wife everything to teach the cheap bum never to take me on a Harry Tour again," Beautricianix at the front door.

"He told me he was going to a conference on yellow bath ducks, I will chop him into little breadcrumbs to feed the ducks in the local open sewer," the wife and added, "Get me Cannymindtrex the lawyer," and because she was enraged and the wife, a servant ran for the lawyer.

"Get me Cannymindtrex," Offaltrex tipping another servant with a gold mark who said, "I am not running halfway round town for a gold mark," so went to the local where waitress service existed for those wanting watery onion soup.

And the little minded man Cannymindtrex appeared, "Two women, one chain of shops, divide by two gives fifty percent to the girls and none to you," Cannymindtrex.

"Bananas I will be broke," Offaltrex.

"Bananas you will remain Managing Director on a hundred thousand marks a year," Cannymindtrex without emotion for he wore a red lawyers robe.

"I will seek my friend ImasleepasIambored of the Session Court to send you to the galleys with the women," Offaltrex screamed.

Except never saw his friend for Offaltrex was too scared to come out of the cupboard.

"Sign," Cannymindtrex slipping the settlement papers under the cupboard door.

And Offaltrex heard the pitter patter of heavy feet in fluffy pink slippers and trembled as the floor groaned from the wife's weight.

Then a chopper split the door and a big hand took his hair. Worse she gently said, "Cupboards where things that go bump in the night live."

And Offaltrex was afraid of the bumpers so signed his life away.

"Now take this and go," the wife giving Offaltrex a paper bag and in the bag; toothpaste and toothbrush for the wife was not cruel, a change of unmentionables and socks the same colour for she did not want a reputation for meanness. And a yellow duck for a memory. An onion and blue cheese just in case he sneaked away to Beautricianix for the breath.

Under his right arm pit Ba Ba his teddy and only friend that comforted him against the night bumpers.

And a tear ran from teddy and splashed the pavement.

"Where can I go? How can I live on a hundred thousand gold marks a year?" And turned at the bottom of the long avenue to his stately house and saw the wife, Beautricianix and Cannymindtrex thrashing out his empire at a candle lit window.

And a moth flew past and sizzled in the candle for moths are not bright.

"Of course, eureka I am Managing Director and will sack Cannymindtrex and call a shareholders meeting and bribe a no confidence vote in the wife and mistress and get everything back," and dribbled and foamed at the mouth and teddy was happy for teddy wanted back to the drawer it slept in, on silk unmentionables for Offaltrex did not wear scratchy underwear like you.

"I am Offaltrex Purchtrix and Blackhood has not a patch on

me, ha he Ha he, and will send Cannymindtrex to a war galley," and was happy but in the meantime wanted a bed.

"I will not pay for clean linen when I must save my coppers," and sought cheap bunks at an inn in dockland. "I will share the bunk with one tick, three fleas and a waitress so they can share the bill," for he was a cunning mind and competitor of Blackhood. "I will live free for I will complain about the fly in the watered-down parsnip soup, the dirty itchy linen, the waitress that snores, the lack of mint in the warm beer and 10% service charge, and complaints always are quietened by giving them what they want."

Yes, Blackhood who was Harry under a black hoodie for fear of being recognised and hacked to death by a slum tenant had much to learn from Offaltrex.

So Offaltrex found the War Galley Inn, a bed, watered down carrot soup and not a fly in it but a swimming centipede. And he had a phobia about these long-legged nasty biting insects.

"Yee," and jumped off his seat, spilt his soup and the centipede found refuge up his sleeve.

So, he danced wildly casting his clothes away for he felt many legs moving on him, then down his spine to a place that cannot be mentioned.

So, he feared.

At first the cut throats, pimps and distant relations were amused until he dropped his leggings.

"Disgusting, throw him out," they shouted sickened by hairy legs.

So, axes and spears where sent at Offaltrex and all missed for he danced and jumped so many blood feuds were started.

"I am charmed," Offaltrex.

And the centipede was shaken onto a man with an eye patch, one leg and stuffed parrot on his shoulder. "Mummy," he throwing it off and a melee worse than the blood feuds started up.

"Think he is clearing off, does he?" The man with the stuffed parrot and was the mate of a war galley needing volunteers.

And Offaltrex went up the shaky stairs with a waitress seen better days for none of the pretty young girls carrying soup wanted near his hairy spindly legs.

"He will drink that meths and wake up next to me on a war galley, he is a walking Albatross, has he not survived a dozen spears and thirty axes thrown at him? And that centipede never bit him and the cheese wire about his neck went on the wrong neck so we need a new cook too. What luck he will bring the ship," the mate and the parrot nodded agreement and was why the bird was still about, it never nagged.

And the mate stuffed a cracker into the bird's beak and then straightened it out for he wanted it looking smart for he had business with the Landlord.

"The admiralty pays twenty gold marks a volunteer for a war galley," the mate.

"A deal," the landlord and took the marks.

"Here something not right here," the mate looking for his share of marks.

And a centipede crawled from the landlord back to the mate for it must like him something.

"Judas I am stung somewhere because my luck has run out for that Albatross is not here," the mate swelling places girls should not look.

And upstairs on a bunk that sent splinters into Offaltrex so he screeched and moaned, "This is the life to compensate being good all the time," as the past it waitress helped him jump up and down and get more splinters in his places so he screeched louder; for like kids they were jumping on the mattress so there.

"Listen to that Albatross, what stamina," the mate below.

"I attend temples and buy criminals for sacrifice to the Snake god, kick beggars for a laugh and help them hack their limbs off, swindle customers and dream of Blackhood going broke so am allowed this distraction from all my hard work, besides the wife threw me out and my mistress does not want me."

And the past it waitress pored bottles of meths into him so soon he saw three of her, "Three women in a bed for the price of one," Offaltrex happy and then was ill so never saw her open the door as a one-legged mate came up the stairs.

"Plunk," the sound of his wooden leg.

So, the shadow of a parrot fell across Offaltrex who said, "Cough ga cough ga," as cheap meths made him see the press gang as sailors come to drag him to a war galley and a jolly little rowing boat waited for him at the docks.

And was thrown into the jolly rowing boat and fins followed hoping the drunk did stand up for a pee and fall overboard, but he was all tied up so reached a war galley; then was thrown down the ladder to the engine room.

"Cough choke I know you," Offaltrex sure that face was on a gold mark.

And on a hill Bat Wing said to her new friend the old horse, "Glad we are not part of them anymore, they let respectable folk down."

"What do you expect, they are fairies," Old Nag.

"And I am smarter than that idiot Offaltrex for Cannymindtrex never said one hundred thousand gold marks, he just said one copper mark, the cheap kind that we rich folk throw at beggars heated in a fire, copper ones and I am not the one going on a cruise," the Blackhood hoodie.

CHAPTER 54
WOTANIC'S TRIP

And Captain Moronicus Wondrous spent hours sitting outside the throne room every day for he aspired to marry Christina before anyone else.

"I have expectations for I brushed my gums up and down to make them pearly white," Moronicus and had reduced his gums to bleeding sores.

"And shaved with a sharp razor so a shiny shine," so his chin was covered in bandages.

Hair wetted, not a louse to be seen, uniform pressed, breast plate polished so reflected his mind, boring.

"It is only seconds away till I am promoted king," an example of boredom and stupidity.

And a bin out back were daily his flowers went and the bees there fed.

And in his hand a poem by Satirextex he had paid ten marks for.

And Wotanic who was hanging about on a thread for Christina wanted him off on a cruise, "Does not that man take a hint?" She shouted at her maidens and naked barbarians for this princess hoarded her pennies, a cod piece was all they got for decency.

"And I sell all prints, kittens, puppies, sausages, fake cod piece, *all popular cod pieces,"* the oiler again.

And Wotanic noticed Moronicus and said, "I will deliver the poem for you," for at ten marks must be excellent stuff.

And behind closed doors he entered and climbed up the steps to Christina's throne.

"Majesty," Wotanic knew when to grovel, "please sign here to increase your shares in Harry Bros. PLC," and Christina softened and relented toward him.

Perhaps there was some goodness in the man after all?

"Sign here also goddess with a pretty nose," the sickening courtier.

"What?" And her royal lips moved as no petitioners were present, like Moronicus they were on the other side of the closed doors.

"An order to provide poor houses and workshops for the poor," Wotanic and did not tell her it was cardboard boxes and nettle soup and she was increasing his salary.

And dancers whispered, "She thinks she is building more slums but has signed to be guarantee for his overdraft."

"I will silence them when I am king and fund a dynasty as I can live with her for, she has a pretty nose," Wotanic and gave Christina the roses Moronicus was to give her, roses picked by minor relations in plague ridden rags taken from beggars.

"A poem from my heart to you my beautiful queen," and Christina read:

> *"Your soft flesh reminds me of swine.*
> *You blond hair plucked wheat.*
> *Your white teeth long walrus tusks.*
> *Your voice monkey chatter,"* and did not finish.

What could Wotanic expect? Moronicus had only paid ten gold marks!

"She trembles with emotion for me," Wotanic so proposed and puckered his lips for kissing.

And because the roses had his name tags on each she went to check if that rose was indeed Pinkie and that one Porky?

"You will get a reply," his intended promised.

"Soon I will be King of Ball and have many Mistress

Beautricianix's for they are scarlet women and not boring like the wife," Wotanic shaking at the knees at the prospect.

Then fear entered him for he heard Pitter Patter but sighed with relief when he saw it was a child with a message from his fiancée.'

"You are now Admiral of the 21st fleet, Ball awaits your victories over the pirates," xxx and the xxx were in small print not large.

And because he was in shock allowed Pitter Patter to push him into a cart and here a poem awaited him.

Then all his household possessions where thrown in the cart.

"Ouch," was heard for each item thrown in.

"OUCH," for the big items like grand piano.

Then an Admiral's black felt cocked hat was stuffed down HARD on his ears and the pullers of the cart told to make haste to the harbour for a war galley was setting sail.

And of Moronicus, he believed he had been promoted to a captain of a ship and find fame, to defeat pirates and be a hero. But first he must find the illusive pirates to let others defeat so he could return and marry Christina.

"She has given me this chance to prove I am worthy to be king," Moronicus so illustrating there were two Wamba's about.

"No Apes mentioned," Moronicus checking the crew list so went happily to join his ship.

And Wotanic was not happy, he knew the Admiral of the 21st had one ship and it was a war galley in the harbour.

It also had a one-eyed mate with a stuffed parrot who was paid twenty gold marks per volunteer he got to row the galley.

Volunteers that mysteriously disappeared so the war galley never sailed.

And fins always circled that ship.

"The ship leaks so is not seaworthy," a whisper belonging to the mate who added, "bad luck follows the ship, it hits reefs, the boson cannot see, it never has a captain trained to navigate, it is infested with rats, spiders and gout."

And the one-eyed mate was crazy for he fed a stuffed parrot crackers.

And worse the parrot ate them.

And Wotanic read the poem.

"What idiot gave my intended this," he frothed at the lips.

And at the quayside a certain one-eyed mate blew a whistle and shouted, "Crew line up for the admiral."

"Okay dickey," a stuffed parrot replied with a cracker in its mouth.

*

And Apes slept mornings so he could play an organ nights to buy erotic imported fruits and green bottles to drink then eat.

For he liked CRUNCHIES.

And a barracks with unmade beds for maids refused to work while he lived there.

"Ouk," Apes which meant he missed Moronicus and ear bashing and so read brochures the Lost Patrol left.

Harry World Tours.

A sunshine sea holiday.

For you

APES

Look at the guests full of xxx with Topless fairies.

See someone walking the plank.

What fun?

PARTY NIGHT.

Look guests firing catapults at clay pigeons.

WHAT FUN?

Harry World Tours PLC.

Be fed grapes from maidens.

It could all be yours

APES.

Look guests rowing?

Sweating off calories.

BOOK NOW

And visit the lands were bananas come from.

And Apes saw at the bottom palm trees with monkeys swinging about in grass skirts.

"Ouk," Apes excited and on knuckles went to the nearest Harry World Tour outlet.

"Ouk," Apes showing the terrified clerkess the pamphlet.

"Let me deal with this customer," and was an oily whisper and Apes was happy he was getting dealt with by the Boss.

"Sign here," Blackhood before Apes could change his mind.

And produced the biggest banana ever with these words, "From Banana Land."

"Gobble," the greedy ape.

"There is a small rowing boat waiting for you at the harbour, quick swing and terrorise the citizens on the way there, quick go before you never visit Banana World," he under the Blackhood and added, "bananas a metre long," and Apes drooled on the Blackhood, "quick save me from this sticky stuff," "mmm banana flavoured drool."

"I want a rise for this?" The terrified guide showing a black garter to entice Apes to the docks where many garters waited for the heroes of a war galley.

"Ouk," Apes dreaming of those chimps in Banana Land in black garters.

"Come with me for stock valuation is needed, cough," for the urge to be like a rabbit had set upon the oily one.

And here as Aslop fable, *"See the power of a garter, any colour will do."*

"Rubbish, my lawyer is Cannymindtrex and will sue Blackhood till his last penny," the girl for the urge to be a rabbit was not upon her but the urge to fleece a dirty old oily salesman was and immigrate to FAR AWAY FAR LAND before the miser counted the millions, she stuffed in her corsets so looked like a rollie Polly walrus and was so left alone by aspirers on the immigrant ship,

CHAPTER 55
ABSOLUTE FAITH

Throughout Haliput vendors pay Blackhood safety money so heavies will not do to them what was done the monkey.

"And I allow it for it keeps public order," Daghdha trying to think up a good excuse to leave the wife for Morrigan was in town.

And the vendors pray Harry and the Snake god for help to send heavies to their competitors.

For fairies are nasty bunches.

"I am frightened of the wife's mud pack and know there are deities above me that created me, and cannot remember who they are, which frightens me so let Harry and cyclones and earthquakes that send fairies as offerings to these deities just in case they want them.

I want loved by these heavenly unseen beings that left me to the Ballenese, and hide behind the name Good god?

So, I give the fairies impossible laws to follow knowing they will all be sent to hell ha he Ha he Ho," a god in hysterics.

And was the laugh of a demented boy grown up into a demented god because his parents did not love him!

"He haw he haw," the laugh showing the god was paranoid and in his fingers steel balls were played with, just like out that film about a mutiny.

And the laugher gave fairies laws such as,

"Thou shall not kill except in war, land, women, and song; he haw he haw.

Thou shall not have more than one wife; "he haw he haw sob boo Ho," for Morrigan was in town, "but concubines is alright."

"Thou shall not steal; he haw he haw for I made fairies, thieves from birth."

"Thou shall not lie; he haw he haw for I made Harry Blackhood."

And Blackhood has it in for me for he tells stories about me that the gods do not exist?"

"To encourage all the vices and have fairies covert my plastic dinosaurs," that oily whisper.

"I must teach that salesman to respect the gods especially me, I will send a carpet of newts across the land," Daghdha.

"Sales of amphibian traps will increase, I will be laughing all the way to the bank," the whisper.

"That salesman thinks he can outwit me by spreading stuff like, 'Every time you say, "I do not believe in gods one dies,"' well I will send a swarm of flies to darken Haliput," Daghdha and clutched his chest as fairies said, "I do not believe in gods."

"Soon that god will be forgotten and Harry's Swinging Night Land Disco's will be full as fairies to throw away their inhibitions and I will jingle cash all the way to the bank," the salesman not whispering any the more the more.

Then drooled for he saw sales of Aspirin rising.

Then shook as he saw sells of XXX going up.

Then collapsed in ecstasy as he saw sales of nappies going up.

"Hey, wait a minute I do not own Aspirin PLC or Panther XXX or Brand Ajax Nappies the Cheapest in Town," so clutched his chest in despair as he heard Offaltrex, "I do."

"He haw ha Ho he haw," a god laughing in the clouds.

CHAPTER 56   DWARF AND BEAR

There is a statue of a dwarf riding a bear in a park in Haliput and a great favourite with the kids and pigeons for Dog Publishers makes millions of gold marks from selling cheap matinee paperbacks, illustrated by Sampenciltrex of course as kids cannot read anyway, just as well as Satirextex authors the stories. All lies to make kids see Dwarf as the 'Lone Ranger' and Bear as 'Silver' his furry horse.

"And where Dwarf goes so do I for what is good for a squirt dwarf is good for a Grisly," and explains why this mobile kitchen rug got into all sorts of trouble for Dwarf was born anti-social.

Why when Dwarf was at the bar with only hands showing holding a coin was ignored because he was not seen. So climbed the bar and beat the publican blue. So Grisly had to join in too so the publican was torn to shreds.

"Oh, my ancestors oh my corns," the publican did EEK as he was shredded.

'NO PETS ALLOWED especially dwarfs', a sign Grisly ignored.

So, the watch was called and ended with Dwarf riding Grisly into the sunset shouting, "Yaheeeeee," for Dwarf had rebellious ancestry.

And when Dwarf bought pies from that certain pie maker, he did not pay for them, not because a tail hung from the pie, but because Dwarf reckoned the world owned him twenty years filing on that chain when Grisly just snapped it like that.

Dwarf had problems topside.

And what Dwarf ate Grisly ate and went bananas when he found Dwarf staring at the tail hanging from his mouth.

A ringed tail.

Then the watch was called and Dwarf rode Grisly into the sunset shouting, "Gee up you ugly flea ridden bear," and for once Dwarf told the truth.

And happened every time and was loud for Dwarf wore spurs that he dug into the ugly flea ridden bear to make Grisly rear on his hind legs.

"Neeee," something Dwarf wanted so much for Grisly to sound like a horse.

"Grr," Grisly instead and tore up some expensive gardens for them spurs were sure sharp.

So Haliput stayed awake one night knowing gold painted nuggets would trap that horrid stupid Dwarf.

'Free gold tankards and free gold painted pickled eggs to every XXX lover tonight,' was advertised over the pub a centipede had got loose and the pub was chosen as a lucky albatross had once stayed there.

"Gold all mine and none for that greedy bear," Dwarf guzzling meths back at the bar for a bench had been erected just for him to stand on.

"If he can drink this stuff so, can I," the stupid bear.

Then the pair fell flat on their backs as the shadow of What'shisname fell across them; him needing a war galley crew.

And explains why Dwarf and Grisly were sleeping it off on a jolly rowing boat with fins following as all headed to a war galley.

And What'shisname knew the time was right to sell the volunteers to the pirates; why they did pay good for the dancing bear and dwarf to be shot out of a canon that any circus with Monty's cousin thirty times removed is driving the wagons dearly needed; and the ape was the trapeze act without a net a hundred feet up: then he could buy that thatched cottage and an aviary out the back for the stuffed parrot for What'shisname did retire.

"Deliverer this message to the pirates," What'shisname stuffing the message in the stuffed parrot's mouth.

And the parrot flew away to deliver the message and knew otherwise about selling the crew, the crew was Garrison.

*

And because none saw Zoo all thought he was on a Harry World Tour excursion. But they were wrong for having eaten twenty beggars and never had it so good had slept the disease-ridden steaks off amongst the red-hot embers of a house.

"Central heating, fantastic," Zoo and fell asleep.

Then water splashed about from cauldrons of sea anemone got up his nose so he awoke wanting breakfast.

And it was dark and the streets full of revellers going home, the nosey type that scream and wake decent sleeping citizens up.

"A fried egg with them would have been a real treat," Zoo so that night decent citizens got good night sleeps in their cardboard boxes.

"I want Garrison," Zoo and found them not but a tunnel that all the open sewers converged into so it stank just like his old cave.

"Home sweet home," Zoo and moved in.

And from here terrorised those nosy XXX lovers on the way home and one night the watch found him eating without washing his hands first.

"We will tell no one for no one will believe us anyway," the captain of the watch, "if they do, they will send us in there to end up as bad breath in a Zoomorphosis mouth."

But the watch had many loose tongues that told waitresses so Christina heard from courtiers for waitress service existed amongst them too.

"Fall down and worship your pretty queen,
Grovel before her.
Throw your bodies across road rots.

So, your queen can have smooth roads.
Look not upon her ankles,
She the gods chosen,
So, remember what the gods do to rutters?
So, start rutting them road holes."

So, citizens found beggars Zoo had missed and threw them in front of the logs as the mobile throne rolled over holes.

"Yee," and "moan," was heard often and explains why Christina's musicians played loud.

Now at the tunnel a royal finger twitched and a gong bearer appeared and hit a gong so he vibrated often.

So was Zoo when he emerged and did a nasty thing, he ate the gong bearer out of spite at being woken up like that for he had been dreaming of a holiday in Disney World where he walked about unsuspected for beside him Mickey Mouse and Goofy and behind him dinner remains.

"Definitely you will leave Haliput," Christina allowing her Master of Ceremonies to speak for her.

"Why?" Zoo and scratched his bottom, picked his nose and winded something bad so "Cur what a stink?" Was heard much.

Why a royal finger twitched and a hundred archers appeared out of the sewer mist.

"I must think about this?" Zoo and went inside to look for a wok for stir fried archer seemed spicy and exotic; and shows Zoo was worse than Wamba for those archers did deflate Zoo something quick.

But Zoo never thought about those minor little irritating things.

"You are bad for business Zoo; no one is buying my land for sale," Blackhood emerging from the tunnel shadows. I can give you a modern cave on the Haliput road, wall to wall carpet, central heating, the newest gas oven and all the tourists will flock to see you and buy from my vendors roast whole sheep to throw at you. Think about it but be quick there are other monsters I could stick in that cave," and Blackhood thought Garrison.

"What must I do to get this cave?" Zoo.

"Move out" and "secondly eat her outside."

"Thirdly X here."

"She has many soldiers out there," Zoo hoping to haggle for Sky TV.

"Allow me to worry about your touring engagements," Blackhood guiding Zoo to put his X on a parchment, "think of them roast sheep, roast sheep yummy yum," and Zoo did not get SKY for he allowed his stomach to X without a haggle.

And Zoo went out and snarled and roared and was soon following Blackhood disappearing in the darkness of the tunnel.

"Ouch," Zoo as he put his feet down all covered in arrows.

"This way," little smiling hooded relations of Blackhood; the expendables of Harry PLC and Zoo was hungry as he was always for Zoo had worms and never seen a vet.

"Feel better now?" Blackhood waiting for Zoo at the end of the tunnel.

Zoo belched.

And Blackhood showed him his new cave, a mine that a dwarf had dug looking for gold nuggets while Grisly slept not knowing Dwarf when found gold would replace Grisly with many barrels of XXX, waitresses and the latest songs.

"Your name outside in flashing neon lights; famous Zoo because I am your friend," Blackhood and added, "You better have my doctor Leecherex pluck those arrows out."

And Zoo looked at Leecherex who said, "I am safe, he belches on a full stomach and no expendables have emerged from the tunnel."

And Blackhood left Leecherex to worry for him with these words, "This new employer of the master has indigestion so suffers from greed, I better hurry before I end up gastric juice like the expendables," and Leecherex covered Zoo in leeches that

almost sucked the monster dry. "Good the terror is exhausted for a single leech can suck up a pint of monster blood just like that, and I put a hundred on him for good measure. A lucky thing for I work with long needles and a mile of cat gut without pain killers and finished so I must leave in a hurry before Zoo recovers and shakes the leeches off onto me."

"No one can stop me, I have many smiling expendables," Blackhood in the mist.

CHAPTER 57 HEAVE HO A ROWING WE WILL GO

FUTURE

And HMS Victorious now a museum piece were minor relations exchange tickets for your mark then sell you cool fizzy drinks and pies with ringed tails sticking form them.

"Buy here quick models of this here ship," a vendor in a mini Blackhood for only the oily whisper wears a full Blackhood, "free gum if you buy," and kids bought for the gum.

Harry PLC knew how to look after its customers.

HMS Victorious where lucky rowers sweated it out to visit exotic ports and wine beautiful waitresses. Yes, the rowers had the time of their lives sun tanning on the ship's decks.

*

PAST

"Hoist sails." Admiral Wotanic.

"ER admiral sir, this is a war galley, we do not have sails," What'shisname the mate.

"What do you call that?" Wotanic pointing at a single sail all nicely rolled up.

"A sail sir," What'shisname rubbing the stuffed parrot perplexed, this admiral was going to be bothersome, a slippery accident needed arranged for a fin somewhere following a jolly rowing boat. "It has never been used."

"Why?" Wotanic not using his imagination seeing rowers losing weight at the oars.

"Too pretty to unroll; besides this is a galley and that sail is a luxury, perverted thing it is, no place here," What'shisname and did not mention rats had eaten a hole in the sail's middle.

"Well, let us have this luxury for I am not rowing to hell and back," Conan and spat tobacco straight into What'shisname mouth so he gagged.

"Well said there hurrah," the Lost Patrol gathering about Conan.

"Order in the ranks, back to the oars you scurvy sea anemone," Captain Moronicus hoping to impress the admiral for aspirers do not know when to quit.

And none went back to the oars for it was dark and dingy in the engine room and besides they all wanted to look for a scurvy sea anemone for none had ever seen one.

Then a little hairy boson cracked a whip over their heads until a huge hairy hand took it away from him.

"What is your name mutinous scum?" What'shisname addressing the huge hairy hand.

"Wamba, he is Garrison," Wotanic feeling ill for Garrison never washed and did it on purpose to offend them with silks.

"Oh err, Wamba the hero, glad to have you aboard," What'shisname lying good.

"Ouk," this Wamba replied then wrapped the whip about the boson Cutyagizzard'sout neck and produced a banana behind What'shisname right ear.

"How you do that?" What'shisname before a banana skin slapped his face with these words, "Ouk."

And the owner of the huge hairy arm swung off to the rafters to eat his fruit alone and savoured every mouthful.

"We are all Garrison," the real Wamba and a cheer rose and was carried to a far-off open window where sat Christina listening to popular street music below.

"We are rid of them,
Garrison.
Eaters of meat pies with ingredients.

Away as fin food.
Hurrah goody," Satirextex.

And Christina missed the scum Garrison so cried and sent for scribe Scarabink.

'You are pardoned, return at once Garrison.

Christina the Great Illustrious.'

"Now send this to HMS Victorious Scarabink," Christina and behind her Pitter Patter in a muzzle.

And Scarabink found a messenger behind the stables playing dice, drinking cheap stuff from green bottles, and helping himself to tarts.

For his sort are always handsome and the daughters think they are marvellous.

"You will do and to help you sober up I kick here and stamp there and now get a horse, find a saddle, give Wamba this message," Scarabink for he was a little man with several warts on his face and a potato growing between his ears so his attack on the handsome worthless messenger with handfuls of tarts was pure jealousy.

Meanwhile aboard HMS Victorious, Wotanic at the rail finding the gentle sea unsettling while an ape carried What'shisname above to unruffle the sail.

And What'shisname did an excellent job considering he had only a terrified stuffed parrot to help him, one eye and one leg; and for encouragement a huge ape sat near him snarling and breaking matches.

"Oh bother," What'shisname seeing a fin circling in the sea.

"Croak," the stuffed parrot paralysed with fear.

"Look Wamba rockets," Tom smelling of roses for he was innocent.

"Yeh wonder what happens when you light one," Conan with evil intentions for he had been jilted by a princess who had sent him on a cruise.

So sent a distress rocket that landed on bales in the docks.

"Dockland is burning," a beggar behind the bales and added, "Oh bother so am I."

"This ship is not moving?" Wotanic still at the rails; so,

Wamba consulted Book but this was the navy so put Book away.

"The anchor," Conan whispered.

"Hey Apes come down here and hoist the anchor up," then remembering whom he addressed added, "a couple of juicy fruit in it for you."

"EEK," What'shisname as Apes swung down.

Fortunately for him he missed the fin but hit the deck peg leg first and got stuck, and no one bothered to help him for he was just

What'shisname.

And lucky for him The Mage at the rails drinking tea had changed the weather, and with another click The Mage filled the sail and the ship lurched into an adventure.

And Wotanic at the rails lurched too and splashed some place.

Immediately the fin zoomed to him as Wotanic swam towards a little rowing boat dragged at the stern; where he hauled himself up as a mouth full of teeth missed him.

Here Wotanic lay still fearing to breathe for the fin was big and he could see it circling his jolly little boat; so was terrified and mortified.

And here he lay in the blazing sun getting heatstroke listening to the rowdy sea songs coming from his only ship in the 21st Fleet.

And another was submitted to the horrid sea songs for he was chained at an oar.

"Shut them up and give me meths," Drunken Noddy and this is what he heard.

"We are sea rats,
  With bottles of rum.
  We eat tacky Albatrosses,
  So have no luck.
  As got a wife in every port."

A popular sailor's song by Satirextex.

304

And the songs carried to citizens waving goodbye at the docks.

"Sort of miss The Mage," Bat Wing.

"Yeh, even if Womba's a Burke," Old Nag as the pair of beasts sat on their hunches waving goodbye.

Meanwhile a handsome royal messenger stripped off at the quay to the admiration of ladies present. Now the messenger posed in body building stances and wearing leopard skin trunks dived in and splashed his way out to the Victorious and met a fin and never delivered the message. Now an Aslop fable here, *'Vanity beware vanity less Arawan's wagon run you over, and stupid fool should have used a jolly little rowing boat.'*

CHAPTER
58 TEMPEST

"Come and get it?" Someone shouted.

Wamba opened a swivelling eye to find the disturbance, and then opened his other eye. Behind him the shadow of a chameleon stretched and yawned. Lost Marines watched and spread it about Wamba was ugly because he had lizard in his ancestry but was just nasty lies. And because spies are everywhere a splash was heard, some healthy shrieks as fins were about; but spies are tenacious thingamajigs so Christina greeted the lies with these words, "Wamba can be kept in a fish tank and fed flies and one Garrison less."

"Perhaps the girl only sees Garrison as boisterous company when they are not about, then cries for them, definitely ,mental health issues here," Aslop wisely.

Anyway: There stood Offaltrex in chef's hat, except the white was all red stuff, green dyes and a chicken's rubber head hung from a pocket.

"Cock a do da do," the head croaked for it was advertising 'Offaltrex Batteries last longer?'

Worse, the chick was smirking for it died laughing as it clucked, "You cannot catch me."

"Offaltrex, what are you doing here?" Wamba rising, decided navy XXX was strong stuff and collapsed with a moan.

"Not sure but being cook beats rowing. I even got hired help, Alicadabara's here."

"Coming boss," Alicadabara and upon his crew cut his battered wizard's hat and around it a string of sausages.

"Well look what crawled out of a snail?" Conan smirked and spat tobacco over the side, and the wind carried it splattering Wotanic behind in a rowing boat, the jolly type. And he almost fell out gagging as a fin brushed his small boat and he was afraid for he had seen Teeth, Teeth's 2, Teeth's 3, Teeth's 4, and Teeth's Revenge and seen a royal messenger swim for it.

Then sat still as the smell of bacon, eggs, fried potatoes, black sausage and red spotted toadstools and mugs of What'shisname coffee wafted upon him.

"They can eat what they like, I see heaps of sea anemone on the boat's bottom so do not care," Wotanic and was a lie and turned his face and "sob."

And aboard ship Alicadabara happily showed a few inches of wand, "It can wash greasy dishes, cut onions without a tear, score pans, dice carrots and at a click produce Singapore Fish Head Curry.

I am your servant," Alicadabara and he was a bigger liar than Wotanic but knew grovelling had its rewards for he got to lick the pots shiny clean.

And the smell of the greasy fry up made the crew run for the rails and the wind carried stuff to an unhappy rowing boat.

"Boohoo," was heard from the unhappy rowing boat.

Except for real Garrison that could eat anything in any weather.

"Gobble," and the sound of bacon rashers devoured made Wotanic pull his hair OUT so, "EEK," was heard often.

And no one remembered him below manacled at an oar doing all the rowing who was jumping up and down trying to free himself. "Give me greasy fry up," he ranted and was in luck for Alicadabara spilled hot cooking oil down the deck's planking.

"Delicious," Drunken Noddy getting third degree burns.

Then the tempest came:

"Leave rope for me," Alicadabara to Offaltrex as they tied themselves to a kitchen bulwark.

"Looks like we will be eating fish broiled, roasted and baked in beans," Offaltrex joking as a wave left squid, flying fish, stingray, barracudas, fins, baby ones of course, and several green meth bottles with messages in them and an apple barrel.

"Tie me as well," the apple barrel spoke to them.

"Wash away Cutyagizzard'sout, wash away," one cook and his helper replied and a wave did exactly that to the barrel.

"Marvellous Ali do not forget the onions," Offaltrex not wanting to cry.

And Ali knew if his wand were long and strong, he would change his spots and become Alicadabara the Rotten. Yes, the wind blew the single square sail to more shreds.

"Go up there Apes and hold the sail together, we must have power to ride this storm out," The Mage barely able to see through the lashing rain.

A good thing for Apes who went below decks and hid in a swinging hammock that crashed into one wall and the next.

"Ouk," Apes each time he cracked into the walls and lumps grew where no lumps had been before and Apes saw spinning lumps not stars nor bananas.

And above deck The Mage seeing no banana skins fall from the rigging realised he had been APED. "We must have power; I will wave my finger and make the tempest go away.

"Click colicky click," The Mage till his fingers were red and swollen and above him two chariots where Daghdha and Morrigan stood laughing at the ship and crew at the rails and when they saw Wotanic went into hysterics. Here an Aslop's moral, *"Do not put your faith in toads."*

"Are you happy my chick ado?" Daghdha being sickening.

"Yes, but what about some lightening, they must be cold," Morrigan full of toadyism?

"Tanaros," Daghdha shouted, and the Thunder god was busy having waitress service at Filthy Big Bertha's for her French Onion Soup was famous so did not appear in a divine sulphuric poof.

"Oh well I am the Chief god so can do it myself," and Daghdha burned his fingers and saw the disgusted look on Morrigan's face and she said, "I am not amused," so he panicked and sent lightning bolts into Taoist nunneries, theatres, soup kitchens, and frizzled a Buddhist monk good; here another Aslop moral, *"Never get involved with scarlet women."*

"This is the work of the gods, we must have a fairy aboard that is cursed with bad luck, we must man the oars and reach land QUICK," The Mage seeking volunteers.

"Volunteers," Wamba and saw What'shisname still pegged to the deck so grabbed him and threw him down to the oars so now there were two rowers.

"Row or else," What'shisname forcing his stuffed parrot to row so now there were three rowers.

"Poly wants a cracker," the parrot complained.

"Curse the day I got this shower for a crew, my partners the pirates will never forgive me," What'shisname prophesied.

And the pirates were amazed at the sudden storm for they had not eaten the following albatross and here another Aslop moral, *"Eat while you can."*

And so, the pirates believing Tanaros the Thunder god hated one of their number started to throw many of their number to fins below.

Until Captain Red Beard called it a day and got straws and who drew the shortest be catapulted into the sky a peace offering. But first tarred and feathered to be mean, and as the catapult twanged, a burning torch would set the offering alight just to be meaner.

For seafarers are a superstitious lot.

And the burning lit the sky and all saw land, so HMS Victorious and Malicious the pirate ship headed there, Treasure Island.

And the storm abated for the offering collided with two chariots.

""You will wish you were never born," Morrigan putting out the offering on her and Daghdha hoped she did use spurs too.

And in a rowing boat Wotanic was kept amused by Cutyagizzard'sout beating fins away from his apple barrel.

And on a burnt hill in Haliput two friends waited for Victorinus's return. "Wish we had gone," Bat Wing said dreaming of sun tanning in a bikini.

"I know, boring without them," Old Nag still on its haunches now suffering cramp dreaming of ogling himself ill ogling Bat Wing in a bikini.

Postdate: *"I must have Alicadabara's wand and breed it to sell to tired housewives who wear rubber gloves to scour greasy frying pans clean,"* an oily whisper from under a black hood.

CHAPTER 59
TREASURE ISLAND

FUTURE

And the fishy tentacles of Harry Bros. PLC bought land, fresh water, and salt and where coconuts, tore them down using those who owed marks after shipping them out as engine cogs as they could not afford passage, and fed them lashings of Bull Whip; and had them plant rubber palms where the coconuts once dropped and when the price of coconut matting went up, lashed them all into digging the rubber out and planting brand new coconuts.

That made Apes happy.

"Ouk."

Then gruel was added to the lashings to encourage hotels built, swimming pools for tourists, aquariums with orcas, penguins for orcas to rip up, dolphins to loop fiery loops and sharks to shred the dolphins to the cheer of the blood thirsty tourists, and then mermaids to made the tourists think of visiting the sleazy hotel bars.

Yes, Harry knew how to keep his gold marks and make the marks have heaps of ancestors in his deep pockets.

And along the beaches of Treasure Island sponge divers and millionaire yachts and fat fins.

"Yes, this is the best thing Wamba ever did for me," Blackhood viewing all from his Plaza suite at the top of the Mangrove 5 Star Hotel on a future Treasure Island.

About him grovelling minor relations and floozy girls all expendable of course bribed from the beaches for a chance to meet the millionaire Blackhood known for his generous spontaneous diamond ring gifts.

"Wamba, now my great smiling expendables there was a Burke, and now the truth about Treasure Island for your ears only," **Blackhood again in the future forcing himself not to howl.**

*

PRESENT

"Stuff this," What'shisname the mate leaving Charles Drunken Noddy to row to find a place to sulk as men do when they do not get their own way.

And What'shisname cuddled his stuffed parrot to forget the nightmarish voyage.

And found a rug to crawl under.

"Here what's this?" What'shisname kicking the snoring rug and then pulled it over himself by its nose.

"Cannot a Dwarf hibernate through a nightmarish sea voyage?" Dwarf butting What'shisname left good knee which made the mate lean down.

A precarious thing to do.

"Cannot a Dwarf dream of gold mines?" Dwarf butting what he could reach so What'shisname groaned loudly.

Then the rug not liked being pulled by the nose ROARED and savaged the mate up good.

"Yikes," came first then, "groan."

"Come on Grizzly Bear let us go topside and see what is cooking," Dwarf and the vicious rug followed and What'shisname went back to rowing.

"Where is the hula-hula girls," the Burke from the forecastle seeing Treasure Island.

"Maybe the natives ate them?" Conan spitting tobacco at a fin and the fin died just like that. "But it is not the missing grass skirts you should be worrying about but that ship yonder with the Skull and Cross Bone Flag."

"Let them come, Grizzly can handle them all with one

paw tied behind his back," Dwarf not asking the astonished worried bear for an opinion.

And Conan sighed; his retirement dream of smoking tobacco with his feet snuggled up in a bear rug was approaching fast.

And that What'shisname overheard below and deserted much to the annoyance of the single oarsman left.

"What is What'shisname up to serge?" Tom pointing at What'shisname waving a flag from the crow's nest.

So, Wamba consulted Book for there was a section on signals so shouted, "A banana in it Apes if you do that fairy?"

"Ouk," Apes saluting and his salute slapped the Taskmaster Whipthemhard overboard.

"Splash," and "EEK," and "where's that jolly little rowing boat?" As fins were about you know?

"Better look Tom," Conan spitting tobacco into the wind that would carry it towards a jolly rowing boat so "Yuck," was heard.

"Made it, now Wotanic will not be lonely?" Tom and Conan had a look and yes there was Wotanic trying hard to keep his little rowing boat to himself, the selfish man.

"And that reminds me, was that Drunken Noddy manning the engine?" Conan.

"It was Corporal," Tom and beamed with pride that he knew important things.

"Better leave him there and not a word to Wamba, or might ask for volunteers," and spat tobacco onto a crack in the deck over the engine so, "Yuck," was heard below.

"Splat," as What'shisname landed at Conan's feet.

"Ouk," Apes wanting his juicy banana.

"I am sure that Apes meant to hit me with the mate?" Wamba.

"Ouk grunt chatter monkey sounds and raspberry," a rude Apes thinking he was smart and funny.

"Just for that no banana," Wamba.

Why Apes landed in front of Wamba snarling with fangs

wanting to rip Wamba to pieces; of course, with ketchup added first.

"Mummy," Wamba hurriedly searching his pockets for fruit and peanut shells and started running for one does when an angry dastardly ape wants to meet you.

"Pirates ahoy," Dwarf and manned the bolt thrower and sent a bolt pinning Red Beard by his beard to his ship Malicious's wheel which was unfortunate as he was on a collision course with the war galley.

"Scurvy scum," Red Beard in a frenzy ripping his beard free.

"EEK," he swore as that was sore.

Then the two ships collided and ran aground on Treasure Island and in the kitchen of Victorious a cauldron of hot devilled pork splashed across Alicadabara.

"I am going to fizzle someone good for this and I forgot ouch that was hot," Ali.

"Here point the wand out the window at the pirates Ali," Offaltrex and led a steaming wizard to the kitchen window and "Poof" as the wizard's wand frizzled pirates.

And boarding planks became tissue paper so pirates fell into the sea and lucky for them the sea about the beach was shallow, for they had to battle Wotanic in his jolly little rowing boat and Cutyagizzardout and Whipthemhard in the apple barrel, not forgetting the fins of course.

"Away you scurvy landlubbers," a pirate swinging in the kitchen window and landed in the Devilled Pork and remained numb for the mustard was extra hot.

"Ruined he has ruined it," and with wooden spoons the cooks beat the daylights out of the pirate.

So, the pirate jumped out the window he came in.

"He has left a red legging behind, all ruined," Alicadabara and with Offaltrex emptied the cauldron of Devilled Pork out the window.

"Judas Priest," and "what idiot emptied that hot food on me," pirates and "delicious food at last," from Wotanic.

Meanwhile in the kitchen, "Watch my good friend number one ship's cook," Alicadabara and since they were calling themselves friends and being cooks something else seems cooking than food.

So, Ali waved his wand and the cauldron boiled with sea food as if there was not enough.

And outside Red Beard saw an Ape chasing a big fairy his way and then the Ape was swinging the fairy against pirates sending them overboard to join pirates fighting to reach the beach and one, made it since this book is not about gore, fins, sword fishes and giant octopuses living in the waters of Treasure Island.

And a mean homicidal ape of course.

Then Captain Moronicus and his Lost Patrol ran this way trying to keep out of the fighting and look like they were fighting and chopped this way and that about Red Beard so "Groan," and "watch it mate" was heard often and "I am finished being a captain," and "finished living."

Red Beard saw 'MARINES' stitched on their backs; "Very nice," he said from his prostate position then saw stars but was rudely awakened by a Dwarf riding a bear on him.

"Gee up Grizzly," Dwarf and sank his spurs in so Grizzly reared and clawed and ripped here and shredded there so "Oh, is not my lucky day," was heard from underneath them.

And an occasional "Moan."

Then they was gone and Red Beard saw his chance to escape so standing saw a big hairy fairy being chased by an ape coming his way.

"Not again?" The only logical thing to say.

Then this Burke was being beaten by an ape on him so, "Groan," was heard from the Burke and Red Beard often.

"Who are you lot?" Red Beard knowing he should never have eaten that albatross.

"I am Wamba," the Burke and them," Garrison and that is Conan and sweet innocent Tom stealing your treasure chest from your pirate ship that is sinking for The Mage is using magic to sink it. "

"I have read 'Tales of Garrison on the Riverbank' by Dog Publishers so who is the bear and little person?" For Red Beard did not want to annoy Dwarf for being shredded by a grizzly bear once is enough for anyone in a lifetime.

But Dwarf was curious for he thought Red Beard said, "I know where a gold mine is," so had to interrogate using Grizzly of course.

"Please do not throw me overboard?" Red Beard hanging from the jaws of Grizzly watching fins multiply in the sea below like clothes hangers in a cupboard.

"Why not?" Wamba asked free of Apes having thrown a juicy Mango towards the rigging.

"I know where diamonds the size of sheep are buried for this here is Treasure Island and you must keep me safe warm and cosy and not associate me with fins," Red Beard using too many big words so Wamba did not understand apart from diamonds, so wondered away thinking what he could do with diamonds the size of sheep?

"Diamonds is like gold, they can me mined," Red Beard hoping to get Dwarf to open Grizzly's mouth so he could escape.

"What do I want with diamonds the size of sheep for? I want gold nuggets and be fooled by 'FOOLS GOLD'," Dwarf and walked away so Grizzly opened his mouth and Red Beard fell out.

"I am free of these idiots at last," Red Beard dusting bear fur off his shredded clothes and that is when Apes swung down for juicier mango or else so bumped Red Beard overboard.

And lucky for him an albatross flew across the sky and a wave brought a jolly little rowing boat under his flight path so, "Blooming hell what the blazes," Wotanic screamed as Red Beard landed on him.

"Ouk," Apes lying for it was not an accident.

*

Now Garrison gathered on the warm tropical beach where no sharp broken bottles, dead sea gulls, plastic bags, lumps of coral, hamburger wrappers, bikini tops and the bag left behind by the husband off with what was in the bikini top lay about.

"Grovel slurp grovel please do not give me to that dwarf and bear act," Red Beard grovelled as he spoke of spot X where the treasure was buried.

"His savings that are ours," Conan.

And above in a coconut the sole pirate who had swam ashore clinging to a coconut that better not break and fall with him clinging to it, for a nut of a dwarf and nasty bear was under him?

Waiting for someone to shred to bits!

And the sole survivor was learning for he had big ears, full of wax for he never washed them.

Was that treasure not his pension, for years of looting and ravaging passengers and pets while serving Red Beard his captain who got all the fame and glory; yes, the treasure was his by Divine Right.

Yes, and was all lies for this was his first trip and was a minor relation escaping from the Blackhood for that relation was domineering and paid you with promises?

And he was a student of Haliput's School of Architecture.

Give a Archicteturalex was his name.

Another aspirer dreamer schemer who polished the gold throne where Blackhood sat lording it over him by wiping his dirty shoes on him. And at the eating table Give a Archicteturalex sat at the far end watching Blackhood and the others eat hot steaming soups full of crusty crustaceans and croissants and because he sat at the far end got the shells and empty soup bowls to lick.

"I want noticed," Give a Archicteturalex.

And here was his chance so shinned down the coconut tree so "EEKED," much and when down ran through thick bamboo forest that twanged him so, "Ouch," often and gathered spades and shovels and because he had only two hands dropped them so, "Yikes," and "XXX," he complained but got to spot X and dug it up all by himself under the blazing sun so, "Gasp I need a drink gasp of cold-water gasp."

And shifted the real spot X and threw the shovels and spades over a nearby cliff.

Emptied his deep pockets a giveaway sign a Give a Harry

is about and littered the place with broken green cheap meth bottles, crisp packets, bubble gum and a fan club badge of Mickey Jacksonscream on the sand and put a false spot X nearby.

Some inebriated god on a wagon from below did get the blame.

"Gasp," the sound of Give a Archicteturalex collapsing under a bush dreaming of the hotels he did build, quick food chains, sleazy bars for tourists and him to visit he did build here with his treasure.

"No, I am betrayed," Red Beard seeing visions of Dwarf and Bear visiting him behind bushes.

Garrison was not amused; the walk up this hill in this heat was something else.

"Apes," Wamba and Garrison parted to reveal to Red Beard Apes foaming at the mouth, snapping sticks in his hands.

But Dwarf was jealous and Grizzly always wanted what Dwarf had so Red Beard got lots of attention that Give a Archicteturalex wanted and explains why Red Beard sailed over that nearby cliff where spades and shovels had been carelessly tossed over.

And missed them sticking up and landed on something soft scurrying below instead.

A sleepwalker dreaming of hotels and waitresses in sleazy restaurants that every sleazy bar has.

"Give a Archicteturalex is that you?" Red Beard.

"Yes," the minor relation wide awake just like that another Give a Harry feature, able to cheat and swindle at short notice.

"Why are you here?"

"Breaking your fall captain," Give a Archicteturalex lied for a sleepwalker had dragged a treasure chest with him.

"You can have the job of cocktail mixer at the poolside of my 5 Star Mangrove Swamp Hotel, why just think of the floozy pirate girls there so drunk they will think you the most handsome pirate ever," Give a Archicteturalex lied for he did feed Red Beard to his pet giant Pacific Octopus in his fish tank that all good hotel owners keep for emergencies.

"Why you?" And Red Beard grabbed the little sniffling twerp by the throat and throttled away.

"This yours?" Wamba at the cliff edge above and dropped the spot X over.

That with a loud "CRACK" landed on someone?

WHO?

And the little sniffling twerp kneed that someone so someone groaned more.

"That Burke has saved my life, I must reward him or the Snake god will want me as an offering," Give a Archicteturalex leaving a penny on the sand for Wamba and carried the treasure chest to a little jolly rowing boat the tide had brought to the shore.

And twice Give a Archicteturalex had to beat fins off him, sea crocodiles under him, jelly fish wanting to cover him and expose delicate skin to sun burn to reach that jolly rowing boat, for "Am I nuts leaving a penny behind, the Snake god can have the Burke."

Such the stuff the Harry's are made off.

And why Wamba was alone for Red Beard had said, "Within an inch my treasure chest until?"

"Then a Gestamp drops X." Conan and spat tobacco on Wamba who began to smoulder.

"A Burke indeed?" The Mage who dusted magic towards Wamba who suddenly was covered in smelly painful carbuncles.

"Yes, a Burke," Alicadabara getting on in the act and with his tiny wand fizzled so Wamba was made to taste the sea soup in the cauldron first just in case it tasted vile.

"Lovely," Wamba when he should have gagged so Garrison set upon him and Apes beat him with a coconut that split in two on Womba's head.

"Ouk," Apes tasting what was in the coconut so left beating Wamba black and green to find more coconuts to crack on Wamba before they had to be nice again.

"I deserved that," Wamba sitting on an empty turtle shell.

"Maybe you did but I am a captain," Red Beard next to him

for it was a big turtle shell.

"You are pirate scum so me and you are now engine cogs and if you want to complain go ahead," Wamba hoping he would for Wamba had a dark nasty streak that loved to watch bear fisted boxing fights and women wrestle in mud filled with spiders.

"I am mate What'shisname and I am not scum."

"I am Boson Cutyagizzardout and I am not scum."

"I am Taskmaster Whipthemhard and is not scum."

"I am Red Beard and is scum."

"Engine cogs needed," Conan and behind him a homicidal ape in a too small sailors uniform just wanting an excuse to shred scum.

So aboard HMS Victorious shredded scum sat at the oars.

"Row faster scum," Conan the new Taskmaster and whipped scum good so, "Blooming hell," and "bloody heck," and "a little more please," came from the engine room.

And Wamba was not whipped for he was Garrison so was treated special; he got a cushion to sit on as he rowed.

"Squawk," the stuff parrot not likening the whip.

"One beat two beat three beat we dip oars.
  And get whipped hard oh lovely.
  So, row hard scum.
  So, pass the meths.
  Row the boat.
  We are the jolly rowers.
See how fast we row,
  So, row hard scum and the sound of a whip was heard."

"Ouk," also just in case any scum had any ideas of rushing the Task master.

CHAPTER 60   THEY
COULD NOT
GO HOME

" For they had joined the navy.
So sailed east,
To the Great Khan.
Hoping to meet sages,
Who could tell them how to bribe Daghdha,
 So, they could go home.
Some to Filthy Big Bertha's.
Some to get lost in cesspit Haliput.
 Some too wet steamy Tandoori forests.
Some to kitchen vacancies.
Some to nature reserves for dwarfs and bears.
Some to remain cogs."

And missed Wamba so dropped a key down a crack in the deck just above his lap.

"For your eyes only," the note attached said.

For Garrison refused to admit they missed him.

So freed himself the next day after a good sulk and left the key behind.

"Here free me too," Drunken Noddy to Red Beard.

"Listen son someone is needed to row this galley," and left.

"A parrot cannot be expected to row," What'shisname and left.

"Yes and a seaman needs sea air," Cutyagizzardout and left.

So, the engine cog was still chained and did a mental, not to worry he calmed down and took his anger out rowing so knew all about anger management.

Anyway: "Where can we go?" The Lost Patrol.

"To the Land of Confucus," The Mage looking east, he is a pensioner who knows everything. For nothing he will tell us what we want to know."

"For nothing?" Offaltrex disbelieving.

"Yes his wisdom is inside every fortune cookie," The Mage adding, "he has ethics," not expecting Offaltrex to understand.

"Is it like triple vision?" Tom.

"Yes, for it is free and affects those who touch. His cookies of wisdom never fail."

"How do we know he is alive?" Tom and Conan was proud for the boy had wisdom and an argumentative streak that every good barbarian has.

"Even the dead talk through the wiggles of a sacrificial victim," The Mage.

"That is against the law," Garrison united knowing volunteers were sacrificial victims.

"When do we get there?" Offaltrex checking his brochures to see what people who gave away cookies could buy from him.

"At this rate, three years and six days," The Mage and he clicked and a whale appeared and pushed the ship from behind.

"At last, a tea break," the lone engine cog below gasped.

"I smell the cooks are cooking something special?" Wamba and his words unleashed Harold as his knuckles scraped the deck to check the rumor out.

"That **whatever** Harold has eaten the contents of Alicadabara's cauldron of salmon steaks in Hollandaise sauce covered in chopped Broccoli," The Lost patrol complained so Wamba was not popular again so ate alone his ration of cold snails covered in lard to swallow easily.

"I want what **whatever** was ate?" A plucky unwise member

of the Lost Patrol for **whatever** did not like attention drawn to itself for then you were volunteered. So just like that it happened for out of the deck shadows darted and the plucky marine was gone.

"About time I got someone to chat too?" Drunken Noddy below; but it did not stop the others wanting:

"I want a roast horse," that arthritic barbarian Conan.

"That albatross would do nicely," the Burke tempting bad luck so found himself alone again.

"Boar in red wine sauce sprinkled in chopped asparagus," The Mage showing mages were different for they were educated folk.

"Filthy Big Bertha I want," Tom showing the true colors of common as muck Garrison.

"Ouk," Apes agreeing for Big Bertha let him eat the big juicy termites in the wood there.

"I want a soft cushion, some books to read, waitress service and a green bottle of meths," and the engine cog could want all he liked.

*

Now Confucus Land today has a statue of a donkey for a caravan once visited the Great Khan Dim Sun with camels, horses, elephants, mules, and a talking donkey traveling through the secondhand horse flesh markets.

And Dim Sun sent for Confucus who saw a good joke here; "He says he is the donkey god and wants clean vegetables," so put Tootanfoot in a stable with rice, noodles, dried smelly fish, and a stable boy who charged admission to see the only talking donkey in the Middle Kingdom of Confucus.

And the donkey was considered good luck to touch, even if it was seen scratching fleas.

Then one sunny day Tootanfoot saw a war galley because the stable boy was leaving the stable window open, for donkeys tend to stink the place up.

"I am saved," Tootanfoot brayed as he saw the ship was Ballenese forgetting all about a certain war galley needing volunteers; so, he jumped through the open window and trotted as fast as a donkey could down to the docks.

Behind him a stable boy intent on lassoing the donkey for the tourists paid him much to let them touch the lucky donkey, he also sold manure to farmers.

Why already he had thrown away his smelly leather jerkins covered in donkey stuff and wore pink and green silks; and smelled of scented rose water and spoke funny too; and had enough takings to hire a street urchin to get covered in donkey stuff now. A

street urchin he kicked here and there and threw donkey's nibbled carrots at him to feast upon.

But to the people of Confucus this mysterious ship must be lucky for it had a big monkey in a sailor's uniform swinging about the rigging so must be The Monkey King. While below hairy fairies stared at them from the railings, hairy fairies that had been at sea for months, with fat wallets of unspent pay.

"Hey Jimmie want noodle soup and waitress service?" A vendor in a sampan near the Victorious.

"Here Jimmy, I buy your mother-in-law OK?" Another vendor.

"Jimmy want a sexy guide?" Another one and soon they were throwing choppers and chop sticks at each other for each wanted the rich picking of HMS Victorious to themselves; and here an Aslop's fable, *"Share for there is enough blueberries for everyone."*

Then Khan Dim Sun came to the docks in a sedan chair a hundred hands high. Gold and mounted on a thousand backs to heave it about and a guard legion in black silk.

"Trouble brewing," Conan and spat tobacco and hit a vendor and bounced off him and hit another then ricocheted off him to hit Wotanic.

"Wamba line Garrison up on the docks," The Mage not thinking for he was sniffing dried medicines mingled in with the aroma of Wok cooking, "Lovely," he added ogling the waitresses in long silk dresses slit up the side revealing long smooth legs so he dribbled at the mouth and shook; and that should teach the old dirty man but he was full of macho;

them that shave with a blunt razor, eat without teeth, cover themselves in rose water and carry a pack of playing cards! Why playing cards? Only Macho men know what to do with playing cards.

So as The Mage shook, Wamba lined Garrison up on the dock for Dim Sun to inspect and the smile on the Khan's face vanished for Conan picked his nose and flicked the greenie nearby, Tom picked his ears and wiped the wax nearby, Harold snarled showing canines Apes secretly coveted.

"Woof," and Cur cocked his leg nearby.

"Ouk," and Apes carelessly threw a banana skin nearby.

"We are only marines and not with them," The Lost Patrol and added, "He is," pushing Captain Moronicus forward to be nasty hoping to be rid of the aspirer for good.

And The Great Khan was nearby and furious and had many Pitter Patters running to meet Garrison when suddenly: "Hi ho Silver Gee up Grisly," and The Khan was so amused watching a bear take spurs off a dwarf and change positions so the dwarf was raked good by those spurs, forgot all about boiling Garrison in oil, then frying them in sesame seeds and oyster sauce.

"Oh, Great Khan I have spoken to an evil wizard in the ship's kitchen and he assures me these hairy fairies are called Garrison," Confucus wanting away for he had read books that a land called Ball existed beyond the mountain passes of Confucus Land and a sub species of ape lived there called Garrison.

Nasty trouble making thieves as well that loved to drink XXX all day and night. And did not tell The Great Khan these exciting extras for he would wait till The Great Khan had stuffed brass ovens full of his soothsayers and astrologers who had been unable to tell him anything about Garrison.

For Confucus wanted the glory all to himself and the rewards that went with glory, the gold, medals, and top-class waitress service at the Hotel Confucus.

"Tell them the hospitality of Confucus Land is theirs," The Great Khan to a little elf called Grovelatkhan'sfeet whose job was to run down the hundred hands high sedan chair and tell Garrison this. But Dim Sun had not made it clear who was welcome? Was it the shredded dwarf and bear riding a rickshaw or Garrison crowding about The Mage?

"Gasp pant," Grovelatkhan'sfeet as he returned to Dim Sun, "They say, 'Ta very much' and what is your reply oh great lord?" Grovelatkhan'sfeet hoping there was not a reply.

"Have they got any gifts for me?" Dim Sun and Grovelatkhan'sfeet ran all the way down to ask Garrison were the wrapped-up presents were?

"Could give him What'shisname?" Conan.

"He means volunteers," Wamba looking up Book.

"That means Wotanic certainly," Tom and Conan beamed pride.

"Ask Dim Sun want he wants?" The Mage and Grovelatkhan'sfeet struggled back up the hundred hands to Dim Sun.

"I want the dwarf juggler, the bear flying a kite, the ape eating banana skins and the one-legged ventriloquist who uses the stuffed parrot," Dim Sun and sent Grovelatkhan'sfeet back to Garrison.

Meantime Confucus invited The Mage back to his house, The Flowering Green Aphid for tea, special friend rice, boiled duck beak in black bean sauce, star fish soup and tasty fried dandelions in sweet and sour sauce.

"Ouk," Harold accepting the invitation.

"See you at 6 pm then," Confucus giving The Mage a map, "just show this to the rickshaw boys over there."

And the rickshaw boys made shapely curves with their hands, drank imaginary bottles, opened black brief cases showing items to treat, timers, shoes, handbags, carved sea chests and like the vendors in the boats knew there could only be one vendor, so threw choppers about and here another Aslop fable, *Remember the stagecoach times for this city is not big enough for many vendors.*

And Dim Sun waved a finger at Grovelatkhan'sfeet who was crawling up the sedan, anyway, panting and gasping of course leaving sweaty pools everywhere.

"I need a cool refreshing fizzy drink," the sweaty one.

"Sound my gong," Dim Sun to be annoying and a bronze gong the size of a house was hit so Grovelatkhan'sfeet forgot what he had climbed all the way up for so started running down to Garrison but unfortunately he slipped on a caterpillar and flew down the rest of the way, headfirst of course.

"Lazy bugger that Khan," Tom not liking what he saw for volunteers got jobs like that so sympathized.

"Yeh so let us do him good," the barbarian Conan thinking of temples to ravage and girls in slit skirts at street corners needing ravaging.

And the gong summoned a cohort of the guard to sweep away the rickshaw boys and their postcards with revealing pictures of ducks, pagodas, and girls in slit skirts of course.

And Dim Sun summoned Grovelatkhan'sfeet back up with a flick of a royal finger just like her with the pretty ankles does in Ball.

"Master?" Grovelatkhan'sfeet.

"You are sacked."

And rickshaw boys were herded towards a war junk needing volunteers and behind them Grovelatkhan'sfeet about to throw himself off the dock to a waiting fin for he had several wives, heaps of kids and needed money to keep them all in different addresses.

"I am ashamed," Grovelatkhan'sfeet.

"This is not right, volunteers needed," Wamba and they came and sent Tom to fetch King Charles from the engine.

"Gasp, I cannot see anything for the sun is so bright," Drunken Noddy for engine cogs row in semi darkness.

And Wamba took Grovelatkhan'sfeet and held him close so Grovelatkhan'sfeet was afraid for he saw things moving from Wamba onto him, and then the smell of an unwashed barbarian overcame him so he grew faint.

"Please let me throw myself to the fin?" Grovelatkhan'sfeet begged but Wamba did not understand Confucus language.

But Grovelatkhan'sfeet knew the khan should have him boiled in tripe, then covered in Soya sauce and left outside the city walls for the jackals to eat for tripping.

"You come here," Dim Sun to his new messenger who ran all the way up the hundred hands of the sedan.

"Arrest them unwashed barbarians," Dim Sun and the new messenger to save time jumped and landed with a thud near Garrison.

And then Drunken Noddy was lined up and someone had stuck fig leaves in his hair and thrown a red rug on his shoulders, so now Drunken Noddy scratched here and there for it was Cur's sleeping rug.

And no one ever washed that nasty dog.

So Dim Sun summoned his new messenger back up and asked, "Who is he?"

And the new messenger on the way down complained, "Why cannot he ask all the questions at once?" And added, "Pant gasp."

"Our king?" The Mage using finger signs.

"I understand that sign," Dim Sun beginning to froth.

And the new messenger ran all the way to Dim Sun and grunted what The Mage had said.

"Ha he has he," Dim Sun and the guard laughed too and stopped just like that when Dim Sun stopped.

"Why did not you laugh?" He asked the messenger.

"Gasp pant he has he ah," the messenger.

"That is better," the cruel Khan, and "go tell the barbarians I want presents or else?" And shoved the new messenger so he tumbled all the way down to land next to Garrison.

"Gasp pant," was all the new messenger was able to pant so never delivered the message.

"Bonsai," Dim Sun and the cohort charged Garrison.

Now The Mage was examining Alicadabara's bandaged wand and pointed it at the road and the road vanished and a hole appeared with green mist coming from it and the sound of a drunk drinking meths and a red eared hound baying.

"Still works I see," The Mage returning the wand.

"Can I try yours; it has been so long since I had a good working model?" Alicadabara.

"Certainly, old boy," The Mage handing his over and just in case Ali had any ideas had cast a return spell on it so anything Ali cast at him would cast upon Ali, perhaps rabbit ears and a tail.

"Cucumbers," Ali and the hundred hands that were actually two hundred steps up the sedan to the throne became ice that Dim Sun slid down. All the way to the hole in the road.

"Gee up mules." Was heard as Arawan got his wagon into action.

"I have two hundred wives, an aviary to fill with budgies and zoo were my talking donkey escaped, I am needed back home, please let go of me?" Dim Sun.

"Burp," the rude reply from the drunk down there.

And new rickshaw boys appeared from behind bamboo grass and shouted, "Hey sailor you want young pixie girl in slit skirts?"

"We must refrain for we are fairies and need to visit Confucus at The House of the Green Aphid," The Mage and was a sour bunch Garrison was that followed him, thinking of ways of pushing him down that hole, accidentally of course.

"I have eyes in the back of my head, the first fairy that gets too close wears invisible clothes," The Mage and that silenced Garrison for they had to think about that one.

But never mind Wotanic eager to find bargains had waved his wallet above his head. A wallet soon to be emptied for about him shiny alligator shoes, singing crickets to send you to sleep, soft drinks, hard XXX, pixie women postcards and suits made in five minutes.

"You want play Bingo with me? Your number one General?" One of them pixies as she played with Wotanic's buttons on his tunic not pants as this is a respectable story.

"Grunt," the reply from Wotanic as his overheated brain was now empty.

"First you get washed as you smell like them," the pixie meaning departing Garrison following The Mage.

"Grunt," Wotanic's second reply.

And here another Alsop fable, *"Men."*

CHAPTER 61   SNIFF

Flowering Aphid house was covered in green fly and buzzed to the sound of insects. Why butterflies flew over the manicured lawn and in the garden pond water snakes ate frogs.

The shrubbery was jungle as Confucus was one these types that let nature to do its thing, so he was the source of the water snakes, the venomous type.

And over the pond he built an ornamental bridge where he could stand to meditate and watch the snakes eat the frogs.

And Confucus showed his unwashed guests the bridge and here one sat down motionless to fish for the carp Confucus liked to watch.

"If I move the fish will not bite," Harold explaining to you and the mosquitoes loved a target that stayed still, big mosquitoes carrying yellow fever and malaria.

And Cur seeing thingies slithering in the undergrowth of the uncut jungle went instead into the house and chewed expensive rugs to shreds.

For the dog needed training and a good beating.

"Come Mage I will show you a book how to get the better of the good god Daghdha," and Confucus took The Mage to his library and was the last time he ever saw his house because Garrison where in it.

"Here this reminds me of my young days," Conan stuffing Middle Kingdom vases down his leather trousers for he was stealing for barbarians never change their spots.

"Here this white powder reminds me of Filthy Big Bertha,"

Tom remembering waitress service for perhaps he was not as innocent as he seemed to be. And he and Garrison drank many bottles of rice wine so were violently ill on the walls that had beautiful paintings on them, of cranes, ducks, and mountains.

Then staggered about the house falling through paper walls and kicked a stove over and the house burnt down just like that.

"Glad we got out in time," Conan.

And in the library, "You must sacrifice a thousand crocodiles, twenty thousand cobras, a hundred ugly virgins," Confucus and began sniffing the air for he smelt smoke.

"Ugly?" The Mage.

"Daghdha has a wife," Confucus, anyway, a thousand gallons of wine, and a ship to burn and possibly ask him to keep Dim Sun," Confucus.

"There must be a cheaper way?" The Mage.

"There is, make an appointment to see Daghdha and hope he is in a good mood," Confucus.

"How do I make an appointment?" The Mage.

"I have prayer bells."

"Anything else?"

"Send him Wamba."

"And?"

"Try saying sorry on bended knees."

The Mage had a lot of options and the Wamba option was the most attractive the cruel nasty mage.

"Let us go back to the Flowering Aphid for I smell cooking?" Confucus and the first thing he said was, "Where is my house?"

And because he was in shock never saw The Mage sneak away and forgot to charge him for his advice and never gave a book away too.

And an Aslop moral here, *"Do not put your trust in fortune cookies."*

"If anything can restore the harmony of a disturbed brain it is watching relaxing carp swimming," Confucus and went to his bridge and saw fish skeletons for Harold was always greedy.

"Raspberry nuttery," Confucus doing a nuttery on himself.

"Never mind readers I am a powerful mage and will restore his house to itself," The Mage and clicked and just like that the pond was full of sticklebacks, toads, and midges. The house made of wood and the trees oaks and firs.

"I want Confucus Land house and carp," Confucus and did another mental adding, "I hate you Garrison."

And a toad croaked and hopped and Confucus started watching it and so did a water snake and a toad got eaten; yes toads was just as relaxing as watching carp swimming.

And on the road a hurrying mage wondering how to do Wamba, but Wamba was big, hairy, and likely to object to being done.

"Sorry Daghdha, I am sorry," The Mage going for the easy option.

*

Some say What'shisname lost his leg while marooned on a desert Island to cannibals.

Marooned but in an empty beer barrel the pirates had thrown over the pirate ship.

"Business deals have we?" Red Beard as fins fought over What'shisname in the barrel.

"50 50," What'shisname screamed up haggling over the price of rowers.

"Cannot hear anything can you lads?" Red Beard asking Cutyagizzard'sout and task master Whipthemhard who nodded and whistled.

"Help," What'shisname as a fin ate the bottom of the barrel he was in.

"95 of the profit to me," Red Beard feeling greedy.

But no reply.

"OK 99% to me and not a penny more," Red Beard and SILENCE.

Red Beard knew he was being generous. "Take it or Cutyagizzard'sout becomes new mate?"

Then he looked over the side, "Blooming heck what is that

in the barrel?" So hauled the barrel up for dinner was in it, a fin with an extended belly.

"Slit her open me hearties," Red Beard speaking pirate fashion for effect.

And Cutyagizzard'sout was disappointed for his promotion vanished as What'shisname rolled out.

Minus one leg.

And the stuffed parrot was still stitched to his shoulder.

And What'shisname the son of a night soul collector had run away to sea and had a wife in every port and tattoos showing the way to each; just in case he forgot one for a woman whose birthday is forgotten is a nasty piece of work.

And he was riddled with scurvy, malaria, gout, pox and usual ticks and fleas picked up in every port in every Inn in every port he sailed into.

And should have died but was a living germ himself who dreamed of being captain of a luxury cruise liner.

And Cutyagizzard'sout was the boson and got his name from cutting chicken stuff out in markets and allowed the name to stick for he was thick.

A son of a beggar with no ambition.

And no one knew anything about Whipthemhard apart from he whipped skin off volunteers and the one engine cog.

"All the faster to make them rowers row fast so I can meet Red Beard and spend my share of crew sales on good looking pixie women," Whipthemhard getting excited.

And Red Beard was the son of White Bread the son of Black Beard and all pirate scum captains.

And was fulfilling to be the most feared pirate captain of all time by throwing volunteers to fins.

"Fins do not want buckles and shoes but I know a certain salesman in Haliput who does, he ah he Ha," Red Beard going for a cheap imitated pirate laugh.

CHAPTER 62
ZANZIBAR

They did not ask to go to tropical Zanzibar; it was Tootanfoot desperate to be changed back into a fairy was told Alicadabara must go there that as it was, he who made him a donkey.

And here another Aslop fable; *"How can a donkey be made a donkey?"*

"Mumm," Alicadabara fingering his little wand, "Let us try this?" And waved arms heavenward for he was very theatrical, "By the weather, crushed newt kidneys, burnt bat tails, dragon's blood, let Tootanfoot be fairy," but forgot please so only the top of the donkey changed.

"Hey this is not fair?" The donkey desperate to meet a half donkey girl princess.

And the crew did what any no-good lazy fairy crew would, sun tanned and Wamba showed genius by drawing up a drinks waiter rota, and Apes and Grisly put-on aprons to carry cups of crushed oranges.

And where Bear went so did a suspicious Dwarf so hid behind a grass skirt.

And Apes flashed eyelids at members of the Lost Patrol hoping for a romantic sea voyage and when ignored foamed and frothed and sulked up in the rigging.

Even the engine was brought topside.

"Fresh air, thank you oh generous ones," for the engine cog did not want returned to the dark damp engines where he had to row so was practising grovelling.

"No hard feelings Drunken Noddy?" Wamba and handed him crushed ice mixed with crushed whatever Apes had been crushing before sulking which explains the strange things in the ice.

"When I am king again, I will make this Burke row and what am I drinking gasp I have been poisoned gasp," Drunken Noddy falling to his knees and was ignored as Garrison wanted to soak up the sun.

Now Zanzibar has lions and chimps and Morrigan is there behind seven silk veils flashing her eyes and whatever at the Sultan Rideemcameltrix for she wanted Garrison still.

And snakes crawled about ceilings and tree branches and crocodiles swam the harbour. A harbour Garrison just sailed in and Alicadabara and Offaltrex made yummy crocodile stew and Offaltrex stored many bales of crocodile leather with these words, "I am rich," and "wait till Harry hears the jingle in my pocket he ah he Ho ha he will have a sudden chest pain and I will be the rightful Boss."

Anyway: "Who are these hairy fairies?" Rideemcameltrix.

"Vikings," his Chief Advisor lost for anything else to say.

And Rideemcameltrix looked up the FTS index on slave prices and said, "Invite them ashore," planning to turn them into public harem attendants.

"I have never asked for anything," Morrigan lying for her vest was covered in rubies given her by Rideemcameltrix for he understood hip movements, the wiggle of a bottom and was a man whose brains were in his bottom.

"What is it my dove?" He asked opening himself to be mugged.

"I want those Vikings," for she knew it was Garrison.

And Rideemcameltrix sniffed for he saw no profit in this transaction unless; and he moved closer to Morrigan who shoved him away after letting him breath in her perfume and get dizzy of course.

"An armful of Heaven," he croaked and sent for his guard to arrest the hairy Vikings.

Now at the docks The Mage asked the guard this, "Why?"

"Ours is to obey orders blindly" the guard captain and saw Garrison approach him, why there was an ape riding a bear and a dwarf riding the ape.

And a dog foaming at the mouth and the hairy Vikings carried giant axes and what was this ship, The Marie Celeste?

And out the stern window Wotanic escaped with these words, "I hate this lot."

"He will be back," The Mage seeing Wotanic splash in the sea and a fin appear.

"Oh, mummy a fin someone nice save me," the aspiring Wotanic shouted.

"I am safe," Wotanic climbing onto a log that was bigger than the fin and added, "here why am I moving," for the log was the biggest saltwater crocodile ever and took Wotanic for a tourist ride.

"Help oh someone please help me," the unwanted loved one shrieked.

And at the far end of the harbour, he jumped ashore and ran into tall grass and stood on a lion; so, got mauled a little.

"Help someone send the marines," the ugly spotty mauled man.

Then recovering ran on and stood on an elephant trunk that beat the living hell out of him so he would not need an outhouse for a week.

"Why does not anyone want to save me?" The twerp asked the heavens that ignored him.

"Ga," Wotanic staggering into the arms of cannibals with these words, "At last civilisation, I am saved."

"Manna from heaven" the cannibal cook and slammed the lid down on the pot with Wotanic in it for he needed flints.

"I am off as I am no one's bacon," Wotanic and fled and stood on a snake that bit him so he puffed and staggered dazed into the arms of slavers.

"Save me I am snake bit," Wotanic hoping Christmas was early.

"We can sell this skinny one as a toilet attendant," a salver and took Wotanic to Harry Bros. PLC Zanzibar Slave Market and let the snake stuff swell Wotanic three times his size so buyers did think he was athletic and buy.

"Is that meths I smell?" Morrigan frustrated Garrison had done terrible things to the guard, "I did go to hell to be rid of Garrison."

"I will take Garrison," Nerthus suddenly appearing behind Morrigan who was looking out a palace window high up in a tower. And Nerthus was the wife remember and was wearing big black boots with studs.

And kicked Morrigan out the window and she fell into a wagon pulled by mules.

"My petticoats," Morrigan pretending to be a good girl and attempt to pull them down but in fact she was helping them billow out to show off her legs.

"Hi Ya, honey," Arawan not able to believe his luck that a handsome woman had joined him, so spat on his hands, wetted his hair, and forgot to pull up his zip and tuck in his jerkin, the leather jerkin, not gherkin oh never mind.

"Arawan unhand me," Morrigan as a drunk intoxicated with her beauty wanted a cuddle.

So Arawan was slapped here and kicked there so groaned and moaned as his wagon creaked off to hell.

"What is this mess I have landed on?" Morrigan for Arawan had been ill.

"Enjoy your visit in hell," Nerthus who knew hell with Arawan was meth fumed.

And in Zanzibar Apes had eaten many fruits from vendor stalls with Harry Bros. PLC above them, eaten things that the tide washed up, yellow plastic ducks and deflated dinosaurs and Zanzibar like many great cities, allows raw sewage to flow into the rivers, so that explains why Apes is clutching his tummy then falling flat on his face with a thud.

"Natures ingredients are always best and free," a cunning

whisper from a fairy who wears a black hood.

So, Apes rolled in the gutter this way and that and rolled down the stalls.

"That ape must be caught and stuffed," that cunning oily whisper again horrified at mounting repair bills.

And The Mage bought all the stuffed green mambas, scorpions, pickled chameleons, and crocodile suitcases to carry them back to the ship for potions and might explain why in the future Harry howls under a full moon.

And the Lost Patrol got lost and Conan went to find them but ravaged temples instead for habits die hard.

And Cur found love in a dog called Getlostrat and knew the days of bliss where limited for his ship would sail and leave behind an ugly litter and the reason why he did never write.

"Here these Vikings are showing us how to live, not to pay taxes and do what we want any time," the citizens of Zanzibar and looked at the hovels they called home, and the palace the Sultan called his hovel, so threw Rideemcameltrix off the quayside and made a beggar who could not read or write the new sultan just to be different.

CHAPTER
63   THE PAN

And while Victorious sailed home, Nerthus visited Queen Christina. Did not all virgins pray to Nerthus for nine months of hell and a ruined figure? And the question was what had been going on in that green fly infested rose garden?

And Nerthus had a duty to answer her devotees prayers and knew what husband Daghdha and Morrigan had been doing in the cramped back rattan seat of a chariot.

For the wife always knows, for she finds the other unmentionables stuck in a pocket, the diamond tiara under the pillow with these words, 'Happy birthday sexy,' and then she gets a Xmas card with Birthday scored out and a single chocolate square full of wiggling thingamabobs.

Yes, the wife knows.

So told Christina she would bring Garrison home because Daghdha hated them so would be good for his indigestion and gout.

"Why are you telling me this?" Christina suspicious of selling her shares in Harry Bros. PLC.

"I want the 1st May my remembrance day when the young shall dance the May Pole and frolic behind the barn," Nerthus predicting a population boom.

And Christina sighed for that part was easy AND SHE SHOULD KNOW.

"Also, the streets littered with dandelions and a million roasters released to ravage chickens behind haystacks, and to feed the energetic a million boars sizzling and a week's holiday for everyone to recover," Nerthus wanting a statue built to her.

And Christina lost her smile, Blackhood had been teaching her accountancy.

"That sweet man Harry Bros. PLC shall pay dearest because he is a man," Nerthus and Christina smiled.

"How will you get the miser to pay?" Christina was relieved her shares where safe.

"In bandages," Nerthus then saw her husband in another dimension.

"Oh dearest," Nerthus her voice full of honeycomb.

"Heck it is the bag," Daghdha taken by surprise.

"I do not like how you are treating Garrison," and did not add "nor being likened to alligator suitcases."

And Daghdha ignored the wife as he played with the oracle innards of a chicken to see what the weather would be like Tuesdays a.m.

And one never ignores the wife, especially one armed with a heavy frying pan.

"Cheating worm," the wife hitting him on the head, "I know you play bingo with that floozy in the back seat of a chariot," and hit him again but somewhere in the front so pearly white teeth littered the floor.

She was some woman scorned and wanting her husband useless for the opposition so hit him many times here and there and stamped there and there again and again. Oh, it was messy, horrid, and said, "half your kingdom I am entitled too and half I will take, and alimony for the kids that will be brought up to hate you. And if you forget their birthdays, I shall visit you with this," and brought a broom down on him and swept him up into a ball which she played football with; and guess what the ball screamed and yelled something.

What a scorned woman Nerthus was?

"So, you like black sexy suspenders," and tightened one of Morrigan's about his neck.

"Ga," Daghdha.

"And frilly knickers," and stuffed his mouth full of those

she had found in his pockets.

"Yucky," Daghdha naturally thinking they was the wife's.

"Like the whip, do we?" And whipped him good.

"Ga," as the god's mouth was full of frillies.

"And the rack while she paints her toes?" And threw a rack at him so he disappeared under it.

"Ga," managing an extra ga.

"Like rich food, do we?" Nerthus throwing a cauldron of lobsters at him and worse alive and biting.

"Why do not you leave me?" It was a squeak and full of hope.

"And allow her to become Queen of Heaven, you nuts or something," and made him polish her boots with his tongue.

"Yuck," he slurped as they tasted wife, of supermarket trollies, doggy whoopsie bags, dull cooking smells as have to cook on the cheap with twenty kids and not a whiff of perfume, just split milk, and baby sickness pongs.

"And would she wash your smelly unmentionables? And lie awake when you snore? No, I am not moving out to sleep in the chariot. And bet she has never stuffed a boar with sheep or must put up with your 'Windies?' No, it is the Chinese takeaway for her?" And attacked the good god with renewed vigor and eventually hit him so good he went to Peter Pan Land.

What a lesson this woman giving teaching jilted women the world over?

Oh yes, "EEK," was heard before he visited Peter and woke up much later.

"Is that 'nutter' gone" His first sentence then noticed a prayer stuck to his feet.

"Sorry," and was from The Mage.

"I will shred it to pieces for he is part of Garrison I loathe so much because Morrigan the floozy bit hates them," Daghdha then saw another note pinned to a heavy-duty frying pan.

"Answer it," and was from the 'nutter' so Daghdha trembled.

"I will ask Mahannan the sea good to give Victorious

currents to bring it home quickly, and Tanaros to fill the sail with wind and add this note, 'Nerthus has gone to see your wives?' So, they did as they were bid.

And Christina was picking green fly from her roses when news was brought to her of Victorinus's return. So summoned her crowd clearers, her naked barbarian fanners, her musicians and went to the docks for she had read about the Aztec gold and was hoping?

And make Garrison pay a treasure tax, a berthing tax, a drop anchor tax, and a right to Breathe tax and Blackhood knew the taxes would come to him for he was the nasty chancellor that thought them all up.

Bad Blackhood let us hope he eats an OUT-OF-DATE peach and moves into the outhouse.

Blackhood had many charities to support and his minor expendable relations were them.

And he lied telling Christina her 'X' built schools when it built sweat shops for street urchins to knit his designer T shirts.

And Give Archicteturalex was back and told Harry all about Treasure Island for he was a boaster and idiot.

And never noticed Harry's lips quibble as fangs fought to flop out and an urge to howl overcome him for even now at this early stage, he was drinking The Mage's vile potions for longevity.

And at last, Archicteturalex no longer sat at the bottom of the thousand-seater long table for relations were like rabbits; he now sat next to Harry.

"Treasure Island will make me rich," Archicteturalex and never saw Harry smile to hide his true intentions that were murderous and explains why Archicteturalex was an idiot about to meet The Fairy Grim Reaper then Fairy Maker in the Big Sky.

1.   And down at the docks an ape was swinging about the rigging without nappies in a sailor uniform.

2.   And a dwarf was at the ship's wheel.

3.   And a bear was in the crow's nest throwing rose

petals about.

4.　　　　And the crowd swore that was Drunken Noddy at the oars and serve the drunk right.

5.　　　　And the Lost Patrol in polished breast plates waved at the sight seers on the docks and because the real Garrison were hiding the crowd forgot what Garrison was.

And Christina forgot what Wamba was too for Dog Publishers owned by Harry churned out lies, Wamba was blond with blue eyes and handsome and well-equipped places; just what any girl wanted on HP.

For Harry knew ugliness and truth would not sell.

"I have spilt The Mage's wine on his carpets so I could sell them at discount so do not want him back," knowing The Mage did want his money back or else? Why Archicteturalex could pay for soon that minor relation did be upside down in a private dungeon reserved for too ambitious relations so all his cash did jingle out of upside-down deep pockets.

"I have substituted Harold's food with a rubber chicken and sold his supper to a beggar just to get the beggar's takings," and knew Harold was still happy with the rubber chicken that seemed to last forever so must stay away.

"I have sold books to Wamba that are pure rubbish about princesses and dragons," and knew Wamba would not do him for Wamba could barely read but still stay away.

"I told Conan about temples full of priestess wanting ravished and were full of pythons and tigers but by luck a passing circus wagon driven by Monty's cousin thirty times removed was driving full of circus workers waiting to be ravaged so Conan must stay away.

"I sold Tom nothing so am safe with him too," Blackhood but knew Apes would shred him, "I will give him a free mango and that will settle the score," and what about that Dwarf and crazy bear? "I will sell him a map to a gold mine in Siberia and the bear will follow him."

So Blackhood knew he was safe from Garrison in the docks, or was he? Garrison, he knew liked HP agreements for they tore them up behind your back while giving you strange finger signs.

Yes, Garrison was better quarantined at the docks; he did have to look to minor hooded relations crazy enough on the promise of a free dinner to sink the Victorious and all who sailed her.

But Archicteturalex said there was Aztec gold on the ship and the tax inspector did not need to know about it. But I can believe for I am the tax inspector for all gold marks and copper pennies are mine by Divine Right.

He has eh ha slurp dribble," and was the sounds of a greedy merchant and felt no remorse at wanting Garrison drowned, of course after he had emptied the ship of its Aztec gold.

Why Garrison had him to thank for their fame, his Dog Publishing House churned cheap paper backs out on their adventures and if Satirextex employed that monkey full time to write he did make Garrison more famous, of course after they were at the bottom of the harbor for Harry the Black hooded one knew lies made him money.

"Wamba meets Robin Hoodtrex," and "Harold marries Tazanantrex of the chimps," were best sellers and all lies.

Why the sales of grapefruit was up because fairies believed his lies that the sour fruit improved your vitality.

Why the sales of bitter Brussels sprouts was up because he lied saying the green cured constipation when every child knows they cause it so will not eat it.

Why the sales of prunes was up for he said prunes kept away vampires.

And incidentally toilet paper sales was up.

Yes, Harry knew lies kept him in power and floozy fairies at his poolside while you soaked in your bath in chilly water with a floozy yellow rubber duck.

"I must visit Christina and tell her the Victorious is full of poisonous spiders that can only be killed at night, then send in my brave relations to empty the ship of gold slurp dribble cough," as he tended to choke on his long dribbles. "Where is that girl, time means interest and money lost."

And heard, "Fall down and worship she with the pretty

ankles."

"Yes, she has pretty ankles," Harry watching her at the docks waving to GARRISON aboard ship.

"Froth dribble froth," the sound of an angry merchant choking on his own foam, "She must go, I will arrange bad land deals by making her buy the best land out but get the National First Fairy Bank to call in the mortgages for I am the Bank President. She will be broke and borrow from me and then I will sack millions of decent people working for me to raise inflation and make the gold mark worthless so she must borrow more from me.

And send out my greedy relations who feed at my long table for a thousand, send them to brothels, public baths, massage parlors, footballs matches, stagecoaches, lap dance venues; anywhere where two fairies meet to spread slander about Christina so the fairies of Haliput will riot, and send her to? MMMM, the war galley I am about to sink, just where can I send a queen with pretty ankles needing worshipped, perhaps those ankles might make me marks, two gold marks a peek, mm, slurp dribble choke," the Blackhood, *was nothing safe from his greedy oily visions?*

"I will tell her to marry me or else 'See that cage over there, there you will perch so worshippers can see those ankles,' yes and she will choose me for I have infected her with greed.

Why in the bottom of every fairy heart greed lurks and breeds sending signals to fairy brains to buy luxury yachts, Cadillacs, jet planes, mansions and shares in pop idles and must borrow from me so I will own their greedy souls he ah he has slurp dribble," the mean twisted demented Blackhood.

So, because he was choking on his dribble could do nothing to stop Wamba laying his cloak over a puddle for Christina to cross and board the Victorious.

"I must hurry or she will see the pirate treasure chests," Harry Blackhood and ran leaving a trail of saliva was dribbling and it was, "gasp my heart, all those pheasants and geese eaten at my table gasp pant dribble," but made the puddle that Wamba had taken his cloak away so Harry Blackhood disappeared for it was a hole that led to a fin below the pier.

"Splash," was heard and, "Goodness gracious me someone save me," from below the pier as a fin opened its mouth.

And there was a poof of magic as Morrigan afraid without Harry's direction her shares would be wiped out. Of course, she should have left him to the fin for he was swindling her out of every penny she had invested in Harry Bros. PLC.

"I am soaked, not to worry for I can smell gold and its warmth will dry me out," Harry Blackhood and made his way onto Victorious leaving a slug trail as he went.

"Here is your share Christina," Harry heard The Mage and hurried forward and saw a treasure chest opened, many chests opened so had a fit and was unable to stop Christina sending her naked barbarians down the gangplanks with many chests that dropped ruby rings so dock hands who worked sixteen hours a day for Harry Dock Labor PLC picked them up with these words, "At last I can feed my family of ten kids and three wives," and threw their brooms and barrels this way and that and many landed on the deck of the Victorious just where Harry Blackhood lay foaming and fitting.

And Wamba saw it was cruel to let Harry Blackhood see so much gold so shut the chests.

"I am the tax inspector so where is my share?" Harry Blackhood and with shaky fingers opened a chest and got his stubby fingers about a diamond tiara so he shook like jelly.

"Apes come remove this jelly from our ship," The Mage for Harry was shaking so much he had become incontinent so stunk something bad.

And Apes took him away at arm's length of course and above the chimney tops of Haliput asked, "Remove where?" And getting no answer from his apish brain just dropped Harry Blackhood just like that and there was a:

"SPLASH," below as Harry Blackhood went into an open sewer where real spiders lived.

And Harry was afraid of those hairy legs spiders always have so, "EEK," was heard from the sewers and rats the size of footballs lived there too, hungry fats that saw a fat merchant

Xmas come early so, "Ouch stop biting me was heard," but no help came as every fairy knew Harry lied so, "EEK," meant "Oh lovely," and " Ouch stop biting me," meant "ha that tickles."

And as Harry fought his way to his home that no one knew where it was, to sit at the top of a long wooden table, The Mage gave Apes a small ruby to take to the Tax Inspector to keep things legal.

"Ouk," Apes taking the ruby and a bunch of bananas The Mage had given to keep the ape busy and away from the ship. For Apes was dressed in a sailor uniform with no bottom or diapers.

"Ouk," Apes and "Sniff" as Apes had no idea where Harry Blackhood lived then luck was with him, Ape's saw minor relations in lines coming out of the shadows and going into the shadows as they headed to the long table where gruel laced with lemon grass waited.

Not that Harry Blackhood slipped that watery stuff, he ate the lobsters and duck at his end.

"Ouk," Apes asking one relation he caught and getting no answer shook him good till he was holding jelly again.

"Ouk," Apes grabbing another luckless relation and snarled at the relation's so he went white and shook with terror.

"Ouk," Apes and took another and "SLAP," for not all the relations where made of spiders and salt but perfume and roses; so "EEK," was added to Ape's vocabulary as this relation knew how to defend herself against gorillas that frightened little girls in black hoods in shadowy alleys.

So, Apes sat there battered and bruised scratching his head wondering what was wrong with these relations then he noticed something; they were all going in the same direction so he followed them.

And noticed something else, they were all in black hoods so Apes grabbed another relation and there was much, "EEK," as the relation being a modern Goth relation had just blackened his skin with shoe polish and studded himself with pins; very daring indeed but sharp to Apes.

So, Apes took another relation and "RIP," for the hood was

too small and "EEK," came from the relation as Apes was not careful, what he ripped?

"Ouk," Apes and "OoVoo," as Apes doubled as some relations wore mini skirts
under their hoods and they remembered what granny had taught them about dirty old gorillas wanting to give them sweets for a peek under the black hood?

So, Apes sat down black and blue scratching his head wondering how he could get a black hood for disguise and then saw a washing line, why on that line the biggest blackest frilly knickers ever.

At least Apes was in black.

And as the relations entered a dark tenement Apes came through the sooty stained windows, for effect of course.

So "EEK" and "I am done," was heard from the table as long glass splinters rained down and "EEK," from Apes as glass splinters got close to important bites.

Never mind these Give a Copper's bred like rabbits behind haystacks and in barns so do no laced with lemon grass get worried.

"Oh, by the gods it is that homicidal gorilla again," Harry fearing the worst and not a relation tried to stop Apes as he tried to get Harry to understand the ruby was the taxes and that was it, no more. And because even the sight of a small ruby got Harry dribbling Apes knew Harry did not understand so took all night to drum it into Harry no more taxes.

"Ouk," Apes repeated many times and "slurp," was heard from the table as relations drank their gruel laced with lemon grass.

Minor relations who hoped the ape would finish of greedy Harry for they dreamed and aspired to his place at the top of the table, where Birds of Paradise was stuffed with horse meat covered in butter sauce with free ketchup.

But they were out of luck for at midnight the town clock went ding and Apes knew he must return to the ship or turn into a pumpkin on wheels drawn by blind mice and Harry he knew did sit in the pumpkin coach and rub out hot cigars on him.

So, Apes fled out the front door this time as the stained window was busted up and outside, he said, "Ouk," which meant I am lost.

So, The Mage got his wish, it took Apes till the next morning and many drunks to tell him where the docks was.

And at a long table, "Half rations of gruel for the lot of you," Harry Blackhood for he knew his relations wanted him sent to King Arawan and his hell for ever and ever.

Then spend his cash on floozy women and blue painted yachts to cruise the seas with more floozy women sunbathing the decks with these words, "He will never be back, good riddance and more lobster and stuff the gruel."

Yes, Harry Blackhood was loved by his minor relations.

And nightly Haliput's vermin was kept awake by billboards going up advertising, "Wamba wrestles fins in open sewer, tickets bought at," and Blackhood found a look alike minor relation that resembled Wamba, threw a hood over him so none could see his face and threw him in the sewer, of course when all the tickets had been bought.

Too bad the fins won but the crowd knew Wamba always came back the next day alive, and there were many look alike relations available at a certain table eating gruel.

"And besides my relations must pay their keep and being ambitious they are in need of putting down for I am the only BOSS," Blackhood and dribbles over his power and behind him a new barrow full of old Garrison unmentionables and shredded socks that Garrison collectors did pay a fortune to own.

"They like the essences," Blackhood jingling cash and salivated over his pointed shoes.

And the millions boars he paid for the holiday of Nerthus were stuffed with piglets stuffed with yoghurt for they had been cooked in a nearby Indian.

And antelopes were stuffed with elephants for they were big antelopes.

And crows were stuffed with pigeons to answer the pigeon

problem, you know pigeon pooh on the head and statues.

And a pie maker and hunter not belonging to Harry grew rich for the million gallons of wine needed soaked up the greasy pies with strange ringed tails sticking out of them.

And no one minded as there was warm minted beer to wash down the tails.

Yes, a great May party and Nerthus was happy for with so many drunks about there was a population boom and Nerthus sagged with milk and smelled the clouds up with baby stinks.

"I must pull my hood down and sell pies also, there is money to be made from vermin," and sent his minor relations out instead, "BOSS never takes risks," and some relations ended up as pie ingredients as a pie maker and hunter objected to competition.

"Our pies are exactly six inches wide and must have at least one rat and tail and be three inches deep full of rich gravy and a whole onion to hide the flavor of rat," the pie maker and the hunter added, "We do not take kindly to these new traps these minor relations are using that catch a thousand rats a go, why even them randy rats cannot make enough rats to replace them caught, and I will be out of a job," the hunter and about his waist a belt with scalps hanging, scalps from minor relations who were not careful and turned their backs on a hunter and pie maker in a dark alley.

And now were ingredients, "The onion will hide their taste," the pie maker.

But Garrison wanted home to a moat where Womba's socks called from the bottom of the moat, "Wamba where art thou come back and get us on," but home was ash for the fiends had burnt the place up.

Ah nasty foolish fiends but left Filthy Big Bertha's alone, sensible fiends.

"Please stay here," Christina hearing of Garrison's home sickness.

"With you?" Wamba hoping.

"No," it was blunt.

"I understand I never rescued you from a dragon so never

made the grade of prince," Wamba.

And The Mage said, "Quite fool," and Christiana saw in Wamba all that was Garrison and needed quarantined.

And wondered how Garrison won?

And the answer was obvious, they had Wamba who had Garrison.

Then Conan slipped a hand under royal petticoats and squeezed a royal knee hoping he did get to stay in the rose garden, no one need know; he did dress as a gnome.

But the official food taster saw, he whom Blackhood hated.

And the food taster clicked a finger and the whole chorus appeared from behind curtains and sang,

"Worship and adore her,
she is a goddess,
She is divine."

"I am sorry Conan I cannot ride into the sunset on your back and be ravaged," and wanted a mile away from his tobacco breath.

And tobacco splattered over the food taster who shouted, "Yikes."

"I want home," Tom and cried for he missed the waitresses to paint.

And Cur howled and cocked its leg on the food taster who shouted, "Yucky."

"Yes, I miss my tower," The Mage and added, "we shall go but never fear we shall return when needed and beware he in the black hood," The Mage and Christiana had made up her mind never to invite them back for they stunk something bad.

"You mean Harry?" Christina.

"Sis, he has spies everywhere," The Mage as the food taster leaned down with a hand over his ear.

And as citizens bought liver salts from hooded minor relations the next day Blackhood watched a snail somersault and do gymnastics.

"Sign here," Harry Blackhood shoving a saucer of rancid butter sauce forward so the snail signed his X.

So Isisnaphut signed his kingdom away and cursed the day

he crawled out of Harold's deep pocket. Now he was just a tasty snail.

"Now I own the flat world, what next? Harry foaming and pushed his chair aside and went to his accounts room to him was what dad's did on attics with train sets, toy boats in baths and Garrison with waitress in Filthy Big Bertha's.

And seeing his accounts in the black did not cheer him for, "She is not mine," and shut his eyes to sleep and count woolly £ and Kashmir $ jumping over a gate and did not fall asleep. So annoyed Isisnaphut by dropping him into the rancid butter sauce and then heated the sauce up, oh what a cruel Blackhood this was.

But Harry Blackhood had heard his tummy rumbling and was just playing with his food.

"Did I hear gastric juices," Isisnaphut weakly and tried to slime his way off the table with these words, "surely he will not eat me," as he attempted freedom.

"What a large rubbery body you have?" Harry stirring the peppery sauce and flicked a few drops at the snail.

"I eat well," the snail at the table edge.

"What long eye stalks you have?" Harry letting a long strand of saliva fall onto the snail as it went over the table edge.

"All the better to see with," the snail answered from the table leg allowing Harry to know where it was, silly foolish gastropod.

"What a long tail you have?" Harry adding chopped shrimp and watercress to a bowl of noodles for Harry knew watercress was good for Blackhoods for he watched Pop Eye the Sailor films so knew it was full of iron.

"Not a bit of fat," Isisnaphut boasted just reaching the floor and freedom.

"All mine even the shell on his back can be crushed as manure," Harry Blackhood and dropped the snail onto the noodles and pored rancid butter sauce on it.

And Isisnaphut eased Harry's pains and here an Aslop fable: *"Let noodle never show their customers what is in the noodle."*

*

Harry feels the pluck

"Hallo Harry dear," the sweet female voice floated through broken stained glass revealing a Cockney accent; and Harry opened one closed eye Apes had previously closed.

Always looking for a gold mark or the contents of a piggy bank.

"Why dearest been a naughty boy have we?" Nerthus.

"A goddess come collecting," Harry coughing up teeth.

"Could say Harry darling," Nerthus meaning he was a dastardly swine.

"Cost a lot this stained-glass window?" Nerthus pinging shreds out that fell on him so he shrieked and knew this was not a social visit.

"EEK," he moaned.

"Your Christina is making May Day my remembrance day," Nerthus informed him plucking hairs off his head as his black hood was down.

"Ouch," he replied.

And knew the bottom line was near as he felt gold marks crawl deeper into his pockets.

"Dearest Harry you look ill," Nerthus gloating and plucked faster.

"OoVoo," was heard often.

And she drew his tongue out to check for spots and he was amazed it stretched three feet.

And more amazed at the speed it withdrew when released with a splat.

"Groan," was heard.

"Guess who is paying?" Nerthus sweetly so Blue tits appeared and sang summer chirps.

"I refuse," he could not help himself even knowing he had committed suicide, a mark was an adult penny and his by Divine Right.

"My loose teeth?" She pulling three without aspirin to kill the pain and there was much of that for she wanted his gold filings.

"I am sure Haliput will be grateful eating a million boars and millions of gallons of wine dearest? Do not you??" And floated above him and clicked royal fingers and he floated up too.

"Amazing?" Harry trying to see ways of turning halflings into pennies for that is what he paid the cleaners who missed much dirt, and the obvious answer was too "SACK THEM and employ minor relations for free.

"Here honey pie just X here?" Nerthus and Harry grimaced for he knew about X.

And his hand shook as he signed because Nerthus was booting him, from behind of course for she did not like to watch swine suffer.

"And I will make sure I get my share of boar for I am ravenous," Harry Blackhood.

And Nerthus read his greedy thoughts so dropped him from thirty feet with these words: "What a darling you are?"

"Pregnant cow of Heaven," he muttered as his face was buried six inches in the cement floor. Yes, it had been a messy landing with lots of cracking sounds.

And she heard and replied with a royal click outside the broken window.

"Pitter patter," the sound of a thunderstorm above his head.

"Thank you very much," he spluttered.

And she replied with a tornado of newts and toads to make warts.

And smelt his rump on fire as lighting hit it and was grateful for the rain for it put out the fire.

"Thank you," he spat.

"Think nothing of it dear," the goddess lying for she meant it all.

And worse an earwig came and bit him for these insects have large mouths and it spat him out for he was bitter.

Then a centipede bit unmentionables and died. The black rat bit him and got rabies and jumped out the broken window and a cat ate it and so spread rabies everywhere.

Then a ravenous cast away pet, a dog wanted to eat him; but cocked a leg instead.

Then the rain stopped and the insects and beasts had a rest and Harry said, "Thank you very much pregnant cow of Heaven," for he thought she had gone.

"I heard that Harry," and Nerthus threw a weasel amongst the insects and beasts so Harry shouted, "ARGH, my thingamajigs."

And then "Help," but Nerthus was gone just as well.

*

And citizens had their books on Garrison for Satirextex whipped the monkey to write faster' and Sampenciltrex fed the parrot more crackers to chisel statues so the parrot became obese.

Garrison was FAB.

So, Harry Blackhood saw his bank account rise for he was mega rich.

"My first born will be called Ordinary," a beggar with no hope of marrying for he was ugly, leprous, and worse, broke.

"I will have Conan tattooed on my huge chest," a washer woman and showed them to blind innocent boys like Tom.

"Giggle," the innocent boys behind bushes.

Remember they were blind fairy lads.

"This fad will pay for the May Day holiday and those million boars," Harry gloating.

"We want our Garrison heroes who sailed off the edge of the square world,

We want streets and sewers named after them,

Our milking cows,

Their scalps to keep,

And the skin off their backs,

For Garrison is FAD,

So will wear their unwashed unmentionables,

If it is Garrison FAD," beggars and washer women agreed then did throw Garrison mugs, wall posters and thingamajigs stolen from Garrison while they slept into the bin

But for the moment if Dog Publishers was making cash jingle in a Blackhood pocket they was Fad.

CHAPTER
64   PETITIONS

And Harry made his relations write petitions.

"Crack," was heard often and, "Oh my aching arm, perhaps I can hire a minor relation for this whipping job with the promise of a burger," Harry Blackhood and used the whip so, "EEK," and, "Shriek," filled his ears from writers and was soothing music to the miser.

And selected a skinny minor relation to use the whip and thought these selfish thoughts, "He will not last the night, but long enough to get the petitions written and I will eat the burger myself for I am partial to a double cheese treat."

"Oh, Great Queen, Apes is swinging about the rafters of the rooftops and makes finger language at you with raspberry sounds; for the primate is cheeky and wants to be King of Haliput by marrying you.

We the pie makers beg you send the gorilla to a faraway forest full of snakes that might bite the nasty banana eater. An ape that eats all our pies without paying so your citizens go hungry and riot," and was copied by a hundred relations and pie maker became a hundred complaints.

"Crack," went the whip.

And Christina remembered Apes as wanting to marry Harry Blackhood and thought it wise to send the monkey away just in case it became a business relation sent on jobs. Jobs requiring muscle and a brain the size of a peanut; trained as a

Ninja monkey to get rid of her.

"And here is the bill for forty thousand bananas."

"Oh, Great Queen whatever Harold is he costs you cash for he never has any money when he dines out and sends the bill to you. Whatever he is has a stomach that devours a hundred courses in a night, not mentioning breakfast and lunch or tea and muffin with

waitress service," and many minor relations, "EEKED," as they wrote this complaint from many restaurant owners for Harry was jealous for he ate a moldy burger; waste not want not his motto so did not waste the loo paper needed; while that whatever it was Harold ate pies with ringed tails all washed down in gravy. So kicked the skinny runt of a minor relation out of the way, took the whip and whipped the writers to shreds, forgetting it was all lies about Harold.

"Oh, blazes I need more minor relations to take the writers places," Harry and shuffled away into the shadows for relations.

And Postscript was added, "So send whatever away before we have no customers for, he eats with his trousers about his ankles, belches and winds and picks his nose and eats what is found."

And included were many restaurant bills for fifty thousand gold marks.

"He ate the furniture," was added as an explanation.

And Christina knew Haliput would lose the Title of City of Culture if Harold was not sent away.

"Shriek," was heard for atmosphere as quills dipped into ink pots and wrote more minor relation lies:

"Oh, Great Queen, Wamba your intended visits every tailor in town and has had a thousand suits made from golden silk and here are the bills," and it came to a million gold marks and, "He has set a date for the marriage."

And Harry shook all over for the lie was genius and when he recovered booted the skinny relation for not giving out enough whip.

"Oh, Great Queen, Conan has looted the Temple of Nerthus

and ravaged the priestesses and put-up pictures of Morrigan for worship, and we know how Nerthus feels about her?"

And Christina feared Nerthus might come visiting then noticed a bill attached to the complaint, "A Hundred thousand gold marks will compensate the priestesses."

And Christina looked at her money chest and saw moths flying away for it was empty.

"Oh, Great Queen Tom is not so innocent for the boy ravages all the daughters he can find and demands closed sewers for the open ones smell something and the cost of his damage is twenty million gold marks for Haliput is full of daughters and do you want to know the cost of covering the sewers?"

And Christina grew faint.

"Oh Great Queen that nasty dog Cur chases oxen pulling circus wagons and Monty's cousin thirty times removed is driving and the crossed eyed Burke loses control and the wagons have blocked the open sewers; and the rats living in the sewers are using the wagons as ladders to reach the streets, why your palace is **now** rat infested, and Give a Pied Piper Harry wants ten million gold marks to trap them," and Harry had a fit over his lie and because he foamed and shut his eyes the skinny relation whipper took a break.

A short break for Harry Blackhood was known to sleep with an eye open.

And Christina shook and had a fit herself but never mind a petition about The Mage was waiting to be read when she awoke.

"The Mage rides Bat Wing turning citizens into newts and toads for he needs them for ingredients that he sells to citizens to grow warts who then must buy ingredients to get rid of them, and the toad and newts are suing you for damages," and for effect a minor relation had enclosed a toad so Christina screamed and threw the thing out a window and it went down a citizen's back so he screamed all the way home.

"Who threw a toad down my shirt?" He asked everyone he met and they all replied, "Hello warty face, no idea," for we all know what toads give!

But Christina kept numb for the complainer was seven feet tall and all muscle.

"Oh, Great Queen Captain Moronicus and his Lost Patrol billet where they please and the homes they leave are no longer fit for fairies to live in for they are not house trained so send them away fast," and Christina saw a PS ," Moronicus do not forget wants to marry you, think of the cost of all the newspaper you must put down on the floor."

"Oh, Great Queen, Alicadabara with his two-inch wand turned the night watch into donkeys to keep Lord Tootanfoot company and boasts he will marry you and do not forget he is a Fiend, ugly and carbuncle ridden with itchy feet to lie in your bed and cuddle into you on your wedding night." And the many wives of the night watch are suing for maintenance and their girlfriends too.

"Loan Terms," she read and threw the petitions at Cannymindtrex disappearing in red robes with these words, "I will marry none of them lawyer."

So, Christina summoned her sedan chair and improperly dressed dancing girls for they were young and full of flirtatious ideas for they were not married and tied down with sixteen kids and stretch marks places.

And the chorus appeared and sang, "Fall down and worship her with the pretty ankles."

And the naked barbarian fanners stood beside Christina and the crowd gaped when they should have shut their eyes; *for the fanners were all minor relations of Arnie something from Austria so the gapers were in for a thrill of a lifetime.*

And Christina sought Garrison in the gutters where they slept for, they fell there full of XXX the night before so were covered in them rats queuing up to run up circus wagons to escape the life of the sewers.

And Garrison when found Christina sent Sprintex from her high Sedan chair to empty the petitions at The Mage's feet for he was a secret alcoholic so was in the sewer
with his boozing pals.

"We are illiterate," Conan bragged.

But deep-down Garrison were happy they was getting the bung for it meant they were going home to a moat that stunk worse than the open sewers.

Where Womba's socks called, "Where art thou, come get us on," from the bottom of the moat.

And happier they did not have to pay any bills, just leave a gnawed chicken bone as a tip.

And because Harry Blackhood was rubbing his hands and salivating never noticed Offaltrex buy out the wife and mistress's shares in his shops.

"He was a down and out ship's cook so why should I have noticed him?" Harry Blackhood.

And Offaltrex never let on he was getting rich and more rich and even filthy rich in case someone said, "You are one of them, Garrison."

And did not paint his name over the shops just in case he had to pay Garrison bills and so he held no grudges against the wife and mistress so gave them night porter jobs and a tied house out the back, pig pens with these words, "More than what they gave me," and hugged his teddy and added, "Many fairies living in cardboard boxes will envy them." And bought teddy silk pajamas for bedtime.

*

And Bat Wing and Old Nag spent many a happy month above Haliput breathing in its essences so were ill often; so never got around to the interesting stuff in a relationship but did speak these words of wisdom: "Our holiday is over thanks to them lot."

And a hundred years later stalls opened on them hills and other hills as the owners did not want to admit their hill was not the hill these two creatures sat and messed the place up for there was no facilities; and the stalls sold plastic dinosaurs.

"Everyone would leave my restaurant and go eat at the restaurants at the top of his hill were these fabled creatures sat, and worse eat more cheaply and healthy," Blackhood so erected signs on every hill claiming it was the spot of the creatures and had the stalls sell noodles too.

Harry's Chinese Restaurant and sold sweet and sour trotters and noodles.

Harry's Kebabs and sold spicy egg noodles minus eggs.

Harry's Tea and Cakes and sold strawberry flavored noodles.

And shops with revolving restaurants belonged to him, Offaltrex the opposition and yes, the pig pens still existed round the back and tourists paid to see where the wife and mistress lived out their years.

Anyway.

"Garrison is getting the bung, looks like the Burke will want to sit on my sagging back," Old Nag devising ways to buck Wamba off into the sewer.

"Yes, that arthritic dirty old man who turns fairies into newts will want to fly about on me," Bat Wing devising ways to buck The Mage off a thousand feet up.

"I will straighten my back and turn my face to him, then snarl just before I bite a chunk of flesh out of him and he will be so surprised he will just fall off just like that," for Old Nag knew his days as a star attraction Bucking Bronco was over; so was forced to resort to nasty methods.

"My hero," Bat Wing sighed and rubbed her neck against the horse's neck and her scales cleared much fur so thingies were seen, ticks and nits that live on a horse never brushed and left to fend for itself.

And was a lie for Bat Wing as she sighed thought of another hero, a big red and black dragon with soot stains and sighed again and Old Nag felt good he could make a girl sigh twice.

"We can find a hill at The Bridge and sit on our haunches watching them," Old Nag cheerfully.

"Yes, as critics and do nothing as we have done throughout this story," Bat Wing and knew when the old horse was away, she did be flying about with that dragon or worse, in his cave looking at his pressed flower collection!

For bat Wing knew the fiery hot dragon could make a girl sigh three times.

And here an Alsop fable, *"Do not throw away the black address book."*

CHAPTER 65
GREATEST EVENT
SINCE SAILING OFF
THE SQUARE WORLD.

Billboards advertised Garrison sailing into the sunset never to be seen again.

"Hurrah," the crowd for it hated Garrison that was to them a stray dog they had befriended that weed in the best China as the priest came by, and left unmentionables with a strong pong on your 'Welcome' doormat for the priest to stand in.

Not to mention it chewed the carpet too shreds for the priest to trip on and scream as he hit the chewed lamp stand that now fell on him, and since the candle was lit set him on fire so he ran screaming from your house.

"And we donated the balloons to make a party atmosphere," Blackhood, "let this be a lesson in economics," and choked on a big cigar and added, "I will get used to it, the image counts," and dribbled for he knew balloons led to XXX and a baby boom and nappy sales would go up.

And a thousand minor relation heads coughed on small cigars and nodded and dribbled saliva and had fits just like him for money was visualized.

"The image counts," they all agreed.

"Assandeadlyknife my distant relation, you will burst the

balloon that is to take Garrison away, just as it floats over the fin infested sea."

"How Boss?" Assandeadlyknife for he was thick as thick toast.

"Do you own a knife?"

"Yes Boss," and Assandeadlyknife showed Boss his sharp knife and soon red stuff was squirting from his fingers for he was ever so careless as well as thick as thick toast.

"Just be in the balloon OK," and Boss Harry Blackhood ran for a bucket and

coughed these words, "Cough the image counts," then was ill for he was allergic to tobacco.

So once upon a time then an assassin as thick as thick toast sneaked under trampolines and ropes to get close to Garrison.

"Here I bet you do not have a ticket to see Garrison?" A minor relation whose job it was to catch those sneaking under trampolines to see Garrison and then beat them up good with a crowbar.

"EEK," was heard and "Ouch."

Then the black and blue thick as toast assassin crawled under tables and had to crawl fast for horrid things was done his legs; for here under the tables his fingers got stood on and those above some had too much XXX and relieved themselves on him for the latrine was too far away; and others stumped their cigars out on him and rats fought him for scraps here too. And some full of XXX and the ingredients of Coffin Pie were ill on him. And some were tittering Geek girls in heavy laced up boots that were attached to jerking legs so went places and he could not "EEK," for he knew assassins never did.

And so unable to use his legs and fingers and stinking and smoldering something the assassin crawled and moaned away and passed floozy women who giggled and then used their parasols on him; for no one understands the mind of floozy women; then bored of this and in a hurry to reach the drunks at the tables ran all over him, and their stiletto shoes went in his eyes as well as important places.

"Shriek," and "cur blimey that hurts," was heard but no one

took any notice but some did say, "My something stinks?" And sprinkled more perfume about that sprinkled into his sore eyes so made them puff worse.

And being unable to see crawled into the thunder box and out again covered in loo paper. "Something stinks?" The park attendants then seeing the escaping loo paper beat the stink up good with brooms and mops for this was a '5 Star Park.'

Yes, his name was Assandeadlyknife and bumped his head into the big balloon that was to carry Garrison over the sea.

"Here this old rug must be Cur's to sleep on?" Wamba and threw Assandeadlyknife onto the balloon.

"Up here I will wait and use my sharp dagger so the balloon drops to the hungry fins," and cut himself again so really did some medical help; but he was an assassin and trained to be deadly tough and had a bald head.

Assandeadlyknife was his name and bled all over the top of the balloon and they say fins can smell blood ten miles away.

And the balloon basket was filed with pickled snails in jars, bananas and a flock of geese, a herd of cows and treats like gingerbread fairies spread in black molasses.

Yummy and sticky too.

And a portable army loo for they did need one.

But what about him hiding in the balloon above with a red stained dagger, what was he too use.

Never mind assassins were trained to hold it in for days and longer.

"Goodbye citizens," The Mage, "We are sorry to leave but must go home."

And millions nodded agreement and he above in the balloon wished The Mage did hurry for he had been last in the training class and wanted a latrine quick.

But he was an assassin and had a job to do.

"Yes, I have a job to do, curse," and crossed his legs and used a piece of string.

"Hurry up and go," the crowd shouted back.

"Ungrateful fairies," Conan and Apes agreed with an "Ouk."

Then Sprintex arrived from Christina with a note.

"Our pardon," that Burke Wamba.

"Mage be a dear and give me a goose that lays golden eggs?"

And The Mage a fool for a pretty ankle that was showing at the top of a nearby sedan chair agreed.

And Sprintex ran back and Christina greeted the goose with these words, "Hurry and lay a gold egg or it's goose orange tonight girl."

"Quack," the goose and laid a hurried egg and was a miracle for it was a boy goose.

"Here where is my egg?" A bar owner whose bar Dwarf and Grisly had demolished.

"And mine?" A pie maker whose pies Harold had eaten and not paid for.

"And mine?" A waitress in a slit dress for Tom had never paid for the service for he was just an innocent Garrison boy and did not know his ABC.

"Hurry to the palace," Christina and left the rioting mob and The Mage had the fire under the balloon lit so the balloon filled with stifling air; and because the rioting crowd made so much noise no one heard the gasps and screams from the balloon as Assandeadlyknife cooked.

"I must see what all this noise is about?" Harry Blackhood emerging from his house and saw indeed a rioting crowd coming down the narrow street and behind him a thousand minor relations so he could not get back in his house.

And some say the minor relations deliberately pretended to be stuck in his doorway for giggling and "his chips are in," was heard by them in the crowd that ran over Harry Blackhood mugging him as they went.

And muggers know what to do to victims so soon even the moans and groans coming from the flattened black hood stopped.

"Messy, was it?" Old Nag still on the hilltop.

"Yes," Bat Wing but her mind was on a red dragon with soot stains.

CHAPTER 66   NO EVIDENCE

"The balloon,
Fairies attempt to reach the stars.
Spoofed just like that.
And bunged Garrison.
To fins below.
Waiting for the mealy-mouthed parachutes,
That was Garrison coming down," Satirextex.
"That poet certainly comes cheap," Harry Blackhood.

So, a plastic statue was modelled by Sampenciltrex and his monkey. In dockland it stands and seafarers throw pennies at it with these words, "We know Garrison is still amongst the clouds so give us fare winds and no following fins for many of us fall overboard when doing our abolitions in the stern," and explains why sea farers never eat prunes and suffer constipation.

And here Aslop advice, *"Beware then what is in a ship's apple barrel?"*

And at night when sea farers sleep it off in gutters and at Filthy Big Bertha's Sailor's Home scores of black hoodies appear and collect the pennies and take them to Harry Blackhood.

"I am rich drool cough dribble," Harry Blackhood and "must smoke one of these cigars as the image counts cough wheeze pant."

But here the truth about Assandeadlyknife in the balloon cooking on slow heat.

"I must use my dagger and destroy this horrid balloon before I am casserole," Assandeadlyknife.

So, he looked out of the balloon where the heat comes up so was toasted some more with these words, "Where is the jam?" And seeing no sea or fins below knew he must get the balloon to the sea wherever it was but how? And had no idea for he was thick as thick toast without jam.

"That is why I sent him," the BLACKHOOD HARRY dribbling and coughing on a cigar as he read how much he had insured Assandeadlyknife.

And as Assandeadlyknife crawled back inside the balloon his dagger fell out of his pocket and pricked the balloon.

"Hiss," went the balloon.

"Oh, dear what have I done?" Assandeadlyknife for he was thick as thick burnt toast with no butter or jam.

So, rushing air sucked him into the hole he had made so never heard The Mage.

And the rushing air was so loud no one heard what The Mage said too.

But What'shisname thought he said throw unwanted stuff out to lessen the weight or perish.

"So, help me Cutyagizzardout," Whipthemhard and together threw Lord Tootanfoot out of the balloon.

"Bray," Lord Tootanfoot in mid-air with no air to stand on.

"No one wants a half donkey anyway," Cutyagizzardout the nasty animal lover.

And a lucky thing it was a half donkey thingamajig as it had hands to grab a trailing rope.

"We need volunteers to go up and stitch the hole in the balloon," The Mage so volunteers gathered at the opposite end of the basket away from him and counted seagulls nonchalantly.

So, the wicker basket tilted and "Help," was heard as members of that lazy no-good disease-ridden Lost Patrol fell out.

And none perished for they all held onto Alicadabara some place so he shrieked and begged them to let go so pulled him out to.

And not one did let go for they had just air to walk on.

And crawled up Alicadabara lengthening something so he shrieked louder and fainted a good thing too for they stuck their toes in his eyes and mouth so gagged him, just as well for his shrieks were ear piercing and sore.

And clung to each other's chain mail and when that was ripped away clung to unmentionables and when that was ripped away just as Alicadabara awoke he shrieked again at what was in front of him; Tootanfoot who was grabbed by the Lost Patrol so cheer up, none fell to the fins below.

So, these hardy naked marines clung to their mates hairy chests and legs till the fur was ripped away.

Yes, fur for these are members of the Lost Patrol whose mothers danced the Dance of The Maypole under full moons to get husbands for they had warts and moles from drinking vile stuff to attract husbands. And did not know they was better off being single.

And anyway: when the fur was gone there was your mates long curled up black toenails to hold onto so "Yuck I am not clinging to those," was heard then "Yikes," for there was nothing else to cling to except Alicadabara again who clung to a donkey man.

"Bray," was also heard in a high pitch for Alicadabara was not careful what he clung too.

"Volunteers," Wamba as he clung to The Mage to stop himself joining the clingers outside.

And why The Mage helped him, for he did not like Wamba that close for strange things lived in Womba's clothes, things that made you scratch.

"Banana here Apes," The Mage and Apes did not get his banana for, "Ta very much," Wamba and ate the fruit and went up the balloon with a needle and thread. But never got there as Apes was peeved off about the banana so jumped Wamba who had no option but to drop the only needle and thread.

That explains why The Mage was all boggled eyed for he had foamed at the mouth and pulled his long white hair out at the roots.

So writhed in agony now.

"Throw the Burke off," members of The Lost Patrol urged the ape.

"Here that Burke is our sergeant," Conan being a barbarian always wanting a punch up for he had watched to many John Waynetrex movies; so, jumped the marines and shred more fur.

"Order in the ranks," Admiral Wotanic and was thrown overboard.

"Not me too?" Captain Moronicus in his navy feathered hat.

"This is a mutiny so walk the plank," a marine.

"There is no plank," Moronicus saved.

So threw him overboard just like that.

Then Captain Red Beard told the marines he was a pirate and one of them but the marines knew what a captain was so tried to throw him overboard.

And did but he took many of them with him for he was big and muscular and exercised with weights daily and ate his cereals and greens.

But the idiots fighting below undid the balloon's harness so WOSH away it went out to sea where fins waited.

"I am rich," Harry Blackhood clutching the insurance papers and dribbled so it ran from his gums to his feet, "that is why I sent Assandeadlyknife for he is thick and knew he did assassinate himself he ah he Ha," the greedy BOSS using a telescope for fairies were not a backward lot, jut fairies.

"Now I can marry Christina and own Ball and be called King Blackhood."

Anyway: As Cutyagizzardout tried to cut Whipthemhard gizzards out The Mage clicked and scratched for Wamba had been close to him, and Old Nag found himself outside the wicker basket attached to it by harness.

"Well at least it is not me," Bat Wing and went back to dream of a red dragon with soot stains but The Mage had not forgotten her so she pulled the basket too.

And more clicks passed so The Mage was left all alone smoking Conan's clay pipe with satisfaction across his face, for the scratchy thingies did not like tobacco smoke.

"Chirp tweet tweedy," fairies chirped pulling the basket next to a horse and bat.

"Bird sounds to soothe nerves, wish Confucus could be here," The Mage and a pity Harry Blackhood was watching a balloon amongst fins so did notice the basket or stalls selling his out-of-stock goods.

"Do not return with them shoddy goods or else," the minor hoodies remembered so gave them away to Offaltrex and his minor relations for no one would buy them.

Why Offaltrex had sent his minor relations out with baseball bats, bigger ones than Harry's minor relations carried under their black hoodies to impress the minor relations.

"I will sell his goods and let him know how I got them and Harry being a stressed-out workaholic merchant must have ulcers that will groan and pop and send him to hell," the merchant Offaltrex and here an Aslop fable, *"Tinker sailor soldier cobbler airman but never merchant will I be."*

*

"Lay an egg you feathered roast," Christina soothing the goose to make it lay a golden egg; and since it refused stroked its long neck between her hands.

"Bo Ho what have I done?" After she had strangled it, of course.

"I presume Madam has savings," Sprintex always ready at her side to sprint.

"How much have you?" For Christina had learnt much from Harry Blackhood and was to hit a gong to summon Pitter Patter.

So Sprintex swallowed hard and squeaked, "Twenty thousand gold marks," for he was a hoarder saving for a rainy day; and behold it was raining newts and frogs just like that.

And Christina hit the gong and took his savings.

"Put not your trust in princesses," Sprintex as he heard Pitter Patter the Chief Executioner coming for him.

"Ha Ho just joking," the wicked princess with pretty ankles.

"Gasp pant I am so relieved your majesty," Sprintex and wisely did not mention the names he thought to call her.

And a hearse stopped at the palace gates where guards looked the other way for, they had not been paid.

And Harry Blackhood stepped out of the hearse as mist enveloped him.

"Eagor," Harry shouted and Eagor doubling as driver, coachman, valet, bouncer, messenger jumped down for he was huge and gormless *and worse a minor relation.*

And went on all fours so Master could ride him into the palace.

So Eagor added atmosphere.

So, Christina gripped her throne as mist rolled in under the throne room door that suddenly opened to eerie music and there was Eagor with Harry who wore gleaming spurs.

And the door slammed into Pitter patter who would not be chopping for a while for he was moaning and slithering on the floor; and here his head cracked Eagor's chin just as Harry used his gleaming spurs to make Eagor rise on his hind legs.

For effect for Harry always wanted an entrance like that out of the cowboy movies.

But Harry Blackhood was a miser not cow hand so fell off Eagor with a thud.

"Where am I?" Harry as he staggered and tripped over Pitter Patter so his head went into a Confucus Willow Pattern vase and stuck there.

"Boss where art thou?" The gormless monster Eagor and picked up the vase and threw it hard against a wall to save Boss.

So, the vase split open and Harry saw many queens and did not know which to demand marriage from?

And because he was in a spin never saw a wicker basket pulled by magical Garrison at the palace balcony.

"Ga," Eagor for he clapped his hands for there was a chimp

there he could play with for Eagor had no friends; and by the way Eagor could not tell a chimp and ape apart.

"Take the basket full of golden eggs Harry and my debt to you is clear," Christina loosening her senses and Harry dribbled all over the place so slipped on his saliva and landed in the wicker basket. And it was painful for hard gold eggs were there so he moaned and shrieked a little.

"And take the lousy goose too," Christina added and threw the goose on him.

"All mine," Harry Blackhood still seeing many queens," and never saw The Mage click a finger so all the eggs became chocolate eggs that started to melt for Harry sat upon them.

And the real golden eggs floated away to a treasure chest and Eagor never saw where they went for, he was offering a big chimp a banana to play Hopscotch for Eagor had no friends.

"Ouk," Apes for he had no friends either so shared the banana.

"Ga," Eagor happy.

"Sign here?" The Mage handing Harry Blackhood a quill to sign away all debts owed him by Christina.

"Apes come here or else?" The Mage and showed Apes a vision of a circus where Apes would be jumping through flaming hoops and swinging as a trapeze monkey with no net below but buckets full of fins, small ones.

"Ouk," Apes hurrying over no longer interested in Eagor as a friend.

"Take Harry home," The Mage and Apes did just that through the wall so Harry being delicate shrieked.

And Eagor shouted "Ga," to his departing friend begging him to write and cried too.

"Ouk," Apes on top of the Empire State Look alike Building and could not remember his orders for he had a peanut in his hand and head.

"Now my head has stopped spinning so where are the eggs?" Harry Blackhood noticing the receipt for debts cancelled. So was wrath and threw the basket away and demanded Apes take him down; but Apes released now he needed two hands to shell the peanut so let go of Harry who drifted away in the breeze.

And Harry gyrated all the way down to an open sewer that was full of toads and newts for it had been raining recently.

But luck was with the miser for Harry hit the grass so did not catch warts from the toads.

And Eagor followed the fluttering black cloth to the open sewer where he saw a basket with a goose in it so grabbed it with these words, "Ga," for he was huge and gormless thinking Boss would be happy now he had these goodies.

"Shriek," Boss under Eagor's feet for Eagor was disaster prone and stood and kicked Harry his Boss now a black cloth into the sewer where warts waited for a home.

"I must do something about Eagor?" Harry Blackhood crawling out of the sewer and Eagor was so happy to see him he hugged and threw Harry up and down and being gormless forgot to catch Harry when he came down.

Never mind it was supper time so Eagor quickly carried Harry home for watery gruel waited for Eagor at his position at the long table; and Eagor knew Harry could remember where that was? And do not feel sad for Harry for blighters never look skyward for Heaven is there, so look at the pavement for Hell and Arawan are there so feel safe warm and cozy; and Harry found many pennies on the pavement so was content.

Anyway: "What brought you back?" Christina glad but outside the palace an angry crowd for they could see Garrison in a wicker basket.

"No homing instinct," meaning the fairies were useless map readers.

"We want Garrison broiled quartered and hung," the angry crowd.

"Time to leave Princess," The Mage who took the opportunity to lean down and kiss her pretty hand and saw further down her pretty ankles.

For The Mage was a dirty old man and real lucky Christina never felt his saliva dribbling onto her feet or The Mage did feel something kick him hard some place.

"My heroes," was what the blind princess said for she was lightheaded from being rescued from Harry when it was Garrison essence that had fainted her.

CHAPTER 67   RAG

And citizens demanded Garrison get the bung and The Mage promised they would when The Wagon was built?

"What wagon," it just takes one someone.

"This wagon," The Mage showing them a blueprint, "a four-wheeler convertible, hundred boar power."

"Buy one?" Another just takes someone in the angry crowd.

"Cheaper D.I.Y.," The Mage and the crowd agreed for they must be relations of Eagor.

"One wagon?" One of these gormless maybe relations of Eagor and the angry crowd quietened down for they were plain curious.

"Built just like that." The Mage and was a lie.

And some ones whispered amongst themselves and asked again, "One wagon?"

"I promise," The Mage.

"Agreed then, then you clear off right?" Another thick citizens.

"Of course," The Mage looking at a dinner menu from a nearby classy restaurant for Garrison would be sent away to chop down a forest and, in a week, drink many pubs empty of XXX and at the end of the week a wheel 20 feet in diameter finished.

And always a seller of flowers nearby in a large black hoodie for it was Harry's new spy who doubled as valet, mugger and cook, Eagor for Harry was rich because he saved on wages.

And Eagor brought news there was to be a royal wedding so Harry Boss Blackhood put on his finest black hood fresh from a laundry and went to the palace where a new guard replied to his demands to get in with these fruit smelling words: "Ouk."

"Eagor," Harry screamed offended, "fix that chimp."

"Ouk," Apes and crushed nuts in his fingers for he had been insulted.

So Eagor took hold of the nearest thing to mangle between his fingers to show off his strength.

And it was a black shiny hoodie fresh from the Chinese laundry.

"Come on hit me if you dare?" Eagor.

"Ouk," the reply.

"Right on the jaw monkey."

"Ouk," the reply.

And as the two giants threw insults at each other Harry Boss Blackhood limped into the palace unopposed proving that Eagor did indeed come in handy.

"Here just what I need?" Wamba grabbing the black robe no longer fresh from a Chinese laundry; and rubbed Old Nag down for Old Nag had been rolling in straw covered in horse stuff.

"It was Tom Wamba," Conan, Harry heard as he went between Old Nag's legs.

"Only a lad too?" Wamba cleaning Old Nag's bottom with the rag.

"I taught him well," Conan as Wamba dipped the rag in a bucket of disinfectant and then wrung it dry and tossed it aside to Cutyagizzard'sout and Whipthemhard his best friend.

For Wamba saw the shiny rag was no longer black and gleaming but green and smelly so did not want it anywhere near Old Nag who only deserved the best rags.

"Just what I need to wipe my daggers clean," Cutyagizzard'sout and did.

"You hear it was Tom?" He asking Whipthemhard.

And Harry thought a razor-sharp dagger passing his 'bitties' was worth it to learn more.

"When will it be?" Cutyagizzard'sout giving the cut-up rag to Whipthemhard for whip practice.

And Whipthemhard whipped the rag many times.

And the old torn smelly green rag never shrieked once.

"There be a crow moving about that discarded rag?" Whipthemhard told his friend Cutyagizzard'sout.

"Croak," Harry Blackhood seeing if he could imitate a crow there did be deliverance for crows where lucky birds to pirates so Satirextex wrote.

"Then whip it to death for all pirates know crows bring bad luck," Cutyagizzard'sout and Harry swallowed hard and hated Satirextex.

And the rag was whipped to pieces so it jumped this way and that.

"Mummy," the rag.

"Whip it harder friend for the bird speaks Ballenese so must be a were-rag," Cutyagizzard'sout advised and comforted himself with a ration of rum.

"Well, it has stopped withering so give me some of that ration as whipping a crow to pieces is thirsty work," Whipthemhard and the two pirates left the rag.

Then Red Beard appeared with Scarab the royal scribe.

"Soon I will complete the Stories of Wamba and friends," Scarab said.

"Yes, then the citizens will love us again," and Red Beard drew his two cutlasses to stab the dirty shredded rag and although a little breeze the rag blew about here and there so Red Beard missed it.

"Did you hear?" Scarab.

"Tom, yeh a lucky boy," Red Beard and the rag stopped fluttering to hear the better so got jabbed many times by Red Beard who said, "For a minute I thought I had lost my aim."

And so left the rag to slither to any exit to escape these people but met Moronicus and The Lost Patrol.

"Look a rag blowing on the wind, spear men practice time," Moronicus who never bothered about practice time in his life but just felt lucky today.

And the spear men did so Moronicus shouted, "Monkeys could do better," for the rag made sure not a spear pierced it for it was quick.

"We are the guard of honor and must do better if we are to protect Tom and you know who?" The Lost Patrol, and the rag stopped to hear the better so got many spears in it.

And the Guard of Honor took their spears and left.

"I must escape this asylum," the rag spat and caterpillar fashion sought an exit.

So met Wotanic and Drunken Noddy who stood upon the rag and wiped their mailed feet on it for their was much donkey stuff in the yard so blame Tootanfoot.

And the rag stopped withering to hear better: "I hate Tom and know she loves me," Wotanic complained.

"Maybe she will not come back from the honeymoon and I can be king again," Drunken Noddy and drank much cheap meths and spilled much and as they moved on, a thrown away lit barbarian tobacco floated onto the rag so, "Woosh," and the rag jumped this way and that into a bucket of water to put the blazing meths out.

"Oh, look a bit of leg sticking out of that rag, must be a beggar's spare," the pirate What'shisname everyone forgot and tried hard to rip the leg off the rag but failed.

"Nasty selfish dirty rag," What'shisname and booted the rag much till the leg stopped groaning.

Then as he left a half donkey came with a stomach like a goat so chewed away on the tasty rag.

"Ha he Ha he," the rag who liked being tickled and donkey did a tantrum for it did not like its food to talk back.

"At last, I am out of this hell house," the rag meaning the palace as he slid to the steps that led to the courtyard and town.

And rag crawled to Eagor sitting sharing peanuts with Apes for they were friends.

"Look a filthy disease-ridden rag," Eagor.

"Ouk," Apes agreeing.

And a passing flock of crows saw the rag as a hawk in disguise so pecked it good.

And the crows numbered one hundred and all had a peck so rag stayed airborne twenty minutes.

Then rag floated down just as a circus passed driven by Monty the crossed eyed cousin of someone and there where thirty elephants, three dozen covered wagons, many careless fire eaters, tight rope walkers and lions and tigers with long talons. Not forgetting chimps with no nappies.

And Eagor and Apes watched the rag get done real good eating peanuts.

And the rag was kicked into the open sewer where fins left it alone for it stunk bad.

So floated home with these words, "Eagor will wish he was never born."

But Eagor with these words had left with his new friend, "We are out of nuts, lucky my master pays me a penny a month so I can buy more nuts, and we can share them at my house," Eagor for he was thick as bananas and about to wish he never were born.

"*He Ha he Ho,*" a sort of maniacal laugh.

Help me Eagor," the filthy rag crawling out of the open sewer so Apes took fright.

"I will broom this talking disease-ridden rag to save my new friend," so Eagor broomed the rag.

"Ouk," and Apes bit it some for good measure.
"There friend have a nut," Eagor and soothed his new friend and behind them a rag rose from the dusting and Apes shrieked and threw Harry's long, big table at rag and fled.

"Nasty rag," Eagor and threw hundreds of minor relations eating at the big table at rag and ran after his new friend.

And that night Doctor Leecherex left Harry Blackhood's house minus three dozen leech jars and ball of cat gut.

And because Dr. Leecherex had left Harry stopped moaning and groaning.

"What did Tom do?" Harry Blackhood asked himself for he had learnt this by heart

"I know Boss," and was Eagor come out of the shadows so gave Boss a heart attack.

"I will pound his chest as I see Dr. Leecherex do," Eagor and pounded Harry good till Harry thud pounded out of bed where he crawled under the bed where he asked Eagor,

"What tell me please did Tom do?" And hated Eagor and knew it a waste of daylight to beat the daylight out of Eagor for Eagor had no daylight in his skull just cobwebs.

"I have no one to blame for I hired the idiot for a relation needed shelter, perhaps I can send him to Offaltrex as a gift?" Harry the Boss under the bed next to the chamber pot Eagor had not emptied in weeks for he doubled at other jobs so never had time to empty Harry's potty.

"Cur what a stink, if I crawl out there that idiot will do something nasty to me, I know it but I cannot stay here so must risk it," Harry Blackhood the Boss and crawled between Eagor's legs and what he thought was fresh air, but Eagor had eaten too many leeches that had fallen off Harry so suffered an attack of wind.

"Where am I?" Harry unable to think.

"Oh, Boss let me pick you up and show you where you are," Eagor and with willing
hands held Boss high so a head cracked a ceiling and there was a thud and moan.

And a second thud with these words, "Oh dear I think I have killed Boss," as he had dropped Boss and Boss had sprang off the bed springs and hit a nearby bedroom wall with a "Splat."

"Just tell me what you know Eagor then go and wash out the pig pens out back where the minor relations live rent free," Boss and Eagor was so relieved he was not a murderer plum forgot what he was supposed to remember.

"Is he a minor relation of Wamba? For he has warts like him, habits like him, and hates me like him?" Boss asked watching Eagor skip away to the pig pens.

"Tar la," Eagor went skipping away happy thinking of his new friend the chimp or was it a monkey?

CHAPTER 68   EAGOR

A stirring of straw in a kitchen corner and from it a large hand with bolts in it reached for a dog bowl.

"EAGOR" was on the bowl not Rover.

So, his large fingers groped finding blue cheese once cheddar on Black hood's long table.

Searched on finding a gnawed mutton bone and quickly pulled it into the straw.

And Eagor was happy for he remembered what Tom did and his master had thrown him the bone as reward. Was he not lucky Boss gave him straw to sleep in sheltered from the elements? And rose after breakfast sniffing warm air flowing through the doorless coal shed and stretched.

"Master wants me to do Tom."

And Eagor put on rusty mails and belted with rope, sheathed a blunt rubber sword, put a cauldron on as helmet and wrapped a hide around his shoulders.

"Dressed through the kindness of Boss my Master Harry Blackhood."

So sought Tom to do.

"And my parents paid Monty's cousin thirty times removed is driving's circus to take me away and feed me quietly to the big cats; but my name is Give a and serve the long table were my relations eat. And taste my master's food and lock the doors and sleep with the keys under me.

I cannot read for the circus people said a thicko need not worry about that, if I did not drop the elephants I carried on my shoulder on the tight rope with no net.

But was rescued by Boss who cares for me for he whips daily and not hourly like the
circus folk.

And for Boss will bash Tom's lugs,

Pull his nose.

Make a V and poke his eyes,

Tie his fingers in knots and see if he can untie them?

Then throw him to the ground and jump on him heaps.

Then do something nasty but can't think that far ahead but know if I bash Tom and "Cut off his long bits," as Boss wants, Boss said, "Birthdays come yearly and love mine for relations must give me presents, and no one knows yours so you never get a birthday; but when Tom is shredded, I will give you burnt toast spread thick in lard and a candle and get the relations to sing, "Happy Birthday Eagor."

So must cut off Tom's long bits that must be his hair," and Eagor dreamed of his birthday treats.

"And I have paid back Assandeadlyknife for finding Eagor in the circus," Harry Blackhood.

*

And Harry lay amongst gold marks heated from below as minor relations kept a furnace burning.

"I will heal quicker without these," and pinged off leeches out his grilled window onto passing folk so, "EEK," was heard much. "A royal wedding is planned between Tom and my intended and the only consolation is selling tea mugs with their faces on them and will make his ugly like Eagor."

But Eagor was pouring hot water into a bath for Boss to soak in and heard what he was.

"Boohoo I am ugly," Eagor and poured more boiling water into the bath.

"And own these seats that royal watchers must sit on along the wedding route and charge inflated prices. The pomp of marching soldiers needing polish for their boots and I own the polish factories where ten-year-old relations work sixteen hour shifts to make me rich. Eagor is my bath ready? And get my book 'Occult; from the library," Boss and slipped into silk bathing trunks for he was bashful. Black trunks with gold $ printed on them.

And Eagor who had been preoccupied crying that he was ugly had forgotten about adding freezing water to the bath; and because he went in search of a library with these words, "Boohoo I am ugly and what is a library," never heard Boss scream as he lowered himself into the bath.

A Boss too weak from a good leeching and a Boss that sat on the slippery soap.

A Boss that found he knew how to curse Eagor good with these words, "I hate you ugly thingamajig," and Eagor did not know what a thingamajig was so ignored Boss.

"Master needs me to scrub his back," was the sort of servant Eagor was and returned to Boss and was happy to see Boss so lively splashing about the bath as he tried to get out.

"Scrub a dub," Eagor sang happily as he scrubbed red the skin behind Harry Black hood's ears.

"I must get a book on the occult to get rid of Eagor," Harry foamed as soap bubbles left his mouth for Eagor knew a mouth needed a good washing too,

Or the breath did smell and Boss's always did of gold marks he kissed and sucked and cigars he coughed on for image counts.

BUT BEHOLD.

Haliput's betting shops raised the stakes whether it did be a boy or girl.

"He is a commoner like us," a pie maker boasting.

"Lucky boy," a hunter dreaming of pretty ankles he only saw when he groveled and looked up as Christina passed on her sedan.

And was a dangerous thing to do as if the naked barbarian fanners caught you ogling, they beat you with them fans.

Then dragged you under the feet of the chorus girls to make sure you never peeked again.

"It happened in that rose garden," a washer woman and bought a pie.

"But will she wear white?" The hunter with many cages of

rats in a wagon for everyone was in such a festive mood sales of pies with ringed tails were up.

So had bought himself the newest mule wagon painted navy blue with a horn too.

And a war galley had been watered down and disinfected, painted pink, and made ready for honeymooners and its crew given sailor uniforms.

"See this tattoo, Tom did that for me," Whipthemhard and sold that tattoo to the highest royal artefact collector but forgot the tattoo was attached to his skin; for pirates were not the brightest lot.

"See these lashes, done on the Victorious," Cutyagizzard'sout and the bidders knew they did sneak up on him as he slept XXX off in the open sewer and Dr. Leecherex did be one and skin him good for the royal artefact.

For he was just a drunken pirate no one loved.

And royal collectors stole everything they could, the royal loo seat, the whips, even Sprintex for a while till he sprinted away.

"What will you give me?" Christina asked and was happy as the collectors gave her back her loo seat.

"Click," The Mage producing a diamond ring for magic lets you take thingies from expensive jewelers without paying.

"For me," Christina and swooned so The Mage would have to catch her and he did and drooled over her pretty ankles; but she knew what she was doing, a peek and drool was worth a ruby ring at least.

"*I am needing brass buttons and a new robe and perhaps a replacement for Eagor,*" and was a jealous whisper.

And Wamba gave Christina Old Nag; "To carry you and Tom into the sunset," and deliberately gave them the horrid stubborn horse to buck them into the first open sewer the happy couple passed, for he suffered sour grapes. "If I did not have this wart?" He cursed the thing on the end of his nose.

"*I will sell the beast to the knackers yard,*" and was a cruel whisper originating from a Black hood.

And Tom had ideas that went to his head and sneaked into

Christiana's privy to wash her pretty ankles and was booted out with a scrubber, violently with these words, "I like a soak in the bath not annoyed by a boy," so he knew who his BOSS was.

"From Daddy," and was a note stuck to a crate of cheap meths and half empty for daddy was a drunk.

And Tom never saw a single bottle but heard raucous laughter and giggles when Christina and her cronies gathered behind closed doors; but felt the empties as they threw them at him when he sneaked in with these words, "Honey it is me Tom," and these her words, "This is only a marriage of convenience so boy get back to scouring the pots and pans," for she was contemptuous of innocent boys.

So, Tom fled saying, "Another twenty years and I will be an adult and wear the pants in this marriage."

And Moronicus was forced by his men to give from his own pocket, for they knew he was a generous chap with a bag of marks, his last pay for they did not want Christina to send them on another cruise with Garrison for being miserly did not wish to spend their own cash. Cash bought waitress service as well as dinner.

But did not watch Moronicus who bought cheap thread and a basket of silkworms instead with these words, "I will tell Christina they spent their pay in Filthy Big Bertha's so you can stitch your own wedding dress and have them sent on that cruise and be free of them at last."

"And I will give him his present back in the dark royal dungeons to sew a wedding dress for her when I marry her," an ugly twisted whisper from him under the hood again.

"To you to ward off barbarians full of XXX and no sense," Conan and gave a wedding present of garlic and that whisper floated by, *"I will steal that as Eagor needs warded off and his cooking has no flavor."*

"Woof," and Cur licked her pretty ankles so was booted away with these words, "To the pound."

"I will have it plucked and fed to Eagor who will suddenly turn purple and die and be free of the monster," that dastardly whisper again.

"Ouk," and Apes in formal pink ballerina dress gave Christina a bunch of bananas.

"Why thank you very much, just what I always wanted," and gave her gloved hand for Apes to kiss and slurp over.

"For you honey," Tootanfoot giving her his engagement ring for he still intended to marry her.

"Fetch boy," Christina and threw a carrot off her balcony and the donkey could not help itself and leaped after it with these words, "Bray help."

"Thud," was heard way below.

"I will get Eagor to make banana cake for he is a survivor," the hated whisper adding, *"the ring will save me buying one,"* for Harry Blackhood Boss was tight and

then ordered Eagor to bath for, "Your body smells are offensive," and was a lie for Eagor used rose water to wash in when he awoke, rose water he found in crates in sheds belonging to Harry.

"The water is still boiling, now I must get my occult book and summon a new servant for Eagor will be broiled to death ha he has Ho," Harry the evil genius.

"What a lucky yellow duck you are to have me to play with?" Eagor who was happy he had a new friend to splash in the bath with.

"He is not even beginning to toast?" Harry disbelieving what he saw. And saw Eagor in his silk trunks stretched to bursting and the rest of what he saw made Harry violently ill.

"Eagor will clean it up," Harry between gasps of air and being ill, never realized Eagor was thick as toast so was too thick to broil and covered in warts and carbuncles and mold and fungus was better clothed than naked.

"And what will you buy Christina for a wedding present Boss?" Eagor washing his duck friend that went "Quack," when it was squeezed.

"Nothing and fetch me ingredients now," Harry and Eagor thought Harry mean and wicked and cruel and loathsome for not wanting to buy the happy couple just NOT'ING; for Eagor had never gone to school so could not spell.

And dripping wet and naked went out to get ingredients for Harry. And good citizens seeing him screamed, " A monster is coming," for the men were envious and woman peeked with these words, "Someone throw the zombie a lion clothe," and Eagor was happy for they had not called him ugly.

And ingredients were: one custard pie but Eagor could not tell what a custard pie looked like for he just got mutton bones to gnaw from the table so got a pie with a ringed tail.

One adder and a vendor sold him a giant worm for Eagor thought all wiggly thingies snakes.

And the vendor belonged to Offaltrex who had heaps of minor relations so here an Aslop moral: *"Never trust relations who own nothing."*

Two silver fish so Eagor bought two smelly rotten fish from a vendor who saw him coming for Eagor stood out in a crowd.

One fresh vulture egg and Eagor bought an ostrich egg from the local fair for he knew a chicken egg was small and a vulture egg big so this was a big egg.

The fin off the back of a fin and a Chinese restaurant sold him dried jerky with these words of assurance, "WA Ho hey ding do ah," which translated means stupid European Burke.

A jar of molten lava and Eagor was happy for he just followed Cur to where doggies make a mess and had his jar of baby larva.

A single nose hair from Filthy Big Bertha and Eagor knew this was dangerous for this woman took tantrums with him for frightening her waitresses so Eagor just ran straight up to her, grabbed her hair so she stretched at a silly angle and pulled a handful of hairs out of her nose.

"Boss will be happy I have brought extra, perhaps he will give me another birthday for the thick lard was nice and stuck to my teeth, yummy," for Eagor was thick as toast and no relation of mine.

And some mercury, and Eagor had seen horror movies and knew mercury was arsenic and all things bad so surprised Cur and dunked the dog in an open sewer then wrung the dog dry, so every drop of poison was not spilled.

"Now I have my mercury that will kill anything, I hope Boss is not planning making me drink this?" And Eagor drank some to sample just in case Boss was not giving him any.

"Mumm, strawberry flavor," and encouraged Eagor to eat one of the silver fish that tasted of rotten kippers and encouraged by these exotic tastes sampled all the rest.

"I better get more ingredients and did much to the annoyance of Filthy Big Bertha who screamed the house down with these words, "I cannot catch you but just wait till your Boss comes visiting, will he get it."

And Eagor to buy these goods crossed barbed wire fencing boundaries, swam piranha infested sewers, beat up many muggers who wanted his ingredients, was hit by lightning thrice, and risked his life hiring Monty's cousin thirty times removed is driving and his coach pulled by short sighted mules to get back to Harry just before midnight like the fairy tales said.

Then remembered he had not bashed Tom till he was pulp or cut his long thingies which was his hair with these words, "I will tell Master I have as not too upset him for I love my kind caring master very much."

Perhaps Eagor belongs to you, maybe fell off the roof rack when he was a toddler and you kept on driving?

CHAPTER 69
FAGGOTS

And through graveyards a thing picking Wolf bane.

"He loves me, he loves me not," and ended with, "he hates me," which made the horrid creature covered in bolts in its neck wrath, so smashed expensive gravestones, round barrows and heaved a weeping willow over the cemetery wall onto elopers taking a breather from their pursuing parents; but never mind no one ever complained as the monster was so big and ugly.

Ugly a word it was advised to never use in its *ugly* evil looking presence or else.

And the thing was Eagor.

Out to fox Tom somewhere in the palace and cut off his long bits.

"A mistake lad," Conan spitting tobacco that the wind blew onto pursuing parents so stopped them dead.

"You taught me dad?" Tom.

"Dad?" Conan looked closely at the innocent boy, no there were no big ears or beaked nose or drooping chin, why the boy was handsome so could not be his.

"It is a mistake because after you see her pretty ankles all ankles look the same and you will turn to warm mint beer and saddle Old Nag and loot temples before the rest of us do in May Day Holiday," Conan advised.

"So, I will ride into the sunset a rich boy," the boy had

learned well.

"And on Old Nag?"

And the boy thought hard but some of Wamba had rubbed off so could not think well.

"It is my fault, I bought you that cod piece with a trap door and let you into the rose

garden," Conan wishing it were him marrying into riches and famous relations to sponge off. "Maybe you can get further on Bat Wing?"

"But I will be king and ravage lots of servants," Tom and if Conan did not know he was innocent would have distanced himself for Tom had not identified what sex he would be ravaging.

"Leave it to the kid to grow up into that royal world, you are Garrison and Filthy Big Bertha is laying on a special for your coming-of-age party, lots of French waitresses dishing out your favorite, onion soup," Conan seeing if the boy did not come, he could have more for himself for Blackhood had rubbed off on him.

"Gee tell me," Tom and Conan ordered more warm beer and charged Christina's account so never heard Eagor groan, "Master hates me and flowers never lie.

Boohoo.

And wants Tom fixed.

Boohoo and hates me and must do Tom for I love Master that calls me ugly Boohoo."

So stopped in a royal rosary to see if the first flower lied so ignored the temple bells ringing for a hurried wedding.

And Tom lurched over his table spilling XXX and feared that if he missed the wedding bells, he did be an engine cog; never mind the pink elephants and rats spinning in front of his eyes cheered him up doing imaginary circus acts.

"Drunk as a newt but have saved his life burp," Conan who being a barbarian saw pink horses and temples gyrating in front of his eyes.

"I want to be king not an engine cog," Tom and was ill all over Conan who minded a lot for he had a wedding to attend for he had an idea, to replace Tom at the alter so sought a bit of uncrowded sewer where washer women were not washing clothes.

"I will be clean in no time," but saw pink fins coming so ran screaming into a wall
with this sound, "THUD," and fell asleep.

"Where is the faggot?" Tom's intended at the altar.

"Never fear oh great queen we will find him," Wamba putting Book away for Book just told him what royalty did to faggots. "We must save him Mage."

"We?" And added, "What for?" For he knew what happened to accomplices.

"Because" but Wamba did not know for he was Wamba.

"Where is my slice of wedding cake," Harold dribbling over The Mage's sandals.

"That is why," Wamba triumphantly but was short lived.

For The Mage sighed which meant volunteers needed.

And Eagor in a rose garden knew what the last rose there said, "He really does hate me," and "I must go fix Tom who never hurt a fly."

And just then a royal page attracted by the sound of shredding rose petals looked in and quickly averted his eyes, for in the brilliant sunshine a thing with bolts in its neck, and carbuncles the size of melons the result of sleeping on unchanged straw for straw costs money.

"I am Tom are you, Tom?" Eagor thinking he was funny for he had no idea what Tom looked like for Boss never paid him so could not buy a souvenir mug with Tom's face on it.

So, the page ran and ran this way and down way sideways and through coal mines but made it to Christina's.

"The boy did what to my roses?" And all saw Christina move her fingers and heard Pitter Patter coming.

"Flee," The Mage not wanting to meet him.

"Are you Tom?" Eagor asked many but none would say for they heard Christina scream, "The engine cog did what?"

*

"Never here when you need her, typical woman," The Mage

and here an Aslop fable.

'If women were there when needed aspirin sales did slump.'

"Book says nothing on the subject except bribe Pitter Patter for a quick clean job," Wamba but had no cash for Blackhood took it all in H.P. Payments and Filthy Big Bertha the rest in alimony payments for Wamba knew many waitresses.

"Sod them," The Mage and disappeared in a green pool.

But Wamba was saved from Pitter Patter for Apes crashed through the priceless palace-stained glass window with these words of fame, "Ouk." Then threw Wamba over his shoulders and smashed through another priceless stained glass palace window.

Apes liked the sound of tinkling glass; it reminded him of Xmas and bananas stuffed with sage and onion and presents and his birthday was soon so making sure Wamba did not forget.

A banana with a candle stuck in it and a holiday to the Congo would do nicely or else.

Then Apes remembered Wamba was always tapping him for cash earned at street corners dancing to an organ grinder as a monkey; so, threw Wamba back through another priceless stained-glass window.

"Ouk," Apes buggering off.

"Surprise," Christina entering with Pitter Patter in slippers so he was not heard. And saw the glass everywhere and a peanut and knew Apes was involved.

"Tie the Burke up for he can join the faggot as kindling," for she was wrath.

And Wamba dropped Book as he was set upon and was dangled from a pole so did not know what to do but said without Book these words:

Wait for it nice, sweet-smelling words that pretty ankles like.

"For you I sought,
The fairest bud,
Not from fear,
But from respect.

So feared harming a petal.
That is your body most dear to me.
My queen.
I adore,
For thee I fight dragons.
Without thought.
The bud I love most,
My queen."

And Pitter Patter and guards and courtiers cried and worse his queen was amazed prose was uttered from him for she knew him as a Burke.

"Satirextex?"

"Wamba."

So, Christina sat.

And a green mist spread from underneath her.

For The Mage was already sitting there invisible.

"What pretty ankles," The Mage for he just could not help himself.

"Take them all, engine cog them in rancid butter sauce," for she was really wrath.

"I am not with them," The Mage lying.

"They are fags," she screamed.

"Less insults please," The Mage.

"Broil them alive," her royal person.

"I will be tough," The Mage.

Then Eagor appeared at a broken window and she screamed louder for he was ugly.

And an orange slime spread from Eagor with bits of custard pie in it for atmosphere and effect for Harry Blackhood was making an entrance. Custard pie the remains of the ingredients Eagor was sent for.

But then smelt the meths and trembled.

"Your ingredients were off, where was the silver fish?" Arawan from green sulfur asked.

"Eagor?" Harry asked immediately knowing it was a mistake to send Eagor for ingredients. And Harry felt one wiggling in his pocket so ate it to get rid of the evidence.

"If you want THING released from hell to help you one must replace THING for a year," Arawan hoping for Christina.

"One," Harry for he wanted rid of just one monster.

"Is THING obedient?" Harry.

"As long as you feed it."

"I will give you Eagor for a year and you feed and keep him too."

"I knew he hated me boohoo," Eagor and sobbed.

SHAME.

"You get THING for six months," Arawan.

"Why?"

"Not enough custard pie."

"So?"

"I love custard pie."

"OK," And Harry put his X down.

There was a puff of smoke and the orange mess shrunk.

"Eagor can wipe it off," then Harry realized Eagor would not be around so cackled and had a fit of heaven.

"Er what is your name," Harry asked THING.

"THING."

"Well THING wipe this orange mess up."

"Cannot do."

"Why not?" Harry going for the whip he used on poor Eagor whom he hated.

"Not in the contract which is to fix Tom."

So, Harry whipped THING so found himself dangling from a rafter with the whip stuck somewhere.

Then Harry fell with a thud for Eagor was not there to catch him, hug and crush him.

"You are supposed to be obedient?"

"I am but whipping is not in the contract."

"What then?"

"I work an hour a week and get paid 168 gold marks. And I do not like my sleeping quarters, where is your bed, Harry?" And THING encouraged Harry to tell him by seeing if Harry could stretch like rubber.

But Harry could not of course so there was much snapping

and moaning sounds.

"When is working hour?"

"Midnight Tuesdays," THING.

"Today's Tuesdays," Harry seeing Garrison and Tom fixed tonight then get Cannymindtrex the lawyer whose surname was Give a to investigate this contract.

And only six hours to midnight.

"Er what do you eat?"

"Steak ten times a day," THING stuffing Harry down the loo till a gold mark
showed, then rolled Harry down the palace stairs and out a window into a barrel of swill on a passing wagon.

Then THING went to bed and ate his supper and was a messy eater to wait till midnight.

And a miracle happened, Arawan did not take Eagor for, "I cannot look at him, every mirror in hell will smash. Judas that man is plain ugly, I cannot take him, he can stay with the living," and Arawan left Eagor in a broom cupboard to surprise the cleaners for Arawan had a sense of humor.

CHAPTER 70   BOOM

The night watch called, "Full moon," smothering his bell and lamp for he was afraid of sleepers with wool stuffed in their ears who did not want to jump out of bed and put his bell somewhere; up his nose perhaps?

So, they slept soundly.

And in a broom closet Eagor found candle and flint for he was not safe with matches. And by luck lit the candle and did not burn the palace down for he had his lucky rabbit foot in his pocket.

"But with much puffing put the fire out on me," Eagor cheerfully and, "Ah ha a fake door," and fell through it because he pushed it for, he was too thick as toast to look for a secret handle; besides with the flames out on him all was blackness so can forgive the ugly monster with big warts.

And followed steps downwards and stomped so heavily the steps broke and Eagor stumbled forward through closed door after closed door. "*Perhaps Apes was needed to eat the termites?*" Aslop.

So missed the dungeon where two mates hung from a wall by their thumbs for a princess rubbed up the wrong way rubbed you up the wrong way.

Here an Aslop fable, '*Make sure you have plenty of diamond tiaras when dealing with spoilt princesses.*'

"I am not amused," The Mage whose fingers where in mini vices so could not click and for good measure dried ear wigs littered the floor as every princess in a fairy tale knows, **stops**

mages dead using magic spells.

And in a dark inn Apes sat on a rafter shelling peanuts and contributed to the conversation with, "Ouk," about freeing The Mage and Wamba.

Notice Wamba was mentioned last as an afterthought.

"What are we waiting for?" Dwarf demanding action.

"For an idea," Conan for Garrison was thick.

"How many guards has she?" Red Beard asked.

"A thousand paid out of wedding presents," Moronicus.

"Fair odds," Cutyagizzard'sout whipping out his disemboweling daggers and a thumb dropped off.

"I have my two-inch wand," Alicadabara waving it as two toads appeared and spread warts amongst the waitresses for Garrison had their own variety of warts.

Ones that are long and skinny with a hair at the end.

"Shish, no one tell the monkey above," meaning Apes had sprouted warts on his baboon place and might rip and tear and bang his chest over shredded Garrison.

And Apes was so happy eating nuts never noticed the elephant tail either.

"But what is that?" Moronicus seeing the strange machine Abracadabra had made and hired street urchins to drag in with the promise of watery gruel with Californian raisins.

"Slurp," the urchins at the inn drinking their gruel with a landlord ready to boot them out as soon as the last droplets of gruel had been licked up.

"A dwarf Blitzkrieg wagon," Alicadabara nominating Dwarf for a suicide mission.

"That is right get us dwarfs to do the bashing," and jumped into the driver's seat.

Then the room filled with squeals as the engine cogs started up.

Swine muck shot out the exhaust covering Moronicus.

Then Dwarf released the brake and pulled a rope and a canon boomed and a wall vanished.

"Come on boys, let us rescue our mates," and drove away

over the landlord who did not want them to leave for some must pay for damages.

"I hate Garrison ouch," famous last words of a landlord and who cares about him, he puts too much froth on the beer head so is hated by those who pay too many taxes.

"Them who charge us too many taxes and wear silk ties and are all Give a Harry PLC," Aslop counting his shares in Harry Plc.

But as this is a happy story and the urchins seeing the publican on his back, ran over him, stomped, and kicked him to make sure he would not come too, then ransacked his inn with these words, "We are drunk" so were put in the stocks happy.

And after for the next month had enough money to eat roast boar with waitress service and a bath of course for the urchins stunk of cardboard boxes.

And Conan left a note behind, "Bill Christina."

And along cobbled streets the Blitzkrieg machine squeaked and met a copper who raised his hands with these words, "Where is the tax disc."

"We dwarves take no chances," Dwarf and, "hit the bacon to get speed," Conan and, "run the onion peel over then call him a peeler," and none owned up to this. And it was not an onion they peeled as that was an excuse for jokes about coppers being related to onions for all had read Sherlock Holmes who must have eaten onions raw.

So rutted **Peel** rolled into a sewer and moaned, "Full moon and all is well," but was a lie as he was ill full of rut marks and rats that lived in the sewer so had the plague too.

Then THING found him so he screamed, "I am dead cannot you see I am dead so leave me alone," the night watch onion yelled.

And THING heard him so did not eat his clogs as that was wood for the nasty night watch never said his prayers at night or kissed teddy Good night so there so got his just deserts.

Then followed Garrison for THING liked the smell and squeaks. And they thought of the Charge of The Light Brigade and the engine cogs fine horses and were riding the wagon to Glory and was a misconception put about by Satirextrex to help sell his pulp rubbish about Garrison and make him, Harry the Bounder richer.

For when they went out the wall, they saw THING following them and so showed the engine cogs frying pans and talked of rashers if speed was not got up.

"SQUEAL," the engine cogs and the war wagon hit the sewers and disappointed the fins for the wagon floated.

"What a relief," Conan and the rest sighed and gave fingers to the circling fins, and for animal lovers, the engine cogs got to rest.

And THING sat on the top of the wagon waving to terrified onlookers shouting, "We are Garrison," so was associated with them inside and plans were made to be rid of them.

"Where must they be going?" A terrified onlooker not fled yet.

"To free Wamba," a suggestion by an aspiring hood hoping they inside the wagon did join Wamba and she be promoted to the top of the long table.

"Let us free Wamba and the wagon will leave us alone," another brighter terrified onlooker and the aspiring cousin vanished as that was not supposed to happen, she did blame the monkey, no, chimp, the ape of course as it could only answer with an 'OUK.'

And the horrified onlookers stuck these signs along the sewer:

"Wamba this way."

The path to a maintenance slipway and a maintenance team working to unplug a pile of banana skins blocking the sewers, thus stopping the fins migrating to the jolly sea and never return as they did be ORCA food.

"Here what is that thumping music, I saw Jaws and there must be fins near us, we better get to higher ground and rest," a worried maintenance worker.

"Yes, Frederick Maintenance worker number 789, and eat our cucumber sandwiches."

"Yes, Sarah maintenance worker 564 with chopped

garlic and drink our warm minted watered-down beer," maintenance worker 321 and pulled an XXX flask from a hip pocket as 321 had more than food on his mind for he was thinking with his bottom.

"That is no fin," Sarah who had taken this job to pay off her student loan and cleared off quick.

"Here I am not drunk yet so come back," 321 watching a vanishing hem line and was wrath so beath Frederick 789 who was a shrimp and why THING only ate 321 as never saw the shrimp.

And the wagon with a bloated THING on it went up the slip way towards the palace gates.

"Gurgle," Frederick 789 finishing the xxx flask in one go not believing his luck, made it to the top, went to bushes to be violently ill as drinking that much XXX has that effect and was paralytic, just as well as Sarah 564 was hiding from THING in those bushes and now stunk so beat the bats and chipmunks out of Frederick 789.

But there is a happy ending here, passing washer women on a float emptied their soapy water out all over Frederick who now smelt of soap and so did Sarah, who had enjoyed beating hibernating escaped pet shop rats out of Frederick 789, so was either going to pull the shrimp into her hiding place and examine him for more animals in the folds of his clothes, or continue beating the innards out of him.

We will leave you to figure which option she chose to make the tale happy again.

ANYWAY

And Harry Blackhood had bribed Wotanic and Drunken Noddy to sprinkle garlic
dust over THING to do THING good; and of course, dried earwigs for Eagor was not available; just as well as Eagor could not tell the difference between an ear wig and a cobra.

"I will make you King Charles and let you Wotanic marry Christina," Harry and was lies to make them work dastardly deeds.

"Dastardly is in the genes ha he Ho ha he Ho," an oily whisper boasting his vermin blood for he knew Christmas was coming and other religious ceremonies were gifts were given to HIM not the gods and got away with it for he was blackmailing the good god Daghdha for he knew about Morrigan and a wife that beat the day lights out of cheating husbands.

Of course, when THING had done Tom as steaks was expensive and when Eagor came back might get ideas so THING must go.

And Harry walked to the palace to see his work done with these words, "386 marks an hour THING costs to run THING I must be nuts."

And Christina was having second thoughts about ridding Ball of Wamba because of his poetry.

For she never had poetry written her just aspirers giving her advice how to rid her roses of aphids.

"Is Wamba more than a wart? Has he a romantic heart instead of a selfish streak? I am young rich and spoilt and do what I want and did with Tom that innocent boy who asked me to help him study the nocturnal habits of lady birds.

If I marry Wamba, Harry Blackhood will spend all his time trying to do him so will leave me alone.

Perhaps I was hasty with Wamba, I will visit him and see if he can recite poetry as he is stretched on the rack?"

And Eagor fell into a room full of interesting things.

"I hear something," Eagor as the room is lit as they always are in movies. So saw twenty green crocodiles wanting to eat him.

"I will climb this rope to get away from them," Eagor and pulled the rope and a python fell on him as well as two thousand angry vampire bats disturbed in their upside-down sleep.

So, he hid in a sarcophagus with pictures of Egypt on it.

And fled as he screamed for mummy hidden in it was now hanging onto his shirt tails and here an Aslop fable. *"Do as mummy bids, get the shirt tail tucked in."*

So Eagor kicked over an aviary.

"Nice chirpy bird," Eagor as the hungry giant Condor he had let loose wanted to eat him.

And as The Mummy strangled him and the bats sucked his blood, the python squeezed the life out of him, and the Condor pecked his teenage parts so he fell into a pool.

"Brr this water is cold," for the crocodiles had left it for they was cold blooded reptiles, lucky Eagor.

Who shouted, "Help poor Eagor never learnt to swim."

So never heard an answer from the other side of the dungeon wall.

"Who asked for help?" Pitter Patter afraid the two prisoners might escape.

And outside the palace Dwarf shouted, "Fire the canon lads," and the palace gate went 'POOF,' for it was poof.

And THING followed.

"What noise is this?" Christina asked on the dungeon stairs.

And more BOOMS followed as Conan was getting carried away.

"Oh, what tickled my pretty ankles," Christina as a cannon ball went by and after turning left and right for a hundred yards, as dungeon stairs are long and creepy, the ball smashed through two walls, one where Eagor was learning to swim and the other were Pitter Patter was, so the wall crumbled with The Mage and Wamba.

The Garrison was free.

Anyway, more action

"I believe in Harry," Wotanic not believing in anything good.

"Bugger him," Charles sure his kingdom was not worth it behind Wotanic but a bottle of meths was.

And were about to dump the dried garlic when Harry appeared.

"Not getting nervous, a deal is deal," and behind Harry a thousand hooded shadows with meat cleavers.

"Here what the blazes," as a crowd angry with no

executions, no wedding, no Garrison to insult roared into the palace grounds and carried the three of them to the palace and down to the damp crocodile infested dungeons where an ugly monster waited for them.

Who was the ugly monster?

*

Except Eagor was free and in a hurry to escape the twenty crocodiles chasing him he brought them to Harry.

"*(&^," Harry as Eagor pretending not to notice him passed him.

"I am eaten," Wotanic and was.

"Blooming idiotic monster," Drunken Noddy and went to Monster Land where bad boys go.

"Burp," Arawan happy to see Harry.

"I will summon my lawyer so do not get ideas?" Harry warned and shouted "Oh Cannymindtrex where art thou come here quick or sacked."

And why Cannymindtrex opened a hundred black cockerels and mixed their blood with a hundred freshly dug worms and drank the lot with a flagon of wine for courage to visit Harry.

And anyone doing that deserves to visit Arawan.

And all he had to do instead was follow the call:

"Cannymindtrex where art thou?"

"I am coming with my bill," and seeing the war wagon and beasts and worse, Garrison in it, so trebled it.

And Garrison got here as:

"I read The Trojan Horse and know there is garrison in there coming to save Wamba," and takes just one palace guardsman with three stripes to know what to do.

Light a cigar and throw it into the open bits on the wagon and wait.

And soon burning was smelt and the wagon stopped.

Then screams and the palace sergeant stood back as angry onlookers from the sewers rushed in to find Garrison and were so many pushed the war wagon out of the way, into the palace moat that was as infected with soggy royal teddy bears, TED the bear, royal Noddy nappies and meths from dropped opened meth bottles not even Garrison could survive that.

"Hello Arawan, it is us," Garrison in the wagon.

And Arawan had an alcoholic fit brought on by them.

But happiness is never far away as he cheered seeing Harry, now he could use the three-story rack bought from Harry to give rackers a view of heaven up there.

The portable air pump to pump Harry up so he did really know what a swollen head was.

And a Barbie Doll that said, "Harry, I hate you," to make Harry sad but with Harry did make him happy.

See more happiness.

"Cannymindtrex take this," Blackhood handing him the contract for THING.

And Cannymindtrex recognized overtime for his nose sniffed and wiggled like as if he was vermin.

"I am still the Boss," Harry recognizing greed.

So Cannymindtrex wagged his finger, "Watch it Boss or you stay here. I am a lawyer and soon to be Boss," for Boss was in Hell.

LIMBO LAND

And Arawan now snored for an empty green bottle rolled in his lap.

And this was limbo where the dodo lived, the first refueling place for Arawan on his way home. "Burger Queen," in neon above him flashed.

And Arawan had Harry and Cannymindtrex in his wagon.

"Quick push the drunk off," Harry and Cannymindtrex used to taking orders did with these words after, "What have I done, I will blame Garrison," for they had pushed Arawan off Limbo Land so he fell away in a mist heading for HELL.

Except Cannymindtrex went blue and purple for his flowing red lawyer's cape was about the wheel like a brake.

"I hate you Cannymindtrex," Harry for the wagon was full of Garrison and whatever; perhaps twenty green greedy crocodiles, Harry now noticing the wagon was not empty.

And the occupants then went back to shredding each other.

Then a flying clam appeared in a poof and was full of the gods.

BEHOLD they were noisier than the waggoner's.

BEHOLD was pulled by winged octopus, lobsters, and mermaids.

BEHOLD loaned from Mahannan god of the sea as the gods where fed up with their own squabbling beasts.

BEHOLD Mahannan's giant clam on wheels the only thing big enough to carry all the gods.

BEHOLD it was collect time.

WORSE the Pregnant Cow of Heaven sat on a throne at the back of the calm and about her wives.

WORSE holding frying pans.

And the waggoner's fell silent.

"EEK," Cannymindtrex squeaked.

"Welcome to Limbo." Daghdha nervously to the wife.

"Look about this contract?" Blackhood.

Daghdha knew nothing of it except the wife was smirking, worse....giggling.

It might be Blackhood but he had face to preserve for his XXX friends were about.

"What contract?" Daghdha twinkling an eye and Blackhood found he was holding an asp that hissed.

"That was silly dear," the wife.

"Look here god, we want home," the waggoner's.

Then Ape threw a banana and none noticed Blackhood and Cannymindtrex sneaking off.

"No chimp throws a skin at me," Daghdha and looked to see if the pan was coming.

"They do for they are Garrison and do not believe in us," Nerthus.

"Do not believe in us, why they cannot do that?" Daghdha.

"They are fairies dear."

"Look are you lot finished, we want home to our moat where trout float belly upwards," Garrison and added, "before no one believes in you and us all poof away."

"Look at yourself dear," Nerthus.

And he saw he was fading into poof metaphysics.

"For it is metaphysics what you cannot see do not exist so you do not have to believe in
what you cannot see," Nerthus who had a degree in Lobotomy.

Then Harold found a cauldron and wooden spoon full of junk for that is where junk floated.

And Harold stuffed the sea food pulling the clam into it and lit a fire under the cauldron for he had not found a fast-food outlet.

And seafood objected and went nuts with the waggoner's who went walnuts shrieking.

"Hey that is my sea food," Mahannon the sea god and jumped out of the calm and found his bottom half had faded away for Harry had let a secret out, "Get rid of guilt and do what you want with these magic words, ten marks a word, 'I do not believe in gods.'"

"EEKS," he shrieked as a natural thing to do.

"Stuff this," Daghdha and threw a spear at Wamba but it went poof.

"Phew," Wamba and heard a pan descend for Nerthus and the wives were Garrison fans thanks to Dog Publishers.

"Was worth it," Daghdha as a lump grew then poofed.

"Cheated," Harold as the sea food poofed.

And Cur sighed relieved as the lobster hanging some place dogs needed to embarrass owners went poof.

"So how do we get out of here?" Cutyagizzard'sout complained to The Mage.

"So, click Mage," Red Beard.

And The Mage did and clicked away.

"Bugger him, who needs him?" What'shisname.

"We do for he took everything except the weevils," Conan stuffing weevils into his clay pipe.

"Book," Wamba.

And Red Beard kicked Book away for he was a mean pirate who had a hook in his pants that must have hurt something.

"I hate you hate you," Wamba and jumped on Red Beard and did not need spurs for his toenails were long and sharp, so made a mess of Red Beard's proud asset, "The girls love my hairy chest," and only he believed this.

*

And Arawan awoke with a headache and found Womba's mailed feet in his mouth and a bear on his head fighting Apes.

And Dwarf fought Cutyagizzard'sout and Whipthemhard on his sclerosing liver.

And Dwarf had spurs on.

And everyone else in the wagon ran over Arawan this way and that just to be annoying.

"Blow this for a laugh," Arawan and shook them off.

"Where are you going, you are supposed to torture us?" They all asked amazed at being ignored.

"Home."

"Can we come?" They asked and sure Arawan replied with these words, "Never not even to unblock the latrine, never."

"That is not fair, what is good for you is good for any Dwarf."

"Grr," Grisly added.

"What are you hiding, diamonds?" Cutyagizzard'sout.

"A spot marked X," Red Beard.

"A princess?" For he was a Burke.

So Arawan threw a sign at them that landed right way up so they could read the BIG
letters, THIS WAY HOME.

And as they read Arawan faded away as no one believed in the devil anyway.

"HOME," Wamba and read no more for he was thick as toast.

"THIS WAY," Conan for these words he knew which made him the best barbarian scout on the Wilderness Trail.

"Trash," Arawan shouted at them from a shadow.

"We are going home," The Lost Patrol and danced together for they were fairies.

"Ouk," Apes and skinned a banana.

And the lot of them ran through the mist that shrouded the real world and so exited Limbo.

"Never come back," Arawan called after them and threw suitcases full of their
unmentionables and socks at them for flies had been attracted to hell because of them.

And when you exit Limbo, you come out where the clouds are so, "Blooming heck," and "EEK," and "mummy," was heard.

Then thud lots of times but they was lucky for they landed on a thousand relations partying below so had soft landings.

But Lord Tootanfoot was aloft from Trash and exited by himself so "Brayed," all the way down and headed for a pitchfork sticking up some careless farmer had put in the ground.

And luck was with the donkey for he landed on a fir tree that bent and shot the donkey man onto a haystack, and in front of him, "Route 66," and Tootanfoot knew this was the way home so trotted off in the wrong direction towards Amity Island and heavy thumping music.

"He has he has," wicked goblins escaped from Noddy TV behind the sign thinking their joke fun.

CHAPTER 71 MARRY ME OR ELSE

"Here the spot where The Mage sunbathed while over that hill Christina was at the mercy of a **Fiend.**

And there Amity Island where the rich and famous come," the tourist guide in the future and added, "watch where you dribble that ice cream kid," for the kid was dribbling it over a sunbathing floozy topless starlet.

And the kid had saved all his pennies from polishing chain mail at stagecoach stations to come here, in the home of dribbling ice cream on a star to get noticed and into films.

Then leave his footprint in cement in Bolly Wood.

And instead, the tourist guide kicked him off the beach, and on his back a guitar, and his head curly greasy black hair and his pelvis gyrated as he walked.

"Blue Hawaii ," was stitched on his jerkin's back.

"Gm," the pelvic gyrater.

And the **Fiend** who had fled up Highway 66 was Boss dragging Christina and behind them Cannymindtrex and a marriage settlement.

"Ge up mules," Boss and whipped the stubborn mules to a frenzy so they hurtled down Route 66 at 100 mph.

"ZOOOOOM," they went.

See Boss had left not a second too soon to put his wicked plans into action since falling out of Limbo right on top of Cannymindtrex for the devil looks after his own.

"Splat," the sound and "moan," under the SPLAT so was a soft landing for Boss.

And Boss Harry Blackhood tied Christina across Route 66 with these words, "Marry
me or the holiday makers of May Day will rut you good, a million wagons with mules and horses doing donkey thingamajigs and dropped nappies just being changed, so fresh nappies," Boss and showed Christina were to X.

"I am not an accomplice but a witness to the signature X and get commission," Cannymindtrex.

"Never," Christina for she had been to the movies so knew a handsome prince always rescued the damsel in distress. But in this story the prince has a name, Wamba.

Then sounds of the first holiday maker for he was Braying.
"I am Ballenese and half donkey,
No one loves me,
Boohoo.
I eat carrots and mash,
I sleep on a four-poster stuffed with hay,
So, eat my bed to make me grow.
My top half fairy,
the bottom all ass.
I am Ballenese and proud of it bray."
"Lord Tootanfoot help," Christina.

"That ass will not save you," Boss.

"You do not understand, help me from him for he wants to marry me."

"Marry me Christina and we can honeymoon in that field of clover."

"Clear of Jackass," Blackhood slapping donkey on the snout and added, "I never went as a kid to donkey rides at the beach, so never knew donkeys can turn nasty," as donkey did a donkey on him for donkeys got teeth like giant rats.

"Mine all mine," Tootanfoot dribbled untying the cheap string Fiend had used to tie
up Christina; and dropped some carrot on her.

"You are not well my lord," Christina tried reasoning and

added, "touch a single hem of my petticoat and I will show you what a terrified princess can do to a donkey."

"Promises," for he was worse than The Mage.

"Oh, look a carrot," Christina pointing at a field knowing reasoning was out but carrots were in, especially with cheap Super Market mayonnaise dressing.

So Tootanfoot looked for the juicy carrot so missed Boss sneaking up on him with a plank with a nail sticking out at his end.

But felt it.

"Who can save me?" Christina and clutched her bosom and fainted as Rout 66 trembled with holiday makers.

Now The Mage could for he was on Route 66 where movie stars flooded in and out of Hollywood Boulevard.

And left their footprints in wet cement and their shoes for the cement was made by Harry Bros. PLC, sticky stuff.

"Who hates me so to plague me with these midges?" The Mage as he blistered from bites so swelled and looked ill so did not rescue Christina.

"Scratch scratching," sounds were heard.

And was the midges fault for they liked the suntan lotion he had on; bought on the cheap from a passing salesman with a black hood; who had minions to sell his goods but, "habits die hard," the hooded one for he had smelt The Mage's pennies ten miles away.

Yes, the lotion was vile and reminded the midges of the green swamps of home for it was.

Thirty million midges gorged themselves on The Mage who shouted, "Help."

And to be generous to the midges they stayed with him for they knew what was rumbling down Route 66.

Holiday makers and who would save poor Christina?

"Ah I see through swollen midge bitten eyes Blackhood hitting Tootanfoot with a carrot," The Mage and should have been looking above him.

Anyway, Garrison fell through the air out of Limbo with

the greatest of ease and there was no net under them. Just The Mage ogling Christina again serve him right and what happened next.

"It is a long way down," Wamba shouted and stuck Cur underneath him for a soft landing.

So, he shrieked for Cur had other ideas so bit him some place.

"Ouk," Apes getting excited for he was a disturbed primate who did not faint at the sight of the red sauce.

"And I gave up the sea for these fools," Red Beard and because he was remembering Geisha Girls never saw Cutyagizzard'sout, Whipthemhard and What'shisname get above him, for they knew with such a fat captain they did have a soft landing; and Wamba was above them and Cur then Apes and the rest of them.

"Siss do not mention his name so he will not look up," for Garrison knew how to be sneaky.

And Wotanic and Drunken Noddy where not with Garrison but still heading down? For as Wotanic looked out the hole where Garrison had left Limbo grinning thinking them done good and proper, he got the whiff of meths for Noddy had found Arawan's secret hidey hole where an emergency store of XXX was kept.

"Burp," the second warning something was amiss behind.

"You are drunk?" Wotanic accusing Noddy at last.

"No, I am not."

"What are those bottles then?"

"Empty ones."

And the third warning all was amiss was when Noddy staggered and pushed him out of Limbo so he was above Garrison, never mind still above Red Beard the fat captain so would get a soft landing and below them all The Mage.

Then Drunken Noddy fell asleep and fell out.

And the rush of chilly air sobered him up.

"Turnips and daffodils," he swore going blue watching solid ground rush up to meet him.

And Conan showed genius for he took hold of a passing

goose on the way to Amity Island to foul up the beaches.

And Apes, Eagor and THING needed many geese to hold onto and THING ate his for he had not been fed his steaks.

And below a speck scratching itself covered in midges as Route 66 bounced to the approaching holiday makers.

"I will click my fingers so I will not crick my spine when I lift Christina onto safety," The Mage thinking of peeking at pretty ankles just before SPLAT happened.

"Thank goodness someone left this black rag on the road that broke my fall," Wamba.

"Think I burst this one?" Conan shaking off donkey fur.

"A goose has hit me," The Mage and then THING hit him for he had no geese to hold onto.

Then twenty green crocodiles and the rest landed on that black rag.

"My hero," Christina and did not specify whom so Garrison hated each other which they did anyway.

And the last to hit the black rag was What'shisname whose peg leg nailed the rag to the road.

"I am not amused with Garrison," The Mage for she had not called him "hero," so clicked and Conan walked about like a tin soldier with no marbles topside.

"I will twist his arm so," Harold to make Conan wake up.

"Ouk," Apes using it as an excuse to be nasty.

And the geese pecked all The Mage's hair off so he was really peeved and about to click again when the road became full of rushing holiday makers.

"What the blazes," his last words as a million tourists ran over him, with wagons and nappies needing changed.

And Wamba carried Christina behind a bush with these words, "I have rescued her and her perfume fills me."

"Help," as What'shisname tried to get his peg leg free and was his last words as mules with tourists on them went over him, mules who had eaten up a field of prunes.

"Go help your mate," Conan and pushed Cutyagizzard'sout to help the pegged one and all knew it was magic that made him ask a mate to lay down his life for a mate.

"What'shisname was never a mate of mine, never sharing the profits of sold crews with me so can stay pegged," Cutyagizzard'sout but climbed to the top of his mate as a mobile cinema passed pulled by a hundred oxen for holiday makers need entertainment on the move.

"Go help your mates," Conan and pushed Red Beard who was ready for him so together they fell into the crowd.

"Sniff sob I will miss him at The Bridge," Wamba.

Then Wotanic and Noddy landed on The Mage so he did not click again.

And was the silence that saved Garrison.

Yes, so quiet after the million holiday makers had passed and there lay Garrison with many nappies, sinks and wagon wheels on them; the ones that leave rut marks behind.

And the black rag took shape and stood and it was Harry Blackhood.

"Master who hates me I love you," Eagor happy to see Boss and hugged so bones where heard to snap. "I am going home to my warm cozy straw and gnawed mutton bones, thank you kind master," and kind master wanted Eagor dead.

"Yes home," Garrison chorused.

And The Mage tried to cover his ears and failed for he was trying to shake off the vampire bats who had joined the midges to bite and suck his tasty blood marinated in a Harry lotion.

Then green sacred crocodiles and THINGS and Garrison clung to him demanding he send them home with clicks.

"They are tearing me limb from limb as well as stealing my wallet and unmentionables," The Mage so clicked and Blackhood was upended and shaken by unseen hands till a magic carpet dropped out of a deep pocket, and there was a tourist footprint on it.

"That is soiled goods, here is a penny for it," The Mage.

"This will take the crew back to Malicious and Victorious so goodbye," The Mage and put up with their handshakes and tears of farewell and promised not to throw their postcards out and to send them Xmas cards.

And was lies just to get rid of them so sent the carpet flying.

And there were no parachutes on the flying carpet for The Mage did not want them returning.

"They are thieving sea scum for they stole what they found in my pockets," and laughed for his pockets were full of thingamajigs you did not want, creepy scorpions
and newts and toads for potions.

Yes, the sea scum took his black diary with the best waitress names at The Bridge.

And his cash as well for waitresses is not cheap.

His lucky rabbit foot.

His butter scotch candy so The Mage had nothing to suck but do not worry Apes gave him a banana, "Ouk," Apes being friendly hoping to be sent to a forest full of floozy gorillas.

And The Mage promised all the vampire bats, crocodiles, and thingamajigs he did send them back to the dungeon so fleeced the rag again for a large chest in his back pocket.

"Why me" The rag annoyed.

"Because you are the greedy miser who all want to hear gets fleeced," so The Mage fleeced good and clicked all the horrid dungeon things into it, where they made such a mess miser knew he could not sell the chest anyway.

Except to Wamba if he had a chance to say dragons had messed it up.

"I want the dungeons instead of level 9 hell and that red eared hound," THING and rolled up the bandages on his leg to reveal gnaw marks and there waiting for a coroner a white tooth belonging no doubt to the hound.

"Howl," the invisible red eared hound knowing it was being mentioned.

"Are you sure?" The Mage liking the idea of THING in Haliput to eat Harry Black hood out of business.

For no one likes an oily miser.

"Yes, I want to be free for Black hood's steaks are so small. I want freedom to eat at the restaurants of Haliput and mug the dungeon visitors," THING and The Mage was so worried he did get blamed changed his click so THING did be free every ten years to annoy Harry.

And the sacred green crocodiles and Mummy and vampire bats and boars and that mammoth were all happy for they could terrorize the dungeons .

Except THING who had to wait ten years so said, "I have been had."

And The Mage saw a broken broom stick sticking out of Harry's chest pocket.

"It is broken so cannot be sold so finders weepy keepers peepers," and clicked and sent Wotanic and Noddy away."

"I could have sold that as kindling," Harry and checked his pockets in case anything else was showing.

And as he searched tinkled a crate of green meth bottles kept for an emergency sale to Arawan.

"You owe those two as much in pay," The Mage and sent the crate after Wotanic who screamed, "Blooming heck a crate full of meths has landed on my head."

"I am the best navy dish washer ever so let me come home with you?" Alicadabara hoping to learn The Mage's magic and turn the former into a duck, "And cook the best duck ever," for he was obsessed with duck and added, "Duck orange, duck curry, duck oriental, sweet and sour duck," see what I mean.

And The Mage knew wizards needed to keep together or Garrison did get ideas so agreed.

"Ouk," Apes wanting to come too and fluttered his eyelashes so The Mage gave in for he had a vision, of Apes in a waitress outfit serving him marmalade on toast, kippers, and porridge as he read the morning paper, the Times of course for mages are not common like us.

And sent Alicadabara and the chimp to his tower and threw in a chest of tools and a wagon load of timber for the tower needed mending.

Then felt tugging at his left foot and claws shredding his right so saw Dwarf clinging
to his left foot with big brown eyes. "We are orphans please let us live at The Bridge," and then saw on his right foot Grisly with bigger brown eyes, "Grr," the bear pleaded for what was

good for that smelly dwarf was good for a bear.

"The pain of shredded feet," so poofed them away and limped here and there as he clicked his right foot all better.

"Grisly promised to be a rug during winter," The Mage having ideas about getting Grisly stuffed to be on the safe side.

"I do not want anything," and was Harry Blackhood fearing The Mage did send him to the North Pole with Eagor as company.

"Oh, a rubber duck," for a yellow bath duck had fallen out of a black hood.

"Listen it sounds like a squeak not quack so is faulty," and The Mage gave Harry nothing. But did enlarge the yellow duck and told Garrison to get on.

"Phew he has forgotten me and Eagor," the miser as the ducky flew into the air.

"Click," and just like that Harry and Eagor where in the North Pole.

"I will go insane alone with him," Harry prophesying his future.

"Never mind Boss I managed to catch a fly before we left for supper," and Eagor ate it so Harry got no supper. "And cheer up Boss look at all the ice cubes we can suck," for Eagor was an idiot.

CHAPTER
72 SUNSET

Once upon a time a giant yellow duck flew across the sky away from Route 66 and Garrison was in it dropping litter as they went. Opened bully beef tins to shred sandalled feet below. Brown paper bags that airlines and yellow ducks provide. And KFC chicken bones gnawed right down. Takeaway meals and XXX from gluttonous Garrison men living it up on an unstable flying yellow duck; so, the turbulence was much and so was the disturbance below for these words could be heard: "Blooming Garrison doing that deliberately, Hilda get my bows and arrows, duck chasseur tonight."

"Hey," also was complained below as empty fizzy drink bottles landed on a black hood.

Anyway: "You do not have a horse so cannot ride into the sunset with me," Christina relieved.

"I know a hill in Haliput where a lazy horse sits on its haunches with a bat," Wamba with hope.

"Then go get him, for she planned once he got to her palace to throw him in the dungeon," and better he did jump off the duck forgetting they were a thousand feet up.

"Kiss me dearest," his reply for he had rescued her in the bush remember.

"Why was I cursed with pretty knees," so blanked her mind for she knew she wanted to keep Burke happy for his warts wobbled so was afraid of him.

So, Wamba kissed her and she swooned for Wamba had learned much at Filthy Big Bertha's so she did not want to be rid of Burke, perhaps keep him on a chain, and house train him just in case and there was always a local Super Market with nappies.

"Cannymindtrex where are you?" Wamba and the red caped lawyer managed to appear, and a goose flew away just in case you were wondering how on Earth.

And tucked in the lawyer's belt a bag of bird seed for the duck.

Sign here," the lawyer and whispered to Christina, "Quick divorces my specialty."

"Kiss me quick Wamba," she said and he did and she swooned so signed in a faint and would be her excuse for a quick divorce but Wamba did not sign.

And the princess had bad Girly thoughts, for if the Burke could kiss like that.

"Wife," Wamba and threw her over his shoulder and demanded the duck land so he jumped off with his wife and ran behind bushes to check for silkworm.

"How can I keep him, he is so ugly the citizens will revolt," she coming out of the bushes none the wiser about the habits of silkworms.

And Wamba stopped a passing wagon and threw the driver off and gave him a note.

"When you reach Haliput thirty gold marks for you, come and see me, King Wamba."

And the man could not stop laughing, Wamba his king and because he opened his mouth to laugh swallowed thirty midges that bit his stomach so he "EEK and I need potion, where is that salesman, never here when you need him?" The man.

"I will put this down to a holiday fling and he is not such a Burke as he has made himself out to be for, he is now King," Christina counting the warts on his arms to pass the time to Haliput.

"But what a kisser, perhaps I will lock him in the dungeons

and let him out every full moon and he can chase me about the palace turrets and towers till he catches me of course, then he put a fury arm about my shoulder, happy to be close to the woman he desires."

And she saw thingamajigs moving along that arm to get to her, ticks, lice, and fleas and was mortified and knew once he was locked up, she did throw the key away.

"What have I done?" She asked.

"Why dear, you have caught the most eligible bachelor in the land and made him your husband," the Burke Wamba and added, "Gee up," for he was in a hurry to give everyone in Haliput the news.

CHAPTER 73   KING WAMBA

"Here the four-poster bed the royal couple did not sleep in," a future tourist guide.

"Here the postcard Wamba sent to his chums at the Bridge Inn," showing a square of Ajax outhouse paper with a stamp. "And these stamps are rare as they show both royal heads." And was true for the handsome model posing as Wamba eloped with a chamber maid.

And even Sampenciltrex could not force his monkey to paint Wamba for the monkey broke into hysterical laughter when it looked at King Wamba.

And Cannymindtrex and Offaltrex printed those stamps knowing they did become collector items.

For Harry Blackhood was up north with Eagor looking for frozen reindeer; and since Harry was absent Offaltrex went to town opening stamp collector shops and showed what one could do without a night's sleep. Not forgetting the new chain of spiced chicken drummer outlets called Offal Chicken straight off an Offaltrex farm.

So, Harry did not see Cannymindtrex new chariot pulled by black panthers and leather padded, all very sexy for a lawyer had cash to spend.

And the guide showed the tourists the loft where Wamba slept for a night hiding from Pitter Patter.

"I will not sign," Wamba protested as Christina slipped a

divorce paper through the doorway with these words, "Dearest look out the loft window," and Wamba did and saw an angry mob wanting to burn him, of course after quartering him, of course after strangling him, of course after drawing him and of course after other nasty thingies they did do him for they hated him.

He was Wamba, too ugly to be their Prince Charming.

And the crowd saw him, "Look there is the wart?" They shouted seeing him at the loft window so threw bricks, shoes, alley cats, feral dogs, and beggars at him to encourage King Wamba to leave Haliput.

And King Wamba was hungry so ate the lot except the beggars of course.

"Sign," Cannymindtrex shoving the divorce papers back.

"I am King Wamba," the Burke in the loft so did not see a royal; finger twitch so the palace gates were opened and the crowd rush in.

"Stick a hot poker somewhere," a cruel crowd member who was an ex-employee of Henry V11's uncle as this is an attempt to sprinkle Shakespeare here and not Satirextex.

"Stretch his tongue then slice it off salami sausage fashion," another hungry crowd member fresh out of a movie called Brave Heart to bring Bolly Wood here.

."We must flee dearest," Wamba in the loft.

"We?" Christina and added, "sweetheart if a wart on your head is burned, I did never forgive myself, quick ride Old Nag back to The Bridge Inn, a sacksful of pearls sits idly at the stable door," for she wanted rid of him and the pearls were beads painted white bought from an oily salesman.

"Sniff," Wamba replied for Cannymindtrex had opened the court room door and rioters had set alight Womba's locks.

"Shriek," the princess for he had thrown her across his shoulders and ran, quite forgetting his beloved was now on fire.

"Help," she cried and allowed the angry mob to pull her to safety. But the flames spread all over Wamba who jumped out the window and landed in a water trough and then slid dripping wet into a barn and shut the barn door, then lifted a secret trap door and hid in a meth cellar.

And the meth ignited with a POOF for King Wamba was the hottest celebrity ever.

And Cannymindtrex saw it all so, "Pssst," he pssst outside the wine cellar.

"I recognize a Give a Copper?" Wamba and was correct for the lawyer shoved the divorce papers at him.

"Oh, greatest of Medusa's please sign the divorce papers," the lawyer being insulting about Womba's rural rustic looks.

"Never," Wamba.

"Over here boys and girls," the lawyer so angry rioters thumped at the cellar door.

And Wamba put his X to the divorce paper and was no longer king.

Now an Aslop fable, *"Greedy lawyers always let you down,"* for as Cannymindtrex went to collect his fat fee from Christina he threw the rioters the cellar key.

And two friends on their haunches watched everything till the red stuff began to squirt for violence did nothing for Old Nag but did for Bat Wing.

"Here they are going to throw him off the palace's highest tower, better fly down and rescue the idiot," Old Nag.

"Yes, better," Bat Wing hoping they did hurry up and throw Wamba off for a moat full of leeches was at the bottom for were-wolf and ghoul movies she loved and leeches were second best; especially if that red scaly dragon was in the back seats with her. The naughty flirtatious beast and Old Nag her boyfriend present too.

"Better fly for they just threw him off, and see you later at The Bridge Inn," Old Nag and trotted away so never saw Bat Wing rub her paws as she watched Wamba fall to the moat.

And Wamba fell in the moat and was covered in leeches, billions of them so even the rioters felt pity and left him to get sucked dry with these words, "Maybe he was not that bad looking," but was lies and they knew it.

And even Bat Wing was afraid with all of them leeches

Garrison did notice something wrong with Wamba and blame her, so reluctantly she flew down to pluck him out of the moat.

And what goes round comes round for twenty leeches crawled off Wamba onto her.

Serves her right, the blood lusting violent bat girl.

And outside South Gate the crowd was burning their cereal fields to rid it of Wamba again for Bat Wing dropped Wamba for the twenty leeches had been joined by a thousand more, and in the burning fields the future cornflakes.

Never mind Wamba landed softly on Old Nag walking by.

"Gee up horse," Wamba and the horse bucked him off.

So, the angry mob running about with torches saw he whom they hated and gave chase, all the way to the Dark Witch Filled Woods where Big Ears the Pixy lived. But Wamba had to go through that wood to get home so the witches there in sacred oak groves gave him some extra toes as a joke; long ones so all did notice.

*

And there was a wolf lurking in that wood that did not bite Wamba for it was biting someone else, someone who had got Eagor to carry him south on the promise he could eat all the flies he could catch.

"Will not cost me a thing," the miser Boss for he knew with smelly Eagor flies did always be handy nearby; for the monster knew not what soap was but to spread it on thick toast for Eagor was thick as thick toast. Then poor Eagor blew bubbles and chased them to burst with these words, "Tar la La how happy I am."

And as usual Harry complained to Eagor life was his fault and must look at his feet so Boss would not see his boils on his chin and be reminded of Eagor, so Eagor cried for he knew Boss did not love him, so did a wise thing, dropped Harry Boss so Boss rolled
down a pine lined hillside.

Yes 365 pine trees grew on the hillside and Boss Harry Black hood hit everyone.

"Howl howling, we will go," Boss hearing the wolf as pine

acorns went down his hood so he scratched this way and that.

"What is this a full moon?" Harry Boss for a second ago the sun was out but this is a story so anything happens for Bolly Wood is full of special effects.

And remembered what Dog Publishers wrote to sell horror books, "Were-wolf of the dark lonely streets rips throat out, 'Your throat.'" So, Harry Boss trembled for the howling was near and knew were-wolves lived in Holly Wood for he had seen Jack Nicholson in 'Wolf'.

"I am the were-wolf who rips throats to eat the apple within, howl," Harry Boss heard and scampered through the under bush but the were-wolf scampered faster as it had hind legs built for scampering.

Besides Harry's black robe caught on a tree branch and all his pennies fell out.

"Mine," Harry as he picked them up oblivious to "Grr."

So was the bad breath panting on his face that made Harry look up and there twenty were-wolfs no longer howling but drooling and worse, holding butcher implements.

And knew he was burger.

"Eagor come back Boss needs you quick. Boss is sorry he called you an ignorant sausage face," and Eagor heard twenty miles away for he had big floppy ears.

Had Eagor not been called Elephant Man in the circus by Monty driving before Assassindeadlyknife rescued him.

And the were-wolves feared for pine trees snapped and the wind blew pine needles into them so they shrieked instead of howling.

And Harry felt sorry for them for he knew a monster was coming and then Eagor was
here.

"Master wants me," and Eagor buffed the twenty were-wolves so they ran away with their tails behind their bums.

Except one three-hundred-pound black were-wolf on Eagor's back and Eagor threw it off with these words, "Go claw someone else," onto Boss.

"Naughty puppy," Eagor pulling the snarling were-wolf off

Boss and kicked it away.

"Master it is Eagor who always protects you, speak and make Eagor happy."

"Gitlostsaugagefacemonster," Harry spat and moaned so Eagor was happy.

So Eagor threw Harry across his shoulders and went off to Haliput where straw and mutton bone waited him.

And Harry died on his back for were-wolves rip you to slivers and eat your kidneys you know as well as bitties you need for were-wolves are degenerate thingamabobs that lounge about under full moons reading tabloids.

And Eagor did not know this for he was singing, "Eagor happy, Eagor spank the bad were- puppy, Eagor hug and cuddle master, bad lying flowers I stamp on," on the way home.

And in hell level 9 Arawan could not belief his luck for there was Harry.

"Morrigan will be so happy she will stop nagging me," so Arawan thought but Harry poofed away and can you guess why?

"Cannot a decent woman sleep in this coal shed?" Morrigan awakened.

"Sorry dear, Harry visited," Arawan thinking she did be pleased.

"And you let him go," and she threw a rackful of coal at Arawan and emptied his meths out which was cruel.

And imps and souls felt sorry for Arawan for, "He never rode us on coals with spurs, or swung us so we collided with rocks or made us drink meths and then blow on a
Match like her.

"I am a were-wolf," Harry opening his eyes on Eagor's back and howled. "Mr. Chairman who never dies they will call me," and he fed on Eagor who found his master's attention embarrassing.

"What have I done?" Harry realizing Eagor would be a were-monster and be with him till the end of time.

"Forever master, how lucky you are?" Eagor and howled.

And explains why Harry Blackhood still lives in the future

with an army of tourist guides to sell you green plastic dinosaurs.

"I am thinking of making a movie called 'Howl' in Bolly Wood for extras as were-wolf food come cheaper there than stunt men in Holly Wood," Harry dreaming time away to get Eagor out of his mind.

"Eagor ha, he, Ho ha," Harry showing you he could not get Eagor out of his mind and Harry frothed and foamed at the mouth and gnawed away at Eagor for Harry just might be demented.

"Naughty Boss," Eagor and slapped Harry good so his wolf fangs wobbled this way and that.

CHAPTER 74   KING

"I was king," Wamba boasted in the Bridge Inn as he watched one of his warts floating in his XXX for too much ZZZ makes a Wamba fall to pieces starting with the liver and ending with the thingamajig, and in between the facial warts.

"Away you go," the patrons and added, "There your crown and there the throne," meaning a spittoon and loo and worse Dwarf and Grisly had been acting suspiciously near these objects.

"Ha, he has he," a caged hyena thinking that hilarious and was the background laughter for these beasts are cheaper than an audience paid to laugh.

"Apes," Wamba for Apes was no longer just Apes but Apes the King's Champion and the ape swung down from the rafters dropping banana skins as he went.

"Ouk," it grunted and the patrons threw nuts because they were free at the bar.

"Better than Monty's cousin thirty times removed is driving uncle's circus," patrons as they watched Apes chase nuts. And the patrons waited for the big accident for there was no net underneath, just tables with patrons, the nasty type who took offence to their drinks getting spilled. And just as well Apes learned to swing rafters because them patrons were armed with two handed swords and axes and nets and even a small cage to cram Apes in, for they would sell him to Monty's cousin thirty times removed is driving uncle's circus to pay for the spilt drinks.

And outside a lonely captain manned the guard hut at the bridge playing Solitaire. Inside Big Bertha's marines played with more exciting toys without a thought about him for they had left these words of advice, "Leave your post which we are meant to guard and we throw you in the moat," and showed Moronicus the cement.

And since everyone was in the Inn who did the chopping down of forests, Moronicus built the new hut and the kennel for Cur too, too pass the time for playing with a piece of lonely string can drive one almonds.

"I hate the lot of them," he kept muttering and through his fingers a lead ball went this way and that with an added word, "Cain," and "mutiny," and "Yes hate them hate them hate them," and what happened to the string, "It wanted fine company so threw it on the ground to speak to worms."

And was Harold who helped build the new hut and kennel for he believed he was building a French restaurant for that is what Garrison told him; for they was liar's and him naive. Never mind this is a happy fairy tale so in the blue print a cooking area and table and plastic plates forks and spoons and a primus stove mountaineers use; nearby a tin of snails and a tin opener so see, Harold would be happy eventually after he figured out how to use the tin opener for Vikings used their teeth but poor Harold did not have any. The truth is he was plain thick.

And Cur would never use the kennel for the dog regarded itself as fairy and right now was upstairs being groomed by a waitress who fed him bone soup.

And after getting kicked out of the Inn for using a spitting as a privy, monthly Dwarf and Grisly Bear would come into the bridge to buy supplies and spread lies about their fame, "Yes we skinned twenty Fiends this month," for they was boasters and knew waitresses rewarded their lies with free Peterhead fish head soup.

"Grr," Grisly adding his comment.

And they patrolled the land between the last rip and Inn, which explains why Garrison was able to spend all their pay there.

And a small settlement grew up about Filthy Big Bertha's

and in time tourists would flock here and buy plastic dinosaurs at stalls with Harry Bros. PLC on them.

And Christina was happy with baby Tom and often checked it for warts for she was haunted about Route 66 and a holiday fling.

And since she spent her time looking for warts Harry Blackhood took control for "Six months being fed flies taught me one thing, Eagor must go, six months of his howling, six months without making cash," and everywhere Offaltrex shop signs and not Harry Bros. PLC.

Now Harry sat at the top of his long table, carried to the palace to show all he was in charge.

And "I howl with Boss at the full moon and with Boss run about fields catching rabbits to shred for we are were-thingies, howl," Eagor and was carrying in Yorkshire Puddings and hot gravy and tripped on a begging minor relation and soaked Boss good.

"By the gods what has that monster down to me," Harry Boss jumping about seeking icy water to cool down in.

"Here Boss," Eagor carrying a jar of chilly water and because he was thirsty drank it all.

"I hate you Eagor do you hear, hate you," cruel Boss.

"Boohoo."

And with Wotanic two rowers who never left.

"One can stay seeing pink elephants," Christina who sent daddy shipments of meths to make sure he never asked for the throne back. "And pensioned Wotanic off," and Wotanic turned his little rowing boat into a home from home and nightly rowed ashore and bored waitresses with his adventure tales, but they sat in their frillies for he paid well. Waitresses in frillies may you ask? Yes, for they spilt the carrot soup and needed to dry their dresses by the fire in Wotanic's rented back room. And rabbits fly about the moon would you believe?

Anyway: room service and just as well he had a pension so was content but the waitresses could not wait till, he went home in his jolly rowing boat to pay them, and followed him, and stood up for a wee in his jolly rowing boat and fell off and Wotanic rowed away, happy he did not have to pay, but they did be waiting for him next night and follow him, stand up for a wee and fall into the sea, and was repeated, so were never paid.

"And so, he stays away from me," Christina and his pension was tagged to the inflation rate to make sure he rowed nightly.

And Arawan was depressed so drank more meths for Morrigan had turned out to be a nagging thingamabob whose mouth never shut.

"I will ration his meths as I am not living with a drunk," so Arawan saw pink elephants everywhere and went bananas.

And The Brotherhood who gave Wotanic his first star billing multiplied and their umbrella spread like octopus tentacles over Haliput so sucked in all discontents such as minor relations.

And covered the pavements in mess for they did not use litter bins and worse, did not pick up their doggy messes and use the doggy mess bins.

"Wamba will return," they also whispered too drunks leaning on lamp posts and to lovers in bed for were like bed bugs and even spoke to you in the loo.

"That idiot return?" Harry Blackhood and "howl," for Wamba might stop him ruling and let Little Tom be king. "Fat chance," the greasy oily miser.

*

And in the future Harry trembles at night with nightmares as The Brotherhood whisper in his ear, "Wamba will return."

So, awakens and The Brotherhood hide under his bed, on his closet and in his black hood and chamber pot Eagor forgets to empty.

"Where is that monster I hate for lavender gives me sweet dreams of mummy but this essence gives me nightmares of THING RETURNED," Harry sweating and should be grateful foe he was losing weight the fat slob.

Anyway: "Surely if the ploughman ploughs Womba's

Round Barrow up the swine's following will eat what tasty bits remain, and then to the pie maker and surely Wamba will be dead and NEVER RETURN," the ghastly miser who had black circles under his eyes from lack of sleep. "I am a hundred now and buy potions from Druidtrex to stop my fur flaking off with age, howl, and become frolicsome on full moons and with Eagor run about a rose garden fouling it up to be nasty."

And Druidtrex had a vision, to accidentally add one extra dried earwig to his potion and summon Garrison back for Harry taxed them too much, even their loo seats where taxed on bottom size.

"Promise me Eagor if that happens, you skewer me with a silver sword," Harry pleaded on gangrene hundred-year-old legs.

"How can I skewer the thing I love," Eagor and patted Boss so hard Boss's brain rattled this way and that for Eagor was strong, huge and did not know his own strength as well as being stupid.

"Maybe that extra earwig will give me back my strength and rid me of Eagor?" Harry hoped. "I will get Druidtrex to lift carpets and seek earwigs straight away, he ah he has," Harry for he too kept hyenas in a cage as pets and background laughter.

And many ghosts about him whispered, "Do it Harry for we want to return."

And repeated it so much it became hypnotic and he did it and then slept and the ghosts would not let him waken in case he stopped Druidtrex making the spell for Garrison to return.

"Moan," Harry as he saw Wamba and Garrison float by his eyes for dreams are from the other world.

"Do not worry Boss, Eagor is here to cuddle you to make you feel safe," and Eagor cuddled and the night filled with the sound of breaking bones of course interrupted with these words, "I hate you Eagor."

And who was Druidtrex? Perhaps a mage who knew the secret of long-life parading under a new name for all knew The Mage was he who gave the wolf a bad name in Red Riding Hood.

And went under the name of Foreign investors perhaps?

A forgotten uncle?

Bank interest rates.

Nontransparent governments?

Party elections and your party did not win.

The D.A. says the bones left over were a dogs and not a mobsters?

Perhaps a disgraced official sneaked back in via The Muppets?

Or old black and white movies come too life?

Or the minister on church day rabbiting on about his holiday?

Or Monty's cousin thirty times removed is driving for he is crossed eyed?

Or WOMBA RETURNED and Harry's nightmare come true?

THE END

This marks the end of the manuscript and will follow a double-spaced blank line after the last line of text.

ABOUT THE AUTHOR

Keith Hulse

Keith was an archaeologist, soldier, entrepreneur, Scottish War Blinded Veteran.
Stories come tumbling into my left temple and out the right ear.
Spirit people visit him, his house is full of cats, perhaps why.

BOOKS BY THIS AUTHOR

Planet World, Ant Rider Book One, Illustrated

Ants 169 is so large needed halved.

Book One has Luke finding out his aims and becomes a hero by fighting for human rights.

Full, of adventure, example, Luke ends up a galley rower and saves the ship from pirates.

And like a dog, Utna pines for Luke wondering seashores seeking Luke, his friend, and like a dog, loves his master.

This book is about love, the power of it, it sings across space as Light. Be lit then.

Ceugant Dana, The Oneness; this book is very spiritual.

We are all 'Jock Thomson's Burns.'

Unity of the Spirit even if an insect or a human, all one.

Phoenix, Ant Rider Book Two, Illustrated.

Is concluding part of Ants 169

48439, 187 pages.

Luke concludes his epic struggle against the humanoid Insect Nobles, become this way by gene mixing.

The Insect Queen, Nina and he race to the star ship Phoenix, a human ship that crashed on Planet World in the Time of Myths. What secrets does it hold?

Is the Insect God Enil a human? One way to find out, come join Luke and be his friend.

Ants 169 [Revised Illustrations] Science Fiction

(Ant Rider Book 3)

A mammoth exciting read. Illustrated science fiction. over hundred beautiful pictures, an old book.
Original had 169 illustrations.
A mirror of our ups and downs.
ANTS about the growing pains of Luke in a lion cloth riding a giant black ant.
He roars and GIANT ant Utna clicks.
He fights humanoid Queen Nina of Insect Noble lineage to free human slaves on wonderful Planet World.
A queen needing human genes in her slow reproducing species.
Humans genes give you fingers.
Human genes drop the wings.
Is suspense, thriller, action, romance. About gene shuttling and what IF? A fast colourful thought provoking read.
A must for science fiction fans.
Concluding happy ending for all books.

Ants169 : Non Illustrated (Ant Rider Book 4)

This is the exciting moving non-illustrated version of Ants 169 illustrations,
Books One and Two together.
It is designed for paperback and library submission.
True to the original story, Luke rides a giant Black Ant, Utna in his war against
humanoid insects.
Genetically altered from radiation fallout and gene shuttling.
Adventure and romance with Luke as he fights for humankind.
From boyhood into a man, the pains of growing, physically and spiritually.
Row the Insect war galleys with Luke.
Swim with Luke away from sharks in the Yellow Sea as his galley sinks.
A good action packed read designed to make you want science fiction.

Concluding happy ending for all books.

The Man

illustrated
See the universes The Man saw, colours and songs space gives out if you listen.
This book is full of Deep Space and shows how big space is.
Meet the aliens he meets.
Dine with him in worlds we must discover ourselves.
This book may be classified as horror due to the presence of a vampire.
Can this vampire fly, nope, uses spaceships to fly about universes.
A jolly delightful read.

Mungo

'Lady' or 'Mr.' just imagine these lion humanoids parading Californian beaches, were the beautiful folk resort. These lion people are nice looking and will soon have you ogling, to the jealousy of the other types loitering the warm sand.
Love jumps races and here species. Your siblings one day might bring an alien with a red Mohican hair style instead of the human heavy rock boy next to dinner.
Here lizard folk ruled by queens, such as Carman hates humans, so adventure and war with her against Mungo, King of Lions.
And no one wins in a war as a human star ship arrives and enslaves the lot.
Advanced humans see other humans as undesirables, especially if a 'nutter' rides a lion .
These lizard folk like humans at a barbecue, as the burgers, steaks, and sausages.
No wonder Mungo wars against them. Well, we eat cows, sheep, pigs and fish. That is what these lizards see humans as, dinner.

and an ape more like a mongoose and teddy bear.
and wide.
Mazarrats

Tiberius Grant

Space hero or womaniser,
But a terrific general and conquers
space for humans until he meets the
Snake People where he would be KING.
And his women turn up.
And alien fleets to do battle.
And a human who wants all space and his ships.
And the mad scientist Woo who declares himself
Emperor.
What a mad cap world this Planet Tagget becomes.
Also pushes for morals as futuristic human society is
Worse than the Roman slave economy.

Big Foot, A Betty Lou Spiirit Guide Murder Mystery Comedy

Comedy, illustrated, a ridiculous tale of dark woods and healed
friendships, illustrated.
Full of Big Foot, Red baboons and two hapless lawmen.
A good laugh.

Ghost Wife, A Comedy Melee

74256 words, 159 pages, illustrated.
Oh, Morag dear, you died so do what ghosts do, Rest In Peace.
"Not on your Nelly, I am very much alive, and stop ogling
the medium Con, dear." Plenty of madcap ridiculous fun.
Information on the After Life.
Is comic mayhem, fanciful rubbish to tickle. The ghosts here will

not haunt but make you laugh, so do not worry about holding bibles, these ghosts are clowns.

Ghost Romance, A Comedy Of Errors

A nonstop ghostly ridiculous adventure from Borneo to New York Zoo, with Calamity the orangutan in tow. So, load up on bananas and figs as the ape eats non-stop.

"Ouk," is her only word spoken.

Do not worry about the extras feeding the crocodiles, they come under a dime a dozen and are not in any union, and better, made of indigestible rubber.

Not to worry animal lovers, a vet is on standby by for the sweet crocodiles, sea water variety so bigger, nastier, fierce, and wanting you as food.

This book speaks heaps for food out there, a mixture of local, Indian, Chinese, Portuguese, Dutch, British, you name it, it found a way onto the menu.

Eat more than a banana and drink condensed tea milk to sweeten you up.

Eagor The Monster, A Laughing Tale

Non illustrated version.
84488 words 248 pages
An epic book of giggles.
Aggressive comedy.
The humorous tale of an ugly monster who
cheats on his many girlfriends.
But he is so ugly?
He works for himself although signed up
to do jobs for the HOOD cousins.
Discount salespersons who will sell you what you
do not need, like BAD Granny who hunts were-wolfs
from her zoomed up mobile home.
A were-wolf girl with a pretty ankle who yes, is

one of the ugly monsters' girls.
Come laugh meeting Eagor's other friends,
Such as Badbladder who dresses as Bunnykins,
In his effort to marry Princess Lana.
And the monster treats his friends bad, as
 gets Badbladder to do his job of pulling
twenty carts full of holidaying villagers on
The Blackhood express.
Giggle laugh snort meeting Eagor's enemies, Bear a chili
Addicted bear, Morag a frizzled-out witch, Wee Mary her
apprentice
and a Glasgow hard case who knows how to deal with Eagor,
"Will you marry me monster," as Wee Mary is desperate.
Just a funny silly tale to brighten your day.
All about magic to make you magically aware of life.

Eagor The Monster, A Laughing Tale, Illustrated

as above with pictures

Coachman, A Travelers Laughing Melody

Your monsters are all here getting the BOOT from
some place in the west to Mongolia.
A good gigantic laugh, a book you can put down and easily
start again.

Coachman, A Travelers Laughing Melody, Illustrated

as above but full of pictures

Printed in Great Britain
by Amazon